ICETE Series

The Motif of Hospitality in Theologial Education

The Motif of Hospitality in Theologial Education

A Critical Appraisal with Implications for Application in Theological Education

SOH Hui Leng Davina

Series Editor
Riad Kassis

© 2016 by SOH Hui Leng Davina

Published 2016 by Langham Global Library
An imprint of Langham Publishing
www.langhampublishing.org

Langham Publishing and its imprints are a ministry of Langham Partnership

Langham Partnership
PO Box 296, Carlisle, Cumbria CA3 9WZ, UK
www.langham.org

ISBNs:
978-1-78368-121-1 Print
978-1-78368-222-5 ePub
978-1-78368-224-9 PDF

SOH Hui Leng Davina has asserted her right under the Copyright, Designs and Patents Act, 1988 to be identified as the Author of this work.

All rights reserved. No part of this publication may be reproduced, stored in a retrieval system or transmitted, in any form or by any means, electronic, mechanical, photocopying, recording or otherwise, without the prior written permission of the publisher or the Copyright Licensing Agency.

Unless otherwise stated, Scripture quotations are from the New Revised Standard Version Bible, copyright © 1989 National Council of the Churches of Christ in the United States of America. Used by permission. All rights reserved.

British Library Cataloguing in Publication Data
A catalogue record for this book is available from the British Library

ISBN: 978-1-78368-121-1

Cover & Book Design: projectluz.com

Langham Partnership actively supports theological dialogue and an author's right to publish but does not necessarily endorse the views and opinions set forth, and works referenced within this publication or guarantee its technical and grammatical correctness. Langham Partnership does not accept any responsibility or liability to persons or property as a consequence of the reading, use or interpretation of its published content.

The subject of this work is how the practice of hospitality could transform theological education. While much has been written about hospitality in relation to higher education in general, its relation to theological education is relatively rare. Davina Soh's distinctive contribution is in showing that the hospitality metaphor is firmly grounded in both the Old and New Testaments and that this biblical concept has a significant bearing on the way theological education is undertaken. The work could not have come at a more appropriate time when many theological institutions, especially in the Majority World, are seeking to play catch-up with the West, and in their relentless pursuit of academic excellence, are encountering the same danger of ending up as soulless institutions.

Rev Simon Chan, PhD
Retired Earnest Lau Professor of Systematic Theology,
Trinity Theological College, Singapore

Davina Soh's book is a comprehensive, deep, and useful investigation of the motif of hospitality as a marker and model for good theological education. It successfully traces the motif from its inception, through higher and theological education scholars and then presents a carefully constructed biblical exposition as a conversation partner to her historical material and as a base for her critique. Her subsequent discussion and application to practice, with an eye to the South East Asian situation, will be vital for contemporary practitioners and future scholars in this region of the world, and also for theological educators globally. She has advanced scholarship in the subject of theological education and modeled best practice.

Graham Cheesman, PhD
Honorary Lecturer in Theology,
Queen's University Belfast, UK

Teaching at university level is currently hostage to market-oriented objectives which tend to reduce teacher/student interaction to authoritarian knowledge transfer. Davina Soh's book has the potential to breathe new life into the relationship by its exploration of the concept of hospitality. Expertly drawing on a variety of research-based disciplines and careful biblical exegesis, she develops a coherent picture of how educative relationships can be enriched by attention to the marks of authentic hospitality. While she is particularly sensitive to the needs of disempowered and multicultural students, and has a special interest in applying her research to Asian educational models, all educators stand to gain from a close study of this book.

Brian V. Hill, PhD
Emeritus Professor of Education,
Murdoch University, Western Australia

Davina Soh's work provides a vital academic contribution to the area of hospitality from a non-Western perspective. The study covers extensive secular and biblical research in the area of hospitality in higher education and theological education. It also includes suggestions on the practice of hospitality within and outside the classroom context.

Hospitality in theological education is a new concept to many educators and will challenge how we do the teaching/learning process for the spiritual formation of students. This research will benefit Christian educators as they learn to extend hospitality to foreign students in a global world where theological institutions are populated by international students.

Ng Tjoh Dju, PhD
Adjunct Faculty Member,
East Asia School of Theology, Singapore

Davina Soh's book is a "game changer" in evangelical theologies of higher education since, if implemented, it will have implications not only for how evangelicals are educated theologically, but will shape lifelong learners, ministers, missionaries, and servants with dispositions that will be inclusive of, vulnerable to, and reciprocal with the many different types of others in a radically pluralistic world. This is thus a dangerous book – don't read it unless you are committed to a reign of God that will feature those from many tongues, tribes, peoples, and nations of the world.

Amos Yong, PhD
Professor of Theology & Mission,
Fuller Theological Seminary, Pasadena, California
Author of *Hospitality and the Other: Pentecost, Christian Practices, and the Neighbor* (2008)

Contents

Abstract xi
Acknowledgments xiii
List of Abbreviations xv

1 Introduction 1
   Research Statement and Hypotheses 1
   Assumptions and Delimitations 3
   Chapter Outline 7

2 The Motif of Hospitality in the Literature of Christian Higher Education and Theological Education 9
   Groundbreakers for Hospitality in Education 10
      Henri J. M. Nouwen 10
         Nouwen's Dual Interest – Psychology and Practical Theology 10
         Nouwen's Development of the Concept of Hospitality . . . 12
         Salient Features of Nouwen's Concept of Hospitality . . . 14
         Contextual Analysis of Nouwen's Concept of Hospitality . . 18
      Parker J. Palmer 25
         Parker J. Palmer's Experience of Community and Contradiction 25
         Palmer's Development of the Concept of Hospitality . . . 28
         Salient Features of Palmer's Concept of Hospitality 31
         Hospitality as an Epistemological Virtue 35
         Contextual Analysis of Palmer's Concept of Hospitality . . 37
      Some Pertinent Interpretive Observations 45
   Hospitality as a Key Concept in Christian Higher Education . . 48
      Hospitality and the Pluralistic Environment 49
      Hospitality and the Academic Life and Community 58
      Hospitality and Classroom Process 62
   Hospitality as a Key Concept in Theological Education 71
      Hospitality and the Pluralistic Environment 72
      Hospitality and the Marginalized 76
      Hospitality and Classroom Process 78
   Summary 81

3   The Motif of Hospitality as Reflected in
     Contemporary Educational Research and Practice, and
     Higher Education Literature 85
         The Emotional and Relational Dimensions in the Teaching-Learning
             Process   86
             Shifting Trends in Higher Education   87
                 From Teaching to Learning   89
                 From Personal Constructivism to Social
                     Constructivism   91
                 From Cognition to Emotion   94
                 Reality: From Then to Now, from There to Here   97
             The Emotional Aspects of Teacher-Student Relationships   99
         Hospitality as a Key Concept in Higher Education Literature 105
             Hospitality and the Teaching Profession   107
             Hospitality and the Academic Life and Community   117
             Hospitality and the Marginalized   125
             Hospitality and Classroom Process   129
         Parallel Practices of Hospitality in Contemporary Higher
             Education Educational Practices   137
             The Practice of Care   137
             The Practice of Inclusion   142
             The Practice of Dialogue   145
         Summary   149

4   The Biblical Basis for the Motif of Hospitality in
     Theological Education. 151
         God as Host   152
             The Practice of Hospitality in the Life of the Israelites 153
                 Reception of the Guest   155
                 Provision of Food and Protection   155
                 Sending Off of the Guest   156
             Israel's Experience of God as Host   156
             Israel's Moral Obligation in Relation to God as Host   162
         Jesus as Guest-Host   166
             The Significance of Jesus' Praxis of Inclusive
                 Table Fellowship   169
                 The Social Functions of Table Fellowship   170
                 The Intent of Jesus' Table Fellowship   172

  Jesus' Instructions on Hospitality from and to Others 182
   The Mission of the Early Faith Communities 182
   The Final Judgment 184
  The Early Faith Communities as Hosts 185
   Homes/Households as Houses of Hospitality 186
   Injunctions to Show Hospitality 191
   Expressions of Hospitality in the Life of Early Faith
    Communities 193
    Worship and Common Meals 194
    Caring for the Needy 195
  Summary 200

5 A Critical Dialogue towards the Application of the Motif of Hospitality in Theological Education **203**
  Hospitality as a Cluster Concept 204
  Constitutive Element 1: Inclusion 205
   Hosts Rather than Hostages 205
   Boundaries as Horizons 209
   Intentional Marginality 213
  Constitutive Element 2: Presence 217
   Embodied Presence of Self 217
    Embodied Presence as Connection to Self 218
    Embodied Presence as Connection to the Other 222
   Articulate Presence to the Other 225
  Constitutive Element 3: Care 231
   Being a Friend to the Other 234
   Listening to the Other 240
  Constitutive Element 4: Reciprocity 244
   Reciprocity, Role Sharing, and Gift Sharing 244
   Reciprocity, Dialogue, and Partnership 250
  Summary 255

6 Conclusion **259**
  Research Statement, Hypotheses, and Findings 259
  Significance, Limitations, and Areas for Further Research 261
  Endword 263

Bibliography **265**

Abstract

Over the past four decades, educational professionals have explored the metaphor of hospitality in an effort to re-envision and re-conceptualize higher education. However, the existing discourses on hospitality in education have not fully explored the metaphor from a biblical perspective. This research thus provides another perspective and voice for the concept of hospitality in higher education – more specifically, theological education – by presenting a biblically informed metaphor of hospitality interpreted by an Asian female theological educator living in Singapore.

Taking an interdisciplinary conceptual approach, this dissertation establishes the viability of hospitality as a practice in theological education for teachers to create a hospitable teaching-learning environment that facilitates the holistic formation of students. It accomplishes this by first examining how hospitality has been proposed by the professionals in the educational arena to address the perennial ills and challenges in Christian higher education, theological education, and higher education. Its interpretation of the biblical metaphor of hospitality then provides the conceptual framework to approach the application of hospitality by teachers in theological institutions seeking to form their students holistically. Instead of working with a single definition of hospitality, this research uses the cluster concept to define hospitality and identifies the constitutive elements of hospitality as inclusion, presence, care, and reciprocity. It proposes ways theological educators can practice at least one, if not more, of the constitutive elements to create an effective environment for facilitating the holistic formation of their students.

Acknowledgments

Embarking on this dissertation was like going on a backpack adventure. With just the essentials in a backpack, the random acts of kindness and gestures of hospitality from strangers and friends along the journey empowered me to reach my destination – the completion of this dissertation.

An important stranger I encountered at the beginning of my writing journey is none other than my supervisor, Dr Graham Cheesman. He graciously received this complete stranger in his office at Belfast Bible College (Northern Ireland) one September morning in 2009, and offered to help her achieve her goal of completing her dissertation proposal during her three-month stay in Belfast. In due course, Graham accepted the formal invitation to be my dissertation supervisor. Without his wise and patient guidance, I would not have been able to see the wood for the trees. With his guidance, I was able to see the big picture as well as the flowers growing at the side of the road.

Accompanying me on my writing journey were two competent guides – my dean, Dr Allan Harkness, and my critical friend, Dr Perry Shaw. I am grateful for their input into my dissertation. Their critical eyes and constructive feedback helped me to hone my thoughts and arguments, and produce a stronger and a more cohesive piece of work.

My long, arduous journey was made more pleasant by the kind acts of hospitality I received from strangers and friends (too numerous to name individually here) who went an extra mile to introduce a friend who could be a resource person for me, to procure much-needed resources which were inaccessible to me, to read and proofread my work, to uphold me in prayer, or to provide financial aid for this academic enterprise. Here, I would like to make special mention of St George's Church, Singapore. Though I was a stranger to the leadership and members, they welcomed me with open arms and covered my program fees for three years and my dissertation examination fee.[1]

---

1. Similarly, the leadership of International Council for Evangelical Theological Education and Langam Partnership extended gracious hospitality to me, a stranger. The publication of this book would not be possible without their partnership. And the valuable assistance from the editorial team of Langham Partnership, especially Vivian Doub and Silke Davison, made the tedious editing process an engaging yet pleasant journey of learning.

Lastly, this writing journey would also have been an impossible venture if not for the enduring support and patient understanding from my family – my parents, who have shown me what hospitality is by their expressions of hospitality to others; my two younger sisters, who have given freely in many ways so that I can be free to pursue my theological studies; and my husband, Casey, who has sacrificed much to empower me to pursue my dreams and fulfill God's calling on my life.

So, to everyone who has helped me to make this dissertation a reality, I would like to say, with a humbled heart filled with gratitude, "Thank you."

Glory be to God!

List of Abbreviations

ASV	American Standard Version
KJV	King James Version
NASB	New American Standard Bible
NIV	New International Version
NJB	New Jerusalem Bible
NKJV	New King James Version
NRSV	New Revised Standard Version

1

Introduction

My interest in the practice of hospitality in education was first piqued by an assignment that I had to do for an educational course which required me to compare how two authors approached a single concept. Prior to that, I had read Henri J. M. Nouwen's "The Second Movement: From Hostility to Hospitality" in his book *Reaching Out* and Parker J. Palmer's chapter "To Teach Is to Create a Space . . ." in his book *To Know as We Are Known*, each separately, at different times of my life. Since both of them employed the motif of hospitality to address the spiritual dimension of education, I decided to use them as the main subjects of my assignment. It was a worthy pursuit because after re-reading their works, I had to pause, reflect, and critically examine my own teaching practices in the light of what they have written about hospitality in education. It also caused me to reflect on the hostile climate that generally characterizes a theological institution – from the business-like administrative staff to busy faculty; from the "No Entry Except Staff" signs in front of offices to the locked prayer room; from teachers' brusque responses to students' queries, to students' scathing comments in evaluating teachers at the end of the course. From my reading and reflection, I began to wonder: "What potential does the practice of hospitality have in transforming our educational practices and endeavors in theological institutions?"

Research Statement and Hypotheses

Prior to this millennium, there was not much sustained interest in the practice of hospitality in the contexts of higher education, Christian higher education, and theological education. The initial works on hospitality in education were that of Nouwen and Palmer and they were written in the 1970s and 1980s respectively. Although works written in a similar vein subsequently appeared, they were few and sporadic. Interest in hospitality as a practice worthy of consideration in educational endeavors has increased since the onset of the 2000s and gained even more momentum in recent years. The Association of Theological Schools (ATS), with support from the Henry Luce Foundation, initiated the Christian Hospitality and Pastoral Practices in a Multifaith Society Project, and awarded eighteen grants to theological institutions for the purpose of exploring ways multifaith elements could be integrated into their curricula during the 2011–2012 academic year.[1] The various reflections, implementations, and reports of those involved in this project were subsequently published in two issues of *Theological Education*, a journal published by the ATS and the Commission on Accrediting of ATS.[2] Their focus was on how students in theological institutions could be taught to minister, as well as offer, hospitality in multifaith contexts. Yet, even with this ongoing interest in the motif of hospitality in theological education, works written on hospitality in education thus far have not explored sufficiently how the biblical concept of hospitality can inform teachers in theological institutions, that is, *theological educators*, in their efforts aimed at the holistic formation of students. Hence, my research statement is:

> That the motif of hospitality is a viable concept for theological education and can be used by teachers in theological institutions to create an environment for facilitating the holistic formation of students.

Supporting this research statement are four hypotheses:

- That the growing body of literature on hospitality in Christian higher education and theological education reveals an emerging literary phenomenon that deserves examination and assessment
- That hospitality appears to be a recurring concept in higher education literature, and that the usage finds parallels in the emotional and relational aspects of learning in contemporary educational practices

---

1. http://www.ats.edu/christian-hospitality-and-pastoral-practices.
2. Graham, "Issue Focus," no. 1; "Issue Focus," no. 2. Since the focus of this work is the creation of a safe and supportive teaching-learning environment that facilitates the holistic formation of students in theological institutions, these two volumes are not included in the literature review because they concern largely the incorporation of the practice of hospitality in relation to multifaith (e.g. Muslim, Buddhist) contexts into the curriculum.

- That an understanding of the biblical concept of hospitality can inform teachers in theological institutions in their goal of education
- That the motif of hospitality can be applied in theological education to create an effective environment for facilitating the holistic formation of students

Assumptions and Delimitations

Working from the assumption that "the teacher has the power to structure the learning environment," an underlying assumption of the present study is that the onus is on the teacher to initiate changes in the teaching-learning environment.[3] Hence, the focus of this study is on how theological educators, as the host to their student-guests, can create a hospitable teaching-learning environment that facilitates the holistic formation of students.

Within the past few years, three handbooks on theological education worldwide have been published in the Regnum Studies in Global Christianity Series.[4] These voluminous works contain discourses addressing the issues, challenges, and trends in theological education around the globe, showing indeed that "the hinterlands of Christian theological education are many and diverse."[5] Recognizing that the contexts of theological education are "unimaginably diverse"[6] and at the same time writing from my perspective as a theological educator in Singapore, the *theological education* that I am focusing on in this study pertains to "*theological education in a theological college, seminary, or divinity school*" that prepares men and women for ministry and leadership, whether as full-time pastors/ministers, or lay leaders in their respective faith communities.[7] Hereafter, in this book, the term *theological institutions* is used generically to refer to these three types of theological institutions. Generally, the focus of theological education in these

---

3. Conde-Frazier, "From Hospitality to Shalom," 173.
4. Werner et al., *Handbook of Theological Education*; Antone et al., *Asian Handbook*; Phiri and Werner, *Theological Education in Africa*.
5. Farr, "Introduction," 9.
6. Kang, "Colonial to Postcolonial," 31; on the types of theological education institutions both around the world and in Asia, see Werner, "Challenges and Opportunities," 20–21; "Perspectives on the Future," 659; see also Harkness, "Introduction," 8–9.
7. Harkness, "Introduction," 8 (original emphasis).

theological institutions is ministerial formation[8] or pastoral formation,[9] with the understanding that *formation* refers to "the whole process of equipping, enabling, raising awareness, shaping or transforming attitudes and values" – an understanding that emerged from and has been in use since the 1965 Gazzada Statement on Laity Formation.[10] In this study, this process will be referred to as *holistic formation* that comprises four key areas: (1) knowing (knowledge), (2) doing (skills), (3) being (character), and (4) feeling (empathy and passion).[11] Ultimately, the goal of theological education is "to form a *person*, not a *professional*."[12]

Based on the assumption that the environment is crucial to learning and transformation,[13] this book is predicated on the general understanding that there are three aspects to the learning environment – physical, intellectual, and emotional.[14] All three aspects have to be considered when creating a teaching-learning environment that promotes learning. However, the central focus of this study will be on the emotional environment, on how the motif of hospitality can inform our creation of a safe and supportive teaching-learning environment that facilitates the holistic formation of students in theological institutions. Nevertheless, in the application of the motif of hospitality, some aspects of the physical and intellectual environments may be discussed.

This book is conceptual in nature, largely based on literature research, because it is exploring an emerging motif in educational works – the motif of hospitality. It seeks to establish the viability of hospitality as a practice in theological education by first examining how hospitality has been proposed by the professionals in the educational arena to address the perennial ills and challenges in Christian higher education, theological education, and higher education. The research then assesses the practice of hospitality from a biblical perspective before proposing how this motif can be applied in theological education. It achieves this by presenting hospitality as a cluster concept of

---

8. Werner, "Challenges and Opportunities," 18.
9. Harkness, "De-schooling the Theological Seminary," 104.
10. Raiser, "Fifty Years of Ecumenical Formation," 440.
11. Carey Baptist College, as cited in Harkness, "De-schooling the Theological Seminary," 105.
12. Witmer, "Seminary," 239 (original emphasis).
13. Gaff, *Toward Faculty Renewal*, 77.
14. Thompson and Wheeler, "Learning Environment," 33.

four constitutive elements that can be practiced by teachers in theological institutions for the holistic formation of students.

This study is aware that the term *higher education* generally refers to education at a degree level and beyond, namely, undergraduate and postgraduate education. However, in this book, the term *higher education* is used to refer to higher education in non-Christian settings. Although the term *secular higher education* may better help distinguish the two educational settings, its use is avoided because of the negative connotations often associated with it. Since this book does not differentiate between Protestant and Catholic, the term *Christian* is used as an inclusive term to encompass both sectors. Correspondingly, *Christian higher education* refers to Protestant/Catholic higher education, and *Christian colleges/universities* refers to Protestant/Catholic colleges/universities.

Besides works written on hospitality from the field of hospitality management, many works have appeared in the last few decades from various disciplines, seeking to address emerging issues in a globalized world through the lens of hospitality. These works cover a broad spectrum of topics, from Christian living[15] to Christian theology;[16] from worship[17] to pastoral care,[18] to evangelism and mission;[19] from unity within the Christian community[20] to interfaith encounters;[21] from multiculturalism[22] to cosmopolitanism;[23] from physical disabilities[24] to sexual inclusiveness;[25] from writing classes[26] to online

---

15. Halverson, *Gift of Hospitality*; Newman, *Untamed Hospitality*.
16. Keifert, *Welcoming the Stranger*; Boersma, "Irenaeus, Derrida and Hospitality"; Russell, *Just Hospitality*; Vondey, "Pentecostal Ecclesiology and Eucharistic Hospitality."
17. Coady, "Hospitality in the Liturgy"; Boersma, "Liturgical Hospitality"; Gilbert, "Hospitality in Sacred Space."
18. Henrey, "Hospitality in Pastoral Care"; Walton, "Welcoming Guest."
19. Arias, "Centripetal Mission"; Koyama, "Extend Hospitality"; Gittins, "Beyond Hospitality"; Park, "Hospitality as Context"; Tomlin, "Evangelism as Catechesis."
20. Reynolds, "Improvising Together"; Tan, "Loving Strangers."
21. Lottes, "Toward a Christian Theology"; de Béthune, "Interreligious Dialogue and Sacred Hospitality"; Kameniar, "Dilemmas"; Yong, *Hospitality and the Other*; Reynolds, "Toward a Wider Hospitality"; Graham, "Issue Focus," no. 1; "Issue Focus," no. 2.
22. Makkhado and Spalding, "Community and Hospitality"; Shryock, "Hospitality Lessons."
23. Dikeç, "*Pera Peras Poros*"; Baker, "Double Law"; Shryock, "Breaking Hospitality Apart."
24. Steele, "Accessibility or Hospitality"; Anderson, *Graduate Theological Education*; Anderson, "Hospitable Classrooms."
25. Gilbert, "Let Us Say Yes"; Binnie and Klesse, "Because It Was."
26. Tremmel, "Hospitality in the Classroom"; Barnette, "Houses of Hospitality," ch. 4.

courses.[27] Given this abundance of literature, this book reviews only English written literature on hospitality within the contexts of Christian higher education, theological education, and higher education. The research also examines contemporary educational practices in higher education, looking at the emotional and relational aspects of learning, and parallel practices of hospitality.

Since metaphors do shape our educational and pedagogical practices,[28] this study seeks to present a "biblically informed metaphor"[29] – the metaphor of hospitality – to teachers in theological institutions for their consideration as they re-conceptualize their role in the holistic formation process of their students.[30] The Bible contains many narratives and teachings of hospitality. However, due to space limitation, this study examines only key biblical passages where hospitality is encountered that could provide a biblical framework of hospitality to assist these teachers in the holistic formation process of students. Moreover, based on the conviction that the Christian practice of "hospitality is [essentially] empowered by the Spirit of the hospitable God"[31] and that "it is the Spirit who enables us to change our guest and host roles,"[32] this study does not include the role of the Holy Spirit in its discussion of divine hospitality.[33] Instead, it only focuses on the role of God as host and Jesus as guest-host when discussing divine hospitality.

This book also contains some personal reflections and narratives from my personal experiences as a female Singaporean Chinese teaching full-time, first in a denominational theological institution, and then an interdenominational one, in Singapore since 1990. These serve as illustrative examples to support my arguments. Even though this work is written from the context of formal theological education, its implications are not limited to formal theological

---

27. Thwaites, "Vigilant Hospitality"; Ascough, "Welcoming Design."
28. Badley and Van Brummelen, "Metaphors," 4, 7.
29. Van Brummelen, *Walking with God in the Classroom*, 33.
30. For more on metaphors and education, see Badley and Van Brummelen, *Metaphors We Teach By*.
31. Yong, *Hospitality and the Other*, 160.
32. Koenig, *New Testament Hospitality*.
33. Amos Yong summarized the role of the Holy Spirit as guest-host in this manner: "The Spirit who is divine guest in the lives of those who receive her is also the divine host who dispenses the economy of God's hospitality" (*Hospitality and the Other*, 126).

education or to Singapore, provided that holistic formation is the goal of theological education.

Chapter Outline

Chapter 2 begins with a discussion of both Nouwen and his friend Palmer, and a selection of their works that are pivotal in discourses concerning hospitality and education. The discussion of these two trailblazers in this initial section will include an examination of the possible factors from the background that could have influenced their thoughts on hospitality, as well as the salient features of their individual concept of hospitality in education. The section closes with some interpretative observations, by way of comparison, concerning their notions of hospitality. Following that is a literature review of works done on hospitality in the contexts of: (1) Christian higher education, and (2) theological education. For each context, the works are grouped by concerns and examined, as much as possible, chronologically, for a clearer picture of how the different issues emerged over time.

Chapter 3 focuses on higher education. It begins by looking at the emotional and relational dimensions in the teaching-learning process. The section following is a literature review of works done on hospitality in the context of higher education. Again, the works are grouped by concerns and examined, as much as possible, chronologically, for the same above-mentioned purpose. From these works, it then draws out three parallel practices of hospitality used by the various authors in their discourses for further discussion: (1) care, (2) inclusion, and (3) dialogue.

Chapter 4 provides the biblical basis for conceptualizing how hospitality can be employed in theological education to facilitate the holistic formation of students. Using the host metaphor as the guiding motif, this chapter looks at hospitality from the perspective of God as host, Jesus as guest-host, and the early faith communities as hosts. The biblically informed metaphor of hospitality is intended to provide the biblical and theological underpinnings for the ensuing discussion in chapter 5, and to help shape the educational and pedagogical practices of teachers in theological institutions seeking the holistic formation of students.

Chapter 5 presents hospitality as a cluster concept and singles out four constitutive elements of hospitality which are drawn from the foregoing discussions in the previous chapters. These four constitutive elements are: (1) inclusion, (2) presence, (3) care, and (4) reciprocity. In the discussion of each element, the implications these elements have for our practice of hospitality in the classrooms of theological institutions are discussed, and suggestions made for its application.[34]

Chapter 6 summarizes and concludes this research. It also makes recommendations for further studies.

---

34. The ensuing literature reviews will show that hospitality, an ancient moral virtue and practice, is discussed by the various authors as a virtue and/or a practice. The focus of this work is on the practice of hospitality.

2

The Motif of Hospitality in the Literature of Christian Higher Education and Theological Education

The academics in the field of hospitality management studies have observed a growing interest in the study of hospitality from other disciplines and perspectives. In the past few decades, published works on hospitality from fields of study such as theology, sociology, history, anthropology, and philosophy, have indicated a recognition of "the potential value of studying hospitality from perspectives not traditionally concerned with the management of commercial hospitality service organizations."[1] This study seeks to broaden the spectrum of enquiry to include education and, more specifically, theological education.

Writing at the start of this millennium, David Smith and Barbara Carvill observed that examining education through the lens of hospitality was a relatively new phenomenon.[2] In their opinion, the "crucial impetus for seeing the significance of hospitality for education came from Henri J. M. Nouwen" and the significance of this metaphor was recognized primarily by Christian religious educators.[3] However, a closer examination of existing literature reveals that this significance was not lost on those involved in higher education,

---

1. Lashley, Lynch, and Morrison, "Hospitality: An Introduction," 1.
2. Smith and Carvill, *Gift of the Stranger*, 87.
3. See Groome, "Spirituality of the Religious Educator"; Seymour, Crain, and Crockett, *Educating Christians*; Cooper, "I Was a Stranger."

Christian higher education, as well as theological education. In fact, since the publication of Nouwen's works in the 1970s and Parker J. Palmer's in the 1980s, the concept of hospitality appears to be a recurring theme in the literature of higher education, Christian education, and theological education.

This chapter seeks to understand the state of the question by first considering the key contributions from two leading authors whose spiritual insights on hospitality still have an influence on educators today. It then reviews literature that relates hospitality to Christian higher education and theological education. The review is structured based on the concerns addressed by the writers, rather than chronologically. However, it seeks to discuss the individual works in a chronological order, as far as possible, to retain a sense of its conceptual development over time. By examining the significant features of hospitality presented in the various works, this review thus provides a conceptual map of the still ongoing discussion of the motif of hospitality.

Groundbreakers for Hospitality in Education

A literature review of the motif of hospitality in education literature must begin with Nouwen and his contemporary, Palmer. Their works are pivotal because many authors made reference to them when developing their own ideas on hospitality. This section outlines the development of the motif of hospitality in the thoughts of Nouwen and Palmer. It also includes a description of the conceptual framework of this motif and an analysis of the contexts that shaped their understanding of hospitality. The section concludes with some pertinent interpretative observations of their contributions to the development of hospitality in education.

Henri J. M. Nouwen

Nouwen's Dual Interest – Psychology and Practical Theology

As stated earlier, Nouwen played a vital catalytic role in promoting hospitality as an important component in education. Nouwen, born in 1932 in the Netherlands, was ordained a priest for the diocese of Utrecht when he was twenty-six years old.⁴ He showed keen interest in psychology as he felt that the discipline dealt with crucial issues of human nature that were often neglected by the church and theology.⁵ This interest led him to enroll in the doctoral program in psychology at the University of Nijmegen in 1957, at a time when clinical psychology was taught purely as a scientific discipline. Dissatisfied with the lack of integration between clinical psychology and religion, Nouwen then enrolled in the program for religion and psychiatry at the Menninger Foundation in 1964. In both instances, Nouwen did not satisfy the requirements for a doctorate degree because he refused to do any empirical research.⁶

Through the recommendation of John F. dos Santos, Nouwen went to the University of Notre Dame as a visiting professor to assist dos Santos in the development of a psychology program at the Roman Catholic university. Initially, Nouwen taught courses in general psychology. However, his "non-scholarly orientation," coupled with being a priest with a pastoral heart, steered him towards courses in pastoral psychology instead.⁷

Nouwen felt that psychology could play a role in religion. He said, "I felt that if I ever stayed in the university I should do theology, even though psychology would be a great help."⁸ Nouwen subsequently returned to the University of Nijmegen and enrolled in a program in theology with the hope of integrating psychology and theology. Ironically, his thesis was not accepted because it was deemed lacking in theological depth.⁹ Henceforth, Nouwen did not seek to pursue further academic studies. In fact, he accepted a teaching position at the Yale Divinity School in 1971 on condition that "he should not be expected to produce a dissertation, nor should the subject be broached in the future" and "what he would write would have to meet only his own criteria and not be measured according to some scientific yardstick."¹⁰

---

4. Biographical information on Henri J. M. Nouwen's life is based on several works (namely, Beumer, *Henri Nouwen*; Ford, *Wounded Prophet*; Jonas, *Beauty of the Beloved*; LaNoue, *Spiritual Legacy*; O'Laughlin, *God's Beloved*).
5. Beumer, *Henri Nouwen*, 24.
6. O'Laughlin, *God's Beloved*, 47, 51.
7. Ibid., 51.
8. LaNoue, *Spiritual Legacy*, 18.
9. O'Laughlin, *God's Beloved*, 53.
10. Beumer, *Henri Nouwen*, 32.

Michael O. O'Laughlin, a close friend of Nouwen, observed that the latter's repeated failures in the field of psychology left such an impact that Nouwen "remained ambivalent about psychology and professionalism in general" all his life.[11] When Yale employed Nouwen, they initially appointed him to be a clinical psychologist, but he abandoned clinical psychology in favor of pastoral psychology, choosing to focus on spirituality and theological issues.[12] However, "his wide knowledge of psychology and theology as well as matters of the spirit combined to make him an excellent counselor and spiritual guide."[13]

Nouwen's Development of the Concept of Hospitality

The concept of hospitality first appeared in *The Wounded Healer*, a book on pastoral care, where Nouwen put forward the Judeo-Christian concept of hospitality as an appropriate response to the wound of loneliness in ministers. To be authentic in their ministry, ministers need to make available their own wounds as a source of healing for others.[14] This is done through the practice of hospitality. Hospitality allows healing to take place because it "allows us to break through the narrowness of our own fears and to open our houses to the stranger."[15] And as a healing power, hospitality must embrace the concepts of concentration and community. The minister as the host needs to "feel at home in his own house" (i.e. concentration) and to "create a free and fearless place for the unexpected visitor" (i.e. community) where the common search for life through mutual sharing of pain may lead to liberation.[16]

In 1972, Nouwen related hospitality to education in a paper, "Education to the Ministry," which he delivered at the biennial meeting of the Association for Professional Education for Ministry at Macalaster College (St Paul, Minnesota). Here, he expressed his concern over the relationship between professional and spiritual formation in the training of future ministers. In his opinion, ministry can be seen as hospitality and "the call to ministry is the call to be a host to the many strangers passing by" in a world that is full of

---

11. O'Laughlin, *God's Beloved*, 56.
12. Ford, *Wounded Prophet*, 116.
13. Vanier, "Gentle Instrument," 262.
14. Nouwen, *Wounded Healer*, xvi.
15. Ibid., 89.
16. Ibid.

fear.[17] "Ministry is to convert hostility into hospitality, to make the *hostis* into a *hospes*, the enemy into a friend," creating "a space where the stranger can cast off his strangeness and become our fellowman."[18]

The seminal thoughts on hospitality penned were developed more extensively in Nouwen's article "Hospitality" – an article which was written while he was working on his book *Reaching Out*. In this work, hospitality is still "the creation of a space where the stranger can enter and become a friend instead of an enemy."[19] Furthermore, it is "an important attitude" that we need to have in an occupied and pre-occupied society. Such a society lacks creative empty space; thus, it prevents new experiences and challenges from presenting themselves to us.[20] With an attitude of hospitality, "we can offer a space where people are encouraged to disarm themselves, to lay aside their occupations and preoccupations, and to listen with attention and care to the voices speaking in their own center" and inner conversion can take place.[21] And in performing ministerial forms of service, one is creating a space that allows the other to dare to approach himself, others, and God.[22]

The culmination of Nouwen's thoughts on hospitality is found in his book *Reaching Out*, a book on Christian spirituality. In this book, Nouwen mapped out three movements of the spiritual life – inward from loneliness to solitude, outward from hostility to hospitality, and Godward from illusion to prayer. When we have reached out to our innermost being, having moved from loneliness to solitude, we will find healing and have the ability to reach out to the strangers walking in our midst. Our vocation as Christians is "to convert the *hostis* into a *hospes*, the enemy into a guest."[23] To be hospitable is to create a friendly space where enemies can be transformed into friends. Hospitality should be "a fundamental attitude toward our fellow human being" which can be expressed in many ways.[24] In fact, "the concept of hospitality might bring

---

17. Nouwen, "Education to the Ministry," 49.
18. Ibid., 50 (emphasis mine).
19. Nouwen, "Hospitality," 8.
20. Ibid., 9–11.
21. Ibid., 11–12.
22. Ibid., 25.
23. Nouwen, *Reaching Out*, 66 (original emphasis).
24. Ibid., 67.

a unifying dimension to all of these interpersonal relationships" – between parents and children, teachers and students, healers and patients.[25]

Salient Features of Nouwen's Concept of Hospitality

Certain distinguishing features stand prominent in Nouwen's concept of hospitality. These features often reappear in subsequent works as a more developed thought or with modifications as determined by the context. The salient features of Nouwen's concept of hospitality are: (1) hospitality as a Judaeo-Christian concept, (2) concentration and community, (3) receptivity and confrontation, and (4) the dual tasks of teaching: revealing and affirming.

1) Hospitality as a Judaeo-Christian concept.

Hospitality is first mentioned as a Judaeo-Christian concept in *Wounded Healer* but without any elaboration.[26] Its elucidation is subsequently found in "Hospitality" and *Reaching Out*.

Hospitality, as seen from three biblical narratives – namely, Abraham and the male strangers at Mamre (Gen 18:1–15), the widow of Zarephath and the prophet Elijah (1 Kgs 17:19–24), and the two disciples on the road to Emmaus and Jesus (Luke 24:13–35) – is a Christian obligation and virtue that involves the receiving of a stranger into one's own house.[27] However, this act of hospitality also gives opportunity for the stranger to become a guest and reveal the gift of promise that he carries with him because "when you open your house for the stranger, you might become his guest."[28] The three men at Mamre revealed themselves as the messengers of the Lord and announced the good news of God's promise of a son to Abraham and Sarah. Elijah revealed himself as a man of God to the widow and blessed her with miracles – her bowl of flour and jar of oil never became empty and her son was raised from the dead. Jesus expounded the Scriptures concerning himself to the two disciples, broke bread with them, and revealed himself as the risen Lord. Herein lies the idea of mutual reciprocity in the host-guest relationship.

---

25. Ibid., 80–81.
26. Nouwen, *Wounded Healer*, 89.
27. Nouwen, "Hospitality," 7; *Reaching Out*, 66–67.
28. Nouwen, "Education to the Ministry," 57.

2) Concentration and community

In *Wounded Healer* Nouwen shared that hospitality as a healing power should embrace both concentration and community.[29] These two encompassing concepts that embody hospitality as a healing power are also employed in Nouwen's other works, albeit in more neutral terms and in the context of Christian spirituality.[30]

In concentration, the host must "be at home in his own house" so that he can pay attention to his guest without being embroiled in his own intentions.[31] The host can do this because he has discovered "the center of his life in his own heart."[32] This necessitates a movement from loneliness to solitude[33] where poverty of mind and heart allows us to be good hosts since this inner disposition "allows us to take away our defenses and convert our enemies into friends."[34] When applied to education, both the host (i.e. the teacher) and the stranger (i.e. the student) need to learn to become at home in their own houses.[35] Poverty of mind allows us to receive new insights from others.[36]

Besides that, poverty of heart creates community as we receive the experiences of others as a gift.[37] Hospitality must also entail community where a free and fearless space is created for the sharing of pain in a world filled with people living in fear, thereby, allowing each guest to find his or her own soul.[38] In this free space the minister, as host, is a guide to the people by sharing his pain.[39] In so doing, he liberates them and gives them hope. It is a paradox, but in this common search for life, "a shared pain is no longer

---

29. Nouwen, *Wounded Healer*, 89.
30. Nouwen, "Education to the Ministry"; "Hospitality"; *Reaching Out*.
31. Nouwen, *Wounded Healer*, 90.
32. Ibid.
33. Nouwen, *Reaching Out*, 101–202.
34. Ibid., 103; see "Education to the Ministry," 51–53. Solitude is described as "the climate of hospitality" (Nouwen, *Reaching Out*, 102).
35. Nouwen, "Education to the Ministry," 53–54.
36. Nouwen, *Reaching Out*, 105.
37. Ibid., 107.
38. The word *place* was used by Nouwen in *Wounded Healer*, 89, but was replaced by *space* in subsequent writings.
39. Ibid., 93.

paralyzing but mobilizing."[40] "Creation of a space" thereafter becomes a catch phrase in Nouwen's definition of hospitality.[41]

Nouwen used adjectives such as *open*,[42] *hospitable*,[43] *empty*,[44] *free*,[45] *fearless*,[46] and *friendly*[47] to describe this space. The friendly empty space is a hospitable space "where a stranger can enter and discover himself as created free – free to sing his own song, speak his own language, dance his own dance, free also to leave and follow his own vocation"[48] – freedom as Henry David Thoreau described, where every person would "be very careful to find out and pursue *his own* way, and not his father's or his mother's or his neighbor's instead."[49]

3) Receptivity and confrontation

For Nouwen, hospitality is not limited to the literal sense, a real physical act of receiving strangers as guests into our homes. It should be a fundamental attitude towards others.[50] In fact, hospitality allows us to have a better understanding of our service to and relation with others.[51] If ministry is seen as hospitality, then the various forms of Christian ministry, namely, teaching, preaching, counseling, organizing, and liturgical celebration, are forms of hospitality.[52] Thus, ministry, or hospitality, creates a space that allows the other to dare to approach himself, others, and God. Furthermore, ministry is not just the work of someone who has a full-time calling to serve God. It is a life-vocation for every believer and "every Christian is called to be a host for the stranger passing by."[53] Seen from Nouwen' perspective, one practices

---

40. Ibid.
41. Nouwen, "Education to the Ministry," 50; "Hospitality," 8; *Reaching Out*, 71.
42. Nouwen, "Hospitality," 5.
43. Ibid., 5, 15.
44. Nouwen, "Education to the Ministry," 50, 51.
45. Ibid., 50; *Wounded Healer*, 89; "Hospitality," 6, 8, 12; *Reaching Out*, 66, 71, 79, 97.
46. Nouwen, *Wounded Healer*, 89; *Reaching Out*, 66, 86, 113.
47. Nouwen, "Hospitality," 6; *Reaching Out*, 79, 95, 97.
48. Nouwen, "Education to the Ministry," 50; "Hospitality," 8; see *Reaching Out*, 72.
49. Thoreau, *Walden*, 68 (original emphasis), as quoted in Nouwen, *Reaching Out*, 72.
50. Nouwen, "Hospitality," 8; *Reaching Out*, 67.
51. E.g. parent with child, teacher with student, or healer with patient; see Nouwen, *Reaching Out*, 81–97.
52. Nouwen, "Education to the Ministry," 50; "Hospitality," 13–25.
53. Nouwen, "Hospitality," 12.

hospitality when one performs any form of Christian service, and hospitality is the attitude we should adopt when serving others.

The reception of strangers as guests involves receptivity and confrontation. We receive the stranger into our homes on his or her own terms and we refrain from imposing the way we think or live upon them as a condition for the care that we are providing.[54] Yet, this unconditional reception must be balanced with confrontation – an articulate presence, a presence within boundaries.[55] The articulate presence of the host in the house then offers "a point of orientation or a frame of reference" and is "available to the guest as a healer, supporter or guide when needed or asked for."[56] Nouwen quoted Gabriel Marcel to elicit this inseparable nature of receptivity and confrontation: "If we devote our attention to the act of hospitality, we will see at once that to receive is not to fill up a void with an alien presence but to make the other person participate in a certain plenitude. To provide hospitality is truly to communicate something of oneself to the other."[57]

4) The dual tasks of teaching: revealing and affirming

Hospitality in teaching is creating "a space where students and teachers can enter into fearless communication with each other and allow their respective life experiences to be their primary and most valuable source of growth and maturation."[58] In a safe environment where there is mutual trust, teachers and students "become present to each other not as opponents but as those who share in the same struggle and search for the same truth."[59] Teaching in such a hospitable space allows for mental and emotional development and demands a teacher do two things: reveal and affirm.[60] The teacher reveals by helping the student see that he is carrying a hidden yet valuable gift that he can offer. This gift, when revealed, needs affirmation. In this process of revealing and affirming, the teacher, as a good host, helps the guest to develop

---

54. Nouwen, *Reaching Out*, 98.
55. Ibid.
56. Nouwen, "Hospitality," 26.
57. Ibid., 27.
58. Ibid., 14.
59. Ibid.
60. Ibid., 15; *Reaching Out*, 87.

this hidden gift, enabling the student to continue his search with renewed strength and confidence.

Teaching becomes ministry when teachers make their lives available to their students, offering their life experiences, their loneliness and intimacy, their doubts and hopes, their failures and successes as a context in which students learn. "The teacher moves beyond the transference of knowledge and is willing to offer his own life experience to his student so that paralyzing anxiety can be removed, new liberating insight can come about, and real learning can take place."[61] Vulnerability is demanded in this common search for meaning in life. Instead of being obstacles to learning, we make our weaknesses creative.[62]

Contextual Analysis of Nouwen's Concept of Hospitality

Biographers who wrote about Nouwen have observed that his books were often birthed from specific events in his life[63] and as he wrestled with the paradoxes in his own life.[64] Since Nouwen's works on hospitality were published during his years at Yale (1971–1981), these writings probably reflected the concerns of his heart and the complexity of the society then. This section analyzes three perceived contexts, namely, the social, intellectual, and personal, to show how they come to play a crucial role in his conceptualization of hospitality.

1) The perceived social context

Nouwen observed that people were living in a world filled with fear and hostility. People had ambivalent feelings towards strangers.[65] Every stranger was viewed as a potential enemy who was out to harm us. A foreboding presence of fear and distrust threatened our interpersonal relationships.[66] Nouwen believed that hospitality could serve as an antidote to counter the pervasive attitude of fear and hostility.

Furthermore, a widespread authoritarian spirit seemed to pervade educational institutions. In *Creative Ministry*, a book which Nouwen wrote while he was still teaching in the University of Notre Dame, he lamented

---

61. Nouwen, *Creative Ministry*, 114.
62. Ibid., 115.
63. Beumer, *Henri Nouwen*, 45.
64. Ford, *Wounded Prophet*, 16, citing Palmer's assessment of Nouwen's books.
65. Nouwen, "Education to the Ministry," 49; "Hospitality," 3–4; *Reaching Out*, 68–70.
66. Durback, *Seeds of Hope*, 36.

the violent teaching process which is competitive, unilateral, and alienating.[67] This competitive academic climate was probably not limited to Notre Dame. The education system at the Yale Divinity School promoted success and prestige, often leading to rivalry and isolation.[68] Nouwen's close friend Robert A. Jonas wrote that, in Nouwen's judgment, "the lack of a cohesive, supportive spiritual community" was a chronic problem among the students, faculty, and staff of seminaries in America.[69] Nouwen believed that teaching should be redemptive – evocative, bilateral, and actualizing.[70]

The situation in the classroom was further oppressed by a resistance to learning, a prevailing phenomenon brought about by a technocratic society, "killing the natural spontaneous curiosity of people and dulling the human desire to know."[71] Students were driven by the need to perform to satisfy the demands of the society as well as their demanding bosses – teachers – at the expense of their personal growth.[72] Furthermore, the education system was ineffective as "solutions are offered without the existence of a question."[73] Instead of allowing questions to surface, teachers simply dished out "prefabricated answers."[74] In such a hostile learning climate, students did not want to become vulnerable and ask questions that were born from within[75] while teachers themselves were too afraid to show themselves to their students.[76] In Nouwen's opinion, religious instruction was conducted in a manner that caused many to regard it as irrelevant because it had no bearing on their personal lives.[77] The Christian faith was reduced to mere

---

67. Nouwen, *Creative Ministry*, 5–10. Although Nouwen did not make explicit mention of the term *hospitality* (ibid., 8–9, 12–13), certain ideas found in the unilateral vs. bilateral teaching process (e.g. the wrong supposition that "it is better [for teachers] to give than to receive" [ibid., 17], and the resistance against "kenotic" self-encounter horror by both teachers and students [ibid., 19–20]) convey strands of thoughts akin to the concept of hospitality which he would elaborate in his future writings.
68. LaNoue, *Spiritual Legacy*, 29.
69. Jonas, *Beauty of the Beloved*, 34.
70. Nouwen, *Creative Ministry*, 10–15.
71. Nouwen, "Hospitality," 13; *Reaching Out*, 84.
72. Nouwen, "Hospitality," 13; *Reaching Out*, 85.
73. Nouwen, "Hospitality," 13; *Reaching Out*, 85.
74. Nouwen, "Hospitality," 14; *Reaching Out*, 86.
75. Nouwen, "Hospitality," 13–14; *Reaching Out*, 85.
76. Nouwen, "Hospitality," 14; *Reaching Out*, 86.
77. Nouwen, "Hospitality," 16; *Reaching Out*, 88.

doctrinal formulations that students were not even aware that Jesus could touch their inner soul and needs. Moreover, in seminaries, students who were preparing to fulfill a divine calling were merely training for a profession rather than for ministry. O'Laughlin observed that, over time, Nouwen viewed "the philosophy of professionalism more and more as something profoundly dehumanizing and simply unchristian" and developed an anti-professional stance.[78]

Living in an age where psychology seemed to provide the answers to human problems and pains, Nouwen was concerned that matters relating to pastoral ministry and Christian spirituality should not be uncritically informed by psychology.[79] In fact, society was so impressed by new findings and contributions from psychology that they "lost sight of the great heuristic potential of ancient concepts such as hospitality."[80] In Nouwen's opinion, psychology and psychiatry only opened our eyes to the rampant alienation and estrangement of many people. Only the biblical concept of hospitality could offer "a new dimension to our understanding of the healing relationship and the formation of a recreating community."[81]

2) The perceived intellectual context

Nouwen's concept of hospitality was influenced by the prevailing ideology and philosophy of his era. In the early 1970s, one of the educational ideals was self-expression.[82] Nouwen advocated this ideal of self-expression in his idea of a free space where one can be free to be himself by highlighting the difference between the German and Dutch words for hospitality. In German, hospitality is *gastfreundschaft* which means "friendship for the guest" while the Dutch word *gastvrijheid* means "the freedom of the guest."[83] Nouwen personally preferred the Dutch understanding since it shows that "hospitality wants to offer friendship without binding the guest and freedom without leaving him alone."[84] His thought was drawn from Thoreau, a transcendental

---

78. O'Laughlin, *God's Beloved*, 45.
79. Mogabgab, "Spiritual Pedagogy," 5.
80. Nouwen, "Hospitality," 7; see *Reaching Out*, 67.
81. Ibid.
82. Smith and Carvill, *Gift of the Stranger*, 87.
83. Nouwen, "Hospitality," 5; *Reaching Out*, 71.
84. Nouwen, *Reaching Out*, 71.

philosopher of the mid-nineteenth century.⁸⁵ Thoreau lived by himself in the woods for two years as an experiment to discover an individual's role and obligation to the society, isolating himself from the society in order to understand it better. When a young friend of his expressed a wish to live like Thoreau, the philosopher's reply was that he desired no one to imitate him but that each should be free to find his or her own purpose in life.⁸⁶

Nouwen's idea of receptivity and confrontation reflected the ideology of Marcel, a leading twentieth-century Christian existentialist whose works focused on the individual's struggle in a dehumanizing technocratic society and how one should interact with the other. The field of psychology also contributed to Nouwen's concept of hospitality. The idea of "being at home in one's own house" was derived from the developmental psychology of the psychoanalyst Erik Erikson.⁸⁷ For Nouwen, intimacy in relationships presupposed self-identity – a concept that is akin to Stage 5 and Stage 6 in Erikson's eight stages of personality development.⁸⁸

3) The perceived personal context

Nouwen personified hospitality in all that he did – writing, teaching, pastoring, and relating to others. His friend Robert Durback even named hospitality as the grace that permeates all his writings.⁸⁹ In the opening lines of Nouwen's first book, *Intimacy: Essays in Pastoral Psychology*, he wrote, "The sources of the following chapters are many: teaching, counseling, discussing, chatting, partying, celebrating, and most of all just being around."⁹⁰ This statement epitomizes his inclusive approach to writing, as well as all other forms of ministry. He was often "in dialogue with the reader"⁹¹ and was "a gracious host to his readers."⁹² After exploring his own ideas and reflecting on his own experiences, he listened to the ideas and experiences of others to arrive at a common understanding which he shared with others.⁹³

---

85. Ibid., 72.
86. Thoreau, *Walden*, 68.
87. Nouwen, "Hospitality," 27.
88. See Yount, *Created to Learn*, 51.
89. Durback, *Seeds of Hope*, 32, 37.
90. Nouwen, *Intimacy*, 1.
91. Durback, *Seeds of Hope*, 34.
92. Ibid., 35.
93. Ibid., 34.

John Mogabgab, who assisted Nouwen in his teaching and writing for five years (1975–1980) while they were working together at Yale Divinity School, made some observations on Nouwen's "spiritual pedagogy."[94] In the classroom Nouwen sought to create a hospitable space for learning at three levels. At the physical level, he would seek out the most inviting classroom for his students. At the spiritual level, each class would begin with prayer "to create a space in which the students' attention will be directed to the one in whose Name they desire to minister."[95] At the intellectual level, the lecture often contained "pastoral examples, personal anecdotes, psychological observations and theological analyses" to provide "points of contact between typical human experiences and the deeper reality of God's Spirit at work in the world."[96]

Nouwen was popular with his students and his affection for them extended beyond the classroom.[97] At Yale Divinity School, Nouwen lived on campus and left his apartment unlocked as a standing invitation to all.[98] He even removed his intimidating library from his office after a student remarked that he had many books. He did not want to make his visitors feel that he was so well read that they had nothing to offer him.[99]

O'Laughlin mentioned that Nouwen spent more time with students than any other faculty members at Yale and his friendships with some of them lasted for decades.[100] Even at Harvard Divinity School, Nouwen was different from those professors who were so busy reading or working that students were not able to find them. In fact, he "never went anywhere alone or even sat down to eat a meal by himself."[101] He also hosted a weekly gathering for students at his house that lasted for two hours.[102] After a simple meal of wine, juice, cheese, and crackers, they would have a short discussion on matters

---

94. Mogabgab, "Spiritual Pedagogy," 4.
95. Ibid.
96. Ibid.
97. LaNoue, *Spiritual Legacy of Henri Nouwen*, 21.
98. Glaser, "Henri's Greatest Gift," 126.
99. Ibid.
100. O'Laughlin, *Henri Nouwen*, 64.
101. O'Laughlin, "Henri the Teacher," 3.
102. Ford, *Wounded Prophet*, 121.

close to their hearts before ending the night by praying the Night Prayer together.

Peter Naus, a former colleague from the University of Notre Dame, recounted that Nouwen believed that "intimate relationships should be hospitable and inclusive."[103] For Nouwen, the Eucharist should be celebrated as "an experience of reconciliation and transformation" to bring people together.[104] It is not surprising then, that when the Eucharist was celebrated every evening in a small octagonal chapel in the basement, every one – Roman Catholic and Protestant – participated.[105] He would encourage the celebrants to go over to strangers to shake hands with them during the giving and receiving of peace.[106]

In his social life, "Nouwen is the consummate host, inviting not only his friends, but even the stranger to his table, pouring a cup of tea, throwing an extra log on the fire, eager to listen to his guest's story and to share his own into the late hours of the night."[107] Being hospitable and reaching out to the stranger was second nature to Nouwen.[108]

In real life, Nouwen was not a perfect human being. In Palmer's opinion, Nouwen's books are "deeply engrossing and engaging precisely because they came out of this ongoing wrestling match between the paradoxes in his own life. He practiced what he preached – and he preached the struggles, sometimes the anguish, sometimes the joy, which he himself was living."[109] Nouwen's friend, Carolyn Whitney-Brown, reportedly commented, "When I remember Henri, I think of two 'books': one is the book that Henri wrote 40 times, yet couldn't quite live; the other is the book that Henri lived for almost 65 years, yet couldn't quite write."[110] Naus, who also observed the "tensions, contradictions, and inconsistencies" in Nouwen's life, wrote that "the paradox is that he [Nouwen] would never have become an inspirational spiritual

---

103. Naus, "Man of Creative Contradictions," 82.
104. Ford, *Wounded Prophet*, 222.
105. Ibid., 123.
106. Ibid., 124.
107. Durback, *Seeds of Hope*, 32.
108. Ibid., 37.
109. As cited in Ford, *Wounded Prophet*, 16.
110. As quoted in ibid., 5.

writer if he lived what he wrote.¹¹¹ Therefore, his personal tragedy was also his gift to others." Struggling to live a life in perfect balance, Nouwen was a wounded man living with many tensions.¹¹² Nouwen himself acknowledged in the foreword of *Reaching Out* that he hesitated in writing the book since he himself was struggling with his own weakness. The encouragement to write came from the words penned by John of the Ladder: "If some are still dominated by their former bad habits, and yet can teach by mere words, let them teach.... For perhaps, being put to shame by their own words, they will eventually begin to practice what they teach."¹¹³

Naus perceived that Nouwen's struggles stemmed from "a deep-seated insecurity" that sought for affirmation in his interpersonal relationships.¹¹⁴ As a friend, Nouwen was generous to a fault. Calling, writing notes, and sending gifts to friends and readers were part of his daily routine. However, as a passionate person, Nouwen had to struggle with negative emotions when his friends did not reciprocate his gesture of friendship.¹¹⁵ With his close friends and family, "he felt a steady yearning for more: more love, more attention, more little reminders that he was special."¹¹⁶ In a newspaper interview in 1994, Nouwen himself confessed, "I need an enormous amount of friendship and love to be well. I'm extremely vulnerable, extremely needy. On the other hand, I think I give a lot."¹¹⁷ This intense cry for affirmation and friendship is also documented by other authors.¹¹⁸

Nouwen's immense emotional need for affection and friendship was further complicated by his struggles with his sexuality. What triggered a severe emotional crisis in Nouwen's life in 1988 was an interrupted friendship with a male colleague in L'Arche Daybreak (Toronto, Canada).¹¹⁹ Nouwen

---

111. Naus, "Man of Creative Contradictions," 84–85.
112. Ford, *Wounded Prophet*, 221–222.
113. As quoted in Nouwen, *Reaching Out*, 16.
114. Naus, "Man of Creative Contradictions," 85.
115. Jonas, *Beauty of the Beloved*, 49.
116. Ibid.
117. As quoted in Jonas, *Beauty of the Beloved*, 63.
118. See Ford, *Wounded Prophet*, 54–55, 222–223; LaNoue, *Spiritual Legacy*, 13; Vanier, "Gentle Instrument," 261–262.
119. Nouwen, *Inner Voice of Love*, xv; see Ford, *Wounded Prophet*, 80; Jonas, *Beauty of the Beloved*, 47–48; LaNoue, *Spiritual Legacy*, 44–45; Ball, "Covenant of Friendship," 91; Naus, "Man of Creative Contradictions," 85–86; O'Laughlin, *God's Beloved*, 75.

suffered a breakdown as a result of this breakdown of friendship. It took him seven months to recover from the emotional breakdown[120] and a couple of years to mend the broken friendship.[121] This was one of the many tensions that Nouwen had to live with – being acutely aware of his sexuality and still remaining faithful to his priestly vow of celibacy.[122]

Undoubtedly, Nouwen's knowledge of psychology and theology played an important role in his conceptualizing of hospitality. His concept of hospitality, focusing on interpersonal relations between people, is relational in nature and stands in stark contrast to the dehumanizing technocratic society in his day. Moreover, "his own pain and anguish, his own thirst for understanding and friendship, gave Henri a deeper understanding of the yearnings, the loneliness, the needs of others."[123] Hence, the practice of hospitality, the creation a free space that welcomes strangers and allows them to be who they are, resonated well with Nouwen, a gentle and sensitive soul.

Parker J. Palmer

Parker J. Palmer's Experience of Community and Contradiction

After receiving his doctorate in sociology from the University of California in Berkeley, Palmer worked for two years as a community organizer before taking up a faculty post that encouraged him to involve students in community work.[124] However, his five-year teaching stint at Georgetown University in Washington was marred by conflict and competition, and left Palmer burned out. Upon reflection, Palmer came to this realization: "I was trying to take people to a place where I had never been myself – a place called community."[125]

Palmer felt that there was "a lack of community in academic life and the larger question of civic community in America."[126] His search for a life in community initiated the Palmer family's move to Pendle Hill in the fall of 1974, a Quaker living-learning community near Philadelphia. What was

---

120. Mosteller "Introduction," viii; see Nouwen, *Sabbatical Journey*, 124.
121. Ball, "Covenant of Friendship," 97; see Nouwen, *Sabbatical Journey*, 124.
122. Ford, *Wounded Prophet*, 152; see Keogh "My Adopted Father," 157.
123. Vanier, "Gentle Instrument," 262.
124. Palmer, *Let Your Life Speak*, 20–21.
125. Ibid., 22.
126. Palmer, *Promise of Paradox*, 55.

initially intended to be a sabbatical leave from work became an eleven-year sojourn.[127] In this Quaker community, about seventy people lived and learned together, hoping "to offer education about the inner journey, non-violent social change, and the connection between the two."[128]

It was in community that Palmer discovered contradictions. He wrote:

> We came seeking a fuller fellowship with others than we had experienced in the suburbs. We found it, but we also discovered a new need for solitude. We came seeking extended family for ourselves and our children. We found it, but we also discovered the need to draw our own family's boundaries more firmly around us. We came seeking to escape certain forces in the world. We have done so, but we have also found ourselves more deeply engaged with the world than ever before.[129]

However, Palmer soon discovered that these were not contradictions; rather, they should be conceived as paradoxes where both poles were true.[130] Since then, paradox has been a recurring theme in Palmer's works, whether it is on educational reform[131] or social change.[132] In jest, Palmer wrote that there was the possibility he could be "one of those writers who have only one book in them, a book they rewrite many times."[133] However, he opted for a more dignified explanation, namely, his fundamental questions that remained unchanged since he first began writing thirty years ago since these constituted the core of his personal identity.[134] Palmer himself admitted, "So at bottom, my longtime fascination with paradox is rooted in my longtime bafflement about myself."[135]

---

127. Palmer, *Let Your Life Speak*, 23.
128. Ibid.
129. Palmer, *Promise of Paradox*, 57.
130. Ibid., 58.
131. Palmer, *To Know as We Are Known*, ch. 7; *Courage to Teach*, ch. 3.
132. Palmer, *Promise of Paradox*, chs. 1 and 3; *Company of Strangers*, chs. 5 and 6; *Active Life*; *Let Your Life Speak*, ch. 6; *Hidden Wholeness*, ch. 4.
133. Palmer, *Promise of Paradox*, xxxiii.
134. Ibid.
135. Ibid., xxxiv.

For Palmer, life can be described as "a whale of a paradox" with "contradiction, paradox, and tension of the opposites" at its core.[136] The phrase "a whale of paradox" was derived from Thomas Merton's journal, *The Sign of Jonas*. In the biblical story of the prophet Jonah, God called Jonah to go to Nineveh but Jonah chose, instead, to board a ship that was going in the opposite direction. Due to a heavy storm, "he was thrown overboard, and swallowed by a whale who took him where God wanted him to go."[137] Merton identified himself with Jonah. He wrote, "Like Jonas himself I find myself traveling toward my destiny in the belly of a paradox."[138] Similarly, Palmer saw himself as traveling towards his destiny in the belly of a paradox.[139]

Instead of struggling to remove tensions in life, Palmer proposed that we should learn to live the contradiction and allow the contradiction to be transformed into paradox.[140] Since a paradox, by definition, is "a statement that seems self-contradictory or absurd but in reality expresses a possible truth," it thereby carries a promise.[141] And "the promise of paradox is the promise that apparent opposites – like order and disorder – can cohere in our lives, the promise that if we replace either-or with both-and, our lives will become larger and more filled with light."[142] This was an insight Palmer gleaned from the Danish physicist Niels Bohr, the 1922 Nobel Laureate in Physics, who wrote, "The opposite of a correct statement is a false statement. But the opposite of a profound truth may be another profound truth."[143] Hence, "learning how to hold life's tensions in the responsive heart instead of the reactive primitive brain is key to personal, social, and cultural creativity: rightly held, those tensions can open us to new thoughts, relationships, and possibilities that disappear when we try to flee from or destroy their source."[144]

---

136. Ibid., 2.
137. Merton, *Sign of Jonas*, 10–11.
138. Ibid., 11.
139. Palmer, *Promise of Paradox*, 1. The word *whale*, as used by Thomas Merton and Parker J. Palmer, is derived from Jonah 1:17 (*dāg gādôl* in Jonah 2:1 of the Hebrew text) but is not translated as such in the English Bibles (cf. *large fish* [NRSV], *great fish* [NASB, NKJV], *huge fish* [NIV]).
140. Ibid., 6.
141. Ibid., xxix.
142. Ibid.
143. As quoted in Palmer, *Courage to Teach*, 65.
144. Palmer, "Broken-Open Heart," 3.

If we hold the tensions of the opposites in our lives creatively, we will be able to encounter new truths that will enrich our lives.

Palmer's Development of the Concept of Hospitality

Palmer described his first book, *The Promise of Paradox*, as an "accidental book."[145] It was a compilation of several of his essays on paradox. His main contention was: By embracing true paradoxes, by espousing a both-and mentality, we can encounter "the other" and "open our minds and hearts to something new," and living with unresolved tension will allow us "to participate in the evolution of a better reality."[146] Similarly, the quest for spiritual truth which is often self-contradictory and non-rational is a quest for what Merton called "life's 'hidden wholeness,' the underlying unity of all things."[147] Hence, God's truth is known through "the complexity of both-and."[148] Although the word *hospitality* was not used, Palmer mentioned the alienation of the heart, the inability to connect with others – a "common malady in modern times, this inability to empathize with the stranger."[149]

The idea of stranger was prominently featured in Palmer's second book, *The Company of Strangers*, a book that addressed the importance of recovering the public life by the church in a fragmented society.[150] Though not related to education per se, Palmer introduced the idea of the stranger and hospitality as central to the biblical tradition. The stranger plays a vital role in public life which, in Palmer's opinion, is "an area of spiritual experience" where God can speak to us in ways and words that we cannot see or hear in our private life.[151] Thus, strangers become "the spiritual guide for our private life."[152] In their presence, with their eyes, we get to look at the outer world with new eyes, thereby gaining a deeper understanding of our inner life. Hospitality is introduced as a quality that we need to relate with the stranger.[153] It acts as a

---

145. Palmer, *Promise of Paradox*, xvii.
146. Ibid., xxx, xxxi.
147. Merton, *Sign of Jonas*, 7; for details, see Merton's poem, *Hagia Sophia*, in McDonnell, *Thomas Merton Reader*, 506–511, esp. 506.
148. Palmer, *Promise of Paradox*, 7.
149. Ibid., 16.
150. Palmer, *Company of Strangers*, esp. ch. 3.
151. Ibid., 63.
152. Ibid., 79.
153. Ibid., 76.

bridge between two realms: the private and public.¹⁵⁴ In showing hospitality, we need to invite the stranger who is found in the public into our private space – be it a physical dwelling place or the inner thoughts and consciousness. In this act of hospitality, we open up our private space and the presence of the stranger may bring new light into a hidden bias or even reveal a hidden treasure in our lives.

It is in Palmer's third book *To Know as We Are Known* that hospitality is discussed in relation to education. In general, the academic climate has inflicted upon educators "the pain of dissociation."¹⁵⁵ Thus, Palmer called for a recovery of connectedness and community in education as an alternative to the prevailing tendency in education to isolate the knowing self from the object to be known. "To teach is to create a space in which obedience to truth is practiced."¹⁵⁶ "Truthful knowing weds the knower and the known" into "in a mutually accountable and transforming relationship, a relationship forged of trust and faith in the face of unknowable risks."¹⁵⁷ And to facilitate this encounter with truth's transformation for students, the teacher must create a space that is open, bounded, and hospitable.¹⁵⁸

In *The Courage to Teach*, Palmer posited that good teaching comes first from knowing oneself as "we teach who we are."¹⁵⁹ Hence, the book first explores the teacher's inner life or the "inner landscape of the teaching self" since the teacher's selfhood is crucial to educational reform.¹⁶⁰ Palmer believed that "*good teaching cannot be reduced to technique; good teaching comes from the identity and integrity of the teacher.*"¹⁶¹ Segueing into the outer form of teaching and learning – community – Palmer redefined teaching in these terms: "To teach is to create a space in which the community of truth

---

154. Ibid., 78.
155. Palmer, *To Know as We Are Known*, x.
156. Ibid., 69. John Mogabgab credited the origin of this statement to Nouwen who formulated it during one of the conversations which the three – Mogabgab, Nouwen, and Palmer – had at Pendle Hill during the falls of 1977 and 1978 ("Spiritual Pedagogy," 4). Palmer too acknowledged that his book *To Know as We Are Known* was birthed from those conversations (xxi).
157. Palmer, *To Know as We Are Known*, 31.
158. Ibid., 71.
159. Palmer, *Courage to Teach*, 2.
160. Ibid., 5.
161. Ibid., 10 (original emphasis); for definitions, see 13–14.

is practiced."¹⁶² "The hallmark of the community of truth is in its claim that *reality is a web of communal relationships, and we know reality only by being in community with it.*"¹⁶³ Knowing, teaching, and learning in community must allow for connectedness. To do so, Palmer advocated the need to see the world in paradox and hold the poles of opposites in a healthy tension. He delineated six paradoxical tensions that should be found in the teaching-learning space.¹⁶⁴ In this pedagogical design, hospitality is presented in the second paradox: "The space should be hospitable and 'charged.'"¹⁶⁵

Hospitality is discussed in Palmer's book *A Hidden Wholeness* in the context of the circles of trust and clearness committee, a Quaker practice that Palmer personally experienced at Pendle Hill. A central practice in circles of trust is the clearness committee, a discernment process used by the Quakers to help their members deal with personal issues.¹⁶⁶ This practice of the Quakers is grounded on two convictions: (1) "our guidance comes not from external authority but from the inner teacher," and (2) "we need community to help us clarify and amplify the inner teacher's voice."¹⁶⁷ It is the true community or circles of trust that will help us to discover the wholeness that is hidden by our broken and divided life. As people of diverse spiritual traditions explore together issues of inner life to discern the "true self" within them, they look for both hospitality and honesty.¹⁶⁸ Circles of trust, thus, must create a safe space that welcomes the soul, allowing for truthful speaking and receptive listening.¹⁶⁹ "We must speak our truth to the center of the circle and listen receptively as others speak theirs."¹⁷⁰ Instead of being inhospitable and

---

162. Ibid., 92; see 97, 123, 135, 153.
163. Ibid., 97 (original emphasis).
164. Ibid., 76–77.
165. Ibid., 76; explained further in 77–78.
166. Originally used to help couples who were contemplating marriage, the clearness committee is now used by the Quakers to help anyone who needs help to think through a problem or make a decision. The committee is comprised of a few selected friends who will give undivided attention to the person seeking help, and ask honest, open questions to help the person "hear more clearly the guidance that comes from within" (ibid., 159; for details on the process, see 156–161).
167. Palmer, *Hidden Wholeness*, 134.
168. Ibid., 81. *True self* is a term used by Merton to refer to the image of God, the soul within us, or what the Quakers term *the inner light* or "that of God" in every person (Palmer, *Let Your Life Speak*, 11).
169. Palmer, *Hidden Wholeness*, 122.
170. Ibid., 130.

responding with our opinions or ideas, we should learn to respond, like in the clearness committee, by asking honest and open questions.

Salient Features of Palmer's Concept of Hospitality

An examination of Palmer's concept of hospitality must begin with an understanding of his friendship with Nouwen which began in the mid-1970s, most likely "around 1976 or 1977,"[171] when they worked together in a Lilly Endowment consultation on spirituality.[172] For two years, during the fall semesters of 1977 and 1978, Nouwen and Palmer, together with Nouwen's teaching assistant at Yale, Mogabgab, met regularly to exchange views on the theme of "Education and Community."[173] Their desire was to articulate a Christian spirituality of teaching that addressed both the educational process and communal aspect of education. The three friends spent the day "talking, praying, laughing, and eating woeful inadequate lunches."[174] This informal and relaxed gathering of friends facilitated the sharing and conceptualizing of ideas and thoughts.

Having read *Reaching Out* even before he met Nouwen,[175] Palmer expressed that he was indebted to Nouwen in regard to the concept of hospitality.[176] In a personal email message to me (22 May 2009), Palmer wrote, "Henri Nouwen... led the way, and I am ever grateful for that." A considerable overlap of ideas about hospitality is discernible in the works of both authors. Yet, the added nuances that Palmer brought to the conversation make his conceptualization somewhat different from Nouwen's. The salient features of Palmer's concept of hospitality are: (1) the stranger and hospitality as biblical concepts, (2) space and community, and (3) receptivity and reciprocity.

1) The stranger and hospitality as biblical concepts

Like Nouwen, Palmer grounded hospitality in the biblical tradition. However, the lens is focused on the stranger in Palmer's presentation of the biblical tradition of hospitality. In *Company of Strangers*, Palmer cited Hebrews 13:1–2: "Let mutual love continue. Do not neglect to show hospitality to

---

171. Palmer, 21 March 2011, email message to author.
172. Palmer, *Promise of Paradox*, xviii.
173. Mogabgab, "Spiritual Pedagogy," 4.
174. Palmer, *To Know as We Are Known*, xxi.
175. Palmer, *Promise of Paradox*, xviii.
176. Palmer, *To Know as We Are Known*, 127, n. 4.

strangers, for by doing that some have entertained angels without knowing it."[177] This citation alludes to the account of Abraham's reception of the three men at Mamre (Gen 18:1-15); however, it also strikes a similar chord in the two disciples' reception of Jesus on the road to Emmaus (Luke 24:13-35).

In both narratives, the stranger is "a bearer of truth," a new truth, reminding us that truth is larger than our own.[178] He is also "a person of promise"[179] who bears two God-fulfilled promises: (1) the promise of covenant – "that God will be faithful to people of faith," and (2) the promise of newness – "that God will continually move among and within us, bringing fresh vitalities and new possibilities to life."[180] As Nouwen put it, "in the context of hospitality guest and host can reveal their precious gifts and bring new life to each other."[181]

Palmer proceeded further by showing the prominence of the stranger in Jesus' teaching: "Truly I tell you, just as you did it to one of the least of these who are members of my family, you did it to me" (Matt 25:40).[182] In the context of Matthew 25, the "least of these" would be the hungry, the thirsty, the stranger, the naked, the sick, or the prisoner. By identifying himself with these who are often treated as objects of fear to be avoided, Jesus reveals the important role the stranger plays in our lives. "The stranger is not simply one who needs us. We need the stranger. We need the stranger if we are to know Christ and serve God."[183] In our every encounter with the stranger we are given the chance to meet the living Christ.

Moreover, in showing hospitality to the stranger, we acknowledge our unity with the needy. "Every hospitable act is an outward and visible sign of our inward and invisible unity," a unity that lies in the word *hospitality* itself, since "*hospes* means both host and guest – the two are really one."[184] Besides, we also need the stranger to help us find ourselves because we are not only strangers to others but also strangers to ourselves. In the stranger, we see "possibilities in our lives which we want to avoid facing" – our vulnerability,

---

177. Palmer, *Company of Strangers*, 64.
178. Ibid., 65.
179. Ibid., 66.
180. Ibid., 67.
181. Nouwen, "Hospitality," 7; *Reaching Out*, 67.
182. Palmer, *Company of Strangers*, 72-73.
183. Ibid., 73.
184. Ibid., 78 (original emphasis).

weaknesses, and sins.[185] We avoid the stranger so that we will not be reminded of our own pain and isolation. However, "to be comfortable with the external stranger we must be comfortable with the stranger within."[186] This idea echoes Nouwen's concept of concentration that calls for the host to be "at home in his own house" (see above p. 15).[187]

2) Space and community

Both Nouwen and Palmer believed in a hospitable space that allowed the stranger to discover who he or she is. However, Palmer further proposed community or circles of trust as an avenue to explore one's true self.[188] Our journey toward an undivided life is guided by the inner teacher or truth within our soul, and the trusted friends in circles of trust who will help us discern the true self within.[189] Instead of choosing to fight or take flight, the circle of trust will help us to respond to the violence of the world in a "third way," the way of nonviolence that does not violate our identity and integrity.[190] The space held within circles of trust makes it "safe for the soul to show up and offer us its guidance."[191] This safe space, which "honors and welcomes the soul," allows us the freedom to make our own discernments as those who are with us encourage and challenge us with their presence.[192] As a result, we are able not only to listen to the inner voice of the soul, but we also have the courage to obey what it says.[193]

This understanding of community in terms of circles of trust has an added nuance to Nouwen's perception of community as "a way of being together that gives us a sense of belonging."[194] In addition, when speaking

---

185. Ibid., 74.
186. Ibid.
187. Nouwen, *Wounded Healer*, 90.
188. Palmer, *Hidden Wholeness*, 11.
189. Ibid., ix.
190. Ibid., 170.
191. Ibid., 22. Although other adjectives such as *creative, focused, free, inviting, meaningful, open, revealing, trusting,* and *trustworthy* have been used to describe this space (Palmer, *Courage to Teach*, 77; *Hidden Wholeness*, 69, 91, 92, 94), the adjective that is more consistently used is *safe* (*Hidden Wholeness*, 66, 72, 73, 76, 91, 122, 136, 144, 152, 170, 171, 183).
192. Palmer, *Hidden Wholeness*, 27, 140.
193. Ibid., 68.
194. Nouwen, *Reaching Out*, 152.

34   The Motif of Hospitality in Theologial Education

about community in higher education, Palmer redefined community as "a capacity for relatedness within individuals – relatedness not only to people but to events in history, to nature, to the world of ideas, and yes, to things of the spirit."[195] It is "a kind of inward version of community."[196] And it is this capacity for connectedness that allows for creative conflicts in classrooms and for learning to take place. Everyone has something to contribute and, by drawing on the pool of knowledge of the group, the knowledge of each individual increases.[197]

3) Receptivity and reciprocity

Palmer lamented that if "ancient hospitality is firstly and primarily a bond between utter strangers,"[198] then "we have lost the ancient sense of hospitality as a bridge between strangers, a bond in which 'lies hidden the idea of humanity and of human fellowship.'"[199] In showing hospitality, we accept the stranger and allow him or her to be who he is, meeting his or her needs without trying to transform him or her into "a modified version of ourselves."[200] This is the receptivity in hospitality that Nouwen spoke of whereby we invite "the stranger into our world on his or her terms, not on ours" (see above p. 17).[201]

Furthermore, "hospitality is always an act that benefits the host even more than the guest."[202] Palmer rooted this idea of reciprocity in the ancient custom of hospitality practiced in nomadic cultures. "The food and shelter one gave to a stranger yesterday is the food and shelter one hopes to receive from a stranger tomorrow" and "the gift of sustenance for the guest becomes a gift of hope for the host."[203] Although Nouwen did not use the term *reciprocity*, he too shared this understanding of reciprocity when he wrote, "When you open your house for the stranger, you might become his guest. When you minister,

---

195. Palmer, "Community, Conflict, and Ways of Knowing."
196. Palmer, "Action and Insight," 328.
197. Palmer, "Community, Conflict, and Ways of Knowing."
198. Palmer, *Company of Strangers*, 76, quoting Meagher, "Strangers at the Gates," 11.
199. Palmer, *Company of Strangers*, 76.
200. Ibid., 77.
201. Nouwen, *Reaching Out*, 98.
202. Palmer, *Courage to Teach*, 51.
203. Ibid.,

you are ministered by those you have invited. When you teach, you might learn from your students."[204]

Hospitality as an Epistemological Virtue

Unlike Nouwen, Palmer perceived hospitality not only as an ethical virtue but an epistemological virtue as well. As a bearer of truth, the stranger is an agent used by God to introduce us to strangeness of truth. Hence, "to be inhospitable to strangers or strange ideas, however unsettling they may be, is to be hostile to the possibility of truth."[205] If hospitality is an epistemological virtue, the classroom, where truth is central, becomes the focal point since it is a place "where stranger and every strange utterance is met with welcome."[206]

Space then becomes pivotal in Palmer's understanding of our quest to know, teach, and learn. This can be gleaned from Palmer's definition of teaching which is elicited from the story of the desert father Abba Felix's conversation with his students.[207] For Palmer, "*to teach is to create a space in which obedience to truth is practiced.*"[208] In the classroom, this space is the teaching-learning space and can refer to: (1) physical space, specifically the physical arrangement of the classroom; (2) conceptual space – the conceptual framework of speech and silence; (3) dramatic space for a personal encounter with truth; and (4) emotional space where feelings can be safely expressed and explored.[209]

To be more inclusive and to reach to a wider reading audience, Palmer later redefined teaching as: "*To teach is to create a space in which the community of truth is practiced.*"[210] Apparently, the word *obedience* had negative connotations that triggered resistance from different groups of readers. Hence, it was replaced by the phrase "community of truth" which represents "a rich and complex network of relationships in which we must both speak and listen, make claims on others, and make ourselves accountable."[211] In

---

204. Nouwen, *Wounded Healer*, 57.
205. Palmer, *To Know as We Are Known*, 74.
206. Ibid.
207. Ibid., 41.
208. Ibid., 69 (original emphasis).
209. Ibid., 75–87; *Courage to Teach*, 76.
210. Palmer, *Courage to Teach*, 92 (original emphasis).
211. Palmer, *To Know as We Are Known*, xi–xii.

the community of truth, truth is a subject that is *"available for relationship"*[212] and *"reality is a web of communal relationships, and we can know reality only by being in community with it."*[213] "The truth we are seeking, the truth that seeks us, lies ultimately in the community of being where we not only know but are known."[214] Knowing is relational. And we develop community with what we know.[215]

Essentially, for Palmer, "to teach, first, is to create a space in which a meeting can occur, a meeting between those who seek truth and the truth which seeks them."[216] For this meeting to take place, the teaching-learning space must consist of three qualities, namely, "openness, boundaries, and an air of hospitality."[217] Hospitality is needed because "a learning space can be painful place."[218] Hospitality enables us to receive "each other, our struggles, our newborn ideas with openness and care."[219] Although hospitality does not remove pain in the learning, it makes it possible to learn painful things – "like exposing ignorance, testing tentative hypotheses, challenging false or partial information, and mutual criticism of thought" in a non-threatening and non-judgmental environment, devoid of competition.[220]

In *Courage to Teach*, Palmer delineates six paradoxical tensions that should be found in this teaching-learning space:

- The space should be bounded and open
- The space should be hospitable and "charged"
- The space should invite the voice of the individual and the voice of the group
- The space should honor the "little" stories of the students and the "big" stories of the discipline and tradition
- The space should support solitude and surround it with the resources of community

---

212. Palmer, *Courage to Teach*, 104 (original emphasis).
213. Ibid., 97 (original emphasis).
214. Palmer, *To Know as We Are Known*, 90.
215. Palmer, *Courage to Teach*, 55.
216. Palmer, "Truth Is Personal," 1054.
217. Ibid., 1054–1055; *To Know as We Are Known*, 71.
218. Palmer, *To Know as We Are Known*, 73.
219. Ibid., 73–74.
220. Ibid., 74.

- The space should welcome both silence and speech[221]

A hospitable teaching-learning is safe even for encountering the dangers posed by difficult topics. Yet, it must not be so devoid of risks and challenges that it lulls us to sleep, causing us to evade or trivialize topics of significance.[222] However, hospitality is not limited to the teaching-learning space. "Good teaching is an act of hospitality toward the young" that benefits the teacher even more than the students for, in showing hospitality to the students, the world becomes a more hospitable place to the teacher.[223]

Contextual Analysis of Palmer's Concept of Hospitality

From the numerous works of Palmer, we can discern the inner and external forces that have influenced his thoughts. Similar to my contextual analysis of Nouwen's concept of hospitality, this section analyzes the perceived social, intellectual, and personal contexts to show the crucial role they play in Palmer's conceptualization of hospitality.

1) The perceived social context

Palmer generally took a rather critical stand against the American society and education system. Although fragmentation of community in American culture can be attributed to "a denial of true self" brought upon by secularism and moralism, Palmer believed that the underlying cause was the "empty self syndrome."[224] People are torn apart because "they have a bottomless pit where their identity should be – an inner void they try to fill with competitive success, consumerism, sexism, racism, or anything that might give them the illusion of being better than others."[225] Since the advent of the Age of Enlightenment with its scientific and technological advancement, the active life is prized above all else.[226] Furthermore, it is assumed, albeit falsely, that

---

221. Palmer, *Courage to Teach*, 76–77. Although John B. Bennett argued that the term *inclusiveness* can better integrate these paradoxes within Palmer's idea of hidden wholeness and connectedness, in my opinion, it is just a preference of terms ("Educational Spiritualities," 180–182). For Palmer, the opposites in the paradox should always be embraced as one (*Promise of Paradox*, 4–9; *Active Life*, ch. 2; *Courage to Teach*, 63–69).
222. Palmer, *Courage to Teach*, 78.
223. Ibid., 51.
224. Palmer, *Hidden Wholeness*, 35, 38.
225. Ibid., 38.
226. Palmer, *Active Life*, 6.

good work can only be produced by competition, not collaboration.[227] Hence, a competitive and individualistic society evolved.[228]

The same spirit of competitiveness hovers over the academic arena. Back in the 1960s, the university was perceived by many as "a place of corruption and arrogance, filled with intellectuals who evaded their social responsibilities and yet claimed superiority over the ordinary folks."[229] Over the ages, it has become a "training ground for competition."[230] Cooperation is even considered cheating.[231] In such a competitive battleground, winners are awarded with abundance and losers with scarcity since the credentials awarded to the winners open the doors to better jobs, wealth, and power.[232] In this sense, "the educational process itself has become a competition over scarce resources."[233]

It is Palmer's conviction that "every epistemology becomes an ethic."[234] The way we know ultimately becomes the way we live. The Western mode of learning that dominates conventional education is objective, analytic, and experimental,[235] and it produces an ethic of detachment and manipulation that has devastating effects on us.[236] It disconnects people as it is rooted in fear.[237] It fears "both the knowing self and the thing known," it "distances self from the world and deforms our relationships with our subjects, our students, and ourselves," and poses a major threat to community.[238] In Palmer's opinion, objectivism – not religious groups or sects – is the major obstacle to community.[239]

Since education seems to be disconnected with the deeper issues of life, Palmer has been working hard for the past four decades to reclaim a "depth-

---

227. Palmer, *Promise of Paradox*, 89.
228. Ibid., 62.
229. Palmer, *Let Your Life Speak*, 26.
230. Palmer, *Promise of Paradox*, 70.
231. Ibid., 70; *To Know as We Are Known*, 37; *Company of Strangers*, 89.
232. Palmer, *Promise of Paradox*, 105–106.
233. Ibid., 105.
234. Palmer, "Violence of Our Knowledge."
235. Ibid.
236. Palmer, *To Know as We Are Known*, 51.
237. Palmer, *Courage to Teach*, 52.
238. Ibid., 55.
239. Palmer, *To Know as We Are Known*, 50–51.

dimension" to higher education.²⁴⁰ In 1994, he initiated the "Courage to Teach" program for K–12 teachers, at the request of the Fetzer Institute, to help K–12 teachers explore the inner landscape of their lives to connect their soul with their vocation that would sustain them in their commitment to teach.²⁴¹ This program has now expanded into the Center for Courage and Renewal, offering programs that help people from the various professions to "reconnect who they are with what they do" through the use of "circles of trust."²⁴²

2) The perceived intellectual context

A person who greatly inspired and influenced Palmer is Merton, a Trappist monk of the Abbey of Gethsemani (Trappist, Kentucky).²⁴³ Merton was a Roman Catholic priest and a prolific writer. Through his writings, he became "a universal religious figure, steeped in Taoism and Zen, hailed by some in the East as an incarnate Buddha."²⁴⁴ Acclaimed as "the hermit of Times Square" and a "pastor" to the peace movement of the early 1960s, he was critical of the involvement of the United States in the Vietnam War.²⁴⁵ Even though Merton lived a life of silence and solitude, away from the hustle and bustle of the worldly life, he was still able to see "prophetically into racism and militarism and became patron saint of social activists."²⁴⁶ We can understand Palmer's affinity with Merton as Palmer himself is an activist in education and social reform. However, Palmer considered himself first a teacher, and it was that calling and passion that precipitated the need for reforms.²⁴⁷ He wrote:

> I am a teacher at heart, and I am not naturally drawn to the rough-and-tumble of social change. I would sooner teach than spend my energies helping a movement along and taking the hits that come with it. Yet if I care about teaching, I must care not only

---

240. Palmer, "Broken-Open Heart," 3.
241. Palmer, *Courage to Teach*, xii. *K–12* is a term used in America, Canada, and some other countries to designate education from kindergarten through twelfth grade (i.e. a total of twelve years of education).
242. Ibid., xv.
243. See Gascho, "Parker Palmer and Christian Nurture," 96–98.
244. Palmer, *Promise of Paradox*, 3.
245. McDonnell, *Thomas Merton Reader*, 3.
246. Palmer, *Promise of Paradox*, 3.
247. Palmer, *Courage to Teach*, 189.

for my students and my subject but also for the conditions, inner and outer, that bear on the work teachers do. Finding a place in the movement for educational reform is one way to exercise that larger caring.[248]

The source of Palmer's concept of paradox can also be traced to Merton. Although Merton withdrew from the world to live a life in solitude, he did not envision a spiritual life that is apart from the so-called secular life. Palmer recounted that in one of Merton's talks to some novice monks, he ended his prayer with this admonition, "Men, before you can have a spiritual life, you've got to have a life!"[249] Merton believed that our spiritual life can be found "in that mess itself, in its earthly realities, unpredictable challenges, surprising resources, creative dynamics."[250] Life, for Merton, is "almost totally paradoxical."[251] Merton himself wrote, "It is in the paradox itself, the paradox which was and is still a source of insecurity, that I have come to find the greatest security," a sentiment that was echoed by Palmer in his writings.[252]

Intellectually, Palmer was also inspired by works that promoted the inseparability of the knower and the known, or the observer and the observed. Drawing from the scientific findings of the chemist Michael Polanyi and the biologist Barbara McClintock, Palmer debunked the myth of objectivism which assumes that the object to be known is divorced from the subject.[253] That *"reality is a web of communal relationships, and we can know only by being in community with it,"*[254] thus, became the cornerstone in Palmer's educational model, the community of truth.[255] Although Palmer believed "these paired and paradoxical modes of knowing" should complement each other, the relational, communal mode of learning remains the key focus in Palmer's epistemology.[256]

---

248. Ibid.
249. Palmer, *Promise of Paradox*, xxvii.
250. Ibid., xxviii.
251. Ibid., 3.
252. As quoted in McDonnell, *Thomas Merton Reader*, 16.
253. Palmer, *To Know as We Are Known*, 27–29; *Courage to Teach*, 56–58, 97–102.
254. Palmer, *Courage to Teach*, 97 (original emphasis).
255. See Gascho, "Parker Palmer and Christian Nurture," 94–96.
256. Palmer, "Community, Conflict, and Ways of Knowing."

Seeing the pitfalls of a self-centered, pragmatic way of knowing, Palmer instead advocated that "good teaching is always and essentially communal."[257] The form of epistemological inquiry he proposed runs against the grain of objectivism. Knowing should be personal, communal, mutual, and transformational.[258] And, instead of a teacher-centered or student-centered classroom, Palmer proposed a subject-centered education where the community of truth gives the subject – the "great thing"[259] – a voice to converse with teacher and students and hold them accountable for what they say or do.[260]

Besides the practice of community living, the Quaker theology and spirituality is yet another influence that shaped Palmer's philosophical thinking.[261] Education, as perceived by Palmer to be the process of "drawing out the learners' truth," is grounded on the Quaker practices of clearness committee and silence,[262] and their theological belief that "all people can come to their own truth which resides within, and that truth is always seeking people out."[263] In fact, "truth is the Hound of Heaven that continually seeks us."[264]

3) The perceived personal context

As one who considers himself "a teacher at heart" and education as his avocation,[265] Palmer is considered by others to be "a teacher's teacher"[266] and even "an extraordinary teacher of teachers (not to mention of deans)."[267] "His power as a teacher comes at the core because he is a learner: curious, always looking for new insights, and seeking new ways of knowing. He pays attention to his surroundings, to the contexts in which he lives, and he is

---

257. Palmer, *Courage to Teach*, 118.
258. Palmer, "Violence of Our Knowledge."
259. Showalter, "Reflections," 165.
260. Palmer, *Courage to Teach*, 119.
261. See Gascho, "Parker Palmer and Christian Nurture," 98–102.
262. Palmer, *To Know as We Are Known*, 83; see 82–83.
263. Gascho, "Parker Palmer and Christian Nurture," 99; see Palmer, *To Know as We Are Known*, 82.
264. Palmer, "Toward a Spirituality," 83; see "Violence of Our Knowledge."
265. Palmer, *Courage to Teach*, 89; *To Know as We Are Known*, xxv.
266. Schmidt, "Review," 497.
267. McDaniel, "Review," 153.

attentive to the people in his life."[268] He is authentic as a teacher because he practices what he teaches, "speaking *out* of his experience and not *about* his experience."[269] "To be with Parker is to be in a learning environment, one that is open, inviting, and filled with light, hope, gentleness, and humor. It's this way because of who he is."[270]

Daniel Liston described Palmer as "an educator oriented toward a contemplative stance," writing "a great deal about ways to enter into this terrain of both the head and the heart."[271] Palmer preferred a reflective approach in his writings, dealing with issues related to the spirituality of education, the educator, and life – issues that he personally encountered as an educator and a non-violent social activist. It is, therefore, not surprising that his writings are often punctuated with personal anecdotes and vivid accounts of his interactions with students, educators, and people of various professions – "public school teachers, physicians, college administrators, lawyers, clergy, philanthropists, and corporate executives."[272] However, Karen Hoffman and Joan Scott mentioned in their reviews of *Courage to Teach* that critics may fault Palmer for "relying too much on the personal."[273] Palmer makes no apology for this for he personally acknowledged that whatever he sees or says will always be influenced by the fact that he is a Christian, a white, middle-class, North American male.[274] Hence, Roberta Clare's observation that, in *Hidden Wholeness*, Palmer only used testimonies of "middle-class Americans – a CEO, teachers (white and African American) and business people" – and omitted the "truly disenfranchised" should be evaluated in like manner.[275] The omission of "those from other classes or cultures who either do not have the freedom or cannot take the many risks involved in expressing the 'counter-cultural' imperatives of the soul"[276] and works of feminist educators

---

268. Beech, "Reflections," 81.
269. Thomas H. Phillips as quoted in Gascho, "Parker Palmer and Christian Nurture," 93–94 (original emphasis).
270. Ibid., 81.
271. Liston, "Contemplating Teaching's Conflicts and Paradoxes," 34.
272. Intrator, "Journey of Questions," xviii.
273. Hoffman and Scott, "Review," 141.
274. Palmer, *Let Your Life Speak*, 22.
275. Clare, "Review, 87.
276. Ibid.

is probably non-intentional and could be attributed to the mix of people Palmer generally interacts with in the course of his work.[277]

Realizing that his writings were reaching an audience beyond Christian circles (i.e. Jews, Muslims, Buddhists, as well as those who do not have ties with any formal religion), Palmer tried, especially in his later works, to build bridges rather than erect walls by using inclusive language.[278] To describe the core of selfhood – the voice of truth that lays claims on our lives, "the image of God in which we are all created"[279] – Palmer used various terms to connect with his readers from diverse beliefs: (1) *true self* (Merton), (2) *original nature* or *big self* (Buddhists), (3) *inner teacher* or *inner light* (Quakers), (4) *a spark of the divine* (Hasidic Jews), (5) *identity* or *integrity* (humanists), or (6) *soul* (popular usage).[280] He also displayed his inclusive stance in his writings through his use of wisdom and insights that came from various spiritual traditions, using stories and poems from diverse sources – Taoism, Hasidic Judaism, Christianity, and a Guatemalan activist – because he believed that "to see truth in the round, we need angles of vision, many voices of varied experience."[281]

Understandably, then, Palmer's choice of words and stories, even his theological understanding that "it is not necessary to accept Jesus Christ as Lord and Savior in order to find in him a paradigm of personal truth"[282] and that "to be saved is to be made whole, to be able to enter the unity that lies beyond all of life's contradictions,"[283] would be considered by most evangelicals, including me, to be veering towards "ideological pluralism" which holds that "all paths are basically equally valid and true and appropriate ways of engaging God (however 'God' may be defined)."[284] Perry W. H. Shaw made the same observation when he wrote in his review of Palmer's books

---

277. See Schmidt, "Review," 498; see also Palmer, "Community, Conflict, and Ways of Knowing."
278. Palmer, *Promise of Paradox*, xiv; *To Know as We Are Known*, ix.
279. Palmer, *Let Your Life Speak*, 11.
280. Palmer, *Hidden Wholeness*, 33.
281. Palmer, *Active Life*, 12.
282. Palmer, *To Know as We Are Known*, 50.
283. Palmer, *Promise of Paradox*, 51.
284. Han, Metzger, and Muck, "Christian Hospitality and Pastoral Practices," 13. In contrast, the term *descriptive pluralism* is merely "an acknowledgment of religious diversity in the United States," and I add, as well as in the other parts of the world (ibid.).

that "Palmer demonstrates no commitment to a metanarrative, seeking to see all narratives as significant in the mutual search for personal truth."[285]

As a person who experienced and overcame three bouts of major clinical depression, Palmer understood the turmoil within the human soul.[286] He confessed:

> Contradiction, paradox, the tension of opposites: these have always been at the heart of my experience, and I think I am not alone. I am tugged one way and then the other. My beliefs and my actions often seem at odds. My strengths are sometimes canceled by my weakness. My self, and the world around me, seem more a study in dissonance than a harmony of the integrated whole.[287]

In Palmer's own acknowledgment, "depression became a school of the spirit" to teach him humility as well as to remind him that his lofty ideas and self-image needed to be brought down.[288] The advice from a spiritual director, that depression is "the hand of a friend trying to press you down to firm ground on which it's safe to stand," helped him to see the ground as a friend rather than an enemy that is holding him up.[289] Moreover, for Palmer, "the best therapy for personal problems comes from reaching out as well as looking in."[290] Besides solitude, it is friends with whom he could reflect on his experiences that helped him through his "long, dark night[s] of the soul."[291] And one of those supportive friends "who ask[s] good questions, who listen[s] well, and who can mirror back honestly" what he heard him say was none other than Nouwen.[292]

Like Nouwen, Palmer's conceptualizing of hospitality is intertwined with his life experiences. The eleven years of community living at Pendle Hill and his Quaker spirituality played a crucial role in transforming Palmer's perspective about knowing, teaching, and learning – from the objective

---

285. Shaw, "Review," 43–44.
286. Palmer, *Promise of Paradox*, xxiv.
287. Ibid., 2.
288. Palmer, "Action and Insight," 327.
289. Ibid.
290. Palmer, *Healing the Heart of Democracy*, 5.
291. Palmer, *Hidden Wholeness*, 36; see "Action and Insight," 327.
292. Palmer, "Action and Insight," 327; *Let Your Life Speak*, viii.

mode to the communal. The relational way of doing things could thus serve as a healing balm to the *trained schizophrenia* in the academic world that trains students to look at reality objectively, apart from their personal lives.[293] Fear distances people from each other, from reality, from truth. And "the only antidote to that fear," as prescribed by Palmer,[294] is the soft virtue of hospitality that has the capacity to support the painful learning process, a soft virtue that also resonated well with the soul of "this gentle Quaker."[295]

Some Pertinent Interpretive Observations

Having traced Nouwen's and Palmer's lives and their conceptions of hospitality, this section concludes with some interpretative observations of their conceptions that are pertinent to the development of the motif of hospitality in education.

Hospitality in education seems to be a response from both Nouwen and Palmer to the violent educational process in the American schools that violates the integrity of teachers and students. Nouwen named the offering of solutions without the existence of questions as one of the greatest problems in the American education system, making it impossible to explore the deeper questions of life.[296] Palmer shared the same sentiment and added that "education dominated by preconceived images of what must be learned can hardly be educational."[297] Rather, it is indoctrination because it has no room for "a live encounter with the unexpected, an element of suspense and surprise, an evocation of that which we did not know until it happened."[298]

Nouwen presented the biblical virtue of hospitality as "a model for creative interchange" between teacher and students[299] while Palmer viewed hospitality as one of the qualities that should characterize a teaching-learning space that allows us to receive "each other, our struggles, our newborn ideas with openness and care."[300] In succinct terms, Nouwen called for a space

---

293. Palmer, "Community, Conflict, and Ways of Knowing" (original emphasis).
294. Ibid.
295. Schmidt, "Review," 499.
296. Nouwen, *Reaching Out*, 85.
297. Palmer, *Active Life*, 74.
298. Ibid.
299. Nouwen, *Reaching Out*, 84.
300. Palmer, *To Know as We Are Known*, 73–74.

where we can encounter each other and Palmer called for a space where we can encounter, not just each other, but also truth.

In seeking to articulate a spirituality of education, each had his own definition of what teaching is. For Nouwen, to teach is to create a space "where students and teachers can enter into a fearless communication with each other and allow their respective life experiences to be their primary and most valuable source of growth and maturation."[301] For Palmer, "*to teach is to create a space in which obedience to truth is practiced*" or "*to teach is to create a space in which the community of truth is practiced.*"[302] For Nouwen, the learning space focuses on teacher and students learning from one another as they "share in the same struggle and search for the same truth."[303] The missing ingredient in Nouwen is the idea of the community of truth where even the subject at the center converses with teacher and students and makes claims upon their lives. The difference in emphasis stems from what each author viewed to be the underlying issue in the society and school that makes learning difficult.

In Nouwen's opinion, the problem in education comes from a production-oriented society that is riddled with fear, competition, and rivalry.[304] Although Palmer agreed that the spirit of competition was a hindrance, he felt that the fault was mainly in "the pain of disconnectedness" that was inherent in the educational process.[305] Hence, the undergirding factor in Palmer's ideology is community.[306] When truth is both personal and communal, when truth can only emerge "between us and among us and through us as we wrestle together with the great and small questions of life," then a hospitable learning space is what makes learning possible.[307]

Many of the ideas proposed by the authors came from their personal contexts. For example, both authors believed that there is a place for silence, especially in a hospitable classroom.[308] The advocacy of silence can be

---

301. Nouwen, *Reaching Out*, 85.
302. Palmer, *To Know as We Are Known*, 69; *Courage to Teach*, 92 (original emphasis).
303. Nouwen, *Reaching Out*, 86.
304. Ibid.
305. Palmer, *To Know as We Are Known*, x.
306. See Gascho, "Parker Palmer and Christian Nurture," 92.
307. Palmer, "Violence of Our Knowledge."
308. Nouwen, *Reaching Out*, 73–77; Palmer, *To Know as We Are Known*, 79–83.

attributed to Nouwen's personal experience in the monastery and Palmer's, in the Quaker community, as well as the wisdom of the Desert Fathers. "If there is a crisis in theological education, it is first and foremost a crisis of the word," Nouwen decried.[309] In the classroom, silence may seem inhospitable to those who "measure progress by noise" but it is needed for truth to emerge.[310] In Bonnie Miller-McLemore's article that explored what contemplative spiritual life is in the midst of day-to-day rigmarole of teaching and parenting, she leveled criticism against Nouwen's call for silence.[311] As a mother, she noticed that words were "sources of self-knowledge, meaning, and relationship" for her toddler son.[312] Though she agreed with the Desert Fathers that silence can keep us from sin and evil, she also believed that "silence can also lead to stagnation and words can build home."[313] No doubt, words can also be "the tools we use to serve God in our calling."[314] Although both Nouwen and Palmer advocated silence, they would nonetheless agree with Miller-McLemore that "the opposition between silence and speech in models of spirituality is a false dichotomy," that is if we take into serious consideration Nouwen's call for a constant movement between polarities and Palmer's call to hold paradox in a creative tension.[315] What Nouwen and Palmer would approve – as Miller-McLemore, Graham Cheesman, and I would also do – is contemplative practice of silence sagaciously counterbalanced by speech.

Similarly, in reacting to an authoritarian educational system that inadvertently produced a spirit of fear in and competitiveness among students, both Nouwen and Palmer advocated the creation of a free space that would allow individuals to be free to be who they are[316] and to receive each other's struggles and ideas with care and openness.[317] Yet, their advocacy

---

309. Nouwen, *Way of the Heart*, 47.
310. Palmer, *To Know as We Are Known*, 81.
311. Miller-McLemore, "Contemplation," 60–61.
312. Ibid., 66.
313. Ibid.
314. Cheesman, "Conversation with Henri Nouwen."
315. Miller-McLemore, "Contemplation," 68.
316. Nouwen, "Education to the Ministry," 50; "Hospitality," 8.
317. Palmer, *To Know as We Are Known*, 73–74.

of a free space is not freedom without limits. For both of them, this free space is always balanced by confrontation and must be bounded."[318]

Hospitality as a Key Concept in Christian Higher Education

As Rebecca Burwell and Mackenzi Huyser noted, "prior to 2001, the notion of hospitality in the context of Christian higher education was a relatively new area of research to explore."[319] Yet, despite being written about two decades earlier, the works of Nouwen (especially *Reaching Out*) and Palmer (especially *To Know as We Are Known* and *Courage to Teach*) served as the catalysts for the growing interest in hospitality in education. These works have prompted other educators to conceptualize how the metaphor of hospitality could address existing and emerging issues in all types of higher education institutions. This section reviews relevant works written by twenty-one authors on hospitality in the contexts of Christian higher education and theological education. Eight of these authors (Burwell and Huyser; Larson; Marmon; Shaw; Smith and Carvill; Stratman) listed the works of both Nouwen (i.e. *Reaching Out*) and Palmer (i.e. *To Know as We Are Known* and/or *Courage to Teach*) in their references. In addition, four others (Hagstrom; Hershberger; McAvoy; Schrag) listed at least a work of Nouwen while two (Call; Wimberly) listed just the works of Palmer. This amounts to about 66 percent of the authors reviewed in this chapter. The majority of the works reviewed here were written from within Western settings. I regret that, with the exception of some writers with educational experience in non-Western contexts (e.g. Wimberly, Shaw), I have not been able to procure literature (if it exists) written on hospitality and higher education within those contexts.

This section reviews relevant post-Nouwen and Palmer literature on hospitality in Christian higher education and shows the multiple facets of this metaphor as it is used in particular contexts by the various authors. The contexts discussed are grouped as follows: (1) pluralistic environment, (2) academic life and community, and (3) classroom process.

---

318. Nouwen, *Reaching Out*, 98; Palmer, *Courage to Teach*, 76.
319. Burwell and Huyser, "Practicing Hospitality," 12.

Hospitality and the Pluralistic Environment

The world we live in today, including Christian colleges/universities, is characterized by a diversity of cultures and traditions. In their writings, Elizabeth Newman and Aurelie A. Hagstrom sought to address the loss of Christian identity in Christian colleges/universities where diverse Christian traditions meet and intersect while Smith and Carvill, and Elizabeth Conde-Frazier, called our attention to the myriad of cultural identities in these academic groves.

Newman's writings about the loss of Christian identity in Christian colleges/universities made their appearances at the turn of the twenty-first century. Newman, who is a Southern Baptist, personally experienced the dissonance between "the privatized world of Christianity and the public world of education" when she taught at a Roman Catholic college – St Mary's College (Notre Dame, Indiana) – for twelve years.[320] In institutions of higher education, faith and knowledge are treated as two separate entities with faith being relegated to the "extra-curricular sphere."[321] This dichotomy has brought about the loss of religious identity and can be attributed to a "malformed gnostic theology" that advocates dichotomy for the sake of peaceful and harmonious living in an environment where diverse faiths co-exist.[322]

Newman believed that Christian identity cannot be separated from the intellectual life of a college or university: "our *knowing* cannot be entirely abstracted from our *being*."[323] She maintained that, in Christian institutions of higher education, we can uphold our particular religious tradition and yet embrace diversity. Since "practices – temporal and tradition-informed ways we engage the world – 'bear epistemological weight'" and shape the knowledge we come to have, Newman proposed the Christian practice of hospitality to welcome the other in our pursuit of truth.[324]

In her first essay, Newman presented hospitality as one's full presence to the other.[325] The practice of "incarnational hospitality" is grounded in

---

320. Newman, "Hotel or Home," 93.
321. Newman, "Who's Home Cooking," 8; "Faith-Knowledge Dichotomy," 131.
322. Newman, "Hospitality and Christian," 79, 81; "Hotel or Home," 97.
323. Newman, "Who's Home Cooking," 9 (original emphasis).
324. Ibid., 9–10.
325. Ibid., 10–13.

God's ever-present generous hospitality and steadfast love, and sustained by the Incarnation.[326] As our Creator, he is always present – sustaining us in his creation. And just as God is fully present to us, we too must be "fully present in our engagement with others, refusing to privatize or abandon those parts of our identity that might sound odd in the world of so-called rational discourse."[327] In this respect, incarnational hospitality as "faithful presence" is different from an objectivistic presence of modernism whereby one must deny one's particularity, and the relativistic presence of postmodernism whereby one is not obligated to welcome the other beyond one's personal preference.[328] Newman supported her idea of hospitality as full presence by drawing on Nouwen's understanding of hospitality as articulate presence or confrontation (see above p. 17).[329]

From these initial thoughts, yet still in the context of the faith-knowledge dichotomy in Christian higher education, Newman expanded her own theological understanding of hospitality in her subsequent works. In her second essay, she argued that vocation is covenantal in nature and it "involves a way of life in communion with others and ultimately with God"[330] that is predicated on trust in our bonds with others and with God.[331] Hence, when teaching and knowing are perceived as a vocation, it needs to be sustained by hospitality as well as testimony and forgiveness.[332] In the midst of diversity, the practice of hospitality "calls us to welcome the other in all of his or her particularity, even to the point of being willing to *suffer* at the hands of the other" simply because God can speak to us through the stranger, who is also a child of God, just like us.[333]

In her third essay, Newman continued from this idea of unconditional welcome of the stranger who could be God's messenger and proposed that "hospitality delights in and is even defined as the welcoming of the other as

---

326. Ibid., 15.
327. Ibid., 11.
328. Ibid., 13, 11.
329. Ibid., 11.
330. Newman, "Faith-Knowledge Dichotomy," 142.
331. Ibid., 144.
332. Ibid., 145.
333. Ibid. (original emphasis).

gift."[334] To do so, we must first acknowledge our human condition – that we are created in the image of God – as gift. By appreciating our existence as gift, "our reasoning must always account or allow space for contingency, for the arrival of the unexpected or new in the form of gift."[335] Just as God is faithful to us, we too need to be faithful to the stranger, practising the same virtues exhibited in God's hospitality in our "intellectual hospitality": (1) patience – bearing with our guests as we seek truth together, (2) courage – being bold to speak and live the truth in love, and (3) charity – being humble and willing to learn and receive from others.[336]

Newman believed that hospitality does not draw boundaries.[337] That prerogative belongs to God. However, hospitality does call for Christian discernment in making distinctions as we engage "with other persons, cultures, ideas, disciplines, knowledge, etc."[338] However, Newman cautioned that hospitality should not be practiced just for maintaining Christian identity in the academy. "The sole reason for practicing hospitality is to participate in what God is already doing so that our efforts will redound to the glory of God. Any preservation of Christian distinctiveness will be a byproduct."[339]

In her fourth essay, Newman gave an interesting perspective on hospitality, contrasting hotel hospitality and *oikos* (meaning, "home"; referring to "a particular place or people") hospitality.[340] Judging from the kind of welcome higher education institutions extend to the other, Newman labeled these institutions "educational 'hotels.'"[341] Hotel hospitality allows people of widely differing ideologies to get along in the common corridor since one's religious convictions and practices are locked away in one's private room. She contended that hospitality is truly practiced "when a concrete sense of place sustains the life of an institution."[342] Only by offering hospitality from the *oikos* can we truly welcome and receive the other because *oikos* hospitality

---

334. Newman, "Hospitality and Christian," 84.
335. Ibid., 85.
336. Ibid., 86.
337. Ibid., 90.
338. Ibid., 91.
339. Ibid., 93.
340. Newman, "Hotel or Home," 92.
341. Ibid., 91.
342. Ibid.

does not dichotomize the spiritual and the material. It is based on Christian understanding of the material world as God's creation and the Incarnation as God's embodied presence in the created world. The *oikos* of Christian hospitality lies in us receiving God's superabundant generosity which then enables us to share from this superabundance. The table manners of *oikos* hospitality allow us to welcome the stranger. However, as we sit together at the table, as we look out for others and allow others to look out for us, we need both courage to speak the truth to others and humility to accept the truth spoken to us.

Newman expanded her conceptualization of hospitality with each new work. Yet, in all her essays, Newman's main concern is that our Christian identity should be integral to our intellectual life. What prevents it from happening is the gnostic tendency to separate faith and knowledge. *Oikos* hospitality, however, makes it possible for us to maintain our Christian identity in the midst of religious plurality because we have a place or a home to welcome and receive the other – an idea that can be traced to her presentation of hospitality as our full presence,[343] of hospitality that is made possible only when we see our existence, as well as the other's existence, as a gift from God.[344]

Newman gave credit to Nouwen only once (and in her first essay) for his idea of articulate presence. However, although Nouwen's and Palmer's works are noticeably missing from her bibliographies, traces of their ideas – for example, the covenantal nature of teaching and the receiving of the other as a gift – can be seen in her writings. We can almost hear Nouwen's and Palmer's voice when Newman wrote that "our status as guests in God's good creation" and "stewards of the gifts God has given" have implications on whatever subjects we teach,[345] and that as hosts, we welcome and receive the other, acutely aware that "because the finite is capable of bearing the infinite, human places always contain the possibility of being epistemologically revelatory."[346]

However, being herself a professor of theology and ethics, Newman provides the theological underpinnings to the practice of hospitality which

---

343. Newman, "Who's Home Cooking."
344. Newman, "Faith-Knowledge Dichotomy"; "Hospitality and Christian."
345. Newman, "Who's Home Cooking," 12.
346. Ibid., 15.

are lacking in Nouwen's and Palmer's conceptualizing of hospitality. Taking on a more proactive stance, she called for an immersion in the Christian practice of hospitality through a more deliberate interdisciplinary approach to teaching and curriculum planning if we truly desire to practice hospitality in Christian colleges/universities.[347]

Another theologian who contributed to the wider conversation on Christian identity and higher education is Hagstrom, a co-participant with Newman in the Hospitality and the Christian College Project that was supported by the Rhodes Consultation on the Future of Church-Related Colleges.[348] Hagstrom observed that church-related schools have downplayed or even forsaken their Christian heritage and identity in the last century.[349] She concurred with Newman that there is a need of "a revival of concrete, integrative practices to sustain the life of the Christian community" for such institutions to remain spiritually vibrant without compromising academic excellence.[350] Hagstrom argued that the Christian academy of higher learning "must recover and appropriate hospitality as a theologically significant moral category" for it to remain a viable educational enterprise.[351] Christian hospitality "is distinctively communal and self-giving, embodying a way of being and thinking about the 'other' or the 'stranger.'"[352] As such, it has the capacity to sustain campus-related issues such as diversity, academic freedom, and scholarly inquiry.

While Newman's approach is more theological/philosophical, Hagstrom's is more biblical/theological. This is especially seen in her second essay where the biblical tradition and practice of hospitality became her platform for discussing intellectual hospitality.[353] However, hospitality to the stranger is more than a "biblical phenomenon"; it is "a moral category."[354] Hospitality should define the Christian moral life. Our acts of hospitality are a participation in and an enactment of the kingdom of God that "overturns

---

347. Newman, "Hospitality and Christian," 92–93.
348. See ibid. 77, n. 9.
349. Hagstrom, "Christian Hospitality," 119.
350. Ibid., 120.
351. Ibid.; see "Role of Charism," 3.
352. Hagstrom, "Christian Hospitality," 120; "Role of Charism," 3.
353. Hagstrom, "Role of Charism," 5–10.
354. Hagstrom, "Christian Hospitality," 122.

discrimination, exclusion, and marginalization in all their forms."[355] Being recipients of God's gracious hospitality as his guests, we must attend to the other with a hospitality characterized by "receptivity, openness, regard for characteristic differences in the experience of others, and efforts to transcend artificial barriers."[356]

Moreover, while Newman focused on our full presence before the other, Hagstrom focused on true dialogue. For Hagstrom, hospitality not only helps to inform issues of diversity on the campuses, it also provides a platform for true dialogue.[357] True dialogue and proclamation go hand-in-hand. "It is precisely in the hospitable proclamation of the gospel that the Christian host community honors truth and maintains integrity."[358]

A new contribution Hagstrom brings to the conversation on hospitality is the idea of tolerance which was mentioned in passing by Newman.[359] For Hagstrom, true dialogue is not "mere 'tolerance'" which "superficially entertains another's worldview, beliefs, and values."[360]

> By contrast, hospitality is incarnational, morally attuned, and prompted by commitments to truthfulness in word and deed. It does not exist as a disembodied attitude toward others, but instead brings concrete strangers together in rituals of peaceful engagement. . . . [H]ospitality surpasses tolerance by demanding a personal, authentic encounter that is self-emptying and open even to those with whom we have deep philosophical, theological, and political disagreements.[361]

The idea of self-emptying refers to Christ's attitude of *kenosis* (meaning, "emptying").[362] "If one is full of oneself and seeking only one's own interests, there is no room for the free space of true encounter and dialogue"[363] – an idea that echoes Nouwen's idea of poverty of heart and mind (see above p.

---

355. Ibid., 124.
356. Ibid., 123.
357. Hagstrom, "Christian Hospitality," 127–130; "Role of Charism," 11–12.
358. Hagstrom, "Christian Hospitality," 127.
359. Newman, "Hospitality and Christian," 85.
360. Hagstrom, "Role of Charism," 13; "Christian Hospitality," 121.
361. Hagstrom, "Christian Hospitality," 121.
362. Ibid., 128–129.
363. Ibid., 129.

15) even though Hagstrom did not quote him in her first essay.[364] But the emptying of self does not imply a rejection of personal identity. "*Kenosis* actually requires an affirmation of one's own identity. Paradoxically, the more one is rooted in one's own identity and tradition, the more open one can be to others."[365]

Hagstrom used the simple imagery of table setting to illustrate how "the religious identity, praxis, and worship of the host are not abandoned in the interchange of hospitality" and how dialogue can take place in Christian colleges/universities.[366] The host sets the table, and guests invited to the table do not take the liberty to change the table setting because it is not done the way they would have done it. And around that table where pleasantries and stories are exchanged, there is also room for "healthy debate and disputation."[367] Undoubtedly, engaging in true dialogue is no simple feat, but a generosity of spirit that welcomes others in the conversation, no matter how diverse the other views may be, can create "a community of reconciliation" in our fragmented world and engender fellowship among people of differing beliefs, ideas, and spiritual traditions.[368]

Christian colleges/universities in the United States are made up not only of people of different theological persuasions but also of different ethnic origins and cultures. The language-learning classroom is a place where we can see people of diverse cultures. Smith and Carvill claimed to be the first to use hospitality as a key metaphor for foreign language education.[369] Choosing to focus their attention on the attitude of teachers and learners in welcoming strangers, they proposed "*that foreign language education prepare [sic] students for two related callings: to be a blessing as strangers in a foreign land, and to be hospitable to strangers in their own homeland.*"[370] The term *strangers* refers to "persons [who] are temporarily in a cultural context where their mother tongue is not spoken and where they interact with native speakers of the host

---

364. In her last footnote, Aurelie A. Hagstrom merely mentioned Nouwen as a reference she had used but did not quote from (ibid., 131, n. 25).
365. Ibid., 129.
366. Hagstrom, "Christian Hospitality," 125; "Role of Charism," 13.
367. Hagstrom, "Christian Hospitality," 126; "Role of Charism," 13.
368. Hagstrom, "Christian Hospitality," 130.
369. Smith and Carvill, *Gift of the Stranger*, 88.
370. Ibid., 57–58 (original emphasis).

country with varying levels of linguistic proficiency."[371] Hospitality, perceived as a spiritual virtue, was considered by them to be an appropriate metaphor to help "*both teachers and students understand and interact with otherness.*"[372]

To help them express their thoughts, Smith and Carvill coined the term "*xenophilic* hospitality"[373] and distinguished it from "*diaconal* or *Good Samaritan* hospitality."[374] Diaconal hospitality responds to strangers who are in distress while "xenophilic hospitality is motivated by the eagerness to receive strangers first and foremost because they come from another nation and culture."[375] And it is their conviction that xenophilic hospitality "must shape the spirit and manner in which learners welcome, acquire, and respond to the foreign language and culture."[376]

Smith and Carvill's concept of xenophilic hospitality has two aspects to it. First, we have and care for a home. Citing Nouwen's (see above p. 15) idea of concentration, they went on to interpret it to mean that we must have our own cultural identity.[377] Hence, "being hospitable means both affirming our own cultural identity and, at the same time, giving the stranger, the other, a loving, welcoming space in which she can be who she is."[378] Clearly, we can see vestiges of Nouwen's and Palmer's idea of receptivity here (see above pp. 17, 34).

Second, we open our home to others and are open to receive from them.[379] Smith and Carvill then employed the embrace analogy of theologian Miroslav Volf to explain this idea.

> In an embrace I open my arms to create space in myself for the other. Open arms are a sign that I do not want to be by myself only, an invitation for the other to come in and feel at home with me. In an embrace I also close my arms around the other. Closed arms are a sign that I want the other to become a part of me while

---

371. Ibid., 58, n. 2.
372. Ibid., 88 (original emphasis).
373. Ibid., 86 (original emphasis); see also nn. 23, 24.
374. Ibid. (original emphasis).
375. Ibid.
376. Ibid., 88.
377. Ibid., 89.
378. Ibid.
379. Ibid.

I at the same time maintain my own identity. By becoming part of me, the other enriches me. In a mutual embrace, none remains the same because each enriches the other, yet both remain true to their genuine selves.[380]

Such a hospitable embrace allows language learners "to encounter the other in a place of give-and-take and of transformation."[381] With this introduction of Volf's concept of embrace, Smith and Carvill help to further elucidate the ideas of receptivity and confrontation in hospitality. In a hospitable embrace, we are able to reach out to others and yet remain ourselves.[382] "Our cultural identity is no longer monochromatic, and through hospitable connection with the stranger we develop a 'spacious heart.'"[383]

Another author who sought to address learning in a multicultural context is Conde-Frazier who is born to parents of Puerto Rican descent in New York City. Having lived a life of invisibility as a person with no presence,[384] Conde-Frazier proposed hospitality as one of the spiritual practices needed for multicultural living.[385] In a segment of her second essay, she discussed how hospitality can be practiced in a multicultural classroom.[386] She believed that "the theological/biblical vision for multiculturalism is that of edification, the healing of wrong arrangements in relationships"[387] and that "the goal of hospitality in the classroom is to create a learning setting in which one can appreciate individual uniqueness, the complexity of group identities (including intra-group differences), and the common human characteristics we share cross-culturally."[388] And the most fundamental thing we can do is to show respect, granting to all visibility for they individually are made in the image of God and are to be valued.[389] As such, hospitality practiced in the

---

380. Volf, "Vision of Embrace," 205, as quoted in Smith and Carvill, *Gift of the Stranger*, 99–100.
381. Smith and Carvill, *Gift of the Stranger*, 101.
382. See Volf, "Introduction," 11.
383. Smith and Carvill, *Gift of the Stranger*, 102. The term *spacious heart* was borrowed from Judith M. Gundry-Volf and Miroslav Volf's book entitled, *Spacious Heart*.
384. Conde-Frazier, "Spirituality," 60–63.
385. Ibid., 69–70; "Hospitality to Shalom," 171–176.
386. Conde-Frazier, "From Hospitality to Shalom."
387. Ibid., 173.
388. Ibid., 174.
389. Ibid., 172.

classroom, initiated by teachers, must make room for the different learning needs (namely, cognitive and affective) and learning styles of the students.

The conversation on hospitality in education is now enlivened by Newman's idea of full presence, Hagstrom's call for dialogue, Smith and Carvill's use of Volf's notion of embrace, and Conde-Frazier's appeal for respect for persons. For each of them, the practice of hospitality is presented as a way of Christian living that can help us to interact with *the other* and *otherness* in the pluralistic environment of Christian colleges/universities (emphasis mine).

Hospitality and the Academic Life and Community

The next context to be addressed is the *academia* or *academe*, which encompasses matters related to the academic life, community, and work.[390] The three essays reviewed here appeared in *Mennonite Life*, a journal published by Bethel College (North Newton, Kansas), and were written by teaching professionals in Mennonite colleges.

In 2003, Dale R. Schrag addressed the problem of inhospitable forces, even cynicism, that were present in the Mennonite colleges. The academic environment is fragile – as evidenced by fragile students, faculty, and administrators. The reason for its fragility is that it "specializes in critique and judgment."[391] He proposed hospitality as practiced in the Benedictine monasteries to counteract this academic culture. Such hospitality requires a "crucified mind" which essentially is an unconditional embrace of the other, accepting students as gifts from God.[392] This practice of radical hospitality can only be nurtured and sustained by the spiritual discipline of prayer. As followers of Christ, we need to practice hospitality "if we are to have a ghost of a chance of dealing successfully and effectively with the inhospitable forces

---

390. For the purpose of this work, since the term *academia* "refers to a community dedicated to higher learning" (Lamont, *How Professors Think*, 2) and the term *academe* "refers to the academic (i.e. higher education) community and environment" (Helms and Rogers, *Majoring in Psychology*, 273), the two terms are used interchangeably.

391. Schrag, "Beautiful Minds," under "The Benedictine Solution."

392. The term *crucified mind* is taken from Bryant L. Myers whose book attempts to integrate Christian witness and transformational development among the poor (*Walking with the Poor*, 18, 216–217). Myers advocated that we should carry out our Christian witness with a crucified mind rather than a crusading mind, a concept which he gleaned from Kosuke Koyama ("Extend Hospitality," 174).

of academe."³⁹³ Addressing the fears of some that an emphasis of hospitality would compromise academic excellence, Schrag proposed that a sense of transcendence, which comes from an open acknowledgment of the presence of God's grace, in a judgmental environment will allow us to more freely affirm others for who they are and not for what they have achieved.

In her response to Schrag's essay, Michelle Hershberger affirmed Schrag's call for the practice of hospitality in the campuses. However, she was mindful that hospitality can get messy when we deal with "angry, lazy, unwilling students."³⁹⁴ Hershberger believed that "true hospitality is not a value neutral environment." She concurred with Nouwen that receptivity must be balanced by confrontation while acknowledging that striking a balance between the two is not an easy task.³⁹⁵

In his essay, Schrag rejected the Karlstadtian solution and Erasmian solution and favored the Benedictine solution as the answer to deal with the inhospitable forces in the academe. Schrag explained that the Karlstadtian solution refers to the leveling of status and is derived from the example set by the theologian Andreas Rudolph Bodenstein von Karlstadt (1486–1541) who, at a certain time of his life, renounced all his doctoral degrees, chose to dress like a peasant, and insisted on being called "Brother Andrew."³⁹⁶ In contrast, the Erasmian solution refers to peer group homogeneity and is derived from the life of Desiderius Erasmus of Rotterdam (1466–1536) who lived in Basel for a time with an equally gifted and knowledgable group of friends.³⁹⁷ For Schrag, faculty members dressing down in order to appear more approachable or admitting only people who meet their criteria only contributes to the already hostile academic environment. Hershberger begged to disagree and took issue with Schrag on the Karlstadtian solution.

Hershberger wrote that linguistic and sociological studies have shown that language and cultural practices do influence our way of thinking. In her opinion, Brother Andrew understood this when he discarded his academic robes and adorned peasant's attire. How we dress or address one another is

---

393. Schrag, "Beautiful Minds," under "The Benedictine Solution."
394. Hershberger, "Response."
395. Ibid., citing Nouwen, *Reaching Out*, 99.
396. Schrag, "Beautiful Minds," under "The Karlstadtian Solution."
397. Ibid., under "The Erasmian Solution."

important because "we set a political climate by our intentional choice of words, rituals, and customs."[398]

> Karlstadt can teach us that we can nurture a climate of hospitality in many ways, one of which is by the language we use. This custom of calling professors by their first names doesn't need to be enforced, for that would not be hospitable, nor does the use of first names imply that such professors dress in inappropriate ways.[399]

Hershberger's comment is valid since academic etiquette differs from culture to culture and from country to country. Hence, she proposed that we should explore the language and customs that we wish to adopt to nurture a hospitable climate.

However, she agreed with Schrag that language alone does not make us hospitable teachers. "Hospitality is impossible work" and can only be achieved as we humble ourselves before God in prayer and corporate worship.[400] We can now welcome and love the stranger because we have experienced God's love and hospitality.

In another response to Schrag's essay, Loren L. Johns voiced his concern about using hospitality as a major paradigm even though he believed that hospitality is a much-needed virtue in Mennonite higher education.[401] Unlike Schrag, he did not believe that a hospitable college would necessarily give Mennonite colleges a marketing edge. "While context is crucial, it is not *everything*."[402] A good education must teach students how to engage critically with subject matters and how to live an authentic Christian life. Such learning is vulnerable and requires a hospitable and safe environment. However, Johns (under "Hospitality as Paradigm") argued that "hospitality is not itself critical engagement."[403] Furthermore, although hospitality may unconsciously be an important factor in college choice, it is more crucial that parents and students "negotiate culture" when making a college choice, taking into consideration

---

398. Hershberger, "Response."
399. Ibid.
400. Ibid.
401. Johns, "Love and Hospitality," under "Hospitality as Paradigm."
402. Ibid. (original emphasis).
403. Ibid.

personal motives, cultural pressures, and competing values.[404] Ultimately, if parents desire their children to be "good negotiators of life" rather than "successful competitors in the marketplace," Mennonite colleges will be the right college choice.[405]

These essays are insightful in that they provide an insider's view of Mennonite higher education. Schrag's presentation of hospitality as an unconditional embrace of the other as gifts of God basically reflects the thoughts of Nouwen and Palmer, even though he did not cite any of their key works on hospitality in education. Although the respondents to his essay agree with him that the spiritual virtue of hospitality is a key to intellectual renewal in Mennonite campuses, they have some reservations about its implementation. Johns questioned the use of hospitality as the major paradigm since hospitality in itself is not critical engagement, an activity which he felt "characterizes the best of education."[406] Here, I take issue with John's argument. I concur with Palmer that "learning spaces need to be hospitable learning spaces not merely because kindness is a good idea but because real education requires rigor."[407] And hospitality has the ability to support that rigor. As Palmer put it, for too long, the academy has been operating on a dichotomy that assigns "the 'hard' virtues of scholarship" to the academic office and "the 'soft' virtues of community" to the student affairs office.[408] Good pedagogy demands a combination of both virtues.[409] Hence, I believe that a hospitable learning space not only invites student engagement but it also encourages critical engagement.

Hershberger, on the other hand, brought to the forefront the messy nature of hospitality which will become more evident when they sit down to determine what hospitable language they should adopt to nurture a hospitable climate in the campuses. Her concern is indeed valid in light of the prevalent cultural diversity in the contemporary society and higher education institutions. This concern will be addressed in the ensuing discussion on how hospitality can be practiced in theological education (see below ch. 5).

---

404. Ibid., under "Negotiating Culture."
405. Ibid.
406. Ibid., under "Hospitality as Paradigm."
407. Palmer, "Toward a Philosophy," 29.
408. Ibid., 30
409. Ibid., 29.

Hospitality and Classroom Process

This section reviews essays that relate hospitality to the classroom process. The term *classroom process* includes teacher planning and classroom process, and focuses "on what the teacher does both in the classroom and in organizing and managing the course."[410] Hence, it encompasses classroom atmosphere, teacher and student behaviors, face-to-face interactions, learning activities, and evaluation procedures.[411]

In the late 2000s, the emphasis shifted from the classroom to the teacher as Christian educators began reflecting on their own teaching practices, envisioning the role teachers could play as hospitable hosts within and without the classroom walls. Conceptualizing teaching as "an act of intellectual hospitality,"[412] "an act of hospitality,"[413] or "the rough trail toward an authentic pedagogy of discipleship" that requires the Christian practice of hospitality,[414] these Christian educators sought to offer practical insights for all teachers seeking to practice hospitality in teaching contexts. It is only in recent years that educators have begun to explore how the practice of hospitality can be employed to teach students about hospitality as a way to interact with others.[415]

Eugene V. Gallagher's treatment of teaching as intellectual hospitality was closely related to his involvement at the Wabash Center for Teaching and Learning in Theology and Religion (Crawfordsville, Indiana). The center, which seeks to support faculty members and institutions in their endeavors to improve teaching and learning, itself is infused with an ethos of hospitality. In his essay, Gallagher focused on the difficult tasks of the undergraduate teachers of theology and religion – the designing and teaching of introductory courses.

---

410. Edwards and Allen, "Perspectives," 180–181.
411. Ibid., 180.
412. Gallagher, "Welcoming the Stranger," 137.
413. Larson, "Creating a Space," 1; "Welcoming and Restoring," 48.
414. Call, "Rough Trail," 79. Carolyne Call's (ibid., 63) understanding of Christian practices was largely influenced by Craig R. Dykstra and Dorothy C. Bass who defined Christian practices as "things Christian people do together over time to address fundamental needs and conditions of humanity and all creation in the light of and in response to God's active presence for the life of the world in Jesus Christ" ("Way of Thinking," 204).
415. Burwell and Huyser, "Practicing Hospitality"; Stratman, "Toward a Pedagogy."

By adopting an ethic of hospitality, teachers are able "to welcome strangers or newcomers to the study of religion or to tackle strange, new topics with open-minded generosity."[416]

> Teaching effectively thus becomes a process of hospitality orchestrating multiple and diverse opportunities for students to demonstrate that they have accurately "heard" the issues, questions, and problems that have been articulated in an ongoing conversation, and that they are able to add their own voices to the discussion in a way that is simultaneously appreciative, respectful, and analytically critical.[417]

Though Gallagher made no reference to Palmer, he expressed similar sentiments where welcoming the strangeness of ideas is concerned.

Likewise, teachers too should welcome the challenge to teach subjects outside their area of expertise. Although being a "utility player" playing multiple positions may be challenging with many potential drawbacks, it also has potential benefits. One of the benefits is that it gives "teachers an opportunity to become more conscious of and to model to their students their own strategies for learning, to show how they strive to situate themselves in a conversation that is new and strange to them."[418] In so doing, the teacher practices intentional marginality which, to me, is an important concept that needs to be addressed when discussing hospitality.

A new idea introduced by Gallagher, as an attitude of intellectual hospitality that teachers and students should foster, is the principle of "methodological belief" formulated by Peter Elbow.[419] Elbow observed that there is a tendency in academic circles to employ a hermeneutic of suspicion through systematic doubting to expose flaws and weaknesses. Such "methodological doubting" should be counterbalanced by methodological belief, "the equally systematic, disciplined, and conscious attempt to believe everything no matter how unlikely or repellent it might seem – to find virtues and strengths we might otherwise miss."[420] In Elbow's proposition, playing the "believing game"

---

416. Gallagher, "Welcoming the Stranger," 137.
417. Ibid., 139.
418. Ibid., 140.
419. Ibid., 140–141.
420. Elbow, as quoted in Gallagher, "Welcoming the Stranger," 140–141.

requires a delicate kind of energy "to keep something energetically open,"[421] enabling teachers and students "to foster an attitude of intellectual hospitality towards each other and their common concerns."[422] Gallagher recounted how he played the believing game in a class, guiding the students to consider the "I'm spiritual but not religious" statement in a hospitable manner. That experiment not only unveiled unexamined assumptions for the students but also helped him "to see clearly the pedagogical potential that balances, at least for a time, often caustic critique with potentially constructive acceptance."[423]

Although Elbow recommended that it is important to play both the believing and the doubting games since "these two games are only halves of a full cycle of thinking,"[424] Gallagher proffered only the believing game probably because it is a more hospitable approach to learning than the hostile doubting game.[425] In my opinion, playing the doubting game is second nature for teachers and students in higher education. Elbow already hinted at it when he wrote: "We learn to play the doubting game 'in general' – not realizing it is a game. What that means is that we learn critical thinking 'in general' – that is, we learn, as it were, to try in general to be more vigilant, try in general to doubt everything."[426]

Another reflective essay is that of Marion H. Larson, exploring the implications of Palmer's oft-quoted definition of teaching: "To teach is to create a space in which the community of truth is practiced."[427] Her essay considered the changes she had to make to create a space and practice the community of truth. She had to re-evaluate what constitutes class participation, the tone her syllabus was setting for the class, and even how she should welcome new faculty.

Like Gallagher, Larson also called attention to "the usual academic practice of presumed skepticism" that seeks to find the flaws in every idea and argument presented.[428] Instead of skepticism, another possible mode

---

421. Elbow, *Writing without Teachers*, 180.
422. Gallagher, "Welcoming the Stranger," 141.
423. Ibid.
424. Elbow, *Writing without Teachers*, 191.
425. Gallagher, "Welcoming the Stranger," 141.
426. Elbow, *Writing without Teachers*, 191.
427. Larson, "Creating a Space"; see Palmer, *Courage to Teach*, 92.
428. Larson, "Creating a Space," 2.

of inquiry could be compassion, as proposed by Mary Rose O'Reilley.[429] In approaching differing ideas, the ability to see flaws should be balanced by the ability to look from a different vantage point to see strengths.

Larson also raised a concern similar to that of Smith and Carvill – that it does not necessarily mean that one must abandon one's own perspective after entering into another's, although there should always be an openness and willingness to be changed by another's perspective (see above p. 56). Like them, Larson drew insights from Volf and suggested using Volf's concept of "double vision" – seeing things "from here" and "from there" – in searching for truth among multiple opinions.[430] Volf derived this concept of double vision from the American philosopher Thomas Nagel.[431] The view "from here" refers to one's own perspective and the view "from there" refers to the perspective of the other. By comparing and contrasting the views "from here" and "from there," "we let their perspective stand next to ours and reflect whether one or the other is right, or whether both are partly right and partly wrong."[432] In our application of double vision, in our willingness to be open to new perspectives and ideas, we may be transformed yet without losing our identities.[433]

Larson ended her essay with an invitation to those working in faculty development to consider how Palmer's definition could be applied in their collegial interactions. She revisited this issue when she wrote "Welcoming and Restoring, Dwelling and Sending."[434] Although this work could belong to the preceding section "Hospitality and the Academic Life and Community" since it concerns academic work, it is reviewed here because it is essentially a continuation of her concept of hospitality, being published a year after her first essay. Moreover, it is reasonable to consider it as part of classroom process since she is addressing faculty developers who are training new, younger faculty members. In this essay, Larson made many poignant and practical suggestions to help faculty developers practice hospitality in their work, thereby energizing one another to teach with renewed vigor.

---

429. As cited in Larson, "Creating a Space," 2.
430. Ibid., 3–4; see Volf, *Exclusion and Embrace*, 250–253.
431. Nagel, *View from Nowhere*; see Volf, *Exclusion and Embrace*, 250.
432. Volf, *Exclusion and Embrace*, 252.
433. Larson, "Creating a Space," 3.
434. Larson, "Welcoming and Restoring."

Throughout her essay, Larson navigated through Palmer's definition of teaching by using Amy G. Oden's four movements in the Christian practice of hospitality – welcoming, restoring the guest, dwelling with one another, and sending forth.[435] In her analysis of early Christian texts regarding hospitality and its specific practices, Oden observed that the practice of hospitality usually begins with welcome where the host receives the guest. The host then restores the guest by addressing the guest's immediate needs. The host and guest then dwell together and share the tasks of common life. The act of hospitality concludes with the host letting go of the guest. The fourth movement of sending forth may include "acts such as blessing, giving food or other supplies for the journey, or giving companions for escort."[436]

The metaphor of hospitality when applied to faculty development would mean that "faculty developers seek to 'create a space' in which their colleagues, as guests, can explore together what it means to 'practice obedience to truth' and, in turn, prepare themselves to host students and each other as we seek to learn together."[437] The movements of welcoming and restoring create a space to welcome, not overwhelm, new colleagues, and to allow them to grow. The movements of dwelling and sending are opportunities to practice obedience to truth. Not only are the new faculty members taught how they can attend to one another hospitably in their engagement with truths (namely, pedagogical, personal and interpersonal), they are thus equipped to practice hospitality in their own classrooms after they have been sent off.

Though Larson's focus in her 2009 essay is on faculty development, the structure and topics discussed are fairly similar to her previous essay. However, the discussion was more extensive as Larson had consulted more recent works on hospitality which helped her to augment the ideas in her earlier work. For instance, Larson included Gallagher's use of Elbow's "believing game" (see above p. 63) when she addressed the pervasive climate of skepticism in the academe.[438] Instead of perpetuating "the academic habit of criticism," we should play the believing game with the first rule always in

---

435. See Oden, *You Welcomed Me*, 145–148.
436. Ibid., 147.
437. Larson, "Welcoming and Restoring," 48.
438. Ibid., 51.

mind – "refrain from doubting the assertions."[439] Instead of looking for errors, we should instead look for "hidden virtues" in ideas we may not agree with.[440]

By using Oden's four movements, Larson has introduced a new element to the metaphor of hospitality in education, namely, the sending off of the guest by the host. Thus far, contributions to hospitality in education are mostly related to the first three movements. The last movement is also an important act in the practice of hospitality. The host is able to let go as "the preceding acts of hospitality have empowered the guest, preparing her for her own responsibilities."[441] Hence, younger faculty members, having been welcomed and restored, and having dwelt with their colleagues, are now "energized and equipped" to become hospitable hosts to the guests in their classrooms.[442] More thought can definitely be given to this last movement in relation to the teacher's empowering of the students and sending them forth (see below ch. 5, esp. p. 250, "Reciprocity, Dialogue, and Partnership").

Like most of the works reviewed thus far, Larson also highlighted the importance of critical presence and confrontation. However, she argued that this should be balanced by boundaries that are like semi-permeable cell membranes, "firm enough to hold, but not so tight that it binds, confines, and cuts."[443] In practicing obedience to truth, "if we fail to challenge and stretch each other, both students and faculty colleagues, we don't do our job; if we disregard each other's boundaries, we may do violence."[444] Though she did not elaborate much on this idea, she has brought Palmer's idea of a bounded space to the forefront, highlighting the need for further scholarly consideration of this aspect of hospitality (see above pp. 29, 36).

Another teacher who attempted to practice hospitality in the classroom is Carolyne Call. Inspired by Ellen L. Marmon's (see below p. 78) attempt in practicing hospitality in her class in a theological institution, Call restructured her Adolescent Psychology class at Saint Mary's College (Notre Dame, Indiana) to experiment with how different her teaching would be if

---

439. See Elbow, *Writing without Teachers*, 149.
440. Elbow, "Believing Game," 19, as quoted in Larson, "Welcoming and Restoring," 51.
441. Larson, "Welcoming and Restoring," 49.
442. Ibid., 52.
443. Westerhoff, *Boundaries of Hospitality*, 83, as quoted in Larson "Welcoming and Restoring," 51.
444. Larson, "Welcoming and Restoring," 51.

she perceived herself as a host and her students as her guests.[445] Drawing on Craig R. Dykstra and Dorothy C. Bass' understanding that Christian practices can help shape communities,[446] Call chose to incorporate the practice of hospitality into her classroom as a way for her diverse group of students to connect as a learning community.[447] Subsumed under the overarching canopy of hospitality are the practices of fellowship, and testimony. Like Marmon, Call realized that practicing hospitality in the classroom was not an easy task. "This was easily the most difficult class I have ever taught," she conceded.[448] And "the difficulty came from the surprising emotional strain of being a hospitable person on a day-to-day basis."[449] At the same time, it was "the most dynamic class" that she have had ever taught.[450]

Call's personal experience reinforced what she had read about hospitality – that "hospitality is not so much a singular act of welcome as it is a way, an orientation that attends to otherness, listening and learning, valuing and honoring"[451] and "hospitality requires not grand gestures, but open hearts."[452] Her struggles with a challenging student caused her to realize that "hospitality does not happen in single, isolated events."[453] Instead, "genuine hospitality requires an orientation of the heart" which is maintained through constant practice, monitoring, reflection, and prayer.[454] In spite of her struggles throughout the entire semester, Call still hoped to practice hospitality in her class again. However, it would have to be "a more realistic and humble embrace of hospitality."[455] And she would definitely continue the community-building practices of sharing food together and hearing personal stories and testimonies.

The focus on teaching hospitality to students appeared in two works in the same issue of the *Journal of Education and Christian Belief* (17, no. 1).

---

445. Call, "Rough Trail," 61; see Marmon, "Teaching as Hospitality" (see below p. 78).
446. Dykstra and Bass, "Times of Yearning," 7.
447. Call, "Rough Trail," 64.
448. Ibid., 71.
449. Ibid.
450. Ibid., 72.
451. Oden, *You Welcomed Me*, 14, as quoted in Call, "Rough Trail," 64–65.
452. Homan and Pratt, *Radical Hospitality*, 16, as quoted in Call, "Rough Trail," 65.
453. Call, "Rough Trail," 78.
454. Ibid., 76, 77.
455. Ibid., 79.

The first essay was written by Burwell and Huyser who experimented with the practice of hospitality as a framework to help students better engage with others outside of the classroom. While the theoretical underpinning of their experiment was based on the Jack Mezirow's transformational learning theory,[456] they were also guided by Mo-Yee Lee and Gilbert J. Greene's four possible stances of students towards cross-cultural learning:

- The stance of ethnocentricism (i.e. low cultural knowledge and low cultural sensitivity)
- The stance of information (i.e. high cultural knowledge and low cultural sensitivity)
- The stance of curiosity (i.e. low cultural knowledge and high cultural sensitivity)
- The stance of reflexivity (i.e. high cultural knowledge and high cultural sensitivity)[457]

Burwell and Huyser wanted to teach students in an urban setting how to be hospitable to those who were different from them in race, culture, or religion; and how to navigate "issues of community change, social action, and diversity and inequality."[458] They designed specific learning activities targeted to help students understand the stances they were operating from. The transformative learning process was further facilitated by accompanying reflections.

The second essay was a response to the decline of dispositional empathy in college students in the United States, and the inability of "self-centered, competitive, confident, and individualistic" college students to engage with people.[459] Initially, hoping to help his students explore "emphatic concern and perspective taking," Jacob Stratman tried to introduce various metaphors

---

456. Burwell and Huyser, "Practicing Hospitality," 13. Jack Mezirow wrote that "transformative learning may be defined as *learning that transforms problematic frames of reference to make them more inclusive, discriminating, reflective, open, and emotionally able to change*" ("Transformative Learning Theory," 22 [original emphasis]). "A frame of reference is a predisposition with cognitive, affective, and conative (striving) dimensions" and could refer to our thoughts, feelings, rules, language, standards, personality traits, or dispositions" (ibid.).
457. Lee and Greene, "Teaching Framework," 4, fig. 1.
458. Burwell and Huyser, "Practicing Hospitality," 14.
459. Stratman, "Toward a Pedagogy," 25, quoting Konrath, O'Brien, and Hsing, "Changes in Dispositional Empathy," 187.

into his teaching. However, his initial attempts were unsuccessful.[460] This was due to his choice of metaphors – the concept of social justice had political overtones while the concept of reconciliation was too theologically profound. Hence, he decided to employ the Christian practice of hospitality to structure his service-learning course that could help the students show more empathy toward the other, even a stranger. In this article, he documented how, by integrating textual analysis, reflection and journaling, and community engagement, he helped students "to think and rethink what hospitality means and looks like in their lives."[461] His sole objective for the class was that "students will be able to construct analytical, reflective, and critical responses to a variety of prompts associated with hospitality."[462]

In both experiments, the authors could not be one hundred percent sure of their success. Burwell and Huyser recorded: "While we do not have specific examples of how we have seen students reflect when operating from this stance [of reflexivity] we do think that this is an integral part to practicing hospitality."[463] However, they reiterated Lee and Greene's advice that at this level of critical reflection the role played by the teacher is of utmost importance. The teacher must be a co-learner in the dialogical reflection process; yet he or she must foster norms to facilitate meaningful dialogue – norms such as "mutually developing discourse procedures, avoiding making dismissive statements, not letting a small number of students dominate the dialogue, and allowing silent moments."[464]

Similarly, Stratman recorded that he was unsure from his students' reflective journaling if all of them achieved his rather unmeasurable "low-stakes objective."[465] However, through the experiment, he felt that he was able "to think more holistically about inviting students to lead empathic lives."[466] Though the results of the experiments could not be adequately assessed, these

---

460. Stratman, "Toward a Pedagogy," 26. The author of the essay is Jake Stratman. In a personal email message to me (24 May 2015), Jacob Stratman explained that "for some odd reason" he used the name "Jake" in that essay.
461. Stratman, "Toward a Pedagogy," 45.
462. Ibid., 44.
463. Burwell and Huyser, "Practicing Hospitality," 20.
464. Ibid., 21, quoting Lee and Greene, "Teaching Framework," 24.
465. Stratman, "Toward a Pedagogy," 45.
466. Ibid.

authors have made a bold step forward by teaching hospitality as a model for students to practice hospitality.

All the essays reviewed in this section are related to the nitty-gritty work of teaching. From the tone of their essays, we can see that both Gallagher and Larson put the onus on teachers to practice hospitality in their teaching. Even when Burwell and Huyser tried to teach students how to show hospitality to others outside of the classroom, they had to first model what hospitality is to their students in the classroom.[467] Hospitality in the classroom – towards strangers and strangeness of ideas – begins with the teacher's hospitality. And in discussing the nitty-gritty work of hospitality, the authors have shared their personal strategies for practicing hospitality, adding to the table of conversation practical ideas such as the believing game, double vision, intentional marginality, the issue of boundaries, and the movement of sending off.

Hospitality as a Key Concept in Theological Education

This section reviews relevant post-Nouwen and Palmer literature on hospitality in theological education and shows the multiple facets of this metaphor as it is used in particular contexts by the various authors. The contexts discussed are grouped as follows: (1) pluralistic environment, (2) marginalized, and (3) classroom process. Though the contexts of theological education discussed here are also contexts discussed under Christian higher education, an examination of the works shows that the emphases of the two academic arenas are somewhat different.

Hospitality and the Pluralistic Environment

Just like Christian colleges/universities, theological institutions teem with people from various cultures and countries. Multicultural diversity in theological education became an issue of concern in the early 1990s and remains even so today. This continuing trend can be seen in the essays of Susanne Johnson, Anne E. Streaty Wimberly, and Molly T. Marshall.

Johnson's essay, "Reshaping Religious and Theological Education in the 90's," was a response to the "multicultural diversity in curriculum content

---

467. Burwell and Huyser, "Practicing Hospitality," 12–13.

and in faculty constituency" prevalent in the American education system and prevailing in theological institutions.[468] Johnson felt that neither foundationalism that holds a transcending set of truth claims acting as a referee to other opinions, nor simple pluralism that uncritically accepts all truth claims were adequate for dealing with diverse hermeneutical options.[469] The alternative strategy to approach diversity she proposed was critical pluralism.[470] In religious and theological education, "*critical pluralism* is a strategy, or a posture of practice and theory, that situates itself in critical dialogue among or between different hermeneutical, cultural, religious, or theological options."[471] Hence, the pedagogical strategy we should employ is critical dialogue since dialogue "permits critical appraisal of the truth claims not only in the other's position (from *inside* that person), but also critical appraisal of one's own culture, tradition, or position, *as seen from the other's vantage point.*"[472] Such reflexive analysis "celebrates diversity and plurality while it also pursues and heightens a sense of particularity."[473] Although she did not cite Volf in her essay, this idea is clearly reminiscent of Volf's double vision (see above p. 65).

Johnson believed that the biblical command to practice hospitality to strangers summons religious and theological educators to confront multicultural issues presented by the contemporary American society.[474] Convinced by John Koenig's argument that "hospitality and partnership with strangers is the hermeneutical key to the entire biblical witness,"[475] she proposed hospitality as the hermeneutical key for critical pluralism.[476] "The very existence of asymmetry in relationships, and the inequity of power, confronts the dominant group with the moral imperative to give hospitality

---

468. Johnson, "Reshaping," 335.
469. Ibid., 340.
470. Ibid., 339.
471. Ibid., 340 (original emphasis).
472. Ibid. (original emphasis).
473. Ibid.
474. Ibid., 341–342.
475. Koenig, *New Testament Hospitality*.
476. Johnson, "Reshaping," 342. It must be noted that John Koenig's treatment of hospitality centered on the ministry of Jesus, the ministry of Paul, and the early church practices as depicted in Luke-Acts. Focusing on hospitality and mission in the New Testament, Koenig argued that hospitality is "the catalyst for creating and sustaining partnerships" with strangers in the proclamation of the gospel (*New Testament Hospitality*, 10).

to the stranger and to place limits on how relative power is exercised."[477] Hospitality, when truly practiced, would bring about: (1) a breakdown in role distinctions, and (2) role reversal, including the voluntary relinquishing of dominance and power by the host.[478] Johnson then proposed that practicing authentic and radical hospitality in religious and theological education would entail a "de-centering of perspective" – an approach to ethics which she found in Thomas W. Ogletree's book.[479] In de-centering, the dominant group makes itself vulnerable by moving from the center to the margins and inviting the strangers into the center. Hence, to de-center our perspectives means "surrendering our tendency to read and to assimilate the experience of others into our own experience."[480] After all, the stranger has his or her own stories to tell that may challenge our self-understanding and worldview or even subvert our assumptions. "Hospitality, in its deepest sense, is a willingness not only to receive the stranger, but also to be changed and affected by the presence of the other, not only personally, but also institutionally, curricularly, and politically."[481]

As with Newman's and Hagstrom's writings, Nouwen's and Palmer's works were also not cited in Johnson's essay. This is understandable as Newman, Hagstrom, and Johnson were addressing an issue – multiculturalism – that was not yet a threat to academic excellence in American educational institutions at the time when Nouwen and Palmer were in conversation about hospitality and the spirituality of education. In her essay, Johnson perceived the asymmetry in relationships and inequity of power as an ethical problem that demands a moral response. Her clarion call was to the dominant privileged group to repent and to create a space where power relationships can be transformed.[482] By so doing, she added a new dimension to Nouwen's and Palmer's notions of hospitality.[483]

---

477. Johnson, "Reshaping," 343.
478. Ibid., 346.
479. Ibid. Thomas W. Ogletree (*Hospitality to the Stranger*, 2) gave credit to the philosopher Paul Ricoeur (*Freedom and Nature*, 126) for the idea of "de-centering of perspective."
480. Johnson, "Reshaping," 347.
481. Ibid., 348.
482. Ibid.
483. See Smith and Carvill, *Gift of the Stranger*, 88.

Johnson herself acknowledged that her essay was inadequate because it had not ventured to see how critical pluralism could be implemented in practice – in the classroom, curriculum, school administration, and faculty development.[484] However, in speaking out for the marginalized, in proposing the de-centering of perspectives, or the practice of intentional marginality, she has articulated the need to attend to strangers who are culturally marginalized.

Also addressing theological education in a multicultural context but about two decades later, M. Marshall, like Johnson, believed that there is a need for "the decentering of dominant privilege in order to make welcome those who bring other capacities and insights."[485] A space must be created for others if we seek inclusive theological education. And the Trinitarian theology of *perichoresis* provides the theological foundation for this idea of creating space for others and otherness.[486]

> *Perichoresis* depicts a relationship of mutuality in which persons draw their identity from being related to others. It is movement, an interplay, of self-giving that calls forth reciprocal sharing of life. By creating space for others, (i.e., Son and Spirit), God lives eternally in communing relationship without demanding sameness.[487]

In God's triune hospitality, there is relational wholeness.[488] By practicing God's triune hospitality, we make space for diversity and make inclusive theological education a reality.

After her positive experience in hospitable kinship circles in Zimbabwe, Wimberly was convinced that theological education needs a relational pedagogical model.[489] Taking into account the cultural diversity and global presence of students, she argued that theological educators should learn to create an environment for hospitable kinship and gift exchange.[490] In a hospitable community, in an environment of openness and trust,

---

484. Johnson, "Reshaping," 349.
485. Marshall, "One Student at a Time," 54.
486. Ibid., 53.
487. Ibid.
488. Ibid.
489. Wimberly, "Hospitable Kinship," 5.
490. Anne Wimberly credited the idea of gift exchange to Anthony J. Gittins (ibid., 4).

"kinship . . . calls us into a communal ritual life in which we sense God's presence with us and God's image in one another," and allows us to give gifts to and receive gifts from the other – "gifts of their distinctive personhood, experiences, thoughts, struggles, hopes, and care."[491]

Wimberly revisited Palmer's idea of the physical, emotional, and conceptual environments that are crucial for learning to take place (see above p. 35).[492] She acknowledged that her views concerning a hospitable learning environment resonated with Palmer's idea of hospitality that receives "each other, our struggles, our newborn ideas with openness and care," and took it a step further by sharing the pedagogical strategies she used in her teaching context – a Western African-American woman teaching in a predominantly African-American-populated seminary with four percent of the students coming from different continents.[493]

Like both Johnson and M. Marshall, Wimberly is also aware of the dynamics of power in the classroom which she highlighted in her essay as the dynamics of *positionality*, a term which she borrowed from Mary Kay Thompson Tetreault.[494] "Positionality comprises aspects of our identities – such as our race or national origin, gender, class, and age – which define our relational position in a particular context and provide a frame of reference out of which our input in conversation emerges."[495] When positionality rears its ugly head in the form of cultural biases or power differentiation, it prevents hospitable kinship and gift exchange from taking place.

The essays of Johnson, M. Marshall, and Wimberly testify to the myriad of cultural contexts in our global community. Though their contexts may differ, they share common concerns such as the need to de-center one's perspective and the need to address issues of power when dealing with multicultural diversity in theological education. While Christian higher education calls for engagement in pluralistic environments (e.g. through full presence, dialogue, embrace, respect), theological education ventures further and calls for empowerment.

---

491. Ibid., 11.
492. Ibid., 5.
493. Ibid., 5–6; see Palmer, *To Know as We Are Known*, 73–74.
494. As cited in Wimberly, "Hospitable Kinship," 4.
495. Ibid.

Hospitality and the Marginalized

By and large, works that specifically relate hospitality to a marginalized group of people in theological institutions are scarce. A recent report and reflection by Sharon M. Tan detailed how the faculty in the United Theological Seminary of the Twin Cities (UTSTC) (New Brighton, Minnesota) developed a theology of theological diversity to guide their educational endeavors and "to cultivate a truly multicultural and antiracist institution."[496] UTSTC is an ecumenical seminary that "has a reputation of being 'open and affirming' to GLBT [sic] students, staff, and faculty."[497] Seemingly a relevant essay, its contents as a report do not add to our conversation on hospitality. Hence, this section only reviews an essay written by Jane McAvoy.[498]

At a time when the metaphor of hospitality was centered on the teaching-learning environment, McAvoy wrote her article as a voice for the marginalized female theological students. From her reflection on the lived experience of women in theological education and Julian of Norwich's understanding of the sin of self-contempt, McAvoy proposed a feminist theology of theological education that would address the marginalized, especially women.

Many female theological students have experienced "silencing" both within and without the classrooms in the "chilly" theological institutions.[499] Hence, McAvoy proposed an educational climate of hospitality as a metaphor for theological education. This calls for hospitable teachers to practice intellectual and psychological hospitality, and ecclesial hospitality in theological institutions that will allow the voice of every student, regardless of gender, to be empowered and heard.[500]

In McAvoy's essay, it is not just lecturers who are insensitive or who have poor interpersonal skills that are silencing female students in theological institutions. The problem lies in the assumption lecturers have – that the "bright young men who have always been successful" in their classes are resistant to education and will fight back when challenged.[501] However, this

---

496. Tan, "Theological Diversity," 117.
497. Ibid., 112.
498. McAvoy, "Hospitality."
499. Ibid., 21.
500. Ibid., 23–25; for more on the categories of hospitality, see Groome, "Spirituality of the Religious Educator."
501. McAvoy, "Hospitality," 21.

does not work with female students. Instead of resisting, they will retreat and silence themselves. The reason: sin of self-contempt. The solution: contrition. Contrition is described as "the process of wearing away self-contempt."[502] Thus, an educational climate of hospitality, created by faculty and institution, is proposed to facilitate this process of contrition that would help female students reclaim their self-esteem.

McAvoy brought up two important points regarding engagement in the classroom. First, citing Gail B. Griffin, she pointed out that to have a voice does not necessarily mean to speak.[503] To have a voice is "to be heard and empowered by one's context."[504] Second, she reminded us that "we should not expect equality in the classroom but rather should strive for an equal engagement in the class according to our relative status."[505] For this, she quoted the black feminist educator and social activist, bell hooks[506] who felt that she, the teacher, also becomes a learner when the community of learners come together. "It positions me as a learner. But I'm also not suggesting that I don't have more power. And I'm not trying to say we're all equal here. I'm trying to say that we are all equal here to the extent that we are equally committed to creating a learning context."[507] McAvoy's two pointers serve to steer us away from digressive discourse and to spur us on toward inclusive discussion. Just as the preceding three have called for a space to be created by the dominant group for those who are culturally different, McAvoy too calls for a space to be created by the dominant group for those living at the margins. Once again, as in the case of pluralistic environment, it is a call for empowerment.

Hospitality and Classroom Process

It took more than three decades after the first appearance of Nouwen's discourse on hospitality in education for educators to translate the concept of hospitality into practices that could be employed in theological classrooms. In

---

502. Ibid., 22.
503. Griffin, *Essays*, 174.
504. McAvoy, "Hospitality," 24.
505. Ibid., 24.
506. The pen name of Gloria Watkins, a black feminist, who chooses to write her name in lowercase letters because "what is most important is the 'substance of books, not who I am'" (Williams, "bell hooks speaks up," 1).
507. hooks, *Teaching to Transgress*, 153, as quoted in McAvoy, "Hospitality," 24.

their essays, Marmon, Shaw, and David M. Rhoads described how hospitality is practiced in their classrooms.

Inspired by Nouwen's *Reaching Out*, Marmon gave her personal account of her journey towards redemptive teaching as a seminary lecturer. After reading Nouwen's thought-provoking interpretation of teaching as hospitality, she was challenged to re-examine her calling as a teacher – to be a host to her guests, her students. Her enthusiasm over this new analogy for teaching was fueled by a better understanding of Christ's encounters with a tax collector (Luke 19) and the Samaritan woman (John 4), her Wesleyan background that has "holiness of heart and life" as an educational goal, and her own research on Transformative Learning Theory.

Marmon soon realized that being a good host was "messy, embarrassing and too much work."[508] In fact, her first attempt at being a good host ended with her doing the unthinkable – apologizing to her students. In that online class, her condescending mindset, that the students were "poor, needy, ignorant beggars," created a barrier to student learning.[509] The situation improved and the class became a learning community only when she welcomed them as guests and the gifts they brought with them. Since then, Marmon has been promoting the redemptive model of teaching. For her, "not having experienced redemptive teaching doesn't excuse us from exploring it as a God-honoring way to facilitate learning."[510]

Whether it is for Christian religious education[511] or theological education,[512] Shaw advocated that a hospitable teaching-learning encounter is pertinent in the spiritual formation of our students. The relational nature of knowing lies at the heart of Christian anthropology and reminds religious and theological educators of their goal as Christian educators: a reconciled relationship with the One who has created us in his image and a reconciled relationship with all of creation.[513] A hospitable environment thus serves as the ideal context to teach for reconciliation – an environment characterized

---

508. Marmon, "Teaching as Hospitality," 36.
509. Ibid., 36, quoting Nouwen, *Reaching Out*, 89.
510. Marmon, "Teaching as Hospitality," 38.
511. Shaw, "Education as Hospitality."
512. Shaw, "Welcome Guest: Theological Education"; "Welcome Guest."
513. Shaw, "Education as Hospitality," 113; "Welcome Guest: Theological Education," under "The Goal of Education"; "Welcome Guest," 17.

by trust, not fear, and reciprocity. These ideas are clearly congruent with those of Nouwen and Palmer.

In addressing theological educators, Shaw added another dimension to his understanding of hospitality as an educational motif. More than just a pedagogical approach, creating a hospitable teaching-learning space is essentially a pedagogical act,[514] even a theological act.[515] The hospitable act of welcoming students as guests in the classroom is a nonverbal visual portrayal of divine reconciling work – God welcoming and reconciling sinners to himself. "It is a profound theological drama, through which the mighty act of divine reconciliation is known by the participants not simply in word but through personal experience."[516] His experiences as a missionary in the Middle East have made him more aware of the communication style of people from high-context cultures.[517] Hence, the ethos of hospitality in our theological institutions and the physical acts of hospitality we extend to one another become lessons in themselves. Our hidden curriculum is "a dramatic enactment of the experience of reconciliation"[518] and "a clear formational experience" that helps shape our students' concept of the ministry – a ministry of reconciliation and healing.[519]

Once again, we are reminded that the practice of hospitality is an enactment of God's divine hospitality; but more specific than that, as proposed by Shaw, it is an enactment of divine reconciliation. We are also reminded of the subtle power of the hidden curriculum. Enacted hospitality has the power to teach profound theological truths about God's hospitality.

Inspired by the hospitality of a teacher (Dudley Riggle, Professor Emeritus of Religion) at Carthage College (Kenosha, Wisconsin), Rhoad's essay contains basically his specific practices of hospitality.[520] His simple yet practical practices include arriving in class before the students, beginning and ending class on time, knowing students' names, communicating with students

---

514. Shaw, "Welcome Guest: Theological Education," under "Prelude."
515. Shaw, "Welcome Guest," 9.
516. Ibid., 8.
517. Namely, through implicit messages and nonverbal coding; see Hall, *Beyond Culture*, 91; Bentley, Tinney, and Chia, "Intercultural Internet-Based Learning," 122.
518. Shaw, "Welcome Guest: Theological Education," under "Education as Hospitality."
519. Shaw, "Welcome Guest," 18
520. Rhoads, "Hospitality in the Classroom," 255.

between classes, letting students know ahead the course expectations, giving prompt and timely feedback to students, and sharing food together as a class. He concluded that "hospitality does not have to do with a series of activities or pedagogical strategies or contextual mechanics. Rather hospitality has to do with relationships."[521]

When it comes down to the nitty-gritty of classroom process, it is the teacher's modeling that is of utmost importance. This can be gleaned from all the three essays reviewed here. However, Shaw's presentation of modeling as a nonverbal enactment of God's hospitality has added an important ingredient to our conversation on hospitality. Although the concept of modeling does appear in Christian higher education literature (e.g. Burwell and Huyser), it is apparent that there are more differences than similarities. After all, each essay is the author's individual narrative of how hospitality is practiced or taught in his or her classroom.

Summary

Having presented a conceptual map of hospitality that began with the conversations between Nouwen and Palmer, this chapter concludes with a brief assessment of the current state of research regarding hospitality in Christian higher education and theological education. Many works on hospitality in Christian higher education and theological education written in the past three decades have been influenced in some way by Nouwen and Palmer. The path cut by these two trailblazers, fundamentally remains unchanged. Hospitality is essentially still the creation of a space that welcomes the other, whether it is a person or an idea. One thing that has changed though is the various authors' explication of who this person or what this idea is, thereby bringing in new nuances to the notion of hospitality in education.

From the literature review, we can also see that there is no one extensive treatment of hospitality in Christian higher education and theological education since each author tends to focus on an aspect of hospitality to address his or her particular area of concern or context. Even though the works reviewed were written primarily from within Western settings, considering that the world is now a global village, the issues they have raised

---

521. Ibid., 261.

are generally universal in nature and relevant for any further conceptualizing of hospitality in education.

For many of these authors, the metaphor of hospitality can serve as a corrective to the existing deficiencies in the liberal higher education system in the United States which also exist in Christian colleges/universities and theological institutions. Initial conversations about hospitality focus on the hostile environment of the academia and teaching-learning environments. Hospitality is perceived as an ethical and intellectual virtue and the discourses generally encourage students, teachers, administrators, and educational leaders to receive each other and each other's ideas with genuine hospitality.

In the context of increasing religious pluralism, ethnic diversity, cultural relativism, and diverse sexual orientations and gender identities, hospitality demands of one to look at the other, the stranger, more intently. It calls for more than mere tolerance. Hospitality reaches out to embrace the stranger, opens a space for the sharing of stories, and may even call for a role reversal for those in positions of power. However, the hospitable embrace need not necessitate an obliteration of our personal identity. Whatever the context of plurality may be, the onus is always on the dominant group to extend an unconditional welcome to those who are significantly different from them.

While educational reforms are not yet implemented nationwide, several individuals have attempted to practice hospitality in their teaching and classrooms. Though a messy task, it is a worthwhile effort that will make significant differences to the classroom experience and learning.

The literature review has revealed several gaps that need to be addressed. Although literature on hospitality in Christian higher education and theological education is slowly expanding, there is still a paucity of literature in the field of theological education. Furthermore, the biblical and theological foundations for the practice of hospitality in theological education is an area of study that has been dealt with only briefly. Though both Nouwen and Palmer presented hospitality from a biblical perspective and cited several biblical Scriptures as support, their interpretation lacked exegetical study of the text. One example is Palmer's interpretation of the cross-examination of Jesus by Pilate in John 18:33–38, in which he categorized Pilate as "the model objectivist" for trying to reduce personal truth – Jesus – to a "what," and so failed to take into consideration the author's world and the textual world.[522] Historically, Pilate, as the Roman governor of Judea, questioned Jesus' claim as "the king of the Jews" to ascertain if this so-called king would be a threat to the Roman Empire.[523] Textually, Pilate represents "the world that refuses the truth about God and itself."[524]

As for Nouwen, he often used Scripture references to support his ideas; however, sometimes his interpretation of the Scriptures seemed to be from his devotional meditations rather than exegetical study of the passages. Dierdre LaNoue noted that "he [Nouwen] made reference to specific passages over seven hundred times in the forty books he wrote."[525] However, she continued, "One must not go overboard, however, in emphasizing his use of Scripture. Nouwen was not a biblical scholar and did not teach from it in an expository manner, with balanced treatment of all of its books."[526] Nouwen's devotional reading of the Bible interpreted the prediction of Peter's death in John 21:18 in terms of spiritual maturity whereby one surrenders in love to a loving God who may lead us in the way of suffering.[527] Hence, even though the thoughts of Nouwen and Palmer on hospitality in education are inspiring, the concept of hospitality in education can be further augmented with an exegetical study of relevant biblical texts, as I have undertaken in chapter 4.

Another lacuna in existing literature is the absence of non-Western voices. This study seeks to fill these gaps and to present a biblically informed metaphor of hospitality that can provide the biblical and theological foundations for the practice of hospitality in theological institutions. The inclusion of an Asian voice offers a view from the other side (using the example of Volf's double vision, see above p. 65) by bringing another cultural perspective to the conversation on hospitality.

---

522. Palmer, *To Know as We Are Known*, 47–48.
523. Brown, *Gospel according to John 13–21*, 868–869.
524. Johnson, *Writings of the New Testament*, 488.
525. LaNoue, *Spiritual Legacy*, 81; see 173–190 for her listing of Scripture passages referenced in Nouwen's books.
526. Ibid., 82.
527. Nouwen, *Reaching Out*, 149–150.

The literature review also shows that hospitality is often discussed in the category of a safe learning environment, thus highlighting the affective dimension in learning which is the focus in the next chapter.[528]

---

528. See Shaw "Welcome Guest," 9.

3

The Motif of Hospitality as Reflected in Contemporary Educational Research and Practice, and Higher Education Literature

The face of education, at all levels, is shaped by societal forces and demands, and has undergone many changes and transformations over the centuries as the world moves from an industrial to a post-industrial society, from the modern to the postmodern era, from a production-based to a knowledge-based economy. With each societal change come new ideas, new demands, and new challenges. Hospitality, with its images of warmth and welcome, offers for at least some of those involved in higher education a viable metaphor for re-conceptualizing education, responding to the challenges posed by an ever-changing society, and addressing a neglected dimension of the teaching-learning – the affective dimension.

The purpose of this chapter is threefold. It seeks to show that: (1) the affective domain plays an important role in learning, (2) the concept of hospitality is a recurring concept in higher education literature, and (3) close parallels to the practice of hospitality are found in the emotional and relational aspects of learning in contemporary educational practices.

The chapter begins by showing the importance of the emotional and relational aspects of the teaching-learning process. It accomplishes this by tracing three paradigm shifts in higher education before discussing the emotional aspects of teacher-student relationships.[1]

Following that is a review of the literature in the field of higher education, including teacher education and curriculum studies, where hospitality is featured as a possible solution to the current ills in higher education.[2] Dissatisfied with the state of higher education, and presented with the challenges posed by the shifting trends in education, as well as the missing emotional and relational dimensions in the teaching-learning process, some of these educational researchers and practitioners have explored the traditional custom of hospitality as an alternative in their efforts to renew higher education.

Lastly, this chapter examines parallels to the practice of hospitality in three contemporary educational practices that have emerged from the literature review – care, inclusion, and dialogue. These three practices have been campaigned for by teaching professionals in higher education and are practiced in higher education institutions. Besides being closely parallel to the biblical practice of hospitality (the content of our discussion in ch. 4), they provide further support for the need for hospitality in theological education.

The Emotional and Relational Dimensions in the Teaching-Learning Process

Since the changing face of education is primarily a reflection of the changing face of the society and its needs, an examination of the changing trends in education will help us to understand the needs of learners today. Our examination of three of these paradigm shifts reveals a move towards the emotional and relational aspects of learning.

---

1. This work only describes paradigm shifts that led to a more relational learning community. It is beyond its scope to discuss the merits and demerits of these shifts although references to relevant literature regarding these issues are given whenever necessary. Writing in relation to the shift from behaviorism to constructivism, Tom H. Brown stated that "neither of these views can be regarded as exclusively right or wrong" ("Beyond Constructivism," 109). I believe this statement is applicable to the various paradigm shifts described in the text.

2. The works included in this literature review are works written from a non-faith based platform (cf. Christian higher education) to a general audience (i.e. the general public). The religious affiliation of these authors, which is sometimes difficult to ascertain, is not a selection criterion.

Shifting Trends in Higher Education

Authors in different parts of the world have acknowledged that the landscape of education has changed and the changes have affected all levels of education – from early childhood to higher education. Peter Jarvis, John Holford, and Colin Griffin discussed thirteen shifts in education, observations gleaned from the British education system, that have occurred over the years. The shifts in emphases are from:

- childhood to adult to lifelong [learning]
- [education of] the few to the many
- education and training to learning
- learning as a process to learning as an institutional phenomenon
- teacher-centered to student-centered [education]
- liberal to vocational and human resource development
- theoretical to practical
- single discipline knowledge to multidisciplinary knowledge to integrated knowledge
- knowledge as truth to knowledge as relative/information/narrative/discourse
- rote learning to reflective learning
- welfare provision (needs) to market demand (wants)
- classical curriculum to romantic curriculum to program
- face-to-face to distance to e-learning[3]

Since Javis, Holford, and Griffin's writing was based on their observations of the British education system, not all of the shifts in emphases in education discussed were applicable globally. For example, the authors perceived the shift from "the few to the many" as largely a British phenomenon. As opposed to the mass education system in the United States, "the British system of education has traditionally been rather elitist, training the few to assume responsible positions in government, the professions and the Church."[4]

In a similar vein, Tom H. Brown, writing from South Africa, cited ten shifts in education internationally – seven of which occurred during the

---

3. Jarvis, Holford and Griffin, *Theory and Practice*, 1–2. The shifts in emphases did not occur concurrently and did not have exact start points. Some began as early as the 1970s (e.g. the shift to student-centered learning, the shift to practical knowledge) (ibid., 5, 7).
4. Ibid., 3.

twentieth century and three that have emerged in recent years.⁵ The first seven of his paradigm shifts are from:

- reproductive [to] productive learning
- behaviorism [to] constructivism
- teacher-centered [to] learner-centered learning environment
- teaching-centered [to] learning-centered activities
- teaching [to] learning facilitation
- content-based [to] outcomes-based approach
- content-based evaluation [to] outcomes-based assessment

The three more recent shifts are from:

- constructivism to social constructivism
- knowledge production to knowledge configuration
- knowledge management towards sense making

Don W. Edgar also gave a descriptive historical account of the paradigm shifts in educational thought and practice in the United States. In his opinion, World War II, the launch of Sputnik into space, and the invention of the World Wide Web are three crucial watershed moments in the American education system, resulting in changing perceptions and expectations about learning.⁶ From his descriptive essay, we can list some of the changes he identified as from:

- recitation literacy (knowledge remembered) to extraction literacy (knowledge understood)
- behaviorism to constructivism (i.e. personal, social, and aphilosophical)
- teacher-centered to learner-centered, knowledge-centered, assessment-centered, and community-centered
- theoretical to practical
- localized community learners to globalized learners

There seems to be a general consensus among educators that these shifting trends have invaded "the sphere of worldwide higher education."⁷ At a conference in Melbourne Australia in 2004, Suxian Zhan and Thao Le cited three changes that have taken place globally:

---

5. Brown, "Beyond Constructivism," 109–112.
6. Edgar, "Learning Theories," 5, fig. 1.
7. Zhan and Le, "Interpersonal Relationship," 2.

- a shift from focus on effective teaching to concern for individual learner's effective learning
- a change from subject-focused curriculum to a competency-focused one
- a great change from stress on learning outcomes to studies of process-oriented learning and teaching[8]

Comparing these lists, we can see that the paradigm shifts are somewhat similar worldwide. This section discusses three shifting trends that bear particularly on our discourse on the motif of hospitality in higher education. The first two trends have been identified by most of the authors: the shifts from teaching to learning, and from personal constructivism to social constructivism. The third paradigm shift, not explicitly mentioned in the above lists, is a more recent development informed by neuroscience research: the shift from cognition to emotion.

From Teaching to Learning

In the mid-1990s, a number of higher education practitioners were advocating a paradigm shift to reshape teaching in higher education – from teaching to learning.[9] The call for a shift from teacher-centered teaching to student-centered learning was not new. During the 1960s, a renewed interested in John Dewey's progressive educational philosophy and the emergence of Jean Piaget's studies of cognitive development contributed to a shift in education, focusing on student learning rather than teacher teaching.[10] However, the process of change was slow and gradual.[11] In 1994, Alan E. Guskin was still commenting that "the primary learning environment for undergraduate

---

8. Ibid.
9. Guskin, "Reducing Student Costs"; Twigg, "National Learning Infrastructure"; Barr and Tagg, "From Teaching to Learning"; Boggs, "Learning Paradigm"; O'Banion, *Learning College*.
10. Jarvis, Holford, and Griffin, *Theory and Practice*, 5; Ültanir, "Epistemological Glance," 199–203.
11. The process of change also affects countries but differently. For instance, it was only in 1997 that Singapore shifted from the efficiency-driven education (1979–1996) "towards a more ability-driven, learner-centered mode of education" (Soh, *Use of Information Technology*, 1; the specific dates were taken from a press release from the Ministry of Education on December 1, 2010, retrieved from https://www.moe.gov.sg/news/press-releases/infosheet-on-singapore-highlighted-in-latest-mckinsey-report-and8220how-the-worldand8217s-most-improved-school-systems-keep-getting-betterand8221). The slow response to worldwide paradigm shifts could be due to the fact that "the Singapore education

students, the fairly passive lecture-discussion format where faculty talk and most students listen, is contrary to almost every principle of optimal settings for student learning."[12] The next clarion call for change was sounded when Robert B. Barr and John Tagg advocated a shift from the traditional, dominant Instruction Paradigm to the emerging Learning Paradigm.[13]

According to Barr and Tagg, there are basically two paradigms adopted by educators in their teaching – Instruction Paradigm or Learning Paradigm.[14] In the Instruction Paradigm, the focus is on transmission of knowledge and teachers are basically deliverers of knowledge and students are passive recipients of knowledge. The late Brazilian educator and social activist, Paulo Freire, termed this the "banking concept of education" – education as merely "an act of depositing, in which the students are the depositories and the teacher is the depositor."[15] To him, as someone who grew up in a poverty-stricken neighborhood and had personally experienced social and economic inequalities in his society, the top-down approach – the teacher as the expert knower and the student's brain merely as a *tabula rasa* or blank slate to be filled – resembled that of an oppressor and the oppressed.[16]

Barr and Tagg noted that "the learning that goes on in Instruction Paradigm colleges frequently involves only rudimentary, stimulus-response relationships whose cues may be coded into the context of a particular course but are not rooted in the student's everyday, functioning understanding."[17] "Knowledge exists 'out there'" and "knowledge comes in 'chunks' and 'bits'

---

journey is closely tied in with the evolution of the modern Singapore state" (Gopinatham, "Fourth Way in Action," 65; see Goh and Gopinathan, "Development of Education"). "Educational reforms have been carried out in parallel, based on the different needs according to the phases of industrialization" (Ng, "Strategic Management," 65).

12. Guskin, "Reducing Student Costs," 20.

13. For a summary chart showing a comparison of the two paradigms in six areas (namely, "mission and purposes, criteria for success, teaching/learning structures, learning theory, productivity/funding, and nature of roles"), see Barr and Tagg, "From Teaching to Learning," 16–17. For a more detailed comparison chart, see McManus, "Two Paradigms," tables 1–5.

14. These terms were used by Robert B. Barr and John Tagg in their proposal for a new paradigm in undergraduate education ("From Teaching to Learning"). This idea is variously described by authors as acquisition metaphor and participation metaphor (Sfard, "On Two Metaphors"), classical teaching to constructivist learning (Lenschow, "From Teaching to Learning," 155), or individualized paradigm and the socially situated paradigm (Martínez, Sauleda, and Güenter, "Metaphors as Blueprints").

15. Freire, *Pedagogy of the Oppressed*, 72.

16. Ibid., 73–74.

17. Barr and Tagg, "From Teaching to Learning," 22.

delivered by instructors."[18] In this paradigm, the teacher plays a dominant role in directing the learning process and students are often sorted, "in the worst cases into those who are 'college material' and those who cannot 'cut it.'"[19] However, in our current Knowledge Age, we cannot have "the one-size-fits-all, production-line model" of education.[20]

On the other hand, in the Learning Paradigm, "a college's purpose is not to transfer knowledge but to create environments and experiences that bring students to discover and construct knowledge for themselves, to make students members of communities of learners that make discoveries and solve problems."[21] Instead of teaching for knowledge transfer, teaching is to help students construct knowledge for themselves. In this paradigm, which has its roots in constructivism, learners themselves play an important role in the learning as they actively discover and construct their own knowledge.

In Peter W. Airasian and Mary E. Walsh's assessment, the shift from a view where truth is given to a view where truth is constructed was welcomed because the teaching practice of "'filling the bucket' of students' heads with facts" was not meeting the intellectual and occupational needs of students.[22] The metaphor of constructivism – "'lighting the flame' of student motivation" – was certainly more appealing.[23] Since the focus is now on student learning rather than teacher teaching or downloading, the learning environment and experiences become essential materials for lighting the flame of student motivation.

From Personal Constructivism to Social Constructivism

As we have just seen, the Learning Paradigm is epistemologically rooted in constructivism where knowledge is a construct created by the learner. However, this is just a broad definition. The term *constructivism* has so many interpretations[24] that to delve into its distinctions would be, as D. C. Phillips

---

18. Ibid., 17.
19. Ibid., 22–23.
20. Gilbert, "Catching the Knowledge Wave," 7.
21. Barr and Tagg, "From Teaching to Learning," 15; see Ramaley and Leskes, *Greater Expectations*, 44.
22. Airasian and Walsh, "Constructivist Cautions," 446, quoting David Elkind.
23. Ibid.
24. See Good, "Many Forms of Constructivism"; Geelan, "Epistemological Anarchy"; Matthews, "Introductory Comments"; Gredler, *Learning and Instruction*.

put it, "a trip into a nightmarish landscape."[25] Margaret E. Gredler noted that constructivism is presently divided into two broad areas: (1) epistemology – "the nature of the disciplines or bodies of human knowledge built up in human history," and (2) educational constructivism – "beliefs about educational practices."[26] For the purposes of this work, we will view educational constructivism as a continuum, with personal constructivism and social constructivism at the two extreme ends.[27]

Basically, all constructivists believe reality and knowledge are constructed by the individual – "objective reality is not perceived directly and that we construct our view of the world based on sensory input of all kinds and the interaction of this input with pre-existing knowledge."[28] However, personal constructivists emphasize "individual cognitive processes"[29] and "believe that we develop our individual view of the world alone."[30] In contrast, social constructivists emphasize the "social co-construction of knowledge,"[31] believing that "we only build knowledge of our surroundings through discourse with others, that is, through social interaction."[32] Personal constructivism can trace its roots to Jean Piaget's theory of cognitive development that focuses on "the individual creation of knowledge and construction of concepts" while social constructivism, developed by Les Vygotsky, gives more attention to

---

25. Phillips, "Opinionated Account," 7.
26. Gredler, *Learning and Instruction*, 19.
27. I am using Michael R. Matthews's terminology here ("Constructivism and Science Education," 362; "Introductory Comments," 7). Alan Pritchard and John Woollard termed them *radical constructivism* and *social constructivism* (*Psychology for the Classroom*, 8–9). The term *radical constructivism* is often associated with Ernst von Glasersfeld (*Radical Constructivism*). Margaret E. Gredler, citing von Glasersfeld as her example, stated that "personal constructivism is a radical view because of the basic belief that reality is not accessible to rational human knowledge" (*Learning and Instruction*, 21–25). Another term for personal constructivism is *cognitive constructivism* (Windschitl, "Framing Constructivism," 140–142; Powell and Kalina, "Cognitive and Social Constructivism"). Gredler also listed a third type of constructivism – *aphilosophical constructivism* – which is not relevant to our discussion (*Learning and Instruction*, 24). Aphilosophical constructivists do not make any assumptions about the nature of knowledge.
28. Pritchard and Woollard, *Psychology for the Classroom*, 9.
29. Windschitl, "Framing Constructivism," 136.
30. Pritchard and Woollard, *Psychology for the Classroom*, 9.
31. Windschitl, "Framing Constructivism," 136.
32. Pritchard and Woollard, *Psychology for the Classroom*, 9; see Lee and Greene, "Social Constructivist Framework"; Hardina et al., *Empowering Approach*, 31.

"the importance of the group (be it the immediate classroom or the wider culture) for the development and validation of ideas."[33]

When Barr and Tagg mooted the idea of the Learning Paradigm, the learning theory undergirding it was that knowledge "exists in each person's mind and is shaped by individual experience" and "is constructed, created, and 'gotten.'"[34] What they proposed was more akin to personal constructivism. The shift towards social constructivism took place when "the concept of knowledge as mental representation" was challenged.[35] Knowledge is more than an individual personal construct; knowledge is co-constructed. The social dimensions of cognition also come to the fore as knowledge acquisition is now viewed as a social phenomenon. Kathleen Carley elaborated the social dimensions as follows:

> The social context, both social structure – *the perceived regularities in the network of ties between individuals and society* – and social knowledge – *that information which is known by 'everyone' in the society* – appears to have an effect on the individual's acquisition of knowledge.[36]

As individuals go about their daily lives and tasks, they acquire knowledge as they interact and communicate with the what and who around them – knowledge of human constructs that are "determined by such things as politics, ideologies, values, the exertion of power and the preservation of status, religious beliefs, and economic self-interest."[37] The learner is not "an artificially objectified and solitary individual isolated from a historical and sociocultural setting."[38] One's gender, race, class/social location, and sexual orientation must be taken into consideration in the construction of knowledge.[39]

Like Katherine C. Powell and Cody J. Kalina, I believe that an effective constructivist learning environment must take into consideration both

---

33. Matthews, "Introductory Comments," 7; Pritchard and Woollard, *Psychology for the Classroom*, 9.
34. Barr and Tagg, "From Teaching to Learning," 17.
35. Gergen, "Social Constructionist Movement," 270.
36. Carley, "Knowledge Acquisition," 381 (original emphasis).
37. Phillips, "Opinionated Account," 6.
38. Phillips, "The Good, the Bad, and the Ugly," 11.
39. See Hussain, "Use of Constructivist Approach."

personal and social constructivism.⁴⁰ However, by shifting the focus from knowledge constructed by individuals to knowledge co-constructed within groups, the importance of the social and relational aspects of learning is underscored. Once again, this shift has significant implications on the learning environment and how teachers teach.

From Cognition to Emotion

The dichotomy between reason and emotion that is deeply embedded in Western philosophical and intellectual traditions finds its roots in Plato's dualistic conception of human as body and soul.⁴¹ The reasoning mind is often contrasted with the "irrational, base, physical desires and passions (the heart)."⁴² Essentially, emotions have been "maligned, neglected, and assigned as a property of the 'other,' as a synonym of deviance,"⁴³ or even a distractor.⁴⁴ Hence, there exists a "suspicion of the emotions."⁴⁵

According to Joseph LeDoux, "through the ages, cognition and emotion have been viewed as separate but equal aspects of the mind. The goal of a theory of mind was traditionally to understand how cognition, emotion, and other mental processes contribute to and interact in the making of the mind."⁴⁶ The lack of interest in the affective aspects of knowing could possibly be attributed to the emphasis on behaviorism,⁴⁷ and the rise of cognitive science in the mid-twentieth century – "an intellectual hegemony . . . that

---

40. Powell and Kalina, "Cognitive and Social Constructivism," 247. For a critique of constructivism (encompassing both personal and social) in education, see Airasian and Walsh, "Constructivist Cautions."

41. Interestingly, the Western notion that beliefs and ideas originate from the mind, and desires and emotions from the heart is rather alien to Chinese thinking. The reason-emotion dichotomy is not found in ancient Chinese philosophy (Hansen, *Daoist Theory of Chinese Thought*, 23; Lin, *Certainty as a Social Metaphor*, 202; Wang, "Confucian Ethics and Emotions," 362; against Yearley *Mencius and Aquinas*). In Chinese thought, the heart is "the central faculty of cognition" and functions "as the organ for thinking, knowing, and understanding" (Yu, "Chinese Heart," 132). It is "the site of both affective and cognitive activities' (Shun, *Mencius and Early Chinese Thought*, 48). And according to Yunping Wang, early Confucians viewed the emotions of human nature as "Heavenly-endowed" ("Confucian Ethics and Emotions," 364).

42. Hansen, *Daoist Theory of Chinese Thought*, 22.

43. Boler, "Disciplined Emotions," 203–204.

44. Patten, "Somatic Appraisal Model of Affect," 87.

45. Oatley, Keltner, and Jenkins, *Understanding Emotions*, 259.

46. LeDoux, "Cognitive-Emotional Interactions," 129.

47. McLeod, "Research," 576–577.

ultimately led to an approach to the mind that intentionally left the study of emotion out."[48] Consequently, until recently, most studies on cognitive issues conducted generally excluded affective factors from their considerations.[49]

However, recent brain research, or neuroscience, has largely disproved "the adage that emotion is the enemy of reason"[50] by showing the dynamic interactions between cognition and emotion in brain functional organization.[51] Through the use of neuroimaging, Jeremy R. Gray, Todd S. Braver, and Marcus E. Raichle researched the "convergence and merging of specialized subfunctions into a single more general function."[52] In their opinion, even though emotion and cognition may be mostly separate entities, the emotional and cognitive factors become inseparable when there is a crossover interaction. "At that point of processing, functional specialization is lost. If the integrated signal has a functional role, emotion and cognition can conjointly and equally contribute to the control of thought, affect, and behavior."[53]

By highlighting connections between cognition and emotion, neuroscience has heightened our understanding of the role of emotion in learning. Rather than the Cartesian slogan, "I think, therefore I am," the catchphrase now would be "I feel, therefore I learn."[54] Thus, since the "Decade of the Brain"[55]

---

48. LeDoux, "Cognitive-Emotional Interactions," 129; see McLeod, "Research," 577; Damasio, "Second Chance for Emotion," 12; Rosiek and Beghetto, "Emotional Scaffolding," 177.
49. Schutz and Lanehart, "Introduction," 67; Imel, *Effect of Emotions*; Zhang and Lu, "Practice of Affective Teaching," 35.
50. Weiss, "Emotion and Learning," 45.
51. Storbeck and Clore, "On the Interdependence"; Pessoa, "On the Relationship"; Patten, "Somatic Appraisal Model."
52. Gray, Braver and Raichle, "Integration," 4115.
53. Ibid.
54. See Immordino-Yang and Damasio, "We Feel, therefore We Learn."
55. President George Bush, with support from the Congress, declared the 1990s as the "Decade of the Brain" so as "to enhance public awareness of the benefits to be derived from brain research" (Bulkeley, *Wondering Brain*, 7).

that started in the 1990s,[56] numerous books[57] and articles[58] on the role of affect in and its implications for education have been published. David Birbeck and Kate Andre noted that in the study of the affective domain, we could be referring to: (1) how teachers relate to students to build a relationship; (2) how teachers arouse the emotions of students as a form of engagement; or (3) how to teach students to understand their emotions and relate them to their actions.[59] Of particular relevance to this study is the first item – the teacher-student relationship.

Neuroscience research has affirmed the mediating role of social and emotional factors on learning. According to Mary Helen Immordino-Yang, findings from a decade of neuroscience research show that: (1) "emotion and cognition are intertwined, and involve interplay between the body and the mind," and (2) "social processing and learning happen by internalizing our subjective interpretations of other people's beliefs, goals, feelings and actions, and vicariously experiencing aspects of these as if they were our own."[60] As a result, educators have been challenged to redesign the learning environment – to take into serious consideration the emotional climate of learning spaces, thereby creating a safe and positive environment, promoting positive relationships that will enhance learning.[61] As a social organ, "the brain . . .

---

56. Ansari, Coch, and De Smedt, "Connecting Education," 37.

57. See Boler, *Feeling Power*; Efklides and Volet, "Emotional Experiences during Learning"; Linnenbrink, "Emotion Research in Education"; Schutz and Pekrun, *Educational Psychology*; de Jong et al., *Explorations*; Schutz and Zembylas, *Advances*.

58. See Hargreaves, "Emotional Practice"; "Emotional Geographies of Teaching"; Fishback, "Learning and the Brain"; Pekrun et al., "Positive Emotions in Education"; Olsson, "Emotion and Motivation"; Dalgleish, "Emotional Brain"; Caine and Caine, "Meaningful Learning"; Cozolino and Sprokay, "Neuroscience and Adult Learning"; Johnson, "Neuroscience"; Perry, "Fear and Learning"; Ross, "Brain Self-Repair"; Sheckley and Bell, "Experience, Consciousness, and Learning"; Taylor, "Brain Function"; Wolfe, "Role of Meaning and Emotion"; Zull, "Key Aspects"; Immordino-Yang and Damasio, "We Feel, therefore We Learn"; Dirkx, "Meaning and Role of Emotions"; Hinton, Miyamoto and Della-Chiesa, "Brain Research"; Ferrari, "What Can Neuroscience Bring"; Immordino-Yang, "Implications"; Patten "Somatic Appraisal Model."

59. Birbeck and Andre, "Affective Domain," 40.

60. Immordino-Yang, "Implications," 98. For other core concepts gleaned from neuroscience research, see Goswami, "Principles of Learning"; Hinton, Miyamoto, and Della-Chiesa, "Brain Research." I chose to cite Mary Helen Immordino-Yang's conclusions because they are more relevant to the motif of hospitality.

61. Sylwester, "How Emotions Affect Learning," 65; Anderson and Carta-Falsa, "Factors," 136–137; Dalgleish, "Emotional Brain," 15–16; Hardiman, "Connecting Brain Research," 266; Hinton, Miyamoto, and Della-Chiesa, "Brain Research," 98–99.

learns best in the context of a trusting relationship."[62] Negative emotions such as fear, stress, and anxiety are barriers to effective learning.[63] Since positive environments and positive relationships promote student learning, attending to the emotional aspects of learning should be an integral part of a teacher's job. As Stephen D. Brookfield put it,

> teaching and learning are highly emotional activities that bring forth strong responses and . . . to feel such emotions is predictable and normal, a sign that you are alive and alert in the classroom. Indeed, it is no exaggeration to say that if classrooms are experienced as emotion-free zones of practice, then something essential to the process of learning and teaching is missing.[64]

Reality: From Then to Now, from There to Here

Paradigm shifts in education in the past decades are undeniably a global phenomenon; yet, it is not easy for changes to take place. For instance, in response to the changing needs of higher education, universities across the United States have implemented several changes to become a more learner-centered *New Academy*, a term coined by Judith Ramaley and Andrea Leskes to describe the college of the twenty-first century.[65] It may appear that "many institutions or educators claim to be putting student-centered learning into practice, but in reality they are not."[66]

Certainly, I see this incongruence reflected in my own situation in Singapore. Although the educational reform "Teach Less, Learn More" was mentioned first by the Prime Minister Lee Hsien Loong in his National Day Rally speech in 2004 to encourage a more student-centered approach to teaching and learning, curricular changes were made in a leading higher

---

62. Cozolino and Sprokay, "Neuroscience and Adult Learning," 15; see Dalgleish, "Emotional Brain," 16.
63. McEwen and Sapolsky, "Stress and Cognitive Function"; Dalgleish, "Emotional Brain," 15–16; Cozolino and Sprokay, "Neuroscience and Adult Learning," 13–15; Perry, "Fear and Learning."
64. Brookfield, *Skillful Teacher*, 95.
65. Ramaley and Leskes, *Greater Expectations*.
66. Lea, Stephenson, and Troy, "Higher Education Students," 322.

education institution only in 2011.⁶⁷ Toh Kok Aun and others cynically commented that there is no difference between Asian classrooms forty years ago and now – they are still "wholly teacher-centered."⁶⁸ "This is not to say that there were no changes instituted over this period. . . . There seems to be some form of seemingly stubborn promulgation of the teacher-centered approach in classroom instruction."⁶⁹ The hesitancy towards change could be due to: (1) Asian tradition and culture, (2) a performance-oriented society, (3) an inertia due to teacher's freedom of choice, (4) organizational structures, and (5) model learned from past experiences.⁷⁰ Paradigm shifts, educational reforms, though highly desirable, do not happen overnight.

Students in Singapore have also described their student life as being "too stressful and tiring."⁷¹ One student remarked: "Let's face it. What counts in the education system and for schools is really the exam results and academic ranking."⁷² Ng Pak Tee concluded that

---

67. Tan, "Teach Less, Learn More." The "Teach Less, Learn More" (TLLM) idea was first mentioned by the Prime Minister Lee Hsien Loong in 2004. This educational reform was part of the "Thinking Schools, Learning Nation" vision cast in 1997 by the then-Prime Minister Goh Chok Tong, a move towards an ability-driven education system (Goh and Gopinathan, "Development of Education," 30). Ng Pak Tee explained:

> According to the MOE [Ministry of Education], TLLM means less dependence on rote learning, repetitive tests and a 'one size fits all' type of instruction, and more on engaged learning through experiential discovery, differentiated teaching, the learning of life-long skills, and the building of character through innovative and effective teaching approaches and strategies. ("Educational Reform," 10)

68. Toh et al., "Teaching," 196. Charlene Tan commented that other Asian-Chinese societies (e.g. Japan, China, Taiwan) also prefer a more didactic style of teaching ("Creating Thinking Schools," 99). We must certainly take social and cultural factors into consideration because "Asian values, especially Confucian teaching, do not endorse an individual's right to question, challenge and demand reasons and justifications for what is being taught" (ibid., 93). The teacher, perceived as an elder, should be revered and respected, and his or her authority should be not questioned (see Yuen and Lee, "Applicability," 544; Martinsons and Martinsons, "Conquering Cultural Constraints," 19; Hassan et al. "Western and Eastern Educational Philosophies"). Writing on adult education in Singapore, Chia Mun Onn remarked, "For a teacher to take a back-seat is very discomforting to the learners" ("Major Differences"). For more on how cultural factors impact learning, see Johnson, "Cross-Cultural Differences"; Volet, "Learning across Cultures"; Economides, "Culture-Aware Collaborative Learning."
69. Toh et al., "Teaching," 196.
70. Ibid., 197–199; see Toh, "Teacher-Centered Teaching."
71. Ng, "Students' Perception," 86. This is from an interview-cum-questionnaire survey, conducted to discover students' responses to the education system change in Singapore, involving students in polytechnics, junior colleges, and universities (ibid., 83–85).
72. Ibid., 86.

to the students, regardless what the rhetoric may be about creativity, in the mean time [sic], mugging for examinations will still bear more material fruits than spending time in exploratory work, since at the end of the day, it is the examination that counts. More efforts and attention will still be channelled in that direction, instead of exploration and experimentation.[73]

A shift to a new paradigm of learning, at least for Singapore, would mean making the education system less obsessive about grades as well as establishing a new model of relationship "that focuses on sharing constructive information and celebrating openness."[74] This new model of relationship that Ng has advocated aligns with our findings on the emotional and relational aspects of learning as well as what contemporary higher education professionals have been advocating.

Though the response to the clarion call for changes in educational practices is generally slow and lagging, nevertheless the shifts in emphases to learning, social constructivism, and emotion have indicated a change in how students learn which in turn demands a paradigm shift in how teachers are to teach. Hence, the practice of hospitality, with its gracious welcome of others, is proposed in this book as a viable metaphor for conceptualizing the work of teachers to better respond to the challenges posed by the changing face of education.

The Emotional Aspects of Teacher-Student Relationships

Even with the Decade of the Brain in the 1990s, Andy Hargreaves observed that "many of those who initiate and manage educational reform, or who write about educational change in general, ignore or underplay one of the most fundamental aspects of teaching and how teachers change: the emotional dimension."[75] Since cognition and emotion are intricately connected, "schooling is an emotionally laden process for students, teachers and parents"[76]

---

73. Ibid., 89.
74. Ibid., 90.
75. Hargreaves, "Emotional Practice," 835.
76. Schutz et al., "Reflections," 343.

and can be "full of spurious emotion."⁷⁷ Looking at the learning community through an emotional lens, "the [entire] school environment creates the context for a variety of emotional experiences that have the potential to influence teaching, learning, and motivational processes."⁷⁸ As such, there is a need for emotional understanding which, as defined by Norman K. Denzin, "is an intersubjective process requiring that one person enter the field of experience of another and experience for herself the same or similar experiences experienced by another."⁷⁹ However, "when individuals mistake their own feelings for the feelings of the other and interpret their feelings as the feelings of the other," emotional misunderstanding takes place.⁸⁰

Hargreaves developed this idea further and mapped out five emotional geographies or five "forms of emotional distance or closeness that can threaten emotional understanding among teachers, students, colleagues, and parents."⁸¹ The five emotional geographies of schooling and human interaction, as mapped out by Hargreaves are as follows:

- *Sociocultural geographies* [forms of distance] – where differences of culture and class can all too easily make teachers on the one hand and parents and students on the other, alien and unknowable to each other.
- *Moral geographies* – where teachers' purposes are at odds with those they serve and where there are no mechanisms to discuss or resolve these differences.
- *Professional geographies* – where teacher professionalism is defined according to a "classical," masculine model of the professions, that creates a distance between teachers and the clients they serve, and that is especially prejudicial to feminine, "caring" ethics of teaching.
- *Political geographies* – where hierarchical power relationships distort the emotional as well as cognitive aspects of communication between teachers and those around them.

---

77. Hargreaves, "Emotional Practice," 839; "Emotional Geographies," 1060; see Brookfield, *Skillful Teacher*, esp. ch. 5.
78. Aultman, Williams-Johnson, and Schutz, "Boundary Dilemmas," 636.
79. Denzin, *On Understanding Emotion*, 137.
80. Ibid., 154.
81. Hargreaves, "Emotional Geographies," 1061.

- *Physical geographies* – where fragmented, infrequent, formalized and episodic encounters replace the possibility of relationships between teachers and students, or teachers and parents (especially in secondary schools) with strings of disconnected interactions.[82]

"How these emotional geographies of teaching are configured is basic to the possibilities of developing the kinds of emotional understanding that are integral to high standards of teaching and learning, good colleagueship, and effective partnerships with parents."[83] Since teaching and learning are emotional practices that can arouse and color feelings, and affect actions, Hargreaves believed that strong positive teacher-student relationships are needed to support the emotional engagement and facilitate emotional understanding.[84]

With the understanding that teaching and learning are emotional practices, when we shift the emotional lens to focus on the classroom, we see a plethora of emotions surfacing and interacting, thereby, impacting the teacher's teaching and the learner's learning. For instance, just as teachers have power (e.g. the power of the grade), students have power (e.g. the power of the will) too. When students wield their power in defiance of teachers, the contest of wills creates "an emotional climate."[85] This issue of power dynamics in the classroom is often exacerbated by the presence of cultural differences.[86] Hence, many educators believe that "in the classroom environment, the interpersonal relationship between teacher and students is an important element contributing to the learning process of students,"[87] "a central component in successful teaching and learning,"[88] or "one of the most significant emotional aspects of teaching."[89] Besides impacting student

---

82. Hargreaves, "Mixed Emotions," 816 (original emphasis), citing J. Bernhard; K. Oately and J. Jenkins; M. Grumet; J. Blase and G. Anderson; S. Lasky respectively.
83. Ibid.
84. Ibid., 812, 815; "Emotional Geographies," 1057, 1060.
85. Conde-Frazier, "From Hospitality to Shalom," 176, citing Lingenfelter and Lingenfelter, *Teaching Cross-culturally*, 19.
86. Conde-Frazier, "From Hospitality to Shalom," 173.
87. Brekelmans, Wubbels, and Den Brok, "Teacher Experience," 73.
88. Aultman, Williams-Johnson, and Schutz, "Boundary Dilemmas," 636.
89. Hargreaves, "Emotional Practice," 838. For higher education, see Churukian, "Perceived Learning"; Frymier and Houser, "Teacher-Student Relationship"; Nichols, "Empowerment and Relationships"; Docan-Morgan and Manusov, "Relational Turning Point Events"; Giles, "Relationships Always Matter." For non-higher education, an area that is beyond the scope

learning, the teacher-student relationship also impacts the professional and personal lives of teachers. However, the scope of the study only allows us to focus on the effects of the teacher-student interpersonal relationship on student learning outcomes.[90]

In the past three decades, many research studies have been conducted to investigate the teacher-student relationship and its relation to: (1) the quality of interpersonal relationships,[91] (2) teachers' interaction in terms of immediacy,[92] (3) students' perceptions of teachers' behaviors,[93] (4) teachers' characteristics,[94] and (5) external institutional policies.[95] Two of these have particular relevance to our discussion at hand – teacher immediacy and perceived care.

Immediacy is defined as "those communication behaviors that reduce perceived distance between people."[96] The distance could be physical or psychological[97] and the behaviors could be nonverbal (e.g. gesture, tone of voice, facial expressions, body postures, movements in class) or verbal (e.g. humor, praise, inclusive language, self-disclosure).[98] Hence, the term *teacher immediacy* is used hereafter in this work to refer to either verbal or nonverbal behaviors or both.

According to the immediacy principle: "People are drawn toward persons and things they like, evaluate highly, and prefer; and they avoid or move away

---

of this work, see Muller, Katz, and Dance, "Investing"; Meyer and Turner, "Discovering Emotion"; Den Brok, Brekelmans, and Wubbels, "Interpersonal Teacher Behavior"; Carr, "Personal and Interpersonal Relationships"; Wubbels and Brekelmans, "Two Decades of Research"; Terry, "Importance of Interpersonal Relations"; Andrzejewski and Davis, "Human Contact in the Classroom"; Newberry and Davis, "Role of Elementary Teachers."

90. For the impact of the teacher-student relationship on the professional and personal lives of teachers, see Hargreaves, "Mixed Emotions"; Brekelmans, Wubbels, and Den Brok, "Teacher Experience"; Brekelmans, Wubbels, and van Tartwijk, "Teacher-Student Relationships"; Spilt, Koomen, and Thijs, "Teacher Wellbeing."

91. Churukian, "Perceived Learning."

92. Gorham and Zakahi, "Comparison"; Velez and Cano, "Relationship."

93. Gorham and Christophel, "Students' Perceptions"; Teven and McCroskey, "Relationship."

94. Kneipp et al., "Impact of Instructor's Personality Characteristics."

95. Zhang, "Study on the Satisfaction."

96. Thweat and McCroskey, "Teacher Nonimmediacy and Misbehavior," 198.

97. Mehrabian, "Inference of Attitudes," 43.

98. Fourteen nonverbal immediacy behavior items are listed in Richmond, Gorham, McCroskey, "Relationship," 583. Twenty verbal immediacy behavior items are listed in Gorham, "Relationship," 44.

from things they dislike, evaluate negatively, or do not prefer."[99] "Interpersonal perceptions and communicative relationships between teachers and students are crucial to the teaching-learning process, and the degree of immediacy between teacher and students is an important variable in those relationships."[100] In their analysis of extant research on immediacy, James C. McCroskey and Virginia P. Richmond concluded that increased immediacy resulted in increased student affinity for the teacher and subject matter, reduced student resistance to teachers' attempts to influence, and increased student motivation and cognitive learning.[101] "The higher immediacy of the teacher, the higher the affective learning of the student,"[102] that is, the higher "the favorable attitudes toward the learning situation."[103]

Interestingly, McCroskey and Richmond highlighted "culture and immediacy" as one of their special concerns since "most empirically based communication theory is heavily biased in the direction of what is normative for the white, middle-class, American culture."[104] Even though their analysis could only examine two studies done on subcultures in California universities, both studies show that, overall, there was a relationship between teacher immediacy and learning although there were some differences regarding the response to specific immediacy behaviors by the various subcultures. A subsequent study conducted with students in higher education from the cultures of Australia, Finland, Puerto Rico, and the United States showed that "whether the norms in the culture favor high or low immediacy, if the teacher is comparatively more immediate, the students' affective learning is enhanced."[105] This conclusion was also true for Japanese college students.[106]

---

99. Mehrabian, *Silent Messages*, 1.
100. Gorham, "Relationship," 40.
101. McCroskey and Richmond ("Increasing Teacher Influence") analyzed research on immediacy at various educational levels of schooling, including higher education (see Richmond, Gorham, McCroskey, "Relationship"; Gorham, "Relationship"; Christophel, "Relationships"; Gorham and Zakahi, "Comparison") that were conducted prior to 1991. For more recent research findings, see Gorham and Christophel, "Students' Perceptions"; Velez and Cano, "Relationship."
102. Richmond, Gorham, McCroskey, "Relationship," 588.
103. Ibid., 575.
104. McCroskey and Richmond, "Increasing Teacher Influence," 113.
105. McCroskey et al., "Multi-Cultural Examination," 303.
106. See Pribyl, Sakamoto, and Keaten, "Relationship."

The pivotal role played by immediacy is further illustrated by research findings that showed that perceived caring effects "increased affective and perceived cognitive learning in the classroom"[107] and can be identified with specific nonverbal immediacy behaviors,[108] and is further enhanced by the use of "explicit verbally caring messages."[109] Working with McCroskey's idea of "perceived caring," Jason J. Teven and McCroskey conducted studies to examine the relation between perceived caring and student learning. Guided by the common assumption that teachers' classroom behaviors affect students' learning, the results of their research are consistent and showed that "the more that students *perceive* their teacher cares about them, the more the students will care about the class, and the more likely they will be to pay attention in class and consequently learn more course material."[110] The key lies in the students' perception. Citing an earlier work of McCroskey, Teven and McCroskey highlighted that since it would be difficult for the teacher to care about every student in a large class,

> [t]hus, it is important for a teacher to learn how to communicate in such a manner that students will perceive that he or she cares about them, whether or not that is the case in reality. *It is not the caring that counts; it is the perception of caring that is critical.* If a teacher cares deeply, but does not communicate that attribute, he or she might as well not care at all.[111]

Besides teacher immediacy and perceived caring within the classroom walls, studies on informal teacher-student interaction beyond the classroom walls have revealed that such interactions too, have positive impact on the students' attendance in class, their academic performance, personal growth and development – cognitively, emotionally, and socially, as well as their aspirations.[112] The results of these studies have thus debunked the myth that teachers influence their students only in the classroom. Patrick T. Terenzini

---

107. Teven and McCroskey, "Relationship," 8.
108. Chory and McCroskey, "Relationship"; Teven, "Relationships."
109. Teven and Hanson, "Impact of Teacher Immediacy," 50.
110. Teven and McCroskey, "Relationship," 1 (emphasis mine); see esp. 8; Teven, "Teacher Caring," 446.
111. McCroskey and Teven, "Goodwill," 1 (emphasis mine).
112. Pascarella, "Student-Faculty Informal Contact"; Lamport, "Student-Faculty Informal Interaction"; Kuh et al., *Student Learning Outside the Classroom*.

and Ernest T. Pascarella believed that thinking that out-of-class interactions with students is simply "mollycoddling" them and not the role of the teacher reflects "at best, little knowledge of effective educational practices and of how students learn, and, at worst, a callous disregard."[113] We can, therefore, concur with Paul Ramsden that "the emotional aspect of the teacher-student relationship is much more important than the traditional advice on methods and techniques of lecturing would suggest."[114]

The findings of this section reveal the need for teachers to rethink their roles and practices in relation to the various emerging emphases on learning, learning within a social context, and, especially, the role of emotion in learning. The emotional nature of teaching and learning calls for the building of strong positive teacher-student relationships and interactions, which is determined by the variables of immediacy and perceived care.

Hospitality as a Key Concept in Higher Education Literature

Dissatisfied with the state of higher education, and presented with the challenges posed by the shifting trends in education, as well as the missing emotional and relational dimension in the teaching-learning process, educational researchers and practitioners have had to explore alternatives to renew higher education. Theodore Mitchell observed that "from the 1930s through the 1970s, the literature of [American] higher education was largely celebratory."[115] He continued,

> Over the past fifteen years a relatively new genre of higher education literature has emerged, one that paints universities in just this way, as institutions populated by venal and small-minded faculty whose selfishness is matched only by their cruelty to each other and to students. Higher education, we have been told over and over again, is rotting from the head . . . .[116]

---

113. Terenzini and Pascarella, "Living Myths," 31.
114. Ramsden, *Learning to Teach*, 75.
115. Mitchell, "Review," 409.
116. Ibid., 410.

Mitchell's observations still hold true today. Writing in the early 1990s, William F. Losito critiqued the education-as-production model of the Industrial Revolution that was still dominating formal education system as "inadequate for generating fruitful ways of thinking, feeling, and responding to individual existential situations of anxiety, alienation, loneliness, low self-esteem, various forms of addiction, and general value confusion."[117] More than a decade later, Steven Bouma-Prediger and Brian Walsh described education in this postmodern age as "an education of upward mobility that results in a pedagogy of disconnection and an ethos of displacement"[118] while Elizabeth Newman argued that the politics of liberalism/pluralism dominating the academy have resulted in "a market approach to education, fueled by self-interest and competition."[119] Thus, Parker J. Palmer and Arthur Zajonc proposed an integrative education to address this problem of disconnectedness, an education that "aims to 'think the world together' rather than 'think it apart,' to know the world in a way that empowers educated people to act on behalf of wholeness rather than fragmentation."[120] For all these educators, and many others, the traditional practice of hospitality presented itself as an attractive alternative approach to address the ills in current education efforts. Hospitality, expressed in the host-guest encounter, was a metaphor that enabled educators "to convey certain meanings of belonging and comfort, protection and inclusion, difference and strangeness, violence and exclusion within everyday encounters between people, objects and places" in the educational arena.[121]

This section reviews the works of the educators who have presented the metaphor of hospitality as a viable model for improving classroom teaching in higher education institutions in relation to: (1) the teaching profession, (2) academic life and community, (3) the marginalized, and (4) classroom process.

---

117. Losito, "Education as Hospitality," 62.
118. Bouma-Prediger and Walsh, "Education for Homeless or Homemaking," 60.
119. Newman, *Untamed Hospitality*, 131.
120. Palmer and Zajonc, "Introduction," 22.
121. Lynch et al., "Theorizing Hospitality," 12.

Hospitality and the Teaching Profession

The term *teaching profession* is used here in a broad sense to encompass ideas related to the teacher as a professional, teacher education, and curriculum studies. Since the 1990s, philosophers of education are increasingly showing concern over the educational state and practices in the United States. We can see this in the essays of Losito, Anthony G. Rud Jr., and Molly Quinn where they voiced their concerns about the gaps in the teaching profession. The metaphor of hospitality was used by each one of them to address these gaps.

In 1991, Losito presented a paper, "Education as Hospitality: The Reclaiming of Cultural Metaphor and Narrative," at the thirty-sixth Annual Meeting of the South Atlantic Philosophy of Education Society.[122] His paper was subsequently published in the meeting's proceedings book. Given the challenges posed by the changing society, he questioned the effectiveness of the education-as-production metaphor, the guiding metaphor for education since the Industrial Revolution.[123] Even the respondent to his paper, Robert J. Mulvaney agreed that such mechanical educational metaphors, including that of teachers as CEOs and key educational officers as cabinets, were poor metaphors for communities of scholars.[124]

Losito, instead, proposed the education-as-hospitality metaphor, "as a complement and corrective to the production metaphor," to guide the conceptualizing of the professional educator.[125] He believed that the openness toward diversity in postmodern epistemology would allow for "both sacred and profane" perspectives to be considered simultaneously.[126] Hence, he sought to elicit the nature and motivation of hospitality by looking first at selected Greek and biblical narratives with the hospitality theme, before looking at how hospitality was practiced among the first-century Christian communities (Rom 12:13) and in the Benedictine monasteries. From this introduction of the tradition of hospitality, Losito then drew on Henri J. M. Nouwen's book, *Reaching Out*, to create more images for his education-as-

---

122. The meeting was held at Furman University (Greenville, South Carolina) on 4–5 October 1991.
123. Losito, "Education as Hospitality," 62–63.
124. Mulvaney, "Hospitality and Its Discontents," 70.
125. Losito, "Education as Hospitality," 63.
126. Ibid., 68.

hospitality metaphor: (1) the creation of a free space for the other to grow, (2) the openness to the "stranger," and (3) the need for confrontation and receptivity. In Losito's evaluation, "the effort of Nouwen to reappropriate hospitality to contemporary society is an excellent starting point for including the metaphor of education-as-hospitality into our own thinking about educational practice."[127]

Though Losito acknowledged that there were "infelicitous aspects" of the metaphor which we should not be obligated to reappropriate for our use, he did not state what these were;[128] but which his respondent Mulvaney felt were crucial for delimiting how the ancient practice of hospitality could be applied in a modern educational setting.[129] Mulvaney's observation is valid, but to be fair, when we take into account that Losito was one of the earliest educators, after Nouwen and Palmer, to advocate the metaphor of hospitality in higher education, it is understandable that Losito was not able to specifically spell out how this metaphor could be applied. However, Losito did add that "the central feature of this metaphoric application would be for the educational community to help individuals create personally meaningful sets of beliefs and understandings."[130] To help generate further thought, Losito did cite some examples to paint a picture of what educators could do to make schools into institutions imbued with a spirit of hospitality. Quoting Martin Buber, Losito described the teacher as host as "the glance of the educator who accepts and receives them all" when meeting students for the first time in class.[131] A school environment that seeks to heal rather than produce would extend a helping hand to the weak and vulnerable and set up policies to proactively respond to exigent social issues, for example, homeless children.[132]

Losito's short paper, one of the earliest works on hospitality in higher education, painted in broad strokes how the education-as-hospitality metaphor could be a possible avenue to enhance current educational practices. Though addressing a wider secular audience and critiquing American higher education in general, Losito was able to present the

---

127. Ibid., 67.
128. Ibid., 68.
129. Mulvaney, "Hospitality and Its Discontents," 72.
130. Losito, "Education as Hospitality," 67.
131. Ibid., 76, quoting Buber, *Between Man and Man*, 112.
132. Losito, "Education as Hospitality," 67–68.

biblical tradition of hospitality, even the Benedictine monastic tradition, as a plausible metaphor for consideration possibly because of America's Christian heritage. Such an approach may not be effective in countries where there is no Christian heritage. However, biblical scholars may not concur with Losito's interpretation of certain biblical passages which he used to support his argument that hospitality played a crucial role in the early Christian and monastic communities. His argument was based on his understanding of the spiritual life as life-as-journey, and of the stranger as person-as-temple (see 1 Cor 3:16).[133] The subject of 1 Corinthians 3:16, even 1 Corinthians 6:19, is clearly a second-person plural, referring to the community of believers, not an individual, as the temple where God's spirit resides. In his perceiving of strangers as "temples of the Holy Spirit, sent by Zeus," Losito erroneously concluded that both the apostle Paul and Nouwen blended pagan beliefs into their Christian understanding.[134] It is doubtful that Paul would subscribe to such a syncretic understanding and Nouwen made no mention of Zeus in *Reaching Out*. Instead, Nouwen in *Wounded Healer* explicitly termed hospitality as a Judaeo-Christian concept.[135] Nonetheless, Losito's metaphor of education-as-hospitality provided a starting point for educators in higher education to reflect more on the theme of hospitality in relation to the teacher as host, a supportive school environment, and inclusive education policies.[136]

The next essay on hospitality in the literature of higher education is found in the book *The Educational Conversation* that addressed the moral dimension of teaching that was missing in teacher education. Rud's essay argued that "learning in comfort and trust is a neglected facet of our schools and a 'gap' in our understanding and appreciation of the conditions of teaching and learning."[137] He proposed an ethos of hospitality in teaching and learning to fill this gap in the educational conversation. His consideration of hospitality in teaching and learning began with his visit to a Benedictine monastery in Charlotte (North Carolina) for he wanted to have a first-hand experience of monastic life to see if monastic practices "could be secularized and applied to the schools" and if they "could serve as metaphoric bridges" for him to

---

133. Ibid., 65.
134. Ibid., 65, 67.
135. Nouwen, *Wounded Healer*, 89.
136. Losito, "Education as Hospitality," 67.
137. Rud, "Learning in Comfort," 119.

articulate his conception of hospitality in education.[138] He discovered that the Benedictine practice of listening could serve as a bridge. "When you listen to a student, the student becomes the teacher."[139] And "if one casts off the mantle of pedagogical invincibility, a teacher probably learns more from students than students learn from the teacher."[140]

But more than that, he discovered that in order to receive others, we must first listen to oneself. Without this "hospitality toward and knowledge of oneself," it would be difficult for one to be hospitable towards others.[141] And this was Rud's main contention – an ethos of hospitality in education would require teachers first to be hospitable towards themselves before they could be hospitable towards the students.[142] He himself felt this was where he differed from Losito's concept of hospitality in education. He personally claimed that his notion of "making oneself ready to welcome others" was derived from his interpretation of the Benedictines, Henry David Thoreau, Nouwen, Palmer, and his own work in teacher renewal.[143] In that context, he also cited Nouwen's use of Mark 12:31, "You shall love your neighbor as yourself."[144] In one way, it is without doubt concentration or being at home with oneself is a prominent feature in Nouwen's concept of hospitality. Writing about Nouwen's concept of spirituality, Dierdre LaNoue cited Matthew 22:34–40 and wrote that Nouwen's idea of spirituality encompassed "three love relationships: with God, self, and others."[145] Indeed, Nouwen used the words of Matthew 22:37, 39 to write about self-knowledge and self-love.[146] However, Nouwen clearly did not use Mark 12:31 in the context of being at home with oneself in *Reaching Out*.

Rud did not explicitly explain how making oneself ready to welcome others could be achieved. From his references to the Benedictines and Thoreau, we may surmise that it entails a "withdrawal to the woods . . . to

---

138. Ibid., 120.
139. Ibid., 121.
140. Ibid., 124.
141. Ibid., 123.
142. Ibid., 128.
143. Ibid., 145, ch. 9, n. 1.
144. Nouwen, *Reaching Out*, 81.
145. LaNoue, *Spiritual Legacy*, 59.
146. Nouwen, *Letters to Marc about Jesus*, 79.

learn, in solitude, to be at home with [one]self."[147] However, he found support for his idea of attending to one's own strangeness in the works of Thoreau, Nouwen, Nel Noddings, and Simone Weil.[148] In order to receive and attend to the other, we must empty all the contents of our soul.[149] And it is only after we have listened to ourselves that we can listen to others.[150] This act of listening is akin to Max van Manen's pedagogical tact or thoughtfulness and immediacy behaviors of eye contact and tone of voice which are ways we can practice hospitality towards our students.[151]

Rud also argued that "hospitality toward self is a central aspect of the Deweyan view of teaching"[152] and cited both Noddings and Seymour B. Sarason for support since Sarason argued that schools and universities should not exist only for students while Noddings considered caring for self first when discussing her centeres of care.[153] In fact, the unique point of Rud's article is his discussion of hospitality in relation to the building of "the good society, of which schooling is an essential and integral part."[154] If democracy is, as defined by Dewey, "more than a form of government; it is primarily a mode of associated living, of conjoint communicated experience,"[155] then hospitality could act "as a *communicative* and thus also *political* virtue, as a generative quality in public life that would ground a common and democratic political involvement."[156] Rud then quoted Nicholas C. Burbules and Suzanne Rice for their definition of communicative virtues:

> These virtues include tolerance, patience, respect for differences, a willingness to listen, the inclination to admit that one may be mistaken, the ability to reinterpret or translate one's own concerns in a way that makes them comprehensible to others, the self-imposition of restraint in order that others may "have a

---

147. Rud, "Learning in Comfort," 122.
148. Ibid., 123.
149. Ibid.; see Noddings, *Challenge to Care*, 16; Weil, *Waiting for God*, 115.
150. Rud, "Learning in Comfort," 122.
151. Manen, *Tact of Teaching*.
152. Rud, "Learning in Comfort," 128.
153. Sarason, *Predictable Future*; Noddings, *Challenge to Care*, ch. 6.
154. Rud, "Learning in Comfort," 127.
155. Dewey, *Democracy and Education*, 91.
156. Rud, "Learning in Comfort," 127 (original emphasis).

turn" to speak, and the disposition to express one's self honestly and sincerely.[157]

When fostered in educational contexts, such virtues not only promote learning and genuine inquiry but also help us to stand in social solidarity with others and contribute to a more civil society.[158]

Definitely, Rud's article looked at hospitality from a different angle and, as promised, he included parallels in educational practice throughout his work. By relating his thoughts on hospitality to van Manen's pedagogy of thoughtfulness, Noddings' pedagogy of care, and William W. Purkey and John Novak's invitational education, Rud was challenging educators to think about the pedagogical implications of hospitality in the classroom.

In her review of the book *Educational Conversation*, not just Rud's essay, Ann M. Phelan expressed her concern that "the authors don't fully recognize the limitations inherent in their own ideological framing of teaching and teacher education."[159] To call attention to that which has been overlooked by the authors of the book, she cited the unpleasant experiences of a female Japanese-American teacher of an elementary school who was marginalized when she tried to adopt a more relational approach to teaching. She reminded the authors that when "they invited teachers to empty themselves, to be open to others, to live by principles of relation and intersubjectivitiy, they must examine what that invitation means for women in the profession."[160] What Phelan highlighted is valid because female teachers, even male or female teachers from a culture different from the dominant culture, seeking to make a difference in their classrooms could be marginalized when they do things differently.

In his response, Rud was delighted that Phelan has indeed located "a 'gap' in the educational conversations."[161] Though he agreed with Phelan in that writing about educational reforms is not sufficient to change the landscape of teacher education, he believed that writing is a transformative activity, albeit

---

157. Burbules and Rice, "Dialogue across Differences," 411, as quoted in Rud, "Learning in Comfort," 127–128.
158. Rud, "Learning in Comfort," 128.
159. Phelan, "Review," 66.
160. Ibid., 69.
161. Rud, "More Than Words," 71.

at the personal level.¹⁶² Definitely, much more need to be done, especially at the social and institutional levels. Quoting Daniel P. Liston, Rud too hoped that the words of his essays, as well as the rest, will not "fall between … institutional cracks" and become merely "empty calls for enhanced directions."¹⁶³

In an essay published in 2010, "'No Room in the Inn'?," Quinn, Associate Professor in the Department of Curriculum and Teaching at Teachers College, Columbia University (New York), invited scholars of the post-reconceptualization movement to consider the living question of hospitality as they reflected on their work in curriculum studies.¹⁶⁴ Using the poetic language of Georg Trakl, she described this question of hospitality as "the step of the stranger" resonating through "the 'silver night' of our academic labors."¹⁶⁵ The call of hospitality is the call "to make room for that which is, in truth, foreign – *other*."¹⁶⁶ This call is relevant to curriculum studies because what lies at the heart of education work is "the encounter with an other."¹⁶⁷

Quinn's essay directed heavy criticism against the academic life in the United States. She depicted academia as hostile and inhospitable, dominated by "the 'herods' of classism, racism, sexism, ablism, and corporate consumerism, among others, and the construction and maintenance of 'Inns of Exclusion' by them," and being "umbilically tied to forces that alienate and dehumanize."¹⁶⁸ Testifying from her own experiences, Quinn felt that, like there was no room in the inn for Mary to deliver baby Jesus (Luke 2:7), there seemed to be no room in the "inn of academia" to welcome curriculum

---

162. Ibid., 71–72.
163. Liston, "Intellectual and Institutional Gaps," 130, 142, as quoted in Rud, "More Than Words," 72.
164. Quinn, "No Room," 101. The post-reconceptualization era of curriculum studies began in the 1980s (Pacheco, *Whole, Bright*, 37). Stated briefly, "at the heart of curriculum development in the postmodern era is a commitment to a robust investigation of cultural, ethnic, gender, and identity issues" (Slattery, *Curriculum Development*, 146). For more on the difference between reconceptualization and post-reconceptualization of curriculum studies, see Pacheco, *Whole, Bright*, ch. 2.
165. Quinn, "No Room," 101. Molly Quinn used Jacques Derrida's translation of Georg Trakl's poem ("Hostipitality," 403).
166. Quinn, "No Room," 101 (original emphasis).
167. Ibid., 102.
168. Ibid., 112, n. 4, 102.

labors.[169] Thus, personally, for Quinn, the hospitality of Mary became a "metaphor for the call of our labors to welcome the child (i.e. student, idea, other – the strange, the new) in our midst" and an invitation "to (re)open the womb of my own room of/for hospitality."[170]

Quinn then broached this living question of hospitality by highlighting several of Jacques Derrida's ideas that could help guide the work of post-re-conceptualization. In the light of her own joyless experiences, Quinn was drawn to Derrida's notion of hospitality as a culture of pleasure and joy that welcomes the other with smiles, just as one would when welcoming a promise.[171] In her understanding, Derrida's concept of hospitality as *"receiving without invitation*, beyond or before the invitation" is radical; "open[ing] itself to an other that is not mine, my hôte [*sic*], my other, not even my neighbor or my brother"[172] unconditionally is impossible.[173] Moreover, Derrida's hospitality/hostipitality binary opposition[174] meant that being open to "the figure of visitation without invitation" might be a "violent experience"[175] or it might also be "the drama of a relation to the other that ruptures, . . . an experience of the Good that elects me before I welcome it, in other words, of a Goodness, a good violence of the Other that precedes welcoming."[176]

When applied to the work of curriculum studies, Quinn felt that hospitality, firstly, could make room for laughter and joy. In her opinion, "principally, perhaps the call of hospitality in our curriculum labors, is the call to joy, a return to the heart – ever, in truth, at the heart of the life of

---

169. Ibid., 104.
170. Ibid.
171. Ibid., 106; see Derrida, "Hostipitality," 358.
172. Derrida, "Hostipitality," 360, 363 (original emphasis). In French, *hôte* denotes both "host" and "guest" (Anidjar, "Note on 'Hostipitality,'" 356).
173. Quinn, "No Room," 106–107. Also known as "the possibility of impossibility," it is "to receive another guest whom I am incapable of welcoming, to become capable of that which I am incapable of" (Derrida, "Hostipitality," 364).
174. The word *hostipitality* was coined by Derrida to highlight that hospitality is "a word of Latin origin . . . which carries its own contradiction incorporated into it, a Latin word which allows itself to be parasitized by its opposite, 'hostility,' the undesirable guest . . . which it harbors as the self-contradiction in its own body" (Derrida, *Angelaki* 5: 3). The hospitality/hostipitality binary opposition can be simply understood as "the welcomed guest [*hôte*] is a stranger treated as a friend or ally, as opposed to the stranger treated as an enemy (friend/enemy, hospitality/hostility)" (ibid., 4).
175. Derrida, "Hostipitality," 360.
176. Ibid., 364.

the mind."¹⁷⁷ Done in the spirit of care, a concept drawn from Noddings,¹⁷⁸ questioning could even be "the play and place of thought," allowing us to "acknowledge, inquire into and indulge in the transformative potential of 'play' and authentic 'interaction.'"¹⁷⁹

Second, a hospitable education that embraces the other would allow us to question and transform power relations embedded within educational practice, as well as to accept "the mystery and 'moreness' of human engagement with the other, including moments of brokenness, stuckness, and vulnerability, as well as progress and possibility."¹⁸⁰ Hospitable teaching, thus, becomes a risky experience because "we do not know what we will discover about the other person or ourselves and how that will impact our lives."¹⁸¹ Yet, Quinn would call for such hospitable education because "teaching as a vulnerable way of being" has a "potentially transformative presence in the lives of the students."¹⁸²

Lastly, though hospitality in curriculum work has its risks, it also has its delights because "in encounters with the otherness that is curriculum, one's identity itself is challenged and transformed: in teaching and learning, we are called to die to a part of ourselves such that the new may be born within us here, too, is the child in our midst we are called to welcome."¹⁸³

In concluding her article, Quinn reiterated her belief that curriculum labors must always live the question of hospitality – "to offer spaces and places of welcome, to invite questioning and conversation, to make, take and remake, room for the strange otherness in our midst that ever calls and questions us."¹⁸⁴ It is ironic but "in our forgetfulness of being . . . , addiction to doing, and prejudice toward progress, we may lose the understanding and experience of what we have loved until now – the inn of our embodied humanity, the home where the heart is, the question of hospitality itself."¹⁸⁵

---

177. Quinn, "No Room," 107.
178. Noddings, *Challenge to Care*.
179. Quinn, "No Room," 108, 107.
180. Ibid., 110.
181. Ibid., quoting Newman, "Hotel or Home," 92.
182. Quinn, "No Room," 110.
183. Ibid., 111.
184. Ibid.
185. Ibid., 111–112.

It seemed Quinn's negative sentiments towards public higher education in the United States were shared by other educators. bell hooks termed it "a corrupt and dying academy"[186] while William F. Pinar described it as "the nightmare that is the present."[187] As a result, receiving a tenure became an unnerving experience, an experience of hooks which Quinn could identify with.[188] In fact, Quinn was even commended by some colleagues when she subsequently chose to give up her tenure.

I agree with JoAnn Phillion, the respondent to Quinn's essay, that Quinn's discourse is "challenging, puzzling, troubling, yet strangely enriching, fulfilling, and generative"[189] and that "Molly had *beautifully* articulated key educational issues and raised key educational questions with her discussion of the *myriad*, and often ambiguous, meanings of the concept of hospitality."[190] However, in terms of readability, Quinn's essay does not fare so well. By looking at hospitality in curriculum studies through a Derridean lens, Quinn's essay is a rather heavy philosophical discourse, even though it contains her personal narratives and experiences in curriculum work. Moreover, being well read in education related literature, Quinn's inclusion of numerous ideas from various authors can overwhelm and confuse readers.[191] This is compounded by her use of picturesque and poetic language in such a philosophical paper.

Nevertheless, from Phillion's response, which is based on her experiences as an educator involved in immigrant and minority education in Hong Kong, the United States, and Canada, it is quite evident that there is a need for renewal in the work of curriculum studies. In her judgment, "inhospitality pervades not only the US [sic] discourse but also the global discourse on immigration."[192] This is her description of the efforts of a university that sought to work towards a more diverse learning environment: "Things on the surface looked good. The secret story was that underneath, an inhospitable discourse,

---

186. hooks, *Teaching to Transgress*, 30.
187. Pinar, *Curriculum Theory*, 4, quoted in Quinn, "No Room," 104.
188. hooks, *Teaching to Transgress*, 1; Quinn, "No Room," 104.
189. Phillion, "Response to Molly Quinn," 121.
190. Ibid., 118 (emphasis mine).
191. Quinn's essay is thirteen pages in length and there are seventy-nine entries in her reference list.
192. Phillion, "Response to Molly Quinn," 118.

though generally unintentional, remained."[193] She also wrote, "Hospitality and its related attributes are missing from much of the discourse I read and from most discourses I engage in such as those at faculty meetings."[194] In her opinion, hospitality, in giving recognition to the other, especially immigrants, and in making learners from ethnic minority groups feel at home would definitely make a difference and give new hope to curriculum studies and education work.[195]

Hospitality and the Academic Life and Community

To improve academic life, community, and work in higher education, "intellectual hospitality" has been proposed by John B. Bennett, and Alison Phipps and Ronald Barnett, as a possible solution to the current ills.

Bennett, who served as faculty member, dean, and administrator in North American higher education, wrote numerous articles and books on hospitality in higher education and academic leadership. In a short essay in 1997, Bennett first broached the ideas of the autonomous self and relational model of higher education, and the collegial ethic of hospitality and thoughtfulness. These themes were further developed in numerous of his subsequent works.

Bennett strongly believed that American colleges and universities were plagued by insistent individualism, resulting in a sense of alienation in the academy.[196] Insistent individualism expresses itself in two forms: first, the aggressive that seeks self-promotion, and second, the passive that seeks self-protection.[197] In short, it is "the disposition to behave in self-absorbed and self-protecting ways and to put self-interest ahead of the welfare of others or a common good."[198] Hence, there was an urgent need "to recover and reappropriate" the relational model of academic community or collegium[199]

---

193. Ibid., 120.
194. Ibid., 121.
195. Ibid., 119–120.
196. Bennett, *Collegial Professionalism*, 12; see "Hospitality and Collegial," 87–90.
197. Bennett, "Academy and Hospitality," 30–31; "Hospitality and Collegial," 87–88; *Academic Life*, 6–10.
198. Bennett, "Academy and Hospitality," 29.
199. Bennett, *Collegial Professionalism*, 12.

whereby individuals are "linked through mutual, covenantal relationships."[200] Using Robert Paul Wolff's definition of an academic community, Bennett envisioned an ideal collegium, as yet not fully attainable, as

> a community of persons united by collective understanding, by common and communal goals, by bonds of reciprocal obligation, and by a flow of sentiment which makes the preservation of the community an object of desire, not merely a matter of prudence or a command of duty.[201]

Bonded by mutual covenantal relationships and common commitments, members in this collegium or covenant community are open to listen and accept criticisms from one another, and they appreciate the individuality and gifting of each individual since "each is essential, not incidental, to the whole."[202]

Bennett too agreed with Nouwen that we need to recover the potential of hospitality for the success of the academe.[203] Hence, it is not surprising that at the heart of the collegial ethic of Bennett's relational model of collegium is the "cardinal academic virtue" of hospitality.[204] For Bennett, hospitality is more than "a bland congeniality": it is an intellectual and moral virtue and an "epistemological necessity."[205] The practice of intellectual hospitality is essentially "the extension of self in order to welcome the other by sharing and receiving intellectual resources and insights."[206] And it is only through this mutual reciprocity, this "faithful, reliable attention of members to each other"[207] that "the collegium as covenant community is created and

---

200. Bennett, "Hospitality and Collegial," 91; for more on collegium, see *Collegial Professionalism*, 27–29; *Academic Life*, ch. 7.

201. As quoted in Bennett, *Academic Life*, 150.

202. Bennett, "Hospitality and Collegial," 91.

203. Bennett, "Academy and Hospitality," 23; "Civic and Moral Virtues," under "I."

204. Bennett, *Academic Life*, 46; "Hospitality and Collegial," 92. In John B. Bennett's initial works, he stated that "hospitality and thoughtfulness are two encompassing virtues that seem essential to the collegium and to constitute the heart of the collegial ethic" ("Academy, Individualism," under "The Heart of Collegial Ethic"; *Collegial Professionalism*, 35–36). Thoughtfulness was subsequently dropped but its essence was incorporated into the concept of hospitality when he described hospitable educators as thoughtful since they were being both reflective and considerate towards others (*Academic Life*, 74).

205. Bennett, "Academy and Hospitality," 23, 25.

206. Ibid., 23; *Academic Life*, 46; see also *Collegial Professionalism*, 36; "Civic and Moral Virtues," under "I"; "Hospitality and Collegial," 92.

207. Bennett, *Academic Life*, 158.

sustained."[208] Hence, "mutual respect, not domination or indifference" characterizes relations among the members of a covenant community.[209]

In Bennett's opinion, teachers can practice intellectual hospitality – sharing and receiving insights between self and others – in their teaching, scholarship, and service.[210] "The hospitable teacher is genuinely open to the particularity of the other and to the possibility that the other who is a learner can also teach."[211] The other is not only his or her students but also colleagues. Ultimately, the hospitable teacher serves by "ensur[ing] that the conditions for hospitable teaching and scholarship are in place and maintained."[212]

Influenced by the late English philosopher Michael Oakeshott, Bennett too proposed the metaphor of conversation as the vehicle to practice hospitality.[213]

> The metaphor of conversation suggests that people with different intellectual interests and histories have important things to say to each other. The process is back and forth – comment or question, followed by response, which in turn generates a rejoinder, and so on.[214]

In this way, we hear and interact with "the multitude of voices, idioms, and other representations of the human achievements and self-understandings that constitute our inheritance."[215] We learn to form meanings and our own humanity as we participate in this conversation. And, "healthy conversations require practicing hospitality" because it requires an air of openness in the acts of sharing and receiving.[216]

---

208. Bennett, "Civic and Moral Virtues," 33; *Academic Life*, x.
209. Bennett, *Academic Life*, 150.
210. Bennett, "Academy and Hospitality," 26–28; "Hospitality and Collegial," 93–95; "Teaching with Hospitality," under "The Gifts of Others and the Rules of Conversation."
211. Bennett, "Teaching with Hospitality," under "The Gifts of Others and the Rules of Conversation."
212. Bennett, "Hospitality and Collegial," 94.
213. Bennett, "Academy and Hospitality," 24; "Civic and Moral Virtues," under "II"; "Hospitality and Collegial," 91; "Liberal Learning"; *Academic Life*, 99–102; "Constructing Academic Community," 58–59, esp. 56.
214. Bennett, *Academic Life*, 99.
215. Ibid., 115.
216. Bennett, "Liberal Learning," under "Openness to the Other."

Bennett acknowledged his indebtedness to Nouwen and Palmer, as well as other authors, for their insights regarding the virtue of hospitality.[217] He echoed Nouwen when he said, "Being hospitable is adverbial in nature. It refers to *how* one relates to others."[218] However, Bennett's focus was on academic hospitality or intellectual hospitality. Yet Bennett's intellectual hospitality as a "radical openness to the other, attending to him or her in sharing and receiving insights and perspectives about self and world[,] ... practicing openness regarding one's position – being willing to review accepted and familiar standpoints, even to abandon them if new insight warrants" reflects Nouwen's idea of concentration (see above p. 15) and Palmer's idea of community (see above p. 33).[219] However, Bennett broadened the practice of hospitality, beyond faculty and students, to include persons in positions of leadership in educational institutions.[220] "Leadership involves practicing hospitality" and "practicing hospitality is a form of leadership."[221]

At the same time, Bennett expressed much of Palmer's sentiments, as well as others, by emphasizing a relational self and promoting the collegial ethic of hospitality in a relational learning community:[222]

> Practicing hospitality creates and expresses this relational community, for it involves an ethic of radical openness in sharing with and receiving from others. . . . To be hospitable is to attend to the reality of the other – to appreciate it without preconditions and to allow it to instruct oneself. "Others" include students, colleagues, and texts – as well as the multitude of practices that constitute human living, that generate health and harmony as well as oppression and hurt. It is in relation to these others that we learn about ourselves and the world.[223]

This understanding clearly aligned with Palmer's idea of a community as "an *ontological* reality, an *epistemological* necessity, a *pedagogical* asset, and

---

217. Bennett, *Academic Life*, xiv.
218. Ibid., 53 (original emphasis).
219. Bennett, "Civic and Moral Virtues," under "I."
220. Bennett, *Academic Life*, ch. 8.
221. Ibid., 185.
222. Ibid., xiii.
223. Ibid., xi.

an *ethical* corrective."²²⁴ However, when analyzed further, it can be deduced that Bennett's philosophical underpinnings for the relational nature of self were derived largely from Alfred North Whitehead's process philosophy.²²⁵ In fact, in a short essay on Palmer's contribution to the spirituality of education, Bennett was of the opinion that Palmer's writings could be strengthened by the philosophical undergirding that comes from relational metaphysics. He felt that Whitehead's philosophy could help to enhance Palmer's thoughts, even resolve some inadequacies and ambiguities about objectivism, hidden wholeness, and paradox.²²⁶

Although Bennett claimed that "Palmer is unusually forthright in describing the dominant ethos of higher education," I am inclined to think that in this area Palmer paled in comparison to him.²²⁷ From his many years of experience as an academician, Bennett made many critical comments about the prevalent insistent individualism in the academe. He identified insistent individualism as "an underlying problem for academe,"²²⁸ adding that present economic challenges are contributing factors to the pervasive competition, alienation, fear, and insecurity within institutions, a consideration which Bennett noted was missing in Palmer.²²⁹

The metaphor of conversation is an important feature within Bennett's notion of the collegial ethic of hospitality. In my opinion, his understanding of conversation as a two-tiered experience – sharing and receiving knowledge, and sharing and offering of analysis and feedback – are especially needful for the multicultural and globalized world in which we live.²³⁰ Incidentally, Bennett also identified six features that commend conversation as the key metaphor for higher education: "the pluralism of our times, the importance of discernment and empathy, the constitution of our humanity, the

---

224. Palmer, "Toward a Philosophy," 25 (original emphasis).
225. Bennett, "Academy, Individualism," under "Relational Nature of Individuality"; *Collegial Professionalism*, xii, 24; *Academic Life*, xiii; see "Constructing Academic Community," 60, n. 3.
226. Bennett, "Educational Spiritualities," 170.
227. Ibid., 171.
228. Bennett, *Academic Life*, 1.
229. Bennett, "Educational Spiritualities," 171.
230. Bennett, "Academy and Hospitality," 24.

incorporation of activity and imagination, experiential and civic learning, and the absence of hierarchy."[231]

I agree with Kerry S. Webb that "Bennett succeeds, ... in painting a perceptive portrait of the relational crisis in higher education and in pointing the way toward a more positive, productive model" not only for the United States,[232] but also for "the global academic community."[233] His vision of the academic community as a covenantal "collegium, rather than as an aggregation of individualists"[234] where we are committed to the welfare of others as conversation partners is definitely worthy of our consideration.[235] However, Webb expressed that she did "not foresee these conversations [between senior and junior faculty members] becoming common place [sic] on college and university campuses in the near future."[236] Bennett himself was aware of this predicament for he wrote:

> Hospitality is always a goal before us. We know we still wrestle with discrimination respecting gender, sexual orientation, and ethnicity – but academe struggles as well with ideological purity, institutional affiliation, and credentials. . . .
>
> Despite being marginalized, academic hospitality remains fundamental to the work and being of the academy – to the pursuit, enlargement, and sharing of learning.[237]

Like Bennett, I too believe that though the task before us may be daunting and challenging, we should still work toward a covenantal and relational community that practices hospitality in pursuit of the common good through open exchange and reciprocity.

Another work on academic life was written by Phipps and Barnett. Both of them felt that the practice of academic life was threatened by the rapid

---

231. Bennett, *Academic Life*, 102.
232. Webb, "Review," 192. Although Kerry S. Webb's evaluation is made with reference to Bennett's book, *College Professionalism*, it can be applied throughout his works on hospitality in higher education.
233. Johnstone, "Review," 179. Although David M. Johnstone's evaluation is made with reference to Bennett's book, *Academic Life*, it can be applied throughout his works on hospitality in higher education.
234. Bennett, *Academic Life*, 142.
235. Ibid., 160.
236. Webb, "Review," 191.
237. Bennett, "Hospitality and Collegial," 95.

social, ideological, cultural, and epistemological changes of globalization. Philosophical and theological in its approach, this article explored "the limits and the possibilities for hospitable academic practice under the exigencies and changing dynamics of academic life."[238]

Phipps and Barnett's insightful observation that the fast-changing realities in our globalized world have created new forms of academic hospitality that challenge us to be open to new possibilities for the practice of hospitality. Besides the epistemological form that welcomes new ideas, which was Bennett's focus, Phipps and Barnett proposed that academic hospitality also "takes material form in the hosting of academics and academic travelers. . . . It takes linguistic form in the translation of academic work into other languages, and it takes touristic form through the welcome and generosity with which academic visitors are received."[239] Undoubtedly, the nature of hosting and guesting will require different expressions of hospitable acts in each of these forms of hospitality.[240]

At the same time, using categories drawn from Rowan Williams, the former Archbishop of Canterbury, Phipps and Barnett suggested that academic hospitality could be conceived of as a synthesis of three modes: celebratory, communicative, and critical.[241] The celebratory mode envisions the ideals of academic hospitality: it is an envisioning "of the academic extremes, of what we prize and what we exclude."[242] The communicative mode considers which form of communication is most appropriate and effective for building bridges across cultural and linguistic divides while "the critical mode sharpens the keen sense of limits and hones the perception of possibilities for practising academic hospitality."[243] In their judgment, Phipps and Barnett believed the ideas of Bennett, Paul Ricoeur, and Derrida could be used to approach these modalities of academic hospitality:

> What we find in Bennett is a view of the potential of academic hospitality for establishing the modes of being which can enable

---

238. Phipps and Barnett, "Academic Hospitality," 238.
239. Ibid., 239.
240. For details, see ibid., 239–243.
241. Ibid., 247.
242. Ibid., 252.
243. Ibid., 250.

the flourishing of the academy again, as he sees it. Bennett's view of academic hospitality is a *celebratory* one. In Ricoeur we find the *communicative* mode in action – academic hospitality may be read as translation and as linguistic hospitality – allowing communication between the pluralities of cultures and languages in ways which may foster understanding. In Derrida we find a critical concern with limits, with the possibility of hospitality, with the nature of justice and its indeconstructability; it is a concept under revision in the face of new movements of peoples, but which both historically and practically cannot be applied universally.[244]

Giving credit to Williams and Bennett, Phipps and Barnett too proposed conversation as a resource for the practice of academic hospitality.[245] In a short concluding paragraph, they explained why they believed that "the art of conversation is the art of hospitality":

> Conversation – in the form of seminar, symposium, conference, the chat in the corridor or the deeper encounters of extremis as life presses and scours out its shape through academic life – enacts hospitality. It gives, speaking, and receives, listening. In the more formal modalities, it ponders, debates, contests, critiques, celebrates and most of all it communicates. . . . Conversation, be it at the level of citation or in the corridor, is the place where ideas and people, meet and greet in celebratory, communicative and often critical modes.[246]

The academic hospitality envisioned by Bennett, and Phipps and Barnett has moved beyond teacher-student classroom interaction which was largely the focus of Nouwen's and Palmer's discussion of hospitality in education. Furthermore, for all three of them, conversation, with its radical openness to

---

244. Ibid., 250–251 (original emphasis). Here, Alison Phipps and Ronald Barnett cited the works on hospitality by Bennett ("Hospitality and Collegial"; *Academic Life*), Paul Ricoeur (*Freedom and Nature*; *On Translation*), and Derrida (*Politics of Friendship*; *On Cosmopolitanism*; Derrida and Dufourmantelle, *Of Hospitality*).
245. Phipps and Barnett, "Academic Hospitality," 253.
246. Ibid.

share and receive, is central to the practice of academic hospitality. These are the new considerations these authors have brought to our table of discussion.

Hospitality and the Marginalized

Just as marginalized groups are an issue in theological education (see above p. 76), marginalized groups are also a concern in higher education – an issue raised by two professionals, Rauna Kuokkanen and Awad Ibrahim.

The first voice for the marginalized – more specifically, indigenous peoples – and their epistemologies was that of Kuokkanen, a Sami woman from Northern Finland who taught at the University of Toronto, Canada. Kuokkanen highlighted the malaise in the academy: epistemic ignorance.[247] Kuokkanen, quoting Michel Foucault, defined "episteme" as "'something like a worldview' and 'the total set of relations that unite, at a given period, the discursive practices that give rise to epistemological figures, sciences, and possibly formalized system.'"[248] Indigenous epistemes is not just indigenous knowledge but also includes "indigenous ontologies, philosophies and presuppositions or conceptual frameworks through which one looks at and interprets the world."[249] Epistemic ignorance is not just a matter of not knowing or a lack of understanding about indigenous epistemologies and epistemes. Epistemic ignorance refers to "ways in which academic theories and practices ignore, marginalize and exclude other than dominant Western European epistemic and intellectual traditions."[250] Fundamentally, it is "a form of subtle violence" since indigenous epistemes "are made to disappear through this invisibility and distance."[251] In both her essays, Kuokkanen held the academy responsible for eradicating epistemic ignorance in its premises.

Even though Kuokkanen recognized that there would be no absolute and satisfying solution to the existing problem, she still believed that hospitality,

---

247. Kuokkanen, "Toward a New Relation"; "What Is Hospitality." Rauna Kuokkanen noted that epistemic ignorance was discussed as "sanctioned ignorance" by Gayatri Chakravorty Spivak (*In Other Worlds*, 199, cited in Kuokkanen, "What Is Hospitality," 60, 62). Spivak perceived sanctioned ignorance as "inseparable from colonial domination." Kuokkanen also noted that Sheila McIntyre called it "studied ignorance" and "privileged innocence" (McIntyre, "Studied Ignorance," cited in Kuokkanen, "What Is Hospitality," 64).
248. Kuokkanen, "What Is Hospitality," 62, quoting Foucault, *Archaeology of Knowledge*, 191.
249. Kuokkanen, "What Is Hospitality," 62.
250. Ibid., 63.
251. Ibid.

"grounded on a sense of social responsibility and reciprocity," could serve the academy in its efforts to accept its responsibility towards indigenous peoples.[252] Seen as "the fundamental openness to the other,"[253] hospitality in the academy would mean both the host (non-indigenous people) and the guest (indigenous people) must assume their responsibilities to build a trusting and reciprocating relationship where host and guest can be "host-guest" and "guest-host" respectively.[254] However, the academy, as the host-guest, must first do its homework. As suggested by the postcolonial critic Gayatri Chakravorty Spivak,[255] doing one's homework involves unlearning one's privilege, behaving as if one is part of the margin.[256] By learning to learn from the other, "not only does one become able to listen to that other constituency, but one learns to speak in such a way that one will be taken seriously by that other constituency."[257] On the other hand, the guest-host not only gives to the host-guest "the gift of the opportunity to learn" but also guides the other as he or she participates actively in this learning process.[258] In the knowing of the other, "the gift of Indigenous epistemes must be recognized, accepted, and respected even if it might not be possible to fully grasp and contain it."[259]

In her second essay, Kuokkanen was even more insistent that the academy should bear the ultimate responsibility to do its homework and address its ignorance so that it could give "an 'unconditional welcome' not only to indigenous people but also to their epistemes, without insisting on translation."[260] She continued where she concluded in her first essay and suggested that indigenous epistemes should be recognized as "a gift to the academy."[261] Here, Kuokkanen highlighted that, contrary to Derrida's notion of the impossible gift where once the gift is recognized as gift, it ceases to be

---

252. Kuokkanen, "Toward a New Relation," 285.
253. Ibid., 267.
254. Ibid., 280, 282.
255. Spivak, *Post-Colonial Critic*, 9.
256. Kuokkanen, "Toward a New Relation," 280; "What Is Hospitality," 78.
257. Spivak, *Post-Colonial Critic*, 42.
258. Kuokkanen, "Toward a New Relation," 282–283.
259. Ibid., 285.
260. Kuokkanen, "What Is Hospitality," 60.
261. Ibid., 65.

a gift, indigenous epistemes must be recognized to make the gift possible.²⁶² Moreover, unlike the logic of exchange,

> in the gift logic of indigenous thought, gifts are not given first and foremost to ensure a countergift later on, but to actively acknowledge the relationships and coexistence with the world without which survival would not be possible. In this logic, the gifts of the land are not taken for granted but recognized by giving back or other expressions of gratitude. . . .
>
> The gift thus implies *response-ability*; an ability to respond, to remain attuned to the world beyond self and be willing to recognize its existence through gift giving.²⁶³

In her essay, "The Gift as a Worldview in Indigenous Thought," Kuokkanen termed this "circular reciprocity" or "ceremonial reciprocity."²⁶⁴ We act responsibly when we receive indigenous epistemes as gifts and reciprocate; in this way, we ensure that "the gift is not taken for granted or misused."²⁶⁵ However, Kuokkanen perceived that the academy may be reluctant to accept the gift as "the gift may threaten the hegemony and hierarchy of epistemes which serve certain interests."²⁶⁶ Furthermore, the academy is entrenched in "the ideology of exchange economy" whereby one gives in order to receive.²⁶⁷

Kuokkanen understood hospitality as "various practices of welcoming guests into a space that is considered, in one way or another, belonging to the guest, whether an individual or a group of people."²⁶⁸ Her concept of hospitality was clearly influenced by Derrida's works. First, radical hospitality "consists, *would have* to consist, in *receiving without invitation*, beyond or before the invitation."²⁶⁹ Second, hospitality must be unconditional.²⁷⁰ Hospitality as unconditional welcome requires the academy to continuously embrace the logic of the gift. In fact, Kuokkanen believed that "the ethics and the future of

---

262. Ibid., 70; see Derrida, *Given Time*, 7, 13–14.
263. Kuokkanen, "What Is Hospitality," 66 (original emphasis).
264. Kuokkanen, "Gift as a Worldview," 89.
265. Ibid., 61.
266. Kuokkanen, "What Is Hospitality," 69.
267. Ibid.
268. Ibid,, 71.
269. Derrida, "Hostipitality," 360 (original emphasis).
270. Derrida and Dufourmantelle, *Of Hospitality*, 25.

the academy require hospitality. Without openness to the other, responsibility to the other, there is no future of and in the academy."[271] This openness and responsibility to the other also challenges the academy to abdicate its role as the sovereign host, assuming a spirit of humility that exhibits "willingness to reciprocate with other epistemes while remaining aware of disparate relations of power, resources, and privilege."[272]

The other voice speaking for the marginalized came from Ibrahim, who was born and brought up in Sudan, and studied in France. He sought political refuge in Canada and was teaching in a college in northwest Ohio at the time of writing. Especially in a post-9/11 United States, he is more acutely aware of his foreignness among those he lives with. Questions supposed to be warm and welcoming – "who are you? where do you come from? what do you want? [sic]" – could be perceived as "unnecessary, if not outright violent."[273] Ibrahim explained, "My hospitality [as shown by others] is conditioned by (1) language (having an accent), (2) my name (assumed to be Muslim from the Middle East), and (3) race."[274] In fact, after coming to Canada and the United States, due to his foreignness, he was often assumed by others to be a Black Muslim. With his foreignness, he sought to discuss how he could be a host and show hospitality in his classroom. He concluded, "It seems that this foreigner is most at 'home' in his classroom. I am able to occupy the position of the host, not in the larger North American society, but in my classroom" – students who were "primarily White, middle-class, females, from Northwest Ohio [sic]."[275] Ibrahim believed that "those who either grow up in a culture or have little material possessions tend to recognize and practice mostly unconditional hospitality."[276] As such, he was able to practice hospitality since he grew up in a culture of unconditional hospitality and poverty, of "an unconditional gift of love, humor, security, patience, humility, and humanity."[277] He sought to provide "a space of open, inverted and unconditional hospitality; where unity

---

271. Kuokkanen, "What Is Hospitality," 74.
272. Ibid., 76–77.
273. Ibrahim, "Question of the Question," 150, quoting Derrida and Dufourmantelle, *Of Hospitality*, 131.
274. Ibrahim, "Question of the Question," 157.
275. Ibid., 159.
276. Ibid.
277. Ibid., 160.

does not mean sameness but working across differences is possible regardless of race, gender, class, ability and sexuality."[278] He hoped that his students, by "experiencing the foreigner, that the foreigner becomes them and they the foreigner."[279] "I want us to meet at the rendezvous of humanity. I want them to *see* and *hear* me, the foreigner, unconditionally. But above all, I want them to set me free, to be myself."[280]

Though Kuokkanen's and Ibrahim's essays were calls for a hospitable space for those at the margins – be it ideas or persons – Ibrahim's narrative, though philosophical in its approach due to Derrida's influence, is the most personal account of what hospitality would mean to the marginalized.

Hospitality and Classroom Process

As defined earlier (see above p. 62), classroom process encompasses classroom atmosphere, teacher and student behaviors, face-to-face interactions, learning activities, and evaluation procedures. Interestingly, hospitality has been a topic of discussion among teachers in higher education composition classes. The essays of Dale Jacobs, Janis Haswell, Richard Haswell, and Glenn Blalock focus chiefly on hospitality as a theory or practice. Another essay in this literature review is written by Tana N. Schiewer and focuses on teacher-student relationships.[281]

Like Rud (see above p. 110), Jacobs' understanding of hospitality was also influenced by the Benedictines' practice of listening.[282] Continuing from an earlier essay where he proposed hope as "a necessary condition of our work as educators attempting to bring change,"[283] Jacobs now attempted to show hospitality, with its elements of listening and availability, as an essential element of hope.[284] Hospitality, for Jacobs, is a relationship of equality,[285] or reciprocity as we have discussed thus far, whereby "the host is not the only one who has something to offer, but rather both guest and host give to each

---

278. Ibid., 159.
279. Ibid., 160.
280. Ibid. (original emphasis).
281. Schiewer, "Teacher-Student Relationships."
282. Jacobs, "Audacity of Hospitality," 566.
283. Jacobs, "What's Hope," 794.
284. Jacobs, "Audacity of Hospitality," 564.
285. Ibid., 576.

other so that the lines between host and guest become blurred."[286] Drawing insights from Gabriel Marcel, Nouwen, and Michele Hershberger, Jacobs too believed in a balance of receptivity and confrontation as we open ourselves to the other and "[lay] our cards on the table."[287] Jacobs termed this open stance to the other as availability[288] or presence.[289] And "being open or available in this way means that we put aside what we *think* we know about our students and colleagues and actually listen to what they have to say in a way that gives serious consideration to their ideas."[290]

So whether it is in classrooms, department meetings, conference sessions or even virtual spaces of interaction, "the key is creating a space for the free exchange of ideas rather than the imposition of ideas by the host on guests" or vice versa.[291] This calls for rhetorical listening which, as defined by Krista Ratcliffe, means "listening to discourses not *for* intent but *with* intent."[292] Such listening not only requires a suspension of our suspicion about the other but also requires us not to view others – our students, our colleagues – as enemies.[293] Moreover, it requires silence, a silence long enough to hear what others have to say.[294]

Critiquing Jacobs in his dissertation, Brandy L. Grabow concluded that "the omission of context in Jacobs' work allows the hospitable metaphor to fit neatly, but falsely elides the considerable power relationships at play among colleagues or instructors and students."[295] Reinterpreting Nouwen's words – "no dialogue is possible between somebody and a nobody"[296] – outside the context of receptivity and confrontation, Grabow pointed out that in the academy, "there is always 'a somebody' and a 'nobody'; there is

---

286. Ibid., 569.
287. Ibid.; see Marcel, *Introduction*; Nouwen, *Reaching Out*; Hershberger, "Response."
288. Jacobs, "Audacity of Hospitality," 565, quoting Marcel, *Introduction*, 23–25.
289. Jacobs, "Audacity of Hospitality," 578, quoting Rodgers and Raider-Roth, "Presence in Teaching," 266.
290. Jacobs, "Audacity of Hospitality," 569 (original emphasis).
291. Ibid., 571.
292. Ratcliffe, *Rhetorical Listening*, 28 (original emphasis).
293. See Jacobs, "Audacity of Hospitality," 568–570.
294. Ibid., 577.
295. Grabow, "Expanding the Metaphor," 26.
296. Nouwen, *Reaching Out*, 99.

always someone with power and someone with less, or none."²⁹⁷ By ignoring the power inequities and potential misreading of one's hospitable act of being open and laying one's cards on the table, Jacobs has made hospitality a risky business that would be difficult to be applied within existing power structures.²⁹⁸

Besides Jacobs, educators like Haswell, Haswell, and Blalock also contemplated the use of hospitality in college writing courses. In their essay, they examined three historical modes of hospitality – Homeric, Judeo-Christian, and nomadic hospitality – and showed how each would look like when applied to five instructional practices (namely, course objectives, shared labor, assignments, response, and assessment).²⁹⁹ In comparison, Homeric hospitality suits the current writing pedagogy that focuses on "group work aimed at a public goal."³⁰⁰ However, they instead proposed "transformative hospitality [which] is especially compatible with college writing instruction, where the focus has always been and must continue to be upon activities powerfully embedded in human change."³⁰¹ For them, *transformative hospitality* was another term for Bennett's intellectual hospitality (see above p. 118). The practice of transformative hospitality allows one's understanding to be transformed by another's perspective and "situates a new triad of pedagogical R's: *risk taking, restlessness,* and *resistance*.³⁰²

The authors stated that they chose the metaphor of hospitality for framing a transformative pedagogy in composition classes because, unlike most metaphors of writing instruction, it allows for a pair of equals – the composition teacher and the writing student.³⁰³ Since transformative hospitality should transform both "teacher and student alike," the authors are right to say that it is an heir to both Judeo-Christian and nomadic hospitality that focuses on radical equality and role reversal respectively.³⁰⁴ Here, I have

---

297. Grabow, "Expanding the Metaphor," 24.
298. Ibid., 26.
299. Haswell, Haswell, and Blalock, "College Composition Courses." For the summarized chart, see 718–719.
300. Ibid., 720.
301. Ibid.
302. Ibid. (original emphasis).
303. Ibid., 724, n. 2.
304. Ibid., 720.

to say that radical equality – "no soul is less than any other in the eyes of the Lord" – may be uniquely Judeo-Christian because in Mediterranean societies, as pointed out by Julian Pitt-Rivers, equality invites rivalry and "reciprocity resides, not in identity, but in an alternation of roles."[305] Like Haswell, Haswell, and Blalock, I believe that "in a world that often functions by separating guest and host, and this includes the world of higher education, there is some argument in recommending that teachers and their students simply go contrary."[306] However, the practice of hospitality in the classroom does not just "reconfigure – re-radicalize, if you will – the notion of student-centered classrooms" of the 1960s, as claimed by the authors.[307] The fact that both teachers and students alike may be transformed would mean that it is no longer a student-centered classroom. As Sean Michael Barnette put it, "a classroom in which transformative hospitality is practiced is not so much student centered as *relationship centered*."[308]

Unlike Jacobs, the three authors have definitely highlighted the practice of hospitality as "complex, tacit, risky, and treacherous, therefore in need of analysis, conscientization, and caution."[309] Yet, these three authors, and Jacobs (albeit less explicitly), argued for the plausibility of its use inside and beyond the composition classrooms which was contested by Matthew Heard as having "no *use* in the economy of value in rhetoric and composition studies."[310] Heard, essentially, was not opposed to the ideas put forth by Jacobs as well as Haswell, Haswell, and Blalock. However, his reading of the philosophical discourses on hospitality and Emmanuel Levinas and Derrida – that hospitality is "not … a practice but a radical, infinite, impractical ideal" – prompted him to present generosity as a more workable alternative.[311] The ethical ideal of infinite hospitality or unconditional hospitality "is not a matter of choice, orientation, or practice but rather of obligation and duty to the 'other.'"[312] Responding to this duty may mean "sacrificing ethics, that is, by

---

305. Pitt-Rivers, "Stranger," 21.
306. Haswell, Haswell and Blalock, "College Composition Courses," 723.
307. Ibid., 709.
308. Barnette, "Houses of Hospitality," 117–118 (emphasis mine).
309. Haswell, Haswell and Blalock, "College Composition Courses," 708.
310. Heard, "Hospitality and Generosity," 330 (original emphasis).
311. Ibid., 318.
312. Ibid., 326.

sacrificing whatever obliges me to also respond, in the same way, in the same instant, to all the others."[313] Hospitality, thus, becomes a burden, "an infinite responsibility" to the extent that in the process of "making the other at home, we shut all of the other others waiting outside the door."[314] On the other hand, generosity is "an attitude that can be learned and perfected . . . . Generosity is within reach: one can choose to give up one's resources, and one can be instructed in how to give *better* or how to give *more*."[315]

Hence, Heard concluded that generosity is more useful as a practice since it can make room for openness, availability, and listening (see Jacobs in above p. 129). Yet, he argued that "radical hospitality needs to be preserved as an ideal that must be pursued endlessly, without the hope that we will someday be able to control, explain, or contain hospitable action."[316] "Hospitality matters because it perpetually hopes for difference. When we 'stand under' hospitality as an infinite responsibility to others, we keep open the possibility that a different idea or person – a different guest – could enter our domain in the next moment and change us."[317] It may even "lead us to shake the entire stratified system of the university."[318]

I personally cannot see the distinction Heard made between "generosity as a practical application" that can be learned and systematized, and "hospitality as an impractical theory" that cannot be measured and quantified.[319] Furthermore, Heard believed that to practice generosity is a matter of one's choice whereas to practice hospitality is one's duty.[320] Although Heard drew upon Levinas and Derrida for his understanding of hospitality as an infinite responsibility, in this point, he overlooked a comment made by Derrida: "If I practice hospitality '*out of* duty' . . . this hospitality . . . is no longer an absolute hospitality."[321] I believe generosity and hospitality are separated only by a thin

---

313. Ibid., 329, quoting Derrida, *Gift of Death*, 68.
314. Heard, "Hospitality and Generosity," 329.
315. Ibid., 317 (original emphasis).
316. Ibid., 319.
317. Ibid., 331.
318. Ibid.
319. Ibid., 317, 318.
320. Ibid., 326, 328.
321. Ibid., 326–330; see Derrida and Dufourmantelle, *Of Hospitality*, 83 (original emphasis).

fine line. The Arabic word *karam* is translated as "generosity" or "hospitality."[322] The subtlety in the difference is also discerned by Stanley Raffel when he stated that "generosity is when you do it everywhere, hospitality when you do the same practices but at home."[323] However, Heard speaks for Haswell, Haswell, and Blalock, for Jacobs, and for me when he argued that hospitality hopes for a difference, for a transformative change not only in composition classrooms but also in all classrooms and all aspects of academic life, including teacher-student relationships and interactions.

The importance of teacher-student relationships is emphasized by Tana Schiewer when she argued that teachers need to play the role of a hospitable host and create a hospitable teaching environment for a more productive classroom and effective learning. Using the idea put forth by Mary Elizabeth Pope, that "the success of a party depends on the hostess,"[324] Schiewer presented three basic ways that the teacher-host could do to create a hospitable learning environment: (1) provide simple instruction, (2) create community, and (3) befriend students.[325]

Writing in a simple manner that is reader-friendly, Schiewer takes a practical approach, giving examples on how teachers can show hospitality in their classrooms. Knowing that the academic prose of the university is foreign to new college students, she suggested that providing a guide, such as Gerald Graff and Cathy Birkenstein's *They Say/I Say*, could help initiate students into academic writing.[326]

Schiewer also realized that teachers are inevitably perceived by students as authoritative figures who have the final say and final authority in the classrooms.[327] This makes it difficult for teachers to build community and to befriend students. To navigate through this delicate balance when building community, Schiewer's first suggestion is the practice of presence. Here, Schiewer introduced Jerry Farber's understanding of presence – the condition

---

322. Shryock, "New Jordanian Hospitality," 36.
323. Raffel, "On Generosity," 126. Although I have used Stanley Raffel's statement to refute Matthew Heard's distinction between generosity and hospitality, I do not agree with Raffel that the practice of hospitality is limited to the home. This work clearly argues otherwise.
324. Pope, "Teacher as Hostess," 107.
325. Schiewer, "Teacher-Student Relationships," 545.
326. As cited in ibid., 546.
327. Ibid.

of being fully present to self and others – as pedagogical mindfulness for our consideration.[328] When we are not fully present, "when we're there but not there, this, in effect, excludes the students, who are reduced to the role of mere onlookers (in lecture) or objects to be manipulated (in 'class-centered' activities)."[329]

Then, to navigate through the delicate balance when befriending students, Schiewer suggested the practice of hospitality. On hospitable behaviors when befriending students, Schiewer referred to an essay written by Marshall Gregory. Teachers who are friends with their students without losing their authority, are those whom students trust and whose critical comments are received as "helpful and productive rather than as mean and destructive."[330]

Schiewer's essay is relatively short – four pages; hence, her discussion lacks both width and depth. For instance, when discussing community building and befriending, the reader needs to refer to her references in order to fully grasp her argument. However, her simple presentation of the host metaphor as a way to conceive teacher-student relationships is easy for readers to understand. And, like those educators writing on classroom process before her who believed in the power of hospitality to transform, she too asserted that

> being fully present, befriending our students, treating them hospitably – all of these behaviors invite us to actively engage our students in a way that holds incredible power to transform. The hospitable teaching environment is not simply "nicer"; it also has far greater potential to be more *effective*.[331]

Interestingly, the same works of Nouwen and Palmer on hospitality in education that sparked further thinking among Christian educators also prompted professionals in higher education working in non-Christian settings to think of education as hospitality. Five out of the thirteen authors discussed here (namely, Bennett; Haswell, Haswell, and Blalock; Rud) listed the works of both Nouwen (*Reaching Out*) and Palmer (*To Know as We Are Known* and/

---

328. Ibid., 546–547; see Farber, "Teaching and Presence," 215.
329. Farber, "Teaching and Presence," 216, as quoted in Schiewer, "Teacher-Student Relationships," 547.
330. Gregory, "Curriculum," 83, as quoted in Schiewer, "Teacher-Student Relationships," 547.
331. Schiewer, "Teacher-Student Relationships," 547 (original emphasis).

or *Courage to Teach*) in their references while two listed a work of Nouwen (i.e. Jacobs; Losito) and another two listed a work of Palmer (i.e. Kuokkanen; Quinn). This amounts to about 70 percent of the works reviewed here. This observation, together with the same observation from our review of Christian higher education and theological education literature (see above p. 48), is a clear indication of the impact Nouwen's and Palmer's conceptualization of hospitality in education has on educators. And, as in the discourses from the circles of Christian higher education and theological education, many of these higher education professionals worked with Nouwen's and Palmer's fundamental idea of hospitality as the creation of a space to welcome the other as they further develop the concept of hospitality to address their particular area of concern or context and to meet the challenges posed by the changing landscape of higher education.

In many of the discourses, there is the call for a relational approach to doing educational work – a call to care, to build community, even the call to allow for emotions. Many of them also share the same sentiments with Losito, that "the characteristics of hospitality do not *imply* a particular practice or policy for school."[332] Rather, hospitality is perceived as an ethical and intellectual virtue. As with the literature from Christian and higher education, most discourses generally encouraged students, teachers, administrators, and educational leaders to receive each other as well as each other's ideas with genuine hospitality. And in the context of global diversities in our contemporary world, hospitality demands one to look at the other – the stranger – more intently, including the indigenous epistemology that comes along with the stranger. However, a noticeable difference is the inclusion of the voices of philosophers such as Derrida and Ricoeur, and feminist thinkers such as hooks and Noddings, in their discourses.

As is the case with Christian higher education and theological education, there is a paucity of literature on hospitality in higher education beyond Western contexts. Almost all the authors, except for Kuokkanen, were addressing the educational scene of North America. Two specifically indicated that they were not raised on American soil – Kuokkanen, who was born, raised and educated in Finland; and Ibrahim who grew up in Africa and studied in France. But again, there is an absence of non-Western voices, a lacuna

---

332. Losito, "Education as Hospitality," 67 (original emphasis).

that this book seeks to address. Furthermore, not much has been said about the practice of hospitality beyond the walls of the classroom or institution. This gap will also be addressed for I believe that hospitality not only has the capacity to sustain academic rigor in the structured intellectual discussions in the classroom but it also opens up opportunities for spontaneous sharing outside the classroom (see below ch. 5).[333]

Parallel Practices of Hospitality in Contemporary Higher Education Educational Practices

As demonstrated above, the prevailing yet worrying state in the higher education arena prompted educators to look at how the metaphor of hospitality, with its positive images of belonging, inclusion, and welcome of strangers and strangeness, could guide contemporary educational practices. In their discussions on hospitality, the pedagogy of care (e.g. Rud; see Quinn), the practice of dialogue (e.g. Bennett; Phipps and Barnett), and the ethic of unconditional welcome, or what I term *inclusion* (e.g. Ibrahim; Kuokkanen), have been variously put forth as possible educational strategies for creating a more relational and supportive learning environment in higher education. Incidentally, these practices were also mentioned in the literature review related to Christian higher education and theological education (e.g. for care, see Burwell and Huyser; for dialogue, see Hagstrom; Susanne Johnson; for inclusion, see M. Marshall). This section thus seeks to examine further how these three parallel practices of hospitality – care, inclusion, and dialogue – are being practiced within the higher educational communities.

The Practice of Care

Teven believed that "caring is an essential attribute of most, if not all, human relationships. In the instructional context, there is substantial evidence that caring is an important characteristic of effective teachers."[334] An effective teaching-learning environment is characterized by "a climate of warmth, understanding, and caring within the classroom."[335] Research in higher

---

333. See Palmer, "Toward a Philosophy," 29–30.
334. Teven, "Relationships," 159.
335. Ibid.

education has revealed that teacher caring is integral to student motivation and learning.[336]

The ethic of care was first introduced by psychologist Carol Gilligan when, through her interview-based study regarding moral decision making, she discovered that men and women speak in different voices – the voice of justice and the voice of care respectively.[337] "While an ethic of justice proceeds from the premise of equality – that everyone should be treated the same – an ethic of care rests on the premise of nonviolence – that no one should be hurt."[338] The language of justice emphasizes rules and rights; the language of care embraces relationships and responsibilities.[339] And, in Gilligan's opinion, "in the representation of maturity, both perspectives converge in the realization that just as inequality adversely affects both parties in an unequal relationship, so too violence is destructive for everyone involved."[340] This understanding clearly differs from that of her mentor, Lawrence Kohlberg, who defined "the highest stages of moral development as deriving from a reflective understanding of human rights."[341]

Gilligan's works on care – focused on ethical and moral dilemmas – were written at a time when education work in the United States was dominated by discourses on ethics and moral reasoning. Writing around the same time was the philosopher and educator Noddings who, too, observed that "ethics has been discussed largely in the language of the father: in principles and propositions, in terms such as justification, fairness, and justice. The mother's voice has been silent."[342] Consequently, Noddings proposed a feminine approach to ethics and moral education – the ethic of care – "rooted in receptivity, relatedness, and responsiveness."[343] Her vision for a caring school stemmed from a need for a new way of doing schooling:

---

336. Hawk and Lyons, "Please Don't Give Up."
337. Gilligan, "In a Different Voice."
338. Gilligan, *Different Voice*, 174.
339. Ibid., 19.
340. Ibid., 174.
341. Ibid., 19.
342. Noddings, *Caring*, 1. Nel Noddings could have been influenced by Carol Gilligan since she quoted Gilligan in her first work.
343. Ibid., 2.

> The traditional organization of schooling is intellectually and morally inadequate for the contemporary society. We live in an age troubled by social problems that force us to reconsider what we do in schools. At a time when thinkers in many fields are moving toward postmodernism – a rejection of one objective method, distinctively individual subjectivity, universalizability in ethics, and universal criteria for epistemology – too many educators are still wedded to the modernist view of progress and its outmoded tools.[344]

For Noddings, the goal of education is the moral life, the "nurturance of the ethical ideal";[345] and education should work towards producing "competent, caring, loving, and lovable people."[346] "Education should be organized around themes of care ... All students should be engaged in a general education that guides them in caring for self, the intimate others, global others, plants, animals, and the environment, the human-made world, and ideas."[347]

Noddings' understanding is that caring is not an individual attribute or virtue: "Caring is a way of being in relation, not a set of behaviors"[348] and "relations, not individuals, are ontologically basic."[349] "The caring attitude that lies at the heart of all ethical behavior is universal."[350] That means, "we recognize human encounter and effective response as a basic fact of human existence."[351] And since relations are ontologically basic, the caring relation is considered ethically basic.[352] The same goes for the desire to be cared for.[353]

Using Martin Heidegger's concept of *dasein*,[354] which in essence is care, as well as "the very Being of human life" and "the ultimate reality in life,"[355]

---

344. Noddings, *Challenge to Care*, 173.
345. Noddings, *Caring*, 6.
346. Noddings, *Challenge to Care*, 154, 174.
347. Ibid., 173.
348. Ibid., 17.
349. Noddings, *Caring*, xiii.
350. Ibid., 92.
351. Ibid., 4.
352. Ibid., 3.
353. Noddings, *Challenge to Care*, 17.
354. Heidegger, *Being and Time*, 66; see ch. 6.
355. Noddings, *Challenge to Care*, 15.

Noddings stated that "a *caring relation* is, in its most basic form, a connection or encounter between two human beings – a carer and a recipient of care," or the one-caring and the cared-for.[356] For this relation to work, the one-caring must practice *engrossment* [or attention][357] and *motivational displacement*[358] while the cared-for must show *responsiveness* or *reciprocity*.[359] In caring, the one-caring attends receptively to the cared-for through listening, looking, and feeling; and sees the cared-for in the best possible light. In caring, the motives of the carer are displaced. Instead, the carer adopts and promotes the goals of the cared-for as her/his own. In order to nurture the ethical ideal and teach the cared-for (e.g. students) how to care, the one-caring (e.g. teacher) has to model care through dialogue, practice, and confirmation.[360]

In applying her theory to practice in schools, Noddings sought to make some practical suggestions as to how a public school could be organized around themes of care.[361] However, her target audience was primarily children. Linda L. Lyman believed that "if belonging to a caring school community contributes to emotional states that enhance learning, then the impact of caring on learning is certainly not confined to a particular age group."[362] Hence, those involved in higher education too have experimented with Noddings' relational care ethics. Within their study group, a group of women in graduate programs utilized a critical ethic of care to guide their

---

356. Ibid. (original emphasis).
357. "Engrossment" means "nonselective attention or total presence to the other for the duration of the caring interval" (Noddings, "Ethic of Caring," 219–220). Noddings has since replaced "engrossment" with "attention" since the former could be misconstrued as infatuation. However, this attention is better conceived as "receptive attention" because the one-caring listens without bias and "is truly open to the other, vulnerable to what she or he is feeling" ("Complexity in Caring," 8, 9).
358. "Motivational displacement" means "her [the carer's] motive energy flows in the direction of the other's needs and projects" (Noddings, "Ethic of Caring," 220).
359. Noddings, *Caring*, 150 (original emphasis). "Responsiveness and reciprocity" refers to the recognition and response on the part of the cared-for of the caring given by the one-caring (*Challenge to Care*, xxv). Noddings admitted that form of responses expressed by cared-for ideas and objects would be different from cared-for people or other living things. She wrote: "And we know that well-tended engines purr, polished instruments gleam, and fine glassware glistens" (ibid., 20). Reciprocity means that caring is reciprocated but because many relations are not equal, "we do not expect the cared-for to balance the relation by doing what the one-caring (or carer) does" (*Caring*, xiii).
360. Noddings, *Caring*, 175–197.
361. Noddings, *Challenge to Care*; "Teaching Themes of Caring."
362. Lyman, *How Do They Know You Care*, 149.

discussions and interactions: (1) critique without negating, (2) examine one's position and privilege in society, (3) examine personal circumstances in relation to one's academic progress, (4) reconstruct self, and (5) lift others.[363] The ethic of care is also crucial in environmental and place-based education, where students learn to interact with the natural world and become more informed to address and make decisions regarding environmental issues.[364] Of utmost importance is

> the development of attentive relationships between a carer and a cared-for (student-student, student-instructor, student-context, participants-learning environment). The goal is to integrate it as a guiding morality in the classroom and as a bridge to the beyond-school world, where it can lead students to right action on behalf of the beings, places, and ideas they value in relationship.[365]

Janet C. Richards experimented with "Caring Conversations" with graduate education majors so that they could have a better understanding of diversity issues and develop relational caring attitudes.[366]

Rud (see above p. 112) considered care as a parallel educational practice to hospitality because the caring relationship, marked by engrossment and motivational displacement, makes it possible for "both openness to receive others, and an ego displacement that would allow reaching out to others."[367] From their ethnographic study, Dwight Rogers and Jaci Webb observed that "it is more than regard or protection, more than affect alone. In the classrooms that we observed, caring is the basis for thoughtful educational and moral decision making, and it requires action."[368] Rather than using the

---

363. Cutri et al., "Honorable Sisterhood."
364. Goralnik et al., "Environmental Pedagogy."
365. Ibid., 420.
366. Richards, "Challenges."
367. Rud, "Learning in Comfort," 127.
368. Rogers and Webb, "Ethic of Caring," 174. Dwight Rogers and Jaci Webb's observations were done on non-higher education. However, what they observed would still be valid for higher education. They also highlighted the ambiguity of the term *caring* – it is open to different interpretations, and it means different things from the teachers' and students' perspectives (for more, see ibid.). For instance, Lynn Isenbarger and Michalinos Zembylas' research listed three categories of caring: pedagogical caring, moral caring, and cultural caring. For them, "there is not simply one kind of caring encompassing all actions and beliefs; there are several kinds as a result of emotional labor involved and the context in which it takes place" (Isenbarger and Zembylas, "Emotional Labour of Caring," 132).

biblical injunction to treat others in the same way you want them to treat you (Matt 7:12; Luke 6:31), Noddings instead advised: "Do unto others as they would have done unto them."[369] This was to encourage one to think of and understand the feelings of the other.

The Practice of Inclusion

The changing demographics brought about by globalization throughout the world are also challenging educational institutions to re-examine the notions of diversity and inclusion within and without their institutional walls. Miroslav Volf observed:

> In recent decades the issue of identity has risen to the forefront of discussions in social philosophy. If the liberation movements of the sixties were all about equality – above all gender equality and racial equality – major concerns of the nineties seem to have been about identity – about the recognition of distinct identities of persons who differ in gender, skin colour or culture.[370]

There has been a growing body of literature on diversity and inclusion addressing the issue of multiculturalism at all educational levels,[371] sexual orientations/gender identities,[372] and disabilities.[373] However, diversity should embrace the whole spectrum of human differences, as Marilyn Loden and Judy Rosener have suggested:

> Diversity is **otherness** or those human qualities that are different from our own and outside the groups to which we belong, yet present in other individuals and groups. **Others**, then, are people who are different from us along one or several dimensions such

---

369. Noddings, "Language of Care Ethics," 55.
370. Volf, "Trinity," 408.
371. Ellsworth, "Why Doesn't This Feel Empowering"; hooks *Teaching to Transgress*; Pang, Rivera, and Mora, "Ethic of Caring"; Richardson and Villenas, "'Other' Encounters"; Baumgartner and Johnson-Bailey, "Fostering Awareness"; Miller, Kostogriz, and Gearon, *Professional Ethics*; Leung and Chiu, "Multicultural Experience"; Schoorman and Bogotch, "Conceptualisations"; Ameny-Dixon, "Why Multicultural Education"; Gupta, "'Multicultural' Classroom"; Kumi-Yeboah and James, "Relevance of Multicultural Education"; Whitsed and Volet, "Fostering Intercultural Dimensions."
372. Rankin, "Campus Climates"; Renn, "LGBT and Queer Research."
373. Sachs and Schreuer, "Students with Disabilities"; Supple and Abgenyega, "Developing the Understanding."

as age, ethnicity, gender, race, sexual/affectional orientation, and so on.[374]

Even the marginalized indigenous ways of knowing that Kuokkanen (see above p. 125) has written about constitute an issue of diversity we have to reckon with.

When dealing with the minority, disabled, or disadvantaged, as Luke Bretherton pointed out, tolerance or respect for the "other," is inadequate:

> Intrinsic to concrete respect is the recognition that the "other" is not the same as me, they possess an irreducible "otherness." Tolerance is ill-suited to promoting such recognition since it involves seeing everyone as the same: autonomous self-reflexive subjects. And while tolerance aims at equality of treatment and a generalised respect, in practice it can often result in discrimination.[375]

Tolerance, merely getting along with others, is inadequate for it fails to see and receive the other (e.g. a mentally handicapped) as a gift.[376] Instead, embrace, as enacted by Volf's metaphor (see above p. 56) and which several authors have mentioned in their discourses (e.g. Larson, Smith and Carvill), serves better in this regard. For Volf, the drama of embrace is enacted through four movements: "opening the arms, waiting, closing the arms, and opening them again."[377] It expresses *"the will to give ourselves to others and 'welcome' them, to readjust our identities to make space for them, is prior to any judgment about others, except that of identifying them in their humanity."*[378] All these require double vision, the ability "to see the world 'from there' and 'from here.'"[379] It is natural for us to see "from here"; however, to see "from there" means: (1) stepping outside ourselves, (2) crossing a social boundary and moving into

---

374. Loden and Rosener, *Workforce America*, 18 (original emphasis).
375. Bretherton, "Tolerance," 90; see Sullivan, "Practice of Inclusion"; Larson, "Classroom Dialogue."
376. Newman, *Untamed Hospitality*, 144.
377. Volf, *Exclusion and Embrace*, 141; for details, see 140–147.
378. Ibid., 29 (original emphasis).
379. Ibid., 250–251.

the other's world, (3) taking the other to our own world, and (4) repeating the process.[380]

Essentially, "the central idea captured by Volf's image of embrace is that of entering into the perspective of another without losing sight of one's own."[381] Charles R. Foster elucidated this idea when he employed Volf's metaphor of embrace to address diversity in theological education.[382] In teacher-student interaction, when we open our arms, we welcome everyone, regardless of their sociocultural backgrounds, into the experience of teaching and learning. By waiting in silence, we communicate our willingness to listen, creating a space for dialogue. Patiently we wait. And when mutual trust is established, we are able to close the arms and engage in a free and deep exchange of ideas and thoughts. We release each other when we open the arms. Having shared, we are now able to respect each other's gifts and differences, and we are also now able to accept the other for who he or she is and encourage the other to return to his or her cultural location. Similarly, in Julia Speller's address to the faculty in Trinity Christian College (Palos Heights, Illinois) at a faculty forum entitled "Relevant Pedagogy and the Dilemma of Diversity" on 4 October 2004, she said,

> The final release is done with the recognition that cultural and racial differences are not problems to overcome or reconcile but gifts to be celebrated. There should not be the naïve notion that all will agree with each other but a mutual respect that appreciates cultural distinctions without needing to fully understand them.[383]

The giving and receiving embedded in Volf's metaphor of embrace is clearly a hospitable approach towards the other who is different.

Research studies have shown that students benefit when they learn among diverse peers.[384] Yet, students in culturally diverse classrooms "who feel unsafe, unconnected, and disrespected are often unmotivated to learn."[385]

---

380. Ibid., 251–253.
381. Larson, "Classroom Dialogue."
382. Foster, "Diversity in Theological Education," 29–30.
383. Kimberly Fabian, "Speller Encourages Faculty to Embrace Diversity," Trinity Christian College news release, 6 October 2004, http://tcc.trnty.edu/new/archive/100604/.
384. Terenzini et al., "Racial and Ethnic Diversity"; Gurin et al., "Diversity and Higher Education"; Chang et al., "Educational Benefits."
385. Ginsberg and Wlodkowski, *Diversity and Motivation*, 3.

Students learn better when they feel they are included in a group, that is, when they feel *respected* by and *connected* to the group.[386] There is a need for "a safe, inclusive, and respectful learning environment."[387] Such a learning environment is necessary because diversity in classrooms can bring about disequilibrium and conflicts[388] and "inequality in classroom interaction has a poisonous effect on trust."[389]

The Practice of Dialogue

Globalization has brought about significant demographic changes across the globe and into the classroom. Learning institutions are now filled with learners from diverse cultural, ethnic, language, and religious backgrounds. In the light of the challenges posed by diversity and multiculturalism in the classroom, Graham Badley argued for the need of a pedagogy of tolerance and reasonableness in higher education institutions so as "to promote a *culture of tolerance, humanism and individuality* and reject the *coercive and dogmatic fundamentalist cultures* now emerging in the East and the West."[390] This could be achieved if we strive to be reasonable to others and engage them in conversations.[391]

Conversation, or dialogue, including questioning, is used as an instructional technique in social constructivist classrooms where learners co-construct knowledge in dialogue with others.[392] Even for Paulo Freire, dialogue plays a crucial role in his problem-posing education and is "indispensable to the act of cognition which unveils reality."[393] Opposing the banking system of education and advocating the critical or progressive education, Freire

---

386. Ibid., 40 (emphasis mine). Establishing inclusion is the first of four mutually dependent motivational conditions for motivating postsecondary students in culturally diverse classrooms to learn. The other three motivational conditions are: (1) developing attitude, (2) enhancing meaning, and (3) engendering competence (see ibid., 37).
387. Ibid., ix.
388. Gurin et al., "Diversity and Higher Education," 362–363.
389. Billson and Tiberius, "Effective Social Arrangements," 90.
390. Badley, "Against Fundamentalism," 414 (original emphasis).
391. Ibid., 417.
392. Mayo, "Dialogue as Constructivist Pedagogy"; Richardson, "Constructivist Pedagogy"; Beck and Kosnik, *Innovations in Teacher Education*; Grant, "Improvising Together"; Kaufmann, "Practice of Dialogue."
393. Freire, *Pedagogy of the Oppressed*, 83.

believed that the teacher and student should participate and construct knowledge together.[394] "Without dialogue there is no communication, and without communication there can be no true education."[395] And, through dialogue, the students become "critical co-investigators" with the teacher.[396] Furthermore, "through dialogue, the teacher-of-the-students and the students-of-the-teacher cease to exist and a new term emerges: teacher-student with students-teachers."[397] And, for Freire, trust should naturally, or logically, emerge from such dialogical education:

> Founding itself upon love, humility, and faith, dialogue becomes a horizontal relationship of which mutual trust between the dialoguers is the logical consequence. It would be a contradiction in terms if dialogue – loving, humble, and full of faith – did not produce this climate of mutual trust, which leads the dialoguers into ever closer partnership in the naming of the world.[398]

It would be like what Oakeshott envisioned: "Different universes of discourse meet, acknowledge each other and enjoy an oblique relationship which neither requires nor forecasts their being assimilated to each other."[399]

Hence, dialogue, viewed from this perspective, is relational, not simply a speech act. However, this may be difficult to achieve when there is imbalance of power. Elizabeth Ellsworth cautioned that

> dialogue in its conventional sense is impossible in the culture at large because at this historical moment, power relations between raced, classed, and gendered students and teachers are unjust. The injustice of these relations and the way in which those injustices distort communication cannot be overcome in a classroom, no matter how committed the teacher and students are to "overcoming conditions that perpetuate suffering."[400]

---

394. Freire, *Pedagogy of Freedom*, ch. 2.
395. Freire, *Pedagogy of the Oppressed*, 92–93.
396. Ibid., 81.
397. Ibid., 80.
398. Ibid., 91.
399. As quoted in Bennett, "Academy and Hospitality," 24.
400. Ellsworth, "Why Doesn't This Feel Empowering," 316.

Floya Anthias, writing about feminism and multiculturalism, also acknowledged this power issue: "Dialogue becomes monologue in the colonial or hegemonic/hierarchized encounter (or may do so depending on the practices of hierarchy). In such a case, dialogue is a way of enabling power, i.e. it is a legitimization tool and there is constrained or enforced dialogue."[401] True dialogue entails "going beyond one's own point of view so that both parties shift their position, not coming closer to each other but developing an alternative vision which is transformative."[402] Anthias' notion of dialogue seems to parallel Marion H. Larson's description of dialogue as embrace (namely, Volf's embrace; see above p. 56):

> From either vantage point, we open ourselves to possibility. We wait long enough to live with an idea that we might not have previously considered. We wrap our arms around an idea, allowing it to become part of us while at the same time maintaining our distinctness. Having inhabited a perspective and allowed it to inhabit us for a long time, we open ourselves again – to let go of this idea (or parts of it) and to signal that we are open for future interchanges.[403]

Clearly, dialogue is a cultural practice that can be colored by several factors such as race, class, gender, and age.[404] As a result, some voices, even indigenous epistemologies, may be intentionally or unintentionally silenced.[405] The absence of a safe environment actually exacerbates this situation. As hooks rightly observed, "it is the absence of a feeling of safety that often promotes prolonged silence or lack of student engagement" in the classroom.[406] However, in hospitable dialogue, we can engage with each other in ways that work against oppressive social formations.[407] If the privileged (e.g. the teacher, the majority) could share their "power," it could create a safe space for dialogue and for multiple voices, especially the minority and marginalized,

---

401. Anthias, "Beyond Feminism," 282.
402. Ibid.
403. Larson, "Classroom Dialogue," under "Classroom of Embrace."
404. Jones, "Cross-Cultural Dialogue," 304–306; Kaufmann, "Practice of Dialogue," 460–462.
405. Kuokkanen, "Toward a New Relation"; "What Is Hospitality."
406. hooks, *Teaching to Transgress*, ch. 10; see Ellsworth, "Why Doesn't This Feel Empowering," 315; Orner, "Interrupting the Calls," 81.
407. Ellsworth, "Why Doesn't This Feel Empowering," 324.

to be heard. hooks personally believed that crucial thinkers who desire to change their teaching practices should themselves cross boundaries and dialogue with other critical thinkers.⁴⁰⁸ True to her convictions, she crossed boundaries and had critical exchanges with several others on separate occasions – a black male scholar Cornel West, a white feminist thinker Mary Childers, and a white philosopher Ron Scapp.

As an educational practice, dialogue not only acknowledges the multiplicity of communicative forms but also creates a safe space that allows for an openness to the other and a reciprocity whereby there is a willingness to receive from the other.⁴⁰⁹ This precisely is an enactment of hospitality: "it gives, speaking, and receives, listening."⁴¹⁰ In short, "the art of conversation is the art of hospitality."⁴¹¹ Dzintra Iliško phrased it this way:

> The pedagogy of hospitality assumes the possibility of dialog as it denotes being oriented to other and the practical accomplishments of articulation. . . .
>
> Dialog means finding a creative and sustainable balance or interaction between dominant values and openness to even contradictory values.⁴¹²

It is more than just understanding each other's perspectives; rather, it is to establish a common, respectful space to acknowledge and engage our differences.⁴¹³ And all this involves listening – "openness to others, sensitivity to listen and to be listened to."⁴¹⁴ Quinn conveyed the same thought with regard to the practice of questioning. "Questioning requires the art of hospitality wherein we are not only open to the radical other it may introduce – listening to, learning from, the stranger who comes even as we question or critique her; but also caring for this other, extending and offering our 'there' to him as well."⁴¹⁵

---

408. hooks, *Teaching to Transgress*, ch. 10.
409. Burbules, "Limits of Dialogue," 262.
410. Phipps and Barnett, "Academic Hospitality," 253.
411. Ibid.
412. Iliško, "Educational Encounters," 201.
413. Ellsworth, "Why Doesn't This Feel Empowering," 324.
414. Iliško, "Educational Encounters," 201.
415. Quinn, "'No Room,'" 108.

The practice of care implies attentive caring towards the other. The practice of inclusion implies respect for the other's otherness. And the practice of dialogue implies an openness to listen to the other and to be listened by the other. All these three educational practices in contemporary higher education involve an "other." Given the fact that hospitality is "other-oriented,"[416] it is, thus, not surprising that professionals in higher education, as well as Christian higher education and theological education, have used the metaphor of hospitality in their efforts to re-conceptualize education for the new global age.

Summary

This chapter began with recognizing the shifting trends in higher education: from teaching to learning, from personal constructivism to social constructivism, from cognition to emotion. The shifts in emphases have shown that effective learning needs a supportive learning environment – characterized by openness and mutual trust among teacher and learners – that allows both teacher and learners to freely explore and connect with both their cognitive and affective parts of self.[417] Inextricably related to this climate of openness and mutual trust is a positive relationship and interactions between teacher and students.

The literature review that followed examined the writings of educators who have looked to hospitality in their re-conceptualizing of higher education amidst the changing educational landscape. In their hospitality-related discourses, contemporary practices of care, inclusion, and dialogue were suggested as possible ways of relating to the other. It is, thus, evident that hospitality allows for the creation of a space in higher education institutions, even theological institutions, "in which teachers and learners [can] develop a stance of openness to the other – the other of the teacher, learners, the subject of study itself."[418]

The concepts of care, inclusion, and dialogue discussed here will emerge, albeit differently, when we explore the biblical practice of hospitality in the

---

416. Kuokkanen, "What Is Hospitality," 71.
417. See Powell and Kalina, "Cognitive and Social Constructivism," 248.
418. Mann, "Personal Inquiry," 122.

next chapter. Both perspectives – contemporary and biblical – then provide the basis for our discussion on how hospitality can be practiced in theological education in chapter 5.

4

The Biblical Basis for the Motif of Hospitality in Theological Education

In the previous chapters, I have explored extant literature related to hospitality in Christian higher education, theological education, and higher education. We have also observed how many professionals in these higher education institutions have cited the practices of care, inclusion, and dialogue as parallel practices of hospitality in their discourses. I have also examined these three practices in the context of contemporary higher education. This chapter seeks to examine the biblical concept of hospitality through the images of God as host, Jesus as guest-host, and the early faith communities as hosts. Based on the understanding that metaphors have a profound influence on our educational and pedagogical practices (see above p. 6), this chapter seeks to present a biblically informed metaphor of hospitality that can help guide theological educators seeking the holistic formation of their students. The findings of this chapter will serve as the basis for us to assess the relevance of our literature findings on hospitality and parallel practices of hospitality in contemporary higher education in relation to theologically grounded concepts of hospitality (see below ch. 5), thus enabling theological educators to conceptualize their educational task in ways that are consistent with their theological beliefs.[1]

In Adelbert Denaux's article on "The Theme of Divine Visits and Human (In)hospitality) in Luke-Acts: Its Old Testament and Graeco-Roman Antecedents," he noted that "for Luke, hospitality is a key to understanding

---
1. See Yeatts, "Why Are We Doing This," 38.

and describing reality: it is an integral part of human life and of the way God cares for his people and Jesus deals with men and women."[2] However, a study of biblical texts reveals that hospitality is a key to understanding and describing reality in both the Old and New Testaments, not just in the writings of Luke. The Israelites experienced God as a gracious host who fed his people and promised a bountiful feast in the messianic age. Jesus himself was the sublime guest-host who came to the world as a stranger but became the ultimate host by offering his body as living bread to the world. He himself practiced the hospitality of the kingdom of God through his table fellowship with not just the rich but also the poor and the marginalized. Moreover, hospitality was an integral part of life in the emerging faith communities of the apostolic age as the Christian believers welcomed one another and received others into their homes.

God as Host

My consideration of God as host is largely inspired by Walter Brueggemann's treatment of the metaphors of sustenance in his voluminous work on the theology of the Old Testament.[3] Brueggemann believed there is a need for a *"contextual shift from hegemonic interpretation ... toward a pluralistic interpretive context"* in the theological interpretation of the Old Testament.[4] Holding the view that Israel's utterances or testimonies regarding God constitute the theological substance of the Old Testament, Brueggemann framed his entire work on the imagery of a courtroom trial since the process of testimony-dispute-advocacy allows for a plurality of witnesses.[5] Through this imagery, he investigates the nature of God as revealed by Israel's core testimony, counter-testimony, unsolicited testimony, and embodied testimony.

---

2. Denaux, "Divine Visits," 258.
3. Brueggmann, *Theology of the Old Testament*, ch. 6. It must be noted the phrase "God as host" has no relation to the divine epithets "LORD of hosts" and "God of hosts." These titles of God frequently appear in various English versions of the Bible, such as the KJV, NASB, and NRSV, but are not related to hospitality. The NIV (1984, preface) translated these titles as "LORD Almighty" and "God Almighty" respectively, retaining the Hebrew sense of God as "he who is sovereign over all the 'hosts' (powers) in heaven and earth, especially over the 'hosts' (armies) of Israel" (see Stallman, "Divine Hospitality," 114–115).
4. Brueggmann, *Theology of the Old Testament*, 710 (original emphasis).
5. Ibid., xvi–xvii.

In his consideration of Israel's core testimony about God, Brueggemann proposed that *"in speaking about Yahweh, Israel regularly moves from the particular to the general, from the verb to the adjective to the noun."*[6] "Nouns used for Yahweh in the Old Testament are metaphors, and there is no one-to-one match between the metaphor and that to which it refers."[7] These noun-metaphors, taken from different aspects of Israel's daily life, "bear witness to Yahweh's elusive constancy" and enabled Israel to understand the constancy and substance of an invisible God.[8]

Brueggemann divided his metaphors into two categories: (1) metaphors of governance that portray the sovereign God as one who orders life in the world (e.g. God as judge, king, warrior, father), and (2) metaphors of sustenance that portray a tender God who nurtures life (e.g. God as artist, healer, gardener-vinedresser, mother, shepherd).[9] Since Brueggemann himself acknowledged that *"the work of voicing Yahweh in nouns is never finished,"* I would like to suggest another noun-metaphor that Israel used to testify concerning the tender God who nurtures life and to express their relationship with him – God as host.[10] This understanding of the centrality of hospitality, and of God as host in the Old Testament is also attested by biblical scholars such as Waldemar Janzen, Robert C. Stallman, and Victor H. Matthews.[11]

The Practice of Hospitality in the Life of the Israelites

Israel derived its noun-metaphors from its experiences of everyday life, "using the human known to throw light on the divine unknown," to articulate its relationship with God.[12] Although terms like *host*, *guest*, and *hospitality* do not appear in the Hebrew Bible, "the lack of Hebrew lexical stock for the field of hospitality should not be construed as an indication that ancient Israel

---

6. Ibid., 230 (original emphasis).
7. Ibid.
8. Ibid., 233.
9. Ibid., 233–261.
10. Ibid., 262 (original emphasis).
11. Janzen, *Old Testament Ethics*; Stallman, "Divine Hospitality"; Matthews, *Old Testament Turning Points*.
12. Caird, *Language and Imagery*, 19.

had no concept of hospitality or that it held the practice in low esteem."[13] The practice of hospitality was part of the fabric of ancient Israelite society, in fact, of the whole ancient Near East. Thus, the image of God as host was most probably generated from the hospitality customs practiced by the Israelites, and it helped them to better understand how God related to them.

The story of Abraham and his three guests in Genesis 18:1–16 is a pivotal passage where the study of hospitality is concerned. In fact, it can be considered "a formative model of hospitality" for both Jews and Christians.[14] The New Testament writer of Hebrews probably alluded to it when he wrote: "Do not neglect to show hospitality to strangers, for by doing that some have entertained angels without knowing it" (Heb 13:2). Abraham's tent was pitched near a cluster of trees at Mamre. One hot day, Abraham was sitting at the opening of his tent when he saw three strangers standing in front of him. He rushed out to greet them with great respect, inviting them to rest under the tree and offering them water to wash their feet and a piece of bread for refreshment. When they accepted his invitation, Abraham acted with great haste to prepare the meal with the help of his wife Sarah and a servant. He served his guests a lavish meal of freshly baked cakes made of fine flour, curds and milk, and the meat of a choice tender calf. He also stood by them under the tree while they ate. Then one of the three men spoke and gave Abraham a promise, a son in a year's time – something unthinkable as Sarah had reached menopause. When they got up to leave, Abraham accompanied them to send them on their way.

This short story introduces to us some behavioral conventions that are basic to Jewish hospitality: the warm reception of guests, the offer of water for washing the feet, the provision of food and shelter, and the sending off of the guests by the host.[15] Similar actions are repeated in other hospitality stories such as the hospitality of Lot to two travelers (Gen 19:1–22), Reuel to Moses (Exod 2:15–22), Rahab to the two spies (Josh 2:1–21), an old man in Gibeah to a certain Levite from Ephraim (Judg 19:1–28), and the rich Shunammite woman to Elisha (2 Kgs 4:8–17).

---

13. Stallman, "Divine Hospitality," 115.
14. Arterbury, *Entertaining Angels*, 71.
15. This work discusses the basic typical actions of hospitality as practiced by the Jews in the Old Testament. For more detailed forms of this social convention, see ibid.

Reception of the Guest

Although hospitality is often initiated by the male host, often the head of the household, extending a warm welcome to the traveler passing by (Gen 18:1-5; 19:1-3; Judg 19:17-20), it is quite possible for females to do likewise (Josh 2:1; 2 Kgs 4:8). Reuel even extended the invitation of hospitality to Moses through his daughters (Exod 2:20). Then, water is usually provided for the guests to wash their feet (Gen 18:4; 19:2; Judg 19:21). Having traveled for long hours on dusty roads, this gesture would probably be gladly received by any guest.

At times, it is the guest who requests hospitality (Gen 24:23; 1 Sam 25:5-8; 1 Kgs 17:10-11). Rebekah responded to the request from Abraham's servant positively (Gen 24:24-25). She ran home to inform her family, and her brother, Laban, hastened to welcome the servant sent by Abraham (Gen 24:28-31). Laban, as a gracious host, provided water for the servant and those traveling with him to wash their feet and straw and fodder for the camels (Gen 24:32). On the other hand, the request for hospitality by David through his servants was rudely turned down by Nabal (1 Sam 25:10-11).

Provision of Food and Protection

The host often provides a meal to his guests (Gen 18:5-8; 19:3; 24:33; implied in Exod 2:20; Judg 19:21; 2 Kgs 4:8) and, if necessary, lodging for the night (Gen 19:2; 24:54; Exod 2:21; Josh 2:1; Judg 19:20). The rich Shunammite woman even suggested to her husband to build a room in the attic for Elijah so that he could stay with them whenever he passed their way (2 Kgs 4:9-10). When Nabal refused to entertain David and his troops, it was his wife Abigail who came to remedy the situation (1 Sam 25:18-31). She loaded her donkeys with bread, wine, grain, raisins, and figs and went without her husband's knowledge to meet David.

As long as the guests remain under his care, the host is responsible for their safety (Gen 19:4-9; Josh 2:3-6; Judg 19:22-25). Protecting one's guests is "a sacred duty" and "the cardinal principle of oriental hospitality."[16] The streets of Sodom and Gibeah were so unsafe that both Lot (Gen 19:3) and the old man (Judg 19:20) insisted that the visitors should spend the night in their homes. Both of their commitments to being good hosts are evident

---

16. Wenham, *Genesis 16-50*, 55.

when Lot offered his two virgin daughters (Gen 19:7–8), and the old man, his virgin daughter and the Levite's concubine (Judg 19:23–24), to the townsfolk who demanded to have the guests so that they could sexually abuse them. John Skinner observed that "Lot's readiness to sacrifice the honor of his daughters, though abhorrent to Hebrew morality (see Judg 19:25, 30), shows him as a courageous champion of the obligations of hospitality in a situation of extreme embarrassment, and is recorded to his credit."[17]

Sending Off of the Guest

We only see the host sending off the guest properly in the story of Abraham's hospitality (Gen 18:16). In Lot's case, it was the two guests who sent him outside the city of Sodom (Gen 19:16). Rebekah was sent off by her family members with their blessings (Gen 24:59–60). Rahab sent her two guests off in an unusual manner – by letting them down the wall of the city by a rope through her window (Josh 2:15). Moses married one of Reuel's daughters and settled down in the land of Midian for a period of time (Exod 2:21). When he left, his father-in-law sent him off with words of peace (Exod 4:18). Even if the stay is brief, once a relationship has been forged, guests are welcome to return to their host's house in the future (Gen 18:14; 2 Kgs 4:10).

The practice of hospitality and the metaphor of God as host thus provided the Israelites speech to utter their relationship with a God who is characteristically elusive.

Israel's Experience of God as Host

Israel's testimony of God as host arose from their personal experiences of God's bountiful provision.[18] In his dissertation, Stallman sought to demonstrate that "the language in the Pentateuch concerning God utilizes a metaphorical perspective in which God is depicted in terms of a host who provides food

---

17. Skinner, *Genesis*, 307.

18. God was a gracious host but his guests were often rude and ungracious guests, violating the host-guest protocol in their disregard for the host's prescribed "menu" and regulations. Inappropriate response to the generosity of the divine host might incur a withdrawal of God's blessings and gracious provision of food (e.g. the curse of hardship and toil on Adam in Gen 3:17–19). This aspect of Israel as ungracious guests is dealt with at length with in Robert C. Stallman's dissertation ("Divine Hospitality"). However, this work does not cover this aspect as its focus is the image of God as host rather than on the guests.

for guests."[19] The experience of God as host or "a provider of food or one who spreads a banquet" began when Adam and Eve were welcomed as guests into God's house – the newly-created cosmos.[20] Matthews described the Garden of Eden as the first gift from God to humankind, making it "the prototypical hospitality tale."[21] "Furthermore, this 'house' is prepared as a home and its 'pantry' is well-stocked in order to provide for the bearers of God's image, the focus of God's favor."[22] As Judith E. McKinlay highlighted, "God is notably careful to stress the divine role of provider: *See, I have given to you* ([Gen] 1:29)."[23]

For Stallman, the idea of God as a gracious host who abundantly provides for his guests is repeatedly seen in the Pentateuch: human beings after the fall and the deluge, Jacob the rude guest, Israel in the wilderness, and the elders at Sinai. The Pentateuch ends with the promise of "a land flowing with milk and honey" – "a land of hills and valleys, watered by rain from the sky, a land that the LORD your God looks after" (Deut 11:11-12). It is a land of abundance, hosted by God so that it could host God's favored guest, Israel. In Stallman's words: "The Promised Land is personified as Yahweh's unique guest who is so abundantly supplied that it, in turn, is suitably prepared to host Yahweh's personal guest, Israel."[24]

The image of God as host is definitely most vividly experienced by the Israelites in their years of wandering in the wilderness through his supply of water to quench their thirst (Exod 15:22-25; 17:1-7; Num 20:8-11) and sufficient provision of manna (Exod 16; Num 11:7-9), and even meat (Exod 16; Num 11:18-34), to fill their stomachs. Moses' recital of the mighty works of God includes God's self-revelation to his people: "I have led you forty years in the wilderness. The clothes on your back have not worn out, and the sandals on your feet have not worn out; you have not eaten bread, and you have not drunk wine or strong drink – so that you may know that I am the LORD your God" (Deut 29:5-6). Duane L. Christensen noted that the emphatic position of "bread" and "wine or strong drink" in the Hebrew text "indicates

---

19. Ibid., 271; see Thompson, *Soul Feast*, 129.
20. Stallman, "Divine Hospitality," 121.
21. Matthews, *Old Testament Turning Points*, 10, 31.
22. Stallman, "Divine Hospitality," 177.
23. McKinlay, "To Eat or Not to Eat," 74 (original emphasis).
24. Stallman, "Divine Hospitality," 257.

that it was supernatural food and water that sustained them up to this point in time."[25] S. R. Driver proposed that the miraculously provided food was a lesson for Israel, that they might learn who God is and their dependence upon him for their sustenance (see Deut 8:2–3).[26] The plentiful provision is again acknowledged by Moses in Deuteronomy 32:13–14:

> He set him atop the heights of the land, and fed him with produce of the field; he nursed him with honey from the crags, with oil from flinty rock; curds from the herd, and milk from the flock, with fat of lambs and rams; Bashan bulls and goats, together with the choicest wheat – you drank fine wine from the blood of grapes.

God's gracious hosting of his guest is further seen in his promise of a land:

> For the LORD your God is bringing you into a good land, a land with flowing streams, with springs and underground waters welling up in valleys and hills, a land of wheat and barley, of vines and fig trees and pomegranates, a land of olive trees and honey, a land where you may eat bread without scarcity, where you will lack nothing, a land whose stones are iron and from whose hills you may mine copper. You shall eat your fill and bless the LORD your God for the good land that he has given you. (Deut 8:7–10)

All these came to pass when Israel reached the promised land and the supply of heavenly manna ceased (Josh 5:12).

It is in Israel's worship, in the Psalter, that we find thankful acknowledgment of God's gracious provision as a host. Peter C. Craigie remarked: "The Book of Psalms as a whole contains Israel's songs and prayers which constitute the response of the chosen people to their revelation from God" that had emerged "out of a life lived in relationship with God."[27] They are "the central repository of the communal faith."[28] In fact, "Israel's faithful speech addressed to God is the substance of the Psalms."[29]

---

25. Christensen, *Deuteronomy 21:10–34:12*, 712.
26. Driver, *Deuteronomy*, 321.
27. Craigie, *Psalms 1–50*, 39, 40.
28. Broyles, *Conflict of Faith and Experience*, 11.
29. Brueggemann, *Psalms*, 15.

Israel gave thanks to a God "who gives food to all flesh" (Ps 136:25) – to those who fear him (Ps 111:5), to the hungry (Ps 146:7) – in due time (Ps 145:15–16). God's abundant provision is not limited to human beings. He also provides for all creatures that he created (Ps 104:10–28). When recounting the forty-year wilderness experience, Israel remembered the quails, the manna that came from heaven, and the water from the rock with an attitude of thanksgiving (Ps 105:40–41). God's continual supply in the wilderness is also remembered in Psalm 78 but in a more sombre tone, "not to recount the past, but to prompt the kind of remembrance that leads to change."[30]

While providing for his people, God the gracious host also protects his people, especially in the wilderness. He did not just "prepare a table in the wilderness" (Ps 78:19) but "he divided the sea and let them pass through it, and made the waters stand like a heap. In the daytime he led them with a cloud, and all night long with a fiery light" (Ps 78:13–14; see Ps 105:39). Without his provision and protection, it would have been impossible for the Israelites to survive the forty years of wandering in the wilderness. God's protective care and provision is also vividly portrayed in Psalm 23. Though commonly known as "The Shepherd Psalm," the imagery of God as host is also present.

In an essay in 1946, Julian Morgenstern noted that "practically all scholars are agreed that it [Psalm 23] presents the Deity in two distinctive roles – shepherd and host."[31] At the turn of the twentieth century, Charles Augustus Briggs and Emilie Grace Briggs described Psalm 23 as a "guest psalm," that expresses confidence in Yahweh, not just as shepherd and guide, but as host – "anointing His guest for the banquet and granting him perpetual hospitality" (see Ps 23:5–6).[32] The guest is given protection, the anointing and cup of welcome, as well as continual residence as guest in the house of the Lord. More recently, Gerald H. Wilson proposed that "in these verses, Yahweh is no longer shepherd but assumes the role of host, while the trusting follower sits as honored guest at his table. The picture is one of the realization of ultimate

---

30. Greenstein, "Mixing Memory and Design," 197.
31. Morgenstern, "Psalm 23," 14. However, Julian Morgenstern's essay essentially advanced E. Power's argument and maintained that Psalm 23 should be interpreted with just the sole imagery of God as shepherd (for this interpretation, see Merrill, "Psalm 23"; Dahood, *Psalms 1:1–50*, 145; Keller, *Psalm 23*; Boice, *Psalms 1–41*).
32. Briggs and Briggs, *Psalms*, 207.

communion with God himself."[33] In analyzing the structure of Psalm 23, Ron E. Tappy perceived two metaphors – shepherd and host. For him there is a "metaphorical harmony within the psalm."[34] As a host, God provides "safe haven and sustenance" for his guest, as a shepherd would for the sheep.[35] Hence, Psalm 23 testifies to God as a host who protects and provides for his guest.[36]

The image of God as divine host who provides for his people also sustained the Israelites when they were in exile. The promise of restoration prophesied by the prophets was often described in terms of agricultural bounty. There would be a plenteous supply of grain, wine, and oil (Jer 31:12; Hos 2:8, 22; Joel 2:19). Famine and hunger would be banished (Ezek 34:29; 36:29–30) when Israel would return to a fertile land with mountains dripping with wine, hills flowing with milk, and rivers flowing with water (Joel 3:18; see Amos 9:13–14; Zech 8:12). And it was none other than God the divine host who would protect and provide for poor and needy Israel (Isa 41:17–20).

This image of God as divine host also includes an anticipation of a future blessing when Israel will be invited to a sumptuous feast hosted by God.[37] The *messianic banquet* is a term referring to "the use of the symbols of food and a festive meal to signify immortality and the joys of the end time or afterlife."[38] At this "messianic" banquet, the presence of the Messiah is to be expected.

The myths of the ancient Near East depict gods gathering together and celebrating victory after a battle with a banquet.[39] Holding coronation banquets was also an ancient Near Eastern custom.[40] Such joyous celebration of feasting and drinking after a victory can also be seen in the Old Testament (1 Sam 11:15; 1 Kgs 1:9, 19, 25; 8:62–65; 2 Sam 6:18). For example, warriors

---

33. Wilson, *Psalms*, 436.
34. Tappy, "Psalm 23," 273.
35. Ibid., 274.
36. See Kraus, *Psalms 1–59*, 303–309; Bellinger and Arterbury, "Returning," 387–395.
37. Stallman, "Divine Hospitality," 120.
38. Smith, "Messianic Banquet," 4:788. Themes associated with the messianic banquet are: "victory over primordial enemies, eternal joyous celebration, abundance of food, the presence of the messiah (assumed), judgment, and the pilgrimage of the nations" ("Messianic Banquet Reconsidered, 67; "Messianic Banquet," 4:789). Our focus is the lavish provision of food and wine.
39. Smith, "Messianic Banquet," 4:789.
40. Oswalt, *Isaiah*, 462–463.

came from far and near, with the intent to crown David, and celebrated for three days (1 Chr 12:38–40). The messianic banquet described in Isaiah 25:6–8 could have drawn from this cultural tradition:

> On this mountain the LORD of hosts will make for all peoples a feast of rich food, a feast of well-aged wines, of rich food filled with marrow, of well-aged wines strained clear. And he will destroy on this mountain the shroud that is cast over all peoples, the sheet that is spread over all nations; he will swallow up death forever. Then the Lord God will wipe away the tears from all faces, and the disgrace of his people he will take away from all the earth, for the LORD has spoken.[41]

Although Isaiah 25 belongs to the often-called "the Apocalypse of Isaiah" (chapters 24–27),[42] John D. Oswalt felt that it is more eschatological than apocalyptic because "the interest is not in triumph outside time but within time," expressing general statements about God's final judgment of cosmic evil and his lordship over the world.[43] These chapters anticipate the end of the old age that is inaugurated by the reign of the Lord of Hosts on Mount Zion and in Jerusalem (Isa 24:23). At the same time, they also look forward to the celebration of the new age, the festive feast that the Lord of Hosts will host for all peoples on Mount Zion.[44] The banquet that God the host serves will be a lavish one. The guests will be served a feast of fat portions of the meat, portions of sacrifices that are reserved for God (Lev 3:3; 4:8–9; Ps 36:8). "But here God is giving the rich food to his people, as the host."[45] Besides that, the guests can enjoy the finest of wines and the best of meats.

The expectation of God as the bountiful host at the end of time can also be found in the literature of the intertestamental period.[46] In apocalyptic

---

41. Gray, *Isaiah*, 428; Kaiser, *Isaiah 13–39*, 200; Oswalt, *Isaiah*, 463; Steffen, "Messianic Banquet," under "The Messianic Banquet in Isaiah."
42. Gray, *Isaiah*, 397; Watts, *Isaiah 1–33*, xliii.
43. Oswalt, *Isaiah*, 440; see Childs, *Isaiah*, 173.
44. Childs, *Isaiah*, 173–174.
45. Oswalt, *Isaiah*, 463–464.
46. As our central focus of this chapter is the Old Testament and the New Testament, rabbinic literature is cited only when necessary. It is important to note that the contents of the Mishnah, Tosefta, Palestinian Talmud, Babylonian Talmud, and the Midrashim "may at times reflect ideas, practices and even statements handed down from earlier phases of

literature, there are references to the eating of the tree of life with the Son of Man in the age to come (*1 En.* 25:2-7; 62:13-16; *Sib. Or.* 2:313-321; 3:616-623; 744-740; *2 Bar.* 29:8; *T. Levi* 18:2-11).[47] In fact, the flesh of the mythical monsters, Behemoth and Leviathan, will become food for all (*2 Bar.* 29:4; *1 En.* 60:24; *4 Ezra* 6:52).[48] The literature of the Qumran community also mentions a meal where the Messiah of Israel would be present (1QSa 2:11-22; for more). Living at the end of days and expecting the Messiah to come any time, the members of the Qumran community "ate communal meals in anticipation of the great Messianic banquet which was to occur in the end of days."[49] And when the Messiah comes, he will "enrich the hungry" (4Q521 2 II, 13). Hence, we can see that Israel's expectation of God as host did not diminish even during the four hundred years of silence.

Israel's Moral Obligation in Relation to God as Host

The land is a prominent theme in the Old Testament. It is a land promised by God and a land given by God to Israel. It was promised to Abraham (Gen 12:7) and to his descendants, Isaac (Gen 26:3) and Jacob (Gen 28:13; 35:12). This promise was more like an elusive dream for the descendants of Abraham as they wandered in the wilderness. After forty years of wandering, standing on the plains of Moab beside the Jordan River, Moses challenged the people of Israel to "go in and take possession" of the land that God had promised to their forefathers (Deut 1:8). And they did, under the leadership of Joshua.

Jewish development, most particularly the days of the second Jewish commonwealth, which commenced with the return to Zion (538 BCE) and building of the Second Temple (c. 516 BCE), and concluded with the destruction of Jerusalem by Titus (70 CE)" (Gafni, "Historical Background," 2).

47. Unless specified, all biblical texts, as well as texts from the Septuagint, Apocrypha, Pseudepigrapha, Josephus, and Apostolic Fathers are taken from *BibleWorks 9* (2013). Citations from the Mishnah in this work are taken from Jacob Neusner, *Mishnah*. Citations from the Dead Sea Scrolls are taken from Florentino García Martínez and Eibert J. C. Tigchelaar, *Dead Sea Scrolls*.

48. The abundance of food and a lavish banquet in the messianic age are also found in rabbinic literature (*'Abot.* 3:19; 4:18). The eating of the Leviathan is also found in the Babylonian Talmud. The Holy One created a male and female Leviathan but "he castrated the male and killed the female preserving it in salt for the righteous in the world to come" (*b. B. Bat.* 74b; text taken from http://www.come-and-hear.com/bababathra/bababathra_74.html#PARTb).

49. Schiffman, "Communal Meals at Qumran," 55; "Eschatological Community," 106; see Cross, *Ancient Library*, 90; Priest, "Messianic Banquet," 228; Dunn, "Jesus, Table-Fellowship," 106.

God has given the land of Canaan to Israel for their possession. A plethora of biblical texts attests to this (e.g. Lev 25:38; Deut 5:31; Ps 105:11). The land is indeed Israel's land. However, there is another perspective that is often left out, that is, the land is God's land. In a footnote, Gerhard von Rad pointed out that in narrative accounts of Israel's possession of the land in the Hexateuch, there are only two instances where God is seen as the owner of the land – Leviticus 25:23 and Joshua 22:19.[50] God laid claim to ownership of the land when he said, "The land shall not be sold in perpetuity, for the land is mine; with me you are but aliens [*gēr*] and tenants [*tôšāb*]" (Lev 25:23).[51] Leviticus 25 addresses the land in relation to the year of Jubilee. The inheritance of each family cannot be sold since God holds the title deed to the land. In other words, "The LORD was the supreme landlord. Israel was his collective tenant."[52] Phrased in the language of a host-guest relationship, it would mean that God was the host and Israel was his guest. This concept was picked up by Janzen who described Israel as "living on its 'inheritance' as God's guests."[53] The same idea is reflected in NRSV's translation of Psalm 39:12 where Israel is described as God's "passing guest."[54]

"The land was an integral part not only of the LORD's faithfulness to Israel, but also of Israel's covenantal obligations to the LORD."[55] God's covenant with Israel includes a land, and "Israel's covenant identity includes being a stranger, an alien, a tenant in God's land – both dependent on God

---

50. Other references to God's ownership of the *'ereṣ*: (1) translated as "earth" (Exod 19:5; Ps 24:1), and (2) translated as "land" (Josh 22:19; Isa 14:2, 25; Jer 2:7; Ezek 36:5; 38:16; Joel 1:6; 3:2).

51. Rad, *Old Testament Theology*, 300, n. 11. In instances where *gēr* and *tôšāb* appear together (see Gen 23:4; Lev 25:23, 35, 47 [twice]; Num 35:15; 1 Chron 29:15; Ps 39:12), *tôšāb* can be regarded as synonymous with *gēr* (Konkel, "תּוֹשָׁב," 4:284) or even as a hendiadys (Kellermann, "גּוּר gûr," 2:448), meaning "resident alien" (Knauth, "Alien, Foreign Resident," 27). On its own, *tôšāb* is distinct from the *gēr* and refers to a foreigner who is a non-proselyte (see rules for participation in Passover meal for the *tôšāb* in Exodus 12:45 and the circumcised *gēr* in Exodus 12:48 and Numbers 9:14) (Kellermann, "גּוּר gûr," 2:448). A *tôšāb* is "possibly less assimilated socially and religiously than the *gēr*" (Konkel, "תּוֹשָׁב," 4:284, citing Vaux, *Ancient Israel*, 75–76).

52. Wright, *Old Testament Ethics*, 201.

53. Janzen, *Old Testament Ethics*, 177.

54. See Hartley, *Leviticus*, 324; Lipiński, "נָחַל," 9:332.

55. Wright, *Old Testament Ethics*, 92.

for welcome and provision and answerable to God for its own treatment of aliens and strangers."[56] This is explicitly expressed in Deuteronomy 10:17–19:

> For the LORD your God is God of gods and Lord of lords, the great God, mighty and awesome, who is not partial and takes no bribe, who executes justice for the orphan and the widow, and who loves the strangers [gēr], providing them food and clothing. You shall also love the stranger [gēr], for you were strangers [gērîm] in the land of Egypt.[57]

The *gēr* can be broadly defined as "a foreigner who is traveling through a land or one who has taken up residence in that land."[58] Such an individual has no familial or tribal affiliation in that community; hence, "he lacks the protection and the privileges which usually come from blood relationship and place of birth."[59] Although the term *gēr* could refer to an Israelite living among foreigners, especially the patriarchs in the Pentateuch (see Gen 23:4; Ps 105:12), it could also refer to a non-Israelite foreigner in the pentateuchal law (Exod 23:9; Lev 19:33–34; Deut 10:19).[60] In the case of the latter, the *gēr* would be considered a resident alien,[61] that is, "a landless foreigner residing with the Israelites under their protection."[62] Though *gērîm* do not have the same social status as the Israelites, they are subjected to the same laws (Exod 12:49; Num 15:16), with a few exceptions (Deut 14:21), and come under

---

56. Pohl, *Making Room*, 16.
57. *Gērim* is the plural of *gēr*.
58. Spencer, "Sojourn," 6:103.
59. Kellermann, "גּוּר gûr," 2:443.
60. Words such as *foreigner* and *stranger* and their cognates can be derived from the Hebrew roots *nkr* and *zwr*. In Deuteronomy, foreigners are categorized under two groups: (1) "*gērim*, who are receptive to the religion of Yahweh," and (2) "*nokrim*, for whom this is clearly not the case" (see Deut 14:21) (Ringgren, "נכר nkr," 9:426). The *gērim* were accorded more preferential treatment than the *nokrim* (see Deut 15:3; 23:20) since the former were more receptive to the God of Israel (Deut 29:9–12; 31:12–13). The *zār* in Deut 25:5 refers to a stranger who is outside the immediate family. It seemed that hospitality was granted to strangers (see Gen 18, 19; in these narratives, the guests were not labeled). A critical attitude towards foreigners appeared in the prophetic writings (Isa 2:6; Ezek 44:7, 9). "Nevertheless, isolation from foreigners or xenophobia does not appear in Israel during the monarchy but is first documented in the period of early Judaism, when the people were living under foreign domination and were concerned for their identity" (ibid.).
61. Knauth, "Alien, Foreign Resident," 29.
62. Christensen, *Deuteronomy 1–11*, 21.

Israel's protection.⁶³ Over the years, "however, under the sign of religious integration, the concept develops more and more toward the proselyte, the non-Israelite who becomes an adherent of the Yahweh faith," having equal rights as the Israelite (see Ezek 14:7; 47:22–23).⁶⁴

Without kin and land, the *gērîm* were in the same vulnerable position as the orphans and widows, and received special protection and care – justice and love – from the divine host of the land (Deut 10:17–19; 24:17–22). All of them were dependent on hospitality for survival.⁶⁵ God loves the marginalized of society, giving them food and clothing.

> Indeed, since Yahweh himself loves aliens, the Israelites were also to love them, remembering that they had been aliens in the land of Egypt. Thus, loving aliens becomes a type of *imitatio Dei* [imitation of God] – realizing our nature as being created in the image of a loving God.⁶⁶

However, as Christopher J. H. Wright rightly pointed out, we can never mimic or copy the actions of God "for clearly there are whole areas of the activity of God that are not available or appropriate for human replication."⁶⁷ Rather than imitating God, loving aliens is a "*reflection of God's character.*"⁶⁸ Remembering their once-bitter plight as aliens and their utter dependency on God, now, the Israelites must be gracious hosts to aliens living among them. In other words, as guests in God's land, they had experienced God's gracious welcome and generous provision. And now, as "hosts" in God's land, they were expected to extend similar treatment to those who were strangers or aliens in their land. However, over the years, the Israelites neglected their duties towards the strangers and the poor. They shut their ears against the voice of God through his prophets. Their inhospitality towards the widows, orphans, aliens, and the poor brought about the wrath of the landlord who took the land away from them (Zech 7:9–14; Jer 7:3–7).⁶⁹ Caring for the marginalized

---

63. Craigie, *Psalms 1–50*, 98; Driver, *Deuteronomy*, 126.
64. Kellermann, "גּוּר gûr," 2:443, 448; see Horner, "Changing Concepts."
65. Kellermann "גּוּר gûr," 2:443.
66. Knauth, "Alien, Foreign Resident," 33; see Brueggemann, *Theology of the Old Testament*, 422.
67. Wright, *Old Testament Ethics*, 37.
68. Ibid., 38 (original emphasis).
69. Richard, *Living the Hospitality of God*, 25–28; Hagstrom, "Role of Charism," 5–6.

was Israel's covenantal obligation to God the host which, when unfulfilled, resulted in God's withdrawal of his generous hospitality towards them.

In summary, the image of God as host was experienced by Israel through God's bountiful provision. God hosted Israel throughout her history – then and in the age to come. God's display of hospitality to his guest can be seen as a pedagogical act to teach Israel to relate hospitably towards the other guests – the orphans, the widows, the strangers – in God's land or God's "home." As Janzen put it, Israel lived "on land given as trust by God, with responsibility *to care* for others in a hospitality imitating [or, more rightly, reflecting] God."[70] In other words, the provision of material needs (i.e. food and clothing) and the protection (i.e. justice) Israel was to accord to the other guests of God is hospitality expressed through care. Hence, the image of God as host is an image of lavish care. Consequently, as hosts in the classroom, theological educators need to embody this concept of care to their students.

Jesus as Guest-Host

The Israelites' expectation of God as host continued into the New Testament as the Jews eagerly waited for the coming of Messiah and the messianic banquet that he would host for his people.[71] The Gospel of John revealed this prevailing messianic expectation in the time of Jesus when the crowd went around looking for Jesus after he miraculously fed a crowd of five thousand (John 6:24–26, 30–31). In feeding the multitudes (namely, the feeding of the five thousand in Matt 14:13–21; Mark 6:30–44; Luke 9:11–17; John 6:5–13; and the feeding of the four thousand in Matt 15:32–39; Mark 8:1–9), Jesus played the role of a host providing food for his people.

Jesus was also a host at the Last Supper (Matt 26:20–29; Mark 14:17–25; Luke 22:14–23) and he even washed his disciples' feet (John 13:1–11). Arland J. Hultgren viewed the footwashing in John 13 as more than an act of humility.[72] It was "a symbolic act of eschatological hospitality" and had soteriological significance.[73] By washing his disciples' feet, like the ancients

---

70. Janzen, *Old Testament Ethics*, 120 (emphasis mine).
71. Cross, *Ancient Library*, 236; Moore, *Judaism*, 365.
72. Hultgren, "Johannine Footwashing," 539.
73. Ibid., 542.

did for the guests, Jesus was symbolically welcoming them into his Father's house as their union with him now allowed them to share his destiny. In the synoptic accounts of the Last Supper, Jesus anticipated a "future sharing of [a] festive meal fellowship" when "he will again eat and drink wine with them at the final banquet in God's kingdom" (Matt 26:29; Mark 14:25; Luke 22:16, 18).[74] In Luke 22:24–30, Jesus too spoke of a dinner which he would host in the kingdom of God for those whose faith in him remained even in times of trials.[75]

Jesus became the supreme host when he offered his body and blood as bread and wine for all people at the cross.[76] He was again host, after his resurrection, when he served his disciples breakfast by the Sea of Tiberias (John 21:12–13).

Jesus' role as host, in providing food for the people, is the bodily enactment of God the host who cares. This point is not missed by the apostle John when he described Jesus, the Bread of Life, personally distributing food to the hungry (John 6:11; cf. the disciples in Matt 14:19; Mark 6:41; Luke 9:16).

At the same time, "Jesus as host . . . cannot be understood . . . apart from Jesus the guest."[77] When Jesus was born, his parents were guests at a single roomed Palestinian home in Bethlehem.[78] "To feed the five thousand, he accepts the loaves and the fish given to him (Mark 6:38–41 and parallels). Even the hosting of the Last Supper takes places in a borrowed hall (Mark 14:13–16 and parallels), and eventually Jesus is laid in a borrowed grave (Mark 15:42–46 and parallels)."[79] Throughout his ministry, Jesus received the

---

74. Heil, *Meal Scenes in Luke-Acts*, 173; see Janzen, *Old Testament Ethics*, 207.

75. Jesus too spoke of the faithful eating in the kingdom of God (Matt 8:5–12; Luke 13:24–30) although he did not cast himself as a host. The kingdom of God is also described by Jesus in terms of a wedding feast (Matt 22:1–14) and a dinner (Luke 14:15–24). Israel's expectation of a messianic banquet with God as host and Jesus' depiction of the kingdom of God metaphorically in terms of a banquet is realized in the marriage supper of the Lamb (Rev 19:7–9).

76. See Shaw, "Welcome Guest," 11.

77. Janzen, *Old Testament Ethics*, 207.

78. Nolland, *Luke 1–9:20*, 105–106. John Nolland's interpretation is plausible since *kataluma* (Luke 2:7), often translated as "inn" (see NASB, NIV, NKJV, NRSV), can mean "dining room" or "guest room" (see NASB, NIV, NKJV, NRSV) in Mark 14:14 and Luke 22:11 (Bauer, *Greek-English Lexicon*, s.v. "κατάλυμα"). A more specific word for *inn*, *pandocheion*, is used in Luke 10:34. Nolland invited us to imagine "an over-crowded Palestinian peasant home: a single-roomed home with an animal stall under the same roof" (*Luke 1–9:20*, 105).

79. Janzen, *Old Testament Ethics*, 207.

hospitality of many and was often a guest at the table of many homes. Jesus dined with people from all walks of life – the poor and the rich, common folks and religious leaders. Besides being taken care of by many unnamed female followers (Luke 8:3; see Matt 27:55; Mark 15:41), Jesus was served by Simon Peter's mother-in-law (Matt 8:14–15; Mark 1:30–31; Luke 4:38–39) and had dinner at Lazarus' home (Luke 10:38–42; John 12:1–8). He was invited to dine both in the homes of Pharisees (Luke 7:36–50; 11:37–54; 14:1–24) and tax collectors (Matt 9:9–13; Mark 2:14–17; Luke 5:27–32; 19:1–10).

Furthermore, as Janzen so aptly pointed out, "the two themes of Jesus the host and Jesus the guest . . . belong inseparably to each other through a characteristic inversion."[80] There is often a reversal of roles where Jesus, the guest, becomes the host. For instance, as a guest in a wedding in Cana, Jesus soon became the host by replenishing the fast-depleting supply of wine (John 2:1–10). In his encounter with two disciples on the road to Emmaus (Luke 24:13–35), "Jesus comes to them as a stranger (they do not recognize him), but they welcome him as a guest, and in breaking bread together, Jesus becomes the host."[81] Both Henri J. M. Nouwen (see above p. 14) and Parker J. Palmer (see above p. 32) made reference to this narrative in Luke in the context of reciprocity. By bringing precious gifts to the host, the guest makes the host his or her guest. Often, Jesus the guest shared divine food with his hosts. In Sychar, Jesus initially requested a drink from a Samaritan woman and ended up offering her the water of eternal life (John 4:5–26). The Samaritans hosted him for two days and received salvation in return (John 4:39–42). Similarly, Zacchaeus received salvation when Jesus was his dinner guest (Luke 19:1–10). Hence, I have entitled this section "Jesus as Guest-Host."

Recognizing that the roles of Jesus as guest and host are fluid, our discussion of Jesus as a hospitable guest-host explores the hospitality of Jesus in terms of his inclusive table fellowship practice and his implicit teaching to his disciples on hospitality.

The Significance of Jesus' Praxis of Inclusive Table Fellowship

The gospel narratives often depict Jesus' open and inclusive table fellowship bringing him into open conflict with the Jewish religious leaders, especially

---

80. Ibid., 208.
81. Pohl, *Making Room*, 31.

when he dined with the marginalized of the Jewish society. He was criticized by the Pharisees for dining with tax collectors and sinners (Matt 9:11; Mark 2:16; Luke 5:30; 15:2). He was also aware that his opponents labeled him "a glutton and a drunkard, a friend (*philos*) of tax collectors and sinners" (Matt 11:19; Luke 7:34). Being labeled "a friend" of these outcasts of society is significant for our study because friendship (*philia*) is akin to hospitality in the Greco-Roman world. Examining non-biblical Greek literature, Gustav Stählin argued that "the whole φιλ-group [cf. *phil* of *philia*] can be used for 'hospitality.'"[82] The word *philos* has multiple meanings in non-biblical ancient Greek texts. In a general sense, it can mean "friend" (i.e. "one who is close or well-known") or "boon companion."[83] However, the verb *phileō* can also mean "to entertain" and the noun *philotēs*, "hospitality."[84] In fact, *philos* ("friend") and *xenos* ("stranger") often occurred together. Stählin even suggested the translation of "guest" for "friend" in Luke 11:6[85] and concluded that "the close relation between friendship and table fellowship found very early expression in hospitality."[86]

Hence, the focus of our discussion of Jesus' hospitality is on his open commensality at the table with controversial dining companions. As Janzen put it, "central to the message manifested by Jesus in the form of hospitality offered and accepted is the identity of those he invited and from whom he accepted hospitality."[87] It is, thus, appropriate for our exploration of Jesus' practice of open commensality at the table to begin with an understanding of Jesus' dinner companions in relation to the act of eating together from a sociological point of view before examining Jesus' intent.

The Social Functions of Table Fellowship

Mary Douglas, a social anthropologist, introduced her analysis of the relation between food and cultural beliefs with this question, "If food is a code, where is the precoded message?"[88] She continued, "If food is treated as a code, the

---

82. Stählin, "φιλέω," 9:148.
83. Ibid., 9:159.
84. Ibid., 9:148.
85. Ibid., 9:159.
86. Ibid., 9:161.
87. Janzen, *Old Testament Ethics*, 208.
88. Douglas, "Deciphering a Meal," 61.

messages it encodes will be found in the pattern of social relations being expressed. And the message is about different degrees of hierarchy, inclusion and exclusion, boundaries and transactions across the boundaries."[89] Her work inspired New Testament scholars to view the meals of the first century as social events with underlying social codes.[90] Meals "replicate the group's basic social system, its values, lines, classifications, and its symbolic world" by: (1) reinforcing defined boundaries, (2) strengthening established roles and statuses, (3) focusing on the internal dimension, and (4) seeking stability and continuity.[91] Our discussion here briefly delineates three messages encoded in the meal traditions of the first century that would help us understand the significance of Jesus' practice of an inclusive table fellowship. From a sociological perspective, meals serve as boundary markers, reinforce social stratification, and promote social bonding.[92]

1) Social boundaries.

As Douglas has shown in her works,[93] food and purity laws governing group practices were "typical boundary building [sic] mechanisms."[94] Bruce J. Malina reiterated this idea when he stated that "purity is specifically about the general cultural map of social time and space, about arrangements within the space thus defined, and especially about the boundaries separating the inside from the outside."[95] An examination of Second Temple Judaism literature shows that "table fellowship could create intimate friendship, so it was increasingly reserved for those whom a person deemed the right kind of companions, who ate the right kinds of food."[96] Likewise, the Dead Sea Scrolls

---

89. Ibid., 61.
90. See Neyrey, "Ceremonies in Luke-Acts"; Malina, *New Testament World*; Bartchy, "Historical Jesus"; Smith, *From Symposium to Eucharist*; Smit, *Fellowship and Food*.
91. Neyrey, "Ceremonies in Luke-Acts," 363.
92. For variations of the encoded messages, see Smith, *From Symposium to Eucharist*, 9–12; Smit, *Fellowship and Food*, 85–96.
93. Douglas, *Purity and Danger*; "Deciphering a Meal."
94. Saldarini, *Pharisees, Scribes and Sadducees*, 215; see Smith, *From Symposium to Eucharist*, 9.
95. Malina, *New Testament World*, 153.
96. Blomberg, "Jesus, Sinners," 44; see 41–43.

indicate that in the Qumran community the purity laws concerning table fellowship functioned as a boundary marker.[97]

Hence, eating with another was a gesture of acceptance.[98] Conversely, to refuse to eat with another showed that one did not accept the other. As a boundary marker, table fellowship indicates "who's 'in' and who's 'out.'"[99] Since one's table companion indicated one's standing within the social system, people preferred to eat with those who were their "social, religious and economic equals."[100] Hence, there is the element of balanced reciprocity – "a symmetrical concern for equivalent benefit for both parties" – in table fellowship.[101]

2) Social stratification

Social stratification is exhibited when like eats with like. This social ranking is further reinforced by the sitting arrangements.[102] The seating order allows others to acknowledge one's social ranking, thus, confirming one's status in society.[103] In any meal setting, there would always be a place of honor and diners were ranked according to their position relative to that place of honor.[104] Hence, where one sat was important and just as important was how one was seated. Dennis E. Smith elaborated that, at a banquet, only those who were free citizens had the privilege to recline.[105] The women, children, and slaves who were present at the meal would have to sit. In a society where honor was "the pivotal cultural value," it is quite understandable that meal times became occasions for one to assert one's honor and to acquire more honor.[106]

---

97. Dunn, "Jesus, Table-Fellowship," 105; Blomberg, "Jesus, Sinners," 43–44; see 1QSa 2:3–10; Josephus, *J. W.* 2:129–133.

98. Bartchy, "Table Fellowship," 796. Scott Bartchy's article is reproduced as "Table Fellowship: Gospels" in the *IVP Dictionary of the New Testament*. The section, "The Significance of Shared Meals," appears with slight revisions and is rearranged in his article, "Historical Jesus" (175–176). Whatever is cited here may also be found in the other two articles.

99. Neyrey, "Ceremonies in Luke-Acts," 381; see Dunn, *Jesus Remembered*, 602.

100. Bartchy, "Table Fellowship," 796; see Smith, *From Symposium to Eucharist*, 9.

101. Neyrey, "Ceremonies in Luke-Acts," 372.

102. Bartchy, "Table Fellowship," 796; Smith, *From Symposium to Eucharist*, 10–11; see Matt 23:6; Mark 12:39; Luke 14:7–10.

103. Smith, *From Symposium to Eucharist*, 10.

104. Bartchy, "Historical Jesus," 177; Smith, *From Symposium to Eucharist*, 11.

105. Smith, *From Symposium to Eucharist*, 11.

106. Bartchy, "Historical Jesus," 178.

3) Social bonding
Generally, those eating together were already connected in some social network. By dining together, the diners formed a bond with one another through the sharing of the event, as well as the sharing of common food or dish at a common table. The sharing at a meal also created a sense of social and ethical obligation.[107] Essentially,

> those who dined together were to be treated equally.... The idea was that a meal that was shared in common and that created a sense of community among the participants should be one in which all could share equally and with full participation. In essence, then, a meal conceived in this way had the potential to break down social barriers and allow for a sense of social ordering internal to the group.[108]

Here, it must be noted that equality operated in tandem with social status. Equal treatment meant "giving everyone their due on an equal basis *according to their relative status.*"[109] Thus, meals not only reinforced group identity; they also promoted group cohesion.[110]

The Intent of Jesus' Table Fellowship

Jesus often sparked controversy by his choice of dinner companions. The Pharisees criticized Jesus for eating and drinking with tax collectors and sinners (e.g. Matt 9:11; Mark 2:16; Luke 5:30).[111] Writing on food as

---

107. Smith, *From Symposium to Eucharist*, 10.
108. Ibid., 11.
109. Ibid. (original emphasis), citing Gregory Nagy.
110. Neyrey, "Ceremonies in Luke-Acts," 378.
111. In Mark 2:16 and Luke 5:30, the scribes were associated with the Pharisees as those who criticized Jesus for eating and drinking with the outcasts of society. G. H. Twelftree stated that some scholars viewed them as two unrelated distinct groups while others viewed them as those Pharisees who were learned in the Law or an elite member among the Pharisees ("Scribes," 733). "The scribes of the Pharisees" appears in Mark 2:16 (NRSV) and "the Pharisees and their scribes" in Luke 5:30 (NRSV), making it possible that the scribes were associated with various Jewish groups in the first century. Joachim Jeremias pointed out that the Pharisaic party within the Sanhedrin were either called "Pharisees" or "scribes" but they never appeared as individual groups within the Sanhedrin (*Jerusalem*, 237, esp. n. 12; see Matt 21:45; Luke 20:19). This work treats the scribes as being closely associated with the Pharisees since they share similar characteristics: (1) They did not approve of Jesus eating with tax collectors and sinners (see Mark 2:16; Luke 5:30; 15:2); (2) They loved to be respectfully greeted in public places and to sit in the seat of honor in the synagogues

boundary-crossing in Luke-Acts, Barbara Rossing claimed that "it is for this reason that Robert Karris makes the stunning claim that 'in Luke's Gospel Jesus got himself crucified by the way he ate.'"[112] I believe Karris' claim holds true for the Gospels of Matthew and Mark too.[113] In this section, we seek to culturally locate the tax collectors and sinners in the first-century world to better understand the significance of Jesus' praxis of inclusive table fellowship.

1) Jesus' dinner companions – the tax collectors and sinners

Appearing only in the Synoptic Gospels, the *telōnēs* (e.g. Matthew the tax collector in Matt 10:3) and the *architelōnēs* (e.g. Zacchaeus the chief tax collector in Luke 19:2) are "technical terms for functionaries in the toll farming system."[114] In the gospel accounts, tax collectors were found in Capernaum (Jesus' "own town" in Matt 9:1; see Matt. 4:13) and Jericho (Luke 19:1), commercial centers where tolls were collected.[115] The taxes collected would flow into the coffers of the Herodian rulers, and, ultimately, the Roman imperial treasury. Consequently, tax collectors were perceived by their fellow-Jews as traitors who had also defiled themselves by working in close collaboration with the non-Jewish enemies.[116]

The right to collect taxes and tolls was obtained through a bidding system and given to the highest bidder. Having paid in advance the expected revenue to those auctioning these collection rights, this system of tax-farming forced tax collectors to collect more than what was imposed as a protection against possible financial loss.[117] They probably pocketed the surplus for their personal gain as well.[118] It is not surprising then, that tax collectors were often

---

(this criticism was leveled against them in Matt 23:6; but addressed only to the Pharisees in Luke and to the scribes in Luke 20:46 and Mark 12:38–39); and (3) They received the same judgment from Jesus (Matt 23:13–35). As such, this work only uses the term *Pharisees* even if scribes are included.

112. Rossing, "Why Luke's Gospel," 229; see Karris, *Luke*, 70.
113. The synoptic accounts of Jesus eating with tax collectors and sinners are not mentioned in the Gospel of John.
114. Donahue, "Tax Collectors and Sinners," 48; for more on Greco-Roman taxation system, see Michel, "τελώνης," 8:88–105.
115. Donahue, "Tax Collectors and Sinners," 54.
116. Harrington, *Gospel of Matthew*, 128; Blomberg, *Matthew*, 156; Witherington, *Mark*, 120.
117. Michel, "τελώνης," 8:99.
118. Harrington, *Gospel of Matthew*, 128.

suspected of dishonesty, bribery, and corruption.[119] Jonathan Klawans even labeled the tax collectors as "the epitome of dishonesty."[120]

Furthermore, tax collectors were often regarded with disdain, especially by pious and devout Jews, because they had compromised on ritual purity. Working as tax agents, they would come in close contact with Gentiles and handle pagan currency that had pagan inscriptions.[121] However, Seán Freyne and John R. Donahue did not perceive ritual impurity as the issue. "The use of money had penetrated right through the society and was now the standard form of exchange even among the day-laborers, widows and other marginalized people."[122] And, according to Donahue, "the toll collectors were not considered to be ritually defiled because of their contact with Gentiles, but were scorned because of their dishonesty, and that the judgment on them remains harsh throughout the Talmud."[123] Hence, tax collectors were probably held in contempt by many because of their dishonesty and disloyalty rather than ritual impurity.

On the other hand, the term *sinner*, among other definitions, could refer to: (1) one who opposes the will of God and lives an immoral life, or who practices a dishonorable trade or a trade that encourages dishonesty (i.e. a non-Pharisaic perspective); or (2) one who does not observe Pharisaic interpretations of the Law (i.e. from a Pharisaic perspective). In essence, a sinner is defined either by moral impurity or ritual impurity.[124] And both of these meanings are found in the gospels although it is used more often by non-Pharisees to describe moral impurity (e.g. Jesus in Matt 9:13; 26:45; Mark 2:17; 14:41; Luke 5:32; 6:32–34; 15:7, 10; 24:7; other individuals in Luke 5:8; 18:13). Interestingly, the Pharisees used the term to denote those who were ritually impure (John 9:16, 24) and morally sinful (Luke 7:39).

Karl Heinrich Rengstorf, however, further defined the sinners who do not abide by the prescribed laws of the Pharisees as *'am ha-ares* [sic] ("people

---

119. Ibid., 126; France, *Gospel of Matthew*, 351.
120. Klawans, *Impurity and Sin*, 109.
121. Albright and Mann, *Matthew*, 105; Mann, *Mark*, 203; Harrington, *Gospel of Matthew*, 128; Hagner, *Matthew 1–13*, 238.
122. Freyne, "Herodian Economics," 39.
123. Donahue, "Tax Collectors and Sinners," 55.
124. Rengstorf, "ἁμαρτωλός," 1:327–329; see Bauer, *Greek-English Lexicon*, s.v. "ἁμαρτωλός."

of the land").[125] William L. Lane concurred with this understanding when he claimed that the term *sinners* is a technical term "for a class of people who were regarded by the Pharisees as inferior because they showed no interest in the scribal tradition."[126] It should not be understood "in the generally accepted sense of 'transgressors of the moral law of God.'"[127] In *The Parables of Jesus*, Joachim Jeremias defined "sinners" as those who lived immoral lives or held dishonorable occupations.[128] His definition remained essentially unchanged in his discussion on the poor in a later work.[129] However, by saying that "Jesus' following consisted predominantly of the disreputable, the *'ammē hā-' āreṣ*, the uneducated, the ignorant, whose *religious* ignorance and *moral* behavior stood in the way of their access to salvation, according to the convictions of the time," he also seemed to imply that sinners were the *'am hā-āreṣ*.[130]

Many scholars, however, are less inclined to equate sinners as the *'am hā-āreṣ*.[131] Looking at the usage in rabbinic literature, E. P. Sanders argued that sinners were not the common people, that is, the *'am hā-āreṣ*.[132] Craig S. Keener also put forth a good argument when he pointed out that it would not make sense for the Pharisees to insist that Jesus should stay away from the sinners when he himself was probably considered as belonging to the *'am hā-āreṣ*.[133]

Thus, the term *sinners* should not be restricted to the *'am hā-āreṣ*. Neither should it be limited to those who do not subscribe to the Pharisaic interpretations of the Law. In Luke 19:7, even the crowd grumbled that Jesus had gone to the house of a sinner when he paid a visit to Zacchaeus who was a chief tax collector. However, we must acknowledge that the Pharisees would definitely use it in this sense. On the whole, the term should be used in the general sense to refer to those who disregard the moral law of God by living

---

125. Rengstorf, "ἁμαρτωλός," 1:328.
126. Lane, *Mark*, 103.
127. Ibid.
128. Jeremias, *Parables of Jesus*, 132.
129. Jeremias, *New Testament Theology*, 109–110.
130. Ibid., 112 (original emphasis).
131. Guelich, *Mark 1–8:26*, 102; Harrington, *Gospel of Matthew*, 128; France, *Gospel of Matthew*, 353.
132. Sanders, "Jesus and the Sinners"; *Jesus and Judaism*, ch. 6.
133. Keener, *Matthew*, 294–296.

immoral lives.¹³⁴ Sinners, therefore, are basically "the notoriously immoral, not merely the ritually negligent."¹³⁵

In the Synoptic Gospels, tax collectors are often paired with Gentiles (Matt 5:46; 18:17), sinners (Matt 9:10; 11:19; Mark 2:15, 16; Luke 5:27, 29; 7:34; 15:1–2; 18:10, 13), and prostitutes (Matt 21:31–32). Jesus saw them in a more positive light (Matt 5:46; 18:17; 21:31–32; Luke 18:10, 13) while one could sense negative vibes when used by the scribes and Pharisees (Matt 9:10; Luke 5:30; 15:2; and possibly Matt 11:19; Luke 7:34). Although Craig L. Blomberg suggested that the grouping of tax collectors with sinners, Gentiles, and prostitutes could be "idiomatic, demonstrating how unwelcome the tax collectors were to the Pharisees,"¹³⁶ it is quite possible that their reputation of being disloyal and dishonest could have caused them to be identified with this disreputable group of people by the over-scrupulous scribes and Pharisees (see Luke 3:13).¹³⁷ Sanders held the opinion that tax collectors and sinners were grouped together because they were traitors.¹³⁸ Tax collectors were "quislings" since they collaborated with the Romans while sinners betray God by rejecting God and his law.¹³⁹ "There was no neat distinction between 'religious' and 'political' betrayal in first-century Judaism."¹⁴⁰ From a grammatical point of view, tax collectors could be considered a subset of sinners.¹⁴¹ In the light of the preceding discussion, both the tax collectors and sinners were generally perceived by others, especially the Pharisees, to be impure, more morally than ritually.

2) Jesus' critics – the Pharisees

Marcus J. Borg spoke of a collision of two social worlds in the first century – the Jewish social world and the Greco-Roman social world.¹⁴² Renewal movements arose among the Jews as they struggled to protect their social

---

134. Nolland, *Luke 1–9:20*, 246; Hagner, *Matthew 1–13*, 238; Keener, *Matthew*, 295.
135. Witherington, *Mark*, 123.
136. Blomberg, *Matthew*, 156.
137. Donahue, "Tax Collectors and Sinners," 59; Freyne, *Galilee*, 192.
138. Sanders, "Jesus and the Sinners," 9.
139. Ibid., 9; *Jesus and Judaism*, 178.
140. Sanders, "Jesus and the Sinners," 9; *Jesus and Judaism*, 178.
141. Wallace, *Greek Grammar*, 280; see Luke 19:7 where Zacchaeus the tax collector was perceived as a sinner.
142. Borg, *Jesus*, 83.

world and identity by promoting an ethos of holiness that demanded separation,[143] with the intent to build "the holy community of Israel, the 'true Israel.'"[144] The Pharisees were part of these renewal movements seeking societal changes towards holiness.[145] Hence, observance of Sabbath, tithing, and purity laws played an important role in this ethos of holiness (e.g. Matt 12:2; 15:2; 23:23; Mark 2:24; 7:1–5; Luke 6:2; 11:38, 42; 13:14; 18:12; John 9:14). Those who did not adhere to their stringent religious requirements were sanctioned through "social and religious ostracism," especially through the refusal of table fellowship[146] since table fellowship was "the high point of their life as a group" in the pre-70s.[147] The need to ostracize is quite understandable if, like Anthony J. Saldarini suggested, the "ethnic groups in the Roman Empire were strong groups, low grid and thus needed to maintain strong boundaries in order to keep the larger Hellenistic-Roman society and culture from absorbing them."[148] The use of the internal rules "to separate, protect and identify," which would be traced back to the restoration programs of Ezra and Nehemiah in the Exile,[149] was "to keep the community whole and its [ultimate] hope pure."[150]

In their attempt to uphold purity, Pharisees would certainly be careful about the state of purity of those who eat with them.[151] As seen from the preceding discussion on tax collectors and sinners, members of these groups would probably not be invited as dinner guests because of the dishonesty

---

143. Ibid., 86–88.
144. Jeremias, *Jerusalem*, 265–266.
145. Borg, *Jesus*, 89; see Saldarini, *Pharisees, Scribes and Sadducees*, 281.
146. Borg, *Jesus*, 89.
147. Neusner, "Mr. Sander's Pharisees," 152; *In Quest of the Historical Pharisees*, 309. However, Neusner cautioned against the idea that they "were only or principally a table-fellowship commune" ("Mr. Sander's Pharisees," 157; *In Quest of the Historical Pharisees*, 316).
148. Saldarini, *Pharisees, Scribes and Sadducees*, 215, n. 34. Anthony J. Saldarini's understanding of grid and group is derived from the work of Jerome H. Neyrey ("Idea of Purity," 117–118) who applied Mary Douglas' (*Natural Symbols*, ch. 4, esp. 62–66) grid/group theory to New Testament studies. Stated simply, "strong 'group' indicates a high degree of pressure to conform to societal norms, as well as a strong degree of pressure for order and control" while "low 'grid' indicates a poor degree of fit and match between individual experiences and stated societal patterns of perception and experience" (Malina and Neyrey, "Jesus the Witch," 37–38).
149. Saldarini, *Pharisees, Scribes and Sadducees*, 216.
150. Perrin, *Rediscovering the Teaching of Jesus*, 103.
151. Bartchy, "Table Fellowship," 796.

associated with them.¹⁵² Besides that, the presence of tax collectors in one's home would render the house unclean (*m. Ṭehar.* 7:6). However, nothing is mentioned in the Mishnah regarding the presence of sinners in one's home. Here, I would agree with scholars like Sanders and Klawans that contact with sinners does not necessarily violate ritual purity rules.¹⁵³

More crucial than determining whether it is the concern for moral or ritual purity that deters the Pharisees from associating with tax collectors and sinners is the fact that purity rules functioned as boundary markers¹⁵⁴ since sharing a meal with another was a symbol of acceptance while refusing to eat together was a symbol of rejection.¹⁵⁵ Judging by Jesus' comment regarding sitting arrangements at the table (Luke 14:10), meals for the Pharisees definitely reinforced one's social ranking. Furthermore, since "table fellowship was at the heart of many Pharisees' self-identity,"¹⁵⁶ it also preserved group identity as well as promoted group cohesion.¹⁵⁷

Hence, Jesus' eating with outcasts was offensive to their Jewish sensibilities because it challenged "the politics of holiness as the cultural dynamic of the society" and threatened "the central ordering principle of [their] Jewish social world: the division between purity and impurity, holy and not-holy, righteous and wicked."¹⁵⁸ Having "a place for everything and everyone, with everything and everyone in its place" to the exclusion of all anomalies, the Pharisees ruthlessly ostracized anyone or anything that was considered an anomaly.¹⁵⁹ Although the Pharisees might not have considered Jesus to be part of their group, they probably did not consider him as belonging to the class of tax collectors and sinners since some of them even invited him to eat with them (Luke 7:36; 11:37; 14:1). However, by eating with the tax collectors and sinners – the impure, not-holy, and wicked – Jesus had transgressed the social boundaries and violated the social code of the day. By identifying himself with them, he would be perceived by the Pharisees as sharing "*their*

---

152. See Klawans, *Impurity and Sin*, 109.
153. See Sanders, *Jesus and Judaism*, ch. 6; Klawans, *Impurity and Sin*.
154. See Dunn, "Jesus, Table-Fellowship," 105.
155. Borg, *Jesus*, 89.
156. Dunn, "Jesus, Table-Fellowship," 103.
157. See Neyrey, "Ceremonies in Luke-Acts," 378.
158. Borg, *Jesus*, 132.
159. Malina, *New Testament World*, 157.

world, not God's world of holiness."[160] It is not surprising then, that he too became an outcast in the eyes of the Pharisees.

3) Jesus' intentional acts

Throughout his ministry, Jesus committed many radical acts: he touched a leper (Matt 8:2–3; Mark 1:40–41) and the tongue of a deaf man (Mark 7:32–33), he stayed in a Samaritan city for two days (John 4:40) and was entertained in the house of Simon the leper (Matt 26:6–7; Mark 14:3). His radical acts challenged prevailing social prejudice and discrimination. Sitting and eating with tax collectors and sinners was also a bold act that overturned conventional social boundaries, hierarchies, and bonding.

However, as Jerome H. Neyrey suggested, Jesus' deliberate choice of dining companions was "no mere lapse of regard for the customs of his day but a formal strategy" to erase the social boundaries that determine "who is eating with whom, where, how or what is eaten."[161] More than just eating, Jesus' table fellowship has been variously termed by scholars as "an acted parable,"[162] "an enacted parable of the grace of God,"[163] "a prophetic symbol,"[164] and an "enacted prophecy."[165] His eating and with whom he ate was intended to teach about the "surprising inclusions" in the kingdom of God.[166] His "radically inclusive, status-leveling, and honor-sharing fellowship at table" was a means to announce and redefine the kingdom of God.[167]

The kingdom of God inaugurated by the coming of Jesus, is radically inclusive. It is not just for the pious elite. It is also for those sinful individuals standing on the fringes of respectability. By eating with the outcast and marginalized, Jesus enacted the far-reaching love and grace of God and broke "the wall of exclusiveness of fellowship and love."[168] His open and inclusive

---

160. Neyrey, "Ceremonies in Luke-Acts," 364 (original emphasis).
161. Ibid., 378, 380.
162. Perrin, *Rediscovering the Teaching of Jesus*, 102.
163. Borg, *Jesus*, 102.
164. Davies and Allison, *Matthew*, 101.
165. Blomberg, "Jesus, Sinners," 61.
166. Ibid., 62; Just, *Ongoing Feast*, 174.
167. Bartchy, "Historical Jesus," 175.
168. Stählin, "φιλέω," 9:160; Koenig, *New Testament Hospitality*, 20; Bartchy, "Table Fellowship," 797.

table fellowship proclaimed God's forgiveness,[169] grace,[170] and compassion.[171] At the same time, his table fellowship is "a sign pointing to . . . the ultimate table fellowship at the messianic banquet where God's hospitality reaches its final fulfillment"[172] and at which the exalted Jesus Christ will be partaking with his faithful ones "from all the people groups on the planet."[173]

When we do a close reading of the various accounts of Jesus' eating with the tax collectors and sinners, we can notice that he was always there as a guest. Andrew McGowan also observed this when he wrote that "Jesus is depicted not as offering hospitality to these marginalized but as accepting their hospitality."[174] Interpreted through the lens of culture, this acceptance of hospitality would imply that Jesus was giving honor to his socially disreputable hosts. This insight came from Perry W. H. Shaw who has been living in the Middle East since 1990. He has written: "In the contemporary Middle East, as in ancient Palestine, the person of lesser status visits the person of higher status."[175] Writing on Mediterranean hospitality, Julian Pitt-Rivers wrote that the visit of a superior person brings honor to all.[176] A biblical example of this is found in the story of Zacchaeus, one who was socially marginalized and without honor (Luke 19:1–10). Zacchaeus, who was hoping to catch a glimpse of Jesus through the thick foliage of a sycamore tree, gladly welcomed Jesus when the latter invited himself over to his house.[177] "The coming of Jesus to share his home is a sign of fellowship"[178] and a "huge gift of acceptance in the eyes of Jesus."[179] Zacchaeus was thus honored by Jesus' visit and by the declaration that "he too is a son of Abraham" (Luke 19:9).

---

169. Jeremias, *New Testament Theology*, 114–115; Neyrey, "Ceremonies in Luke-Acts," 378; Just, *Ongoing Feast*, 196; Witherington, *Mark*, 122; Davies and Allison, *Matthew*, 100–101.

170. Lane, *Mark*, 107.

171. Borg, *Jesus*, 133.

172. Just, *Ongoing Feast*, 79; see Jeremias, *New Testament Theology*, 115–116; Lane, *Mark*, 106.

173. Blomberg, "Jesus, Sinners," 61.

174. McGowan, "Meals of Jesus," 106.

175. Shaw, 7 January 2014, email message to author. Although I cannot find written documentation to support this, I live in a culture that also practices it. For a Chinese living in Singapore, it is culturally more appropriate for a person of lower status to visit someone of higher social status.

176. Pitt-Rivers, "Stranger," 17.

177. Bailey, *Jesus through Middle Eastern Eyes*, 179.

178. Marshall, *Gospel of Luke*, 697.

179. Bailey, *Jesus through Middle Eastern Eyes*, 182.

Furthermore, in a society where guests reclined at the table according to their social rank,[180] where guests sought the seat of honor beside the master of the house,[181] Jesus used meals as occasions to teach status-leveling and honor-sharing. In Luke 14:7–11, Jesus censured those who sought seats of honor during a meal. They instead should learn to humbly defer to others "for all who exalt themselves will be humbled, and those who humble themselves will be exalted" (Luke 14:11).[182] At another meal, the Last Supper, when his disciples were disputing about whom among them was the greatest, he taught them about role and honor reversal: the greater is not the one reclining at the table but the one who serves (Luke 22:27). He did not just teach by words for he continued, "But I am among you as one who serves." His entire life was a life of service and his actions were intentional pedagogical acts (e.g. washing of disciples' feet in John 13:1–17).[183] By eating with those at the margins of the first-century society who probably had no place at respectable dinner tables, Jesus had leveled their social status and accorded honor to them. As McGowan so wittingly put it, "the distinction of Jesus' meal practice was its lack of distinction."[184]

I agree with James D. G. Dunn that "Jesus' table-fellowship must be seen as both a protest against a religious zeal that is judgmental and exclusive and as a lived-out expression of the openness of God's grace."[185] Through Jesus' open commensality, "God's love is vividly painted as condescending. It reaches down even to the lowest level of human society."[186] When the Pharisees questioned why Jesus ate with tax collectors and sinners, Jesus replied: "Those who are well have no need of a physician, but those who are sick; I have come to call not the righteous but sinners" (Mark 2:17; see Luke 5:31–32). In Jesus' eyes, tax collectors and sinners were not "contaminating and deserving to be spurned."[187] In fact, if impurity were contagious, then,

---

180. Smith, "Dinner with Jesus and Paul," 36.
181. Bauer, *Greek-English Lexicon*, s.v. "πρωτοκλισία"; cf. Matt 23:6; Mark 12:39; Luke 14:7; 20:46.
182. Bartchy, "Historical Jesus," 179.
183. Geldenhuys, *Gospel of Luke*, 562.
184. McGowan, "Meals of Jesus," 111.
185. Dunn, "Jesus, Table-Fellowship," 111.
186. Yao, "Table Fellowship of Jesus," 30.
187. Nolland, *Luke 1–9:20*, 246.

holiness would be even more contagious.[188] In the end, in welcoming all, even the marginalized and ostracized, to the table, Jesus is no longer a dinner guest but "the supreme host, welcoming strangers into the kingdom of God."[189]

Jesus' Instructions on Hospitality from and to Others

In one sense, Jesus did not explicitly teach on hospitality. As seen from our preceding discussion, he taught through his acts of hospitality, especially through his open commensality, welcoming anyone and everyone at the dinner table. However, when he sent his disciples to proclaim the good news, he expected hospitality to be shown to his disciples. In the judgment parable in Matthew 25:31–46, those who showed hospitality were rewarded. Though these may not be explicit teachings on hospitality, the significance of these passages cannot be ignored as they became integral to the life and mission of the early faith communities.

The Mission of the Early Faith Communities

Before Jesus sent his twelve disciples (Matt 10:1–42; Mark 6:7–11; Luke 9:1–5) and seventy others (Luke 10:1–16) to preach the gospel, he specifically told them to whom they should go (only in Matt 10:5–6), what they could bring with them, and what they were to say and do.[190] Essentially, they were told to bring almost nothing, not even a bag (Gk. *pēra*), but to eat and drink whatever was provided to them (Luke 10:7) for a laborer deserved his food (Matt 10:10) and wages (Luke 10:7).

In ancient times, it was customary for travelers to carry a change of clothes in a sack and some money in a purse tied to their belt or hung around the neck by a cord.[191] A Cynic philosopher would wander across the country with

---

188. Blomberg, *Contagious Holiness*, 128; see Borg, *Conflict, Holiness and Politics*, 147–149; Chilton, *Jesus' Baptism and Jesus' Healing*, 58–71.

189. Richard, *Living the Hospitality of God*, 31.

190. There are some variations regarding what they could bring among the passages. Scholars had acknowledged that there is no good resolution to this issue (Witherington, *Mark*, 211; Davies and Allison, *Matthew*, 171). We may just have to make room for "the fluidity of oral tradition or the frailty of human memory" (Davies and Allison, *Matthew*, 171). Nolland felt that "the significant variation in the lists between the various Gospels suggests that at least in relation to ongoing mission they were taken to be suggestive rather than exhaustive, and therefore open to flexible application" (*Gospel of Matthew*, 418). This is quite possible as Jesus changed his instructions to his disciples in Luke 22:36 as he prepared them for what would happen after his arrest and crucifixion.

191. Stambaugh and Balch, *New Testament*, 38.

a staff in his hand and a begging bag (Gk. *pēra*) over his shoulder.¹⁹² It could be possible that the disciples were told not to carry a *pēra* so as to distinguish them from Cynic philosophers who begged for their food.¹⁹³ With so many itinerant philosophers and religious teachers in Jesus' time, it would be crucial to know the real from the fraudulent. The *Didache* (c. early first century to early second century), the teaching manual of the early church, even had guidelines for dealing with itinerant teachers and recognizing false prophets.¹⁹⁴ However, John Nolland and I. Howard Marshall suggested that *pēra* in the gospel accounts could refer to an ordinary traveler's bag rather than a beggar's bag.¹⁹⁵ Their interpretation is more probable when we consider the dating of *Didache* and the occurrences of *pēra* in the Bible. The word occurs five times, four of which in the same context (see Matt 10:10; Mark 6:8; Luke 9:3; 10:4), and only in the Synoptic Gospels. Its occurrence in Luke 22:36 favors Nolland's and Marshall's interpretation. Thus, Jesus instructed his disciples not to carry any traveling bag (Matt 10:10; Mark 6:8; Luke 9:3; 10:4) and they were to stay at one place till they leave (Matt 10:11; Mark 6:10; Luke 9:4; 10:7).

Jesus taught an austere style of doing missions because he wanted the disciples to be dependent on the hospitality of people, and, ultimately, the hospitality of God. With nothing much on them, they had to totally rely on the providential care of God to provide for their needs.¹⁹⁶ As Blomberg put it, "the point of Jesus' strictness is not to leave his disciples deprived and defenseless but dependent on others for their *nourishment* ('keep,' v. 10) in every area of life."¹⁹⁷ By traveling without any provisions, the disciples are taught to expect goodwill hospitality from the community.¹⁹⁸ When asked about their mission experience at the Last Supper, the disciples testified that

---

192. Hock, "Cynics," 1:1223.
193. Keener, *Matthew*, 318; Witherington, *Mark*, 210.
194. Lake, *Apostolic Fathers*, 307. E.g. one was a false prophet if he stayed for three days (*Did.* 11:4–5; 12:2) or if he asked for money when he was leaving (*Did.* 11:6). For the text of the *Didache*, see Lake, *Apostolic Fathers*.
195. Nolland, *Gospel of Matthew*, 418; Marshall, *Gospel of Luke*, 353.
196. Geldenhuys, *Gospel of Luke*, 265, 300; Lane, *Mark*, 207; Marshall, *Gospel of Luke*, 350–351, 418; Fitzmyer, *Gospel according to Luke 1–9*, 752; Allen, *Matthew*, 102–103; Hagner, *Matthew 1–13*, 269; Davies and Allison, *Matthew*, 171; Nolland, *Gospel of Matthew*, 418; France, *Gospel of Matthew*, 386.
197. Blomberg, *Matthew*, 172 (original emphasis).
198. Lane, *Mark*, 208; Marshall, *Gospel of Luke*, 353; France, *Gospel of Matthew*, 386.

they lacked nothing even when they carried with them nothing – no purse, bag, sandals (Luke 22:35).

The Final Judgment

Matthew 25:31–46 is the concluding discourse of the eschatological discourse which began when the disciples asked Jesus when he would return to bring in the end of the age (Matt 24:3). It ends with Jesus telling them about the coming of the Son of Man in his glory to judge all the nations. Jesus used the imagery of a shepherd dividing his flock to portray the judgment of all humanity when the Son of Man comes in his glory.[199]

In this judgment scene, the king, Jesus, does what a shepherd does; he separates the sheep from the goats. It is a judgment that separates the righteous from the wicked among the nations. The righteous are then invited to receive their inheritance, the blessings of God's kingdom. And the basis of their inheritance is their treatment towards the "members" of the king's family who were in need (Matt 25:40).

There is much scholarly discussion regarding who the members, or brothers in the Greek text (i.e. τῶν ἀδελφῶν), are.[200] This study identifies the "brothers" as "disciples" since the term is used by Jesus for his disciples (Matt 12:49–50; 23:8; 28:10). This understanding is also "the majority view in church history and among contemporary New Testament scholars, although those who hold 'siblings' to be disciples divide sharply over whether they are specifically missionaries or poor fellow disciples in general."[201] In view of possible persecutions of those associated with Jesus (Matt 5:11; 10:18, 22, 25; 23:34), we will see it as referring to needy disciples, whether they are missionaries or not.

Hence, the righteous are judged by their kind deeds towards the disciples of Jesus when the latter were hungry or thirsty, when they were a stranger or naked, and when they were sick or in prison. Doing these acts of mercy for those associated with Jesus amounted to doing it for the Son of Man (see Matt 10:40–42). And not doing these acts of mercy meant eternal punishment

---

199. The meaning of "all the nations" in Matthew 25:32 has been much disputed (for more, see Hagner, *Matthew 14–28*, 742). This work adopts the view that "all the nations" refers to all humanity since the phrase is used consistently with this sense elsewhere in Matthew (Matt 24:9, 14; 28:19) (for more, see Donahue, "Parable," 14–16).
200. See Hagner, *Matthew 14–28*, 744–745.
201. Keener, *Matthew*, 606.

for the wicked (Matt 25:42–43). The righteous were approved for having done deeds of mercy and the wicked were faulted because they did not do charitable deeds. The unknown stranger in need was none other than Jesus himself.[202] Jesus, "the ultimate host who cares for the neighbor in need no matter who he or she is" is now "the supreme guest who, unbeknownst to us, is in need of our care."[203]

In summary, the hospitality of Jesus is best understood in terms of his roles as both the host and the guest. Jesus is the host who cares and provides for his people, just like God the host did. As such, he fulfilled Israel's expectation of God as host. At the same time, Jesus is also the guest, sometimes the unknown guest, who accepts the hospitality and care from others. Often he is the guest-turned-host. In his dual role as guest-host, Jesus shows and accepts hospitality from anyone and everyone. This is most poignantly enacted through his controversial practice of inclusive table fellowship. By eating with unrespectable tax collectors and sinners, Jesus erased all social boundaries and removed all social rankings, thereby bestowing honor on these marginalized people. Consequently, as hosts in the classroom, theological educators need to consider how this gesture of inclusion can be extended to their students.

The Early Faith Communities as Hosts

Jesus' instructions regarding hospitality in relation to missions (see above p. 182) and the final judgment (see above p. 184) to his disciples did have a continuing impact. This is clearly evidenced by the role hospitality played in the life and mission of the early faith communities, as seen from the New Testament epistles, and especially the Book of Acts.[204] In the words of John Koenig, "the Acts of the Apostles may be read, structurally, as a collection of guest and host stories about the missionary ventures generated in the Spirit-led communities of Jerusalem and Antioch."[205] The movements of the first-century Christians, as depicted in these biblical documents, reflect "the

---

202. Miller, "Israel as Host to Strangers," 570.
203. Han, Metzger, and Muck, "Christian Hospitality and Pastoral Practices," 13.
204. This work does not discuss critical issues related to the selected New Testament documents. The reader is advised to read leading commentaries of these documents which are too numerous to be listed here.
205. Koenig, *New Testament Hospitality*, 87.

mobility of Roman society as well as the practice of private hospitality" in the house churches.[206] Private homes or households played an important role in the practice of hospitality within the life and mission of the early faith communities.[207] Besides presenting how homes/households became houses of hospitality, this section also examines the biblical commands to show hospitality and the expressions of hospitality in the life and mission of the early Christian communities.

Homes/Households as Houses of Hospitality

During the Roman Empire, the extensive travel infrastructure and *pax Romana* made travel much easier and safer.[208] "Land was measured and divided, rivers bridged, canals dug joining rivers and seas, and roads were cut through inhospitable country."[209] Designed and built for use by the military so that the armies could travel in all weather conditions,[210] the roads were soon used for political and commercial purposes, as well as for general travel.[211] As a result, "mobility in the Roman Empire during the imperial period was much higher than in any other ancient society."[212] Weary travelers on a long journey could find lodging in temples, gymnasiums, synagogues, and inns.[213]

Ancient Greek itinerant philosophers reportedly stayed at temples and gymnasiums. Clarence A. Forbes discovered that the gymnasium, among other uses, was also a place for learning where philosophers would conduct lectures.[214] The itinerant philosophers "were received and taken care of by the gymnasiarchs," the public officers in charge of the gymnasiums.[215] In

---

206. Malherbe, *Social Aspects*, 95.
207. Taking into consideration the household context of gatherings of the early faith communities, the word *home* is not limited to the idea of a physical dwelling (e.g. Acts 10:6; 21:6) but includes the idea of a "household" (e.g. Acts 7:10; 10:2).
208. Rosenfeld, "Innkeeping," 136; cf. Paul's experiences, see 2 Cor 11:25–26.
209. Adams, "Introduction," 2.
210. Witherington, *Acts of the Apostles*, 637.
211. Souter, "Roads and Travel," 4:394.
212. Kolb, "Conception," 54.
213. Hock, *Social Context*, 29.
214. Forbes, "Expanded Uses," 33–37.
215. Ibid., 35; esp. n. 24 for Forbes' citation of ancient Greek texts.

his travels, the Greek philosopher Apollonius of Tyana supposedly stayed in temples.[216]

For Jews, the synagogue would be the preferred choice of lodging. Besides being a place for public meetings, communal meals, and charitable activities, the synagogue also served as a courtroom, a school, and even a hostel for travelers.[217] The Theodotus inscription, which was discovered in Jerusalem and generally accepted as pre-70 CE, described a synagogue that was built with a guest room with chambers and water fittings.[218] This synagogue probably functioned as a temporary boarding house for travelers outside of Jerusalem in the first century even though we cannot ascertain the identity of these travelers with certainty.[219]

First-century travelers could also seek shelter for the night in inns. From antiquity, as early as 3000 BCE in the ancient Near East, inns were built along roads to provide lodging for travelers who were mainly the merchants and government officials.[220] As a result of the well-developed travel infrastructure in Roman times, inns of various types mushroomed to cater to the different needs of the travelers, offering a wider range of services.

The Greek word *pandocheion* ("accepting all comers," see Luke 10:30 35), appearing as early as the fifth century BCE, is used mainly for inns in the Greek-speaking regions of the eastern Mediterranean world in the first and second centuries CE, and does not appear in literary sources from the western Roman Empire.[221] These inns served travelers in the eastern Roman Empire

---

216. Philostratus, *Vit. Apoll.* 4.40; 5.20; 8.15, cited in Hock, *Social Context*, 80, n. 34.
217. Levine, *Ancient Synagogue*, ch. 5.
218. Riesner, "Synagogues in Jerusalem," 193–194; Levine, *Ancient Synagogue*, 57–58. The synagogue as a hostel is supported by other evidences, mostly from the post-70 CE period. For specific examples, see Safrai, "Communal Functions," 190–191; Loewenberg, *From Charity*, 142–143.
219. These foreigners could be itinerant pilgrims or even Jews from Rome (Levine, *Ancient Synagogue*, 58), permanent residents of or visitors to Jerusalem (Flesher, "Palestinian Synagogues," 1:34). Nevertheless, it seemed to be a synagogue linked to Diaspora Jews. "Vettenos" was a Roman name; Theodotus' family probably came from Rome. His family could have been "descendants of Jews taken captive by Pompey in 63 BCE" (Levine, *Ancient Synagogue*, 56–57). Paul Virgil McCracken Flesher, in arguing that the synagogue did not co-exist with the Temple in Jerusalem as a religious institution, concluded that the evidence merely confirmed that the only synagogue in Judea was for foreigners but not the locals ("Palestinian Synagogues," 1:33–34).
220. Rosenfeld, "Innkeeping," 134.
221. Constable, *Housing the Stranger*, 11, 13; for more on inns in Greece and Rome, see Firebaugh, *Inns of Greece and Rome*.

from the first to the seventh centuries.[222] As a physical place of lodging, the *pandocheion* was often associated by Greek writers with prostitution, theft, drunkenness, and murder.[223] Besides, the Jewish writer Josephus (*Ant.* 3.276, 451) classified female innkeepers, along with harlots, slaves, prisoners of war, cheating hawkers, and women who left their husbands, as women whom priests could not marry.[224] And in the Mishnah (*m. 'Abod. Zar.* 2:1; *m. Yebam.* 16:7), the integrity of innkeepers was also doubted.[225] The term *inn* was also used metaphorically by philosophers such as Philo and Epictetus to depict "the physical man, whose weak, temporal, and fallible existence contrasts with the superior permanent entity of the rational mind."[226] For Philo, the fool is like those "who, as it were, enter an inn only to fill themselves and vomit in their passions" while Epictetus believed that our transient life on earth, even our possessions, should be treated like a temporary stay at an inn.[227]

On the other hand, the Latin-speaking part of the Roman Empire had different hospitality establishments to cater to travelers' needs.[228] Both the *hospitia* and the *caupona* offered accommodation, as well as food and drink, and it is difficult to distinguish them.[229] Bruce Woodward Frier, studying the

---

222. Constable, *Housing the Stranger*, 7.
223. Ibid., 16. For evidences, especially from Late Antiquity, see ibid., 18–21.
224. Ben-Zion Rosenfeld noted that writings concerning inns in Palestine prior to Josephus did not depict them as places of promiscuity ("Innkeeping," 137–141). "Admitting the problematic nature of argumentation *ex silentio*, one cannot escape the conclusion that, at this phase, inns were not a familiar feature of Jewish life in Palestine" (ibid., 141).
225. See ibid., 143–145. In later rabbinic literature, the inn was painted in a negative light. It was seen as a place where violence and danger lurked. Jewish travelers were exposed to idolatry, theft, verbal and physical violence, robbery, evil innkeepers, and sorcery. For specific examples, see Grossmark, "Inn as a Place of Violence," 57–68.
226. Constable, *Housing the Stranger*, 21–22. The inn as a worldly institution inherent with temptation is found in the writings of early church fathers such as Clement of Alexandria, Hippolytus, Origen, Didymos the Blind, John Chrysostom, Augustine (ibid., 25–29). On a positive note, it is also conceived of as a site for chance encounters and possible conversion and redemption since it is a meeting place for both Christians and non-Christians (ibid., 29).
227. Philo, *QG* 4.33; Epictetus, *Diatr.* 2.23.36–38; *Ench.* 2.11.
228. DeFelice, "Inns and Taverns," 474–476. John DeFelice's article on inns and taverns was based on archaeological findings from Pompeii. The eruption of Mount Vesuvius in 79 CE buried and preserved the city under a carpet of volcanic ash. For a description of the inns and restaurants of Pompeii, see Jashemski, "Pompeian *Copa*."
229. DeFelice, "Inns and taverns," 474, 476. Latin authors were not very consistent in their use of terms for Roman inns. See *A Dictionary of Greek and Roman Antiquities (1890) Online*, s.v. "caupona," Perseus Digital Library, http://www.perseus.tufts.edu/hopper/text?doc=Perseus%3Atext%3A1999.04.0063%3Aalphabetic+letter%3DC%3Aentry+group%3D3%3Aentry%3Dcaupona-cn; Frier, "Rental Market," 27–37. This work discusses inns in general.

rental market in early Imperial Rome, noted that "in literary sources, *caupona* is used almost exclusively for 'inn,' especially 'country inn.'"[230] The term *caupona* carried bad connotations – filth, deceit, vice, violence.[231] Bedbugs were described by Pliny the Elder[232] as "the summertime creatures of the inns."[233] Jérôme Carcopino, writing on the daily life in ancient city of Rome, wrote of keepers of inns and taverns who made the back of their premises into gambling dens and employed prostitutes as barmaids.[234] The Roman philosopher Cicero (c. 106–43 BCE)[235] narrated a story of a traveler who dreamed about a fellow-traveler seeking his help from an evil innkeeper who intended to kill him.[236] Thus, we can conclude with Brian M. Rapske that "the available literary and archaeological sources generally witness to dilapidated and unclean facilities, virtually non-existent furnishings, bedbugs, poor quality food and drink, untrustworthy proprietors and staff, shady clientele, and generally loose morals."[237]

When we consider the ill repute of inns, the parade of nudity in gymnasiums,[238] and the worship of idols in temples (1 Cor 10:20–21), we can understand why first-century travelers preferred to stay in the homes of family members and friends.[239] "Whenever and wherever possible, [Jewish] people preferred synagogue-shelters"; however, the wealthy and traveling scholars preferred home hospitality.[240]

It was common for the well-to-do to entertain their friends and relatives from afar. Such private hospitality was extended to strangers as well since

---

230. Frier, "Rental Market," 33.
231. DeFelice, "Inns and Taverns," 476.
232. Pliny the Elder, *Nat.* 9.154, cited in DeFelice "Inns and Taverns," 483, n. 17.
233. Casson, *Travel in the Ancient World*, 208.
234. Carcopino, *Daily Life in Ancient Rome*, 276. DeFelice cautioned against the general assumption that women working in inns and taverns were prostitutes ("Inns and Taverns," 481; for his argument, see 479–482).
235. Cicero, *Div.* 1.57.
236. Ramsay, "Roads and Travel," 5:393. However, the sources cited by William M. Ramsay are later than first century CE (e.g. Ulpian, Tertullian, and Karl Joachim Marquardt).
237. Rapske, "Acts, Travel and Shipwreck," 15. Brian M. Rapske considered them "fair generalizations" (ibid.). Graffiti found in Pompeii attest to the colorful life in inns and taverns (see Breitenbach, "Pompeian Wall-Scribblings," 529–534).
238. Townsend, "Education (Greco-Roman)," 2:313; see Josephus, *Ant.* 12:241; 1 Macc. 1:14–15.
239. Casson, *Travel in the Ancient World*, 198.
240. Loewenberg, *From Charity*, 143.

the practice of hospitality was regarded as a sacred obligation sanctioned by the religions of that day. The God of the Jewish people loves strangers and watches over them (Deut 10:17–18; Ps 146:9). The Greek god Zeus Xenios, as well as his Roman counterpart, Jupiter Hospitalis, was the protector of strangers.[241] "Each and every stranger had the right of sanctuary and asylum; every wayfarer, as though under the protection of Zeus Xenios himself, was sure to find a host."[242] For the Greeks and Romans, the home was the place where the visitor was warmly received and transformed from the status of stranger to guest.[243] For obvious reasons, the Jews too welcomed strangers of their own kind into their homes. Rabbi Jose ben Joezer (c. 175 BCE) himself said: "Let your house be wide open. And seat the poor at your table ['make . . . members of our household']" (*m. 'Abot.* 1:5).[244]

Home- or household-based hospitality was also practiced by the believers in the early church, as evident in the Book of Acts. When traveling, the apostles stayed with fellow believers. The apostle Peter stayed with Simon the tanner (Acts 9:43; 10:6) while the apostle Paul stayed with the Philippian jailor (Acts 16:27–34), Jason (Acts 17:5–7), Aquila and Priscilla (Acts 18:2–3), Philip the evangelist (Acts 21:8), Mnason of Cyprus (Acts 21:16), and believers in Puteoli (Acts 28:14). After Peter had witnessed to and baptized Cornelius and his household, he was invited to stay for several days (Acts 10:48). Similarly, after Paul had converted and baptized Lydia and her household, he too was invited to stay at her home (Acts 16:15). On the island of Malta, Paul astonished the natives when he escaped unscathed from a viper bite. The chief man of the island, Publius, received Paul and those who were with him and entertained them hospitably for three days (Acts 28:7).

Elsewhere in the epistles, the practice of household-based hospitality was at work as well. Gaius was Paul's host in Corinth (Rom 16:23). Paul personally requested lodging from his friend, Philemon, in Colossae (Phlm 22). He even requested hospitality from the believers in Rome – fellow believers whom he had never met but hoped to see en route to Spain (Rom 15:22–24). In his letters, he also requested hospitality on behalf of his colleagues in the

---

241. Arterbury, *Entertaining Angels*, 38.

242. Firebaugh, *Inns of Greece and Rome*, 29.

243. Stock, "Hospitality," 6:808–812; Arterbury, *Entertaining Angels*, ch. 2.

244. For Jewish hospitality over the centuries, see Greenstone, "Hospitality," 6:480–481; Arterbury, *Entertaining Angels*, ch. 3.

work of the gospel – Phoebe (Rom 16:1–2), Timothy (1 Cor 16:10–11) Mark (Col 4:10), and Zenas and Apollos (Titus 3:13). It is thus evident that home hospitality was practiced by the believers in the early faith communities.

Injunctions to Show Hospitality

Living in the first-century Greco-Roman world, the New Testament writers understood the importance of hospitality. Writing to the various faith communities, they enjoined all believers to practice hospitality (*philoxenia*) (Rom 12:13; Heb 13:2) and to be hospitable (*philoxenos*) (1 Pet 4:9).

Paul exhorted believers in Rome to pursue hospitality (Rom 12:13) and the writer of Hebrews admonished his readers to not neglect to show hospitality (Heb 13:2). In both instances, the word *philoxenia* (literally meaning, "love of strangers") is employed."[245] This could have led some Bible translators to add "strangers" after "hospitality," implying that hospitality is to be shown to strangers.[246]

In Romans 12, "pursuing hospitality" is set within a series of participial clauses (Rom 12:9b–13) that seeks to explain how sincere love is expressed within the faith communities (Rom 12:9a). Immediately preceding it is the call to participate in the material needs (Gk. *chreia*) of the saints (Rom 12:13a). All the occurrences of *chreia* ("need") in the plural (Acts 20:34; 28:10; Rom 12:13; Titus 3:14) refer to material needs such as food, clothing, and shelter.[247] In Acts 28:10, it refers to the material aid given to Paul and his companions by their hosts when they left Malta. This hospitality-related word could be used here in Romans 12:13 since Paul needed the hospitality of the Romans to provide for his mission to Spain (Rom 15:24, 28). Hence, it would seem

---

245. The verb *xenizō* can mean "to surprise" (Acts 17:20; 1 Pet 4:4, 12) or "to show hospitality" (Acts 10:6, 18, 23, 32; 21:16; 28:7; Heb 13:2). Gustav Stählin noted that in the New Testament derivatives of the stem *xen-* (viz. *xenia, xenodocheō, philoxenia, philoxenos*) "belong exclusively to the domain of hospitality" ("ξένος," 5:2). He also highlighted that the compound words, *philoxenia* ("hospitality" in Rom 12:13) and *philoxenon* ("hospitable" in 1 Tim 3:2; Titus 1:8; 1 Pet 4:9), as well as *xenodocheō* ("to show hospitality" in 1 Tim 5:10), a *hapax legomenon*, are found in virtue lists that have an imperative force (ibid., 5:21).
246. See NRSV in Rom 12:13; ASV, KJV, NASB, NIV, NJB, NKJV, NRSV in Heb 13:2 (see Vogels, "Hospitality in Biblical Perspective," 173, n. 35).
247. Moo, *Romans*, 779.

that hospitality was to be shown to needy fellow believers with no explicit reference to strangers[248] or to "traveling Christians unknown to the host."[249]

Similarly, in Hebrews 13, the reminder to practice hospitality (Heb 13:2a) is preceded by the exhortation to let brotherly love (*philadelphia*; literally meaning, "love of brothers") continue (Heb 13:1). However, that such an act of hospitality could be entertaining angels unknowingly (Heb 13:2b) may imply that the guest is unknown to the host (i.e. a stranger). The idea that the stranger might be a divine messenger in disguise is a prevailing motif in Greco-Roman times (see Acts 14:11–12; Homer, *Od.* 17.484–487; Cicero, *Verr.* 2.4.48; *Deiot.* 6.18, *Quint. fratr.* 2.10; Ovid, *Metam.* 8.620–724). Labeled as "theoxenic hospitality" by Ladislaus Bolchazy,[250] one is motivated to treat strangers kindly because "of the belief that the gods or their representatives often visited humans in the form of beggars or strangers."[251] This is akin to what Jesus taught in Matthew 25:31–46, "he Himself is lodged and entertained in the . . . [stranger]."[252] The practice of hospitality could be a spiritual encounter – an opportunity to encounter the Lord Jesus Christ himself. Hence, Ben Witherington III interpreted Hebrews 13:2 to mean hospitality should be shown to "any unknown person"[253] while Criag R. Koester believed that "it also seems likely that care for strangers meant aiding travelers of various sorts, not only those who belonged to the faith community," that is, even non-Christians.[254] Together with the following command to remember those in prison and those who are mistreated (Heb 13:3), the appeal bears close resemblance to Jesus' teaching in Matthew 25:31–46. Hence, hospitality is to be shown to fellow believers and, possibly, strangers who are of the Christian faith.[255]

---

248. Cranfield, *Romans*, 64; Moo, *Romans*, 780.
249. See Witherington and Hyatt, *Romans*, 294; see Käsemann, *Commentary on Romans*, 347; Dunn, *Romans 9–16*, 744; Fitzmyer, *Romans*, 655; Schreiner, *Romans*, 666.
250. Bolchazy, *Hospitality in Antiquity*, 11–14.
251. See Pitt-Rivers, "Stranger," 19; Arterbury, *Entertaining Angels*, 95.
252. Stählin, "ξένος," 5:22.
253. Witherington, *Homilies for Hellenized Christians*, 354.
254. Koester, *To the Hebrews*, 563.
255. Some scholars interpreted Hebrews 13:2 as a reminder to extend hospitality to traveling fellow-Christians (Lane, *Hebrews 9–13*, 512; Ellingworth, *Epistle to the Hebrews*, 694; deSilva, *Perseverance in Gratitude*, 487–488; Witherington, *Homilies for Hellenized Christians*, 354). Paul Ellingworth, however, added that this reference to fellow-Christians was not emphasized (*Epistle to the Hebrews*, 694). George Wesley Buchanan believed that it should be

Rowan A. Greer noted that "it is remarkable that we do not find any clear evidence that hospitality should be practiced by Christians toward unbelievers."[256] Yet, Greer presented Matthew 25:31–46 and Romans 12:13 as two possible passages that deal with hospitality towards unbelievers. His suggestions are disputable because Matthew 25:40 makes reference to "the brothers" (see above p. 184) and, as argued earlier, Romans 12:13 does not seem to include unbelievers. Furthermore, the context of 1 Peter 4 indicates that believers are to be hospitable to one another, namely, fellow believers (1 Pet 4:9).[257] Hospitality, thus, is first and foremost shown to members within a faith community. However, it could also be extended to other members of the larger faith community, the body of Christ – strangers who are fellow brothers or sisters in the Lord.[258]

Expressions of Hospitality in the Life of Early Faith Communities

Our discussion of "Homes/Households as Houses of Hospitality" (see above p. 186) has highlighted the importance of private homes or households as an important location for the practice of hospitality in the early church. Hospitality was "a fitting, requisite, and meaning-filled practice" in the early faith communities and found expression in several aspects of church life.[259] "It was the hospitality of these homes which made possible the Christian worship, common meals, and courage-sustaining fellowship of the group."[260] It was also the hospitality of these homes which made possible the caring of the needy – the poor elderly widows, and traveling Christians.

---

shown first to the immediate faith community and then to strangers of the same faith (*To the Hebrews*, 230).

256. Greer, *Broken Lights and Mended Lives*, 122.

257. Some scholars interpreted hospitality in 1 Peter 4:9 in the context of a house church meeting, that is, hospitality within a local community of believers (Michaels, *1 Peter*, 247; Jobes, *1 Peter*, 280–281; Witherington, *Homilies for Hellenized Christians*, 204–205), while others stressed the need for hospitality to traveling Christians (Kelly, *Epistle of Peter and of Jude*, 178–179; Davids, *First Epistle of Peter*, 158–159; Elliot, *1 Peter*, 751–753), and still others interpreted it to include both the community of believers and traveling Christians (Marshall, *1 Peter*, 144–145; Achtemeier, *1 Peter*, 297).

258. See Bruce, *Epistle to the Hebrews*, 389.

259. Pohl, *Making Room*, 29.

260. Filson, "Early House Churches," 109.

Worship and Common Meals

Private homes and households became the regular gathering place for the early believers to meet for worship – teaching of the Word, prayer, fellowship, breaking of bread, and partaking food together (Acts 2:42, 46; see Rom 16:3–5, 23; 1 Cor 16:19; Phlm 2). "In such a location, hospitality was a natural and necessary practice."[261] Its importance is further seen in the Pastoral Epistles where being hospitable was a qualification for church leadership (1 Tim 3:2; Titus 1:8).

To his pastoral teammates in Ephesus and Crete, Timothy and Titus respectively, Paul reminded them that a bishop must be hospitable (*philoxenos*) (1 Tim 3:2; Titus 1:8). Since being hospitable or practicing hospitality was expected from all believers (see above p. 191, "Injunctions to Show Hospitality"), leaders should also exemplify it. Besides, "it seems to be an assumption that overseers were often also householders (vv. 4–5) [1 Tim 3:4–5], so it is natural that the church should look to them to model this virtue."[262] The same line of reasoning applies to Titus 1:8.[263] Jerome D. Quinn further highlighted the dire straits faced by Jewish Christians fleeing Palestine in the early 60s CE.[264] Thus, hospitality was a primary virtue needed as the churches under Titus' supervision might have had to care for their Palestinian brothers and sisters.

When we consider that "there is no longer Jew or Greek, there is no longer slave or free, there is no longer male or female" because everyone is one in Christ Jesus in God's household (Gal 3:28), we see another expression of hospitality at work in the life of the early church communities.[265] Every believer, regardless of his or her background and status, was to be welcomed, and all should eat together at a common table. In a sense, this is reminiscent of Jesus' inclusive table fellowship. Sadly, the fledgling early faith communities struggled in their efforts to show hospitality to their brothers and sisters in the household of God. The apostle Paul had to rebuke the rich Corinthian believers for their bad table manners – not welcoming the poor when they

---

261. Pohl, *Making Room*, 32.
262. Towner, *Timothy and Titus*, 252; see Knight, *Pastoral Epistles*, 159; Marshall and Towner, *Pastoral Epistles*, 478.
263. Quinn, *Letter to Titus*, 90–91; Marshall and Towner, *Pastoral Epistles*, 163.
264. Quinn, *Letter to Titus*, 91.
265. See Yong, "Guests, Hosts," 75.

came to eat together (1 Cor 11:17–34).[266] When done rightly, "hospitality practices in the Christian community were to portray a clear message – that of equality, transformed relations, and a common life."[267]

Caring for the Needy

As our preceding discussion has shown, hospitality shown to traveling Christians – friends and strangers – was part and parcel of life in the early faith communities (see above p. 191). Widows as well as "itinerant teachers, missionaries, emissaries, and refugees from persecution relied upon a network of Christian homes for shelter and provisions."[268]

Apparently, the early church took care of widows and provided food to them on a daily basis (Acts 6:1). In Paul's instructions to Timothy (1 Tim 5:9–10), a widow, to be eligible for care from the church, must have the reputation for good deeds, such as showing hospitality (*xenodocheō*) and washing the feet of believers. Though washing the feet of guests could be taken as "a symbol for humble service" to believers, it was part and parcel of hospitality from antiquity.[269] By welcoming guests, the widow would have duly discharged her responsibility as the matron of the house.[270] Having shown hospitality to others, the faithful and godly elderly widow would now be shown hospitality by the church.

Though persecutions in the first century were mainly sporadic and local, they still resulted in a scattering of Christians into regions beyond Jerusalem, Judea, and Samaria (Acts 8:4; 11:19).[271] Due to an edict issued by the Roman emperor Claudius, Jews, including Jewish Christians, were expelled from Rome (Acts 18:2). Traveling as refugees or living in a hostile society where believers were ostracized and/or persecuted (see the Epistles of Hebrews, James, and 1 Peter), hospitality promoted solidarity within the Christian community and gave support to those whose faith was tested. Offering hospitality during such precarious times could be a challenging task. Hence, when writing

---

266. Fee, *First Epistle to the Corinthians*, 567–569; Thiselton, *First Epistle to the Corinthians*, 898–899.
267. Pohl, *Making Room*, 32.
268. Lane, *Hebrews 9–13*, 512.
269. Towner, *Timothy and Titus*, 348; See Quinn and Wacker, *Timothy*, 439.
270. Towner, *Timothy and Titus*, 347.
271. Cairns, *Christianity through the Centuries*, 86.

to Christians living among hostile neighbors, the New Testament authors reminded the believers that hospitality was an act not to be neglected (Heb 13:2) and one was to be hospitable without complaining (1 Pet 4:9). Paul even urged the Christians in Rome to pursue (Gk. *diōkō*) hospitality (Rom 12:13b). The verb *pursue* projects a "proactive stance," suggesting that believers should take the initiative to seek out strangers rather than passively wait for strangers to approach them.[272] Taking the preceding admonition – contribute to the needs of the saints (Rom 12:13a) – into consideration, it seems then that the practice of hospitality could be a financial burden.[273] In the light of this, Paul had to urge believers to make an effort to pursue hospitality.

Besides extending hospitality to widows and dislocated persecuted Christians, hospitality was also extended to itinerant teachers, missionaries, and emissaries, a practice that is similar to the hospitality extended to traveling pairs of Jewish rabbis in the first century CE.[274] Being rich in their knowledge of the Torah but poor materially, the rabbis were often invited to homes of individuals.[275] In exchange for food and lodging, they would share their learning at the homes.[276] Jesus likely was following the convention of his day when he sent his disciples out on mission, teaching them to depend on the hospitality of receptive hosts (Matt 10:1–42; Mark 6:7–11; Luke 9:1–5; 10:1–16). The apostles and the early faith communities probably continued this practice. So, like the traveling pairs of Jewish rabbis, traveling ministry workers were to get material assistance in return for the spiritual food they shared. "The missionaries are to allow the host to feed them; they are to sit at the table of the *oikos* not as beggars but as guests."[277]

---

272. Arterbury, *Entertaining Angels*, 108; see Moo, *Romans*, 780, n. 80.
273. Schreiner, *Romans*, 666–667.
274. Koenig, *New Testament Hospitality*, 17.
275. Such a practice was extolled in later rabbinic literature (Loewenberg, *From Charity*, 143–144).
276. A practice of Jesus too as he was invited to homes and share at the table (Luke 7:36–50; 11:37–52; 14:1–14). John Koenig mentioned that the practice of opening one's home and inviting the needy to dinner on the eve of Sabbath existed before the time of Jesus and was practiced in the first century (*New Testament Hospitality*, 16, citing Samuel H. Dresner).
277. Gehring, *House Church and Mission*, 55.

At the same time, this practice of open welcome of strangers could be potentially harmful to the hosts and abused by the guests.[278] As a result, it was common for one to write a letter of recommendation to vouch for the character of another.[279] This convention was to protect the host as well as the vulnerable traveler passing through an inhospitable area. Such a letter would vouch for the character of the guest and allow the guest to be exempted from any test of worthiness. Instead, the guest would be accorded the same status as the letter writer.[280] "To reject the recommended stranger is, of course, a challenge to the honor of the recommender. It spurns his honor, and requires an attempt at satisfaction on his part, under pain of being shamed."[281]

A case in point can be found in 2 and 3 John. In 2 John 10, the elder instructed that hospitality, including greetings (*chairō*), should not be extended to false teachers teaching who did not teach the truth. In the Mediterranean world, the character of either the host or the guest was implicated by his or her counterpart.[282] To welcome a traveling preacher was tantamount to welcoming his spiritual message.[283] Therefore, it would be unwise to associate with one with questionable credentials. Moreover, by not providing a base for their activities, it could curb the influence of these false teachers and the propagation of their erroneous teachings.[284] In this case, inhospitality would protect the vulnerable host because the act of welcome was an expression of solidarity, a participation in their evil deeds which would then result in receiving the same condemnation (2 John 11).[285]

And in 3 John, the elder was writing to Gaius, requesting him to show hospitality to Demetrius because Diotrephes had refused to welcome (*epidechomai*) the elders and his friends (3 John 9–10), thus bringing shame

---

278. Another possible problem posed by the practice of hospitality is the abuse of the hosts' goodwill in providing food, lodging, and provisions to the guests (Arterbury, *Entertaining Angels*, 98–99). This abuse was later addressed in the post-apostolic church manual, *Didache* (see *Did.* 11–12).
279. See Malherbe, *Social Aspects*, 101–103; Arterbury, *Entertaining Angels*, 99–100.
280. Arterbury, *Entertaining Angels*, 99.
281. Malina, "Received View," 187.
282. Arterbury, *Entertaining Angels*, 119.
283. Gehring, *House Church and Mission*, 56.
284. Marshall, *Epistles of John*, 75; Rensberger, *Epistles of John*, 114–115; Smalley, *1, 2, 3 John*, 320–321; for more, see Lieu, *1, 2, & 3 John*, 259–261.
285. Marshall, *Epistles of John*, 74.

to the elder. The verb *epidechomai* is used twice in the New Testament and only in 3 John. The NRSV has translated the same verb differently in these two occurrences, "to acknowledge (someone's) authority" in verse 9, and "to welcome" in verse 10, thus complicating the issue.[286] In the Septuagint, the verb is used frequently with the idea of receiving another as a guest (1 Macc. 10:1; 12:8, 43; 14:23). Furthermore, the use of other compounds of *dechomai* in the sense of warm reception and welcome makes it possible for it to be used with the same sense in 3 John 9.[287] As Barth L. Campbell suggested, "rather than primarily a conflict regarding doctrine, polity, theology, or morality, the contention involving the elder and Diotrephes revolves around the giving and withholding of hospitality."[288] In rejecting those sent by the elder, Diotrephes had also rejected him, the one who sent them (see Matt 10:40; Luke 10:16; John 5:23; 12:44; 13:20).[289] Within the prevalent honor-shame social matrix of the Mediterranean world, such an act was a public display of dishonor and shame.[290] Besides slandering the elder, Diotrephes had also dishonored the elder further by preventing those who wanted to show hospitality to the elder's emissaries and expelling them from the church (3 John 10). Hence,

---

286. Raymond E. Brown's understanding paralleled NRSV's translation. However, he added, "In my view both meanings of *epidechesthai* are present in 9b: the letter was looked upon as an extension of the Presbyter's presence in his role as a member of the Johannine School; his missionaries would have had precisely the same function. The refusal to welcome the missionaries (10d) and to accept the letter (9b) are two sides of the same policy" (*Epistles of John*, 718). See Smalley, *1, 2, 3 John*, 343.

287. Lieu, *1, 2, & 3 John*, 275. E.g. with *ana-* (Acts 28:7); with *apo-* (Luke 8:40; 9:11; Acts 18:27; 21:17; 28:30); with *hypo-* (Luke 19:6; Acts 17:7); with *para-* (Acts 15:4); with *pros-* (Rom 16:2; Phil 2:29). For a more detailed study on Greek words associated with hospitality, see Arterbury, *Entertaining Angels*; esp. 53–54, 92–93, 130–131, 187–189. Likewise, both Abraham J. Malherbe and Margaret M. Mitchell argued that the verb should be translated as "to receive someone as a guest." (see Malherbe, *Social Aspects*, 106–107; Mitchell, "Diotrephes," 299–320). However, Malherbe argued it in the context of letters of recommendation while Mitchell, the context of diplomatic relations.

288. Campbell, "Honor, Hospitality," 338. See Malherbe, *Social Aspects*, 92–112; Malina, "Received View," 171–194; Arterbury, *Entertaining Angels*, 120. For ecclesiastical disagreement, see Marshall, *Epistles of John*, 12–13; Storm, "Diotrephes," 193–202; Strecker, *Johannine Letters*, 100; for doctrinal differences, see Bultmann, *Johannine Epistles*, 261–262; or combination of both factors, see Brown, *Epistles of John*, 738–739; Smalley, *1, 2, 3 John*, 340.

289. See Mitchell, "New Testament Envoys," 641–662.

290. "The social values of honor and dishonor were fundamental to first-century culture, whether Roman, Greek, Egyptian or Jewish" (deSilva, *Introduction*, 125). For ancient sources supporting this premise, see deSilva, *Perseverance in Gratitude*, ch. 1; *Despising Shame*, chs. 2, 3.

Campbell proposed that in writing 3 John, the elder was trying to reclaim his honor, as well as the integrity of the gospel, by writing 3 John.[291]

A clue to the extent of hospitality shown to visiting ministry workers is found in the act of sending off these guests. The elder in 3 John 6 suggested that Gaius would do well by sending visiting preachers on in a way (*propempō*) worthy of God. "*Propempō* is used in the New Testament only for sending a departing traveler on his way."[292] The verb could mean "to accompany" or "to escort someone" (Acts 20:38; 21:5). However, it is more frequently used with the idea "to assist someone in making a journey, *send on one's way* with food, money, by arranging for companions, means of travel, etc."[293] This idea is made even more explicit in Titus 3:13. Titus was instructed to "make every effort to send Zenas the lawyer and Apollos on their way, and see that they lack nothing." Putting it plainly and in practical terms, "sending the missionaries on their way involved providing for their journey – supplying them with food and money to pay for their expenses, washing their clothes, and generally helping them to travel as comfortably as possible."[294] "Essentially, anything that takes place 'from the moment a visitor approaches someone's house until the moment he departs' or even reaches his next destination is considered to be an outgrowth of either hospitality or inhospitality."[295] Viewed from this perspective, we can thereby accept Stählin's statement that "hospitality serves the gospel."[296]

In summary, the location for hospitality in the early faith communities was the private homes or households. Incidentally, the households, like the gymnasiums, temples, and synagogues, were not only houses of hospitality but also centers of learning (see above p. 186).[297] Furthermore, practicing hospitality was a social necessity and a moral obligation for the first-century believers. Marginalized and persecuted because of their Christian faith, the

---

291. Campbell, "Honor, Hospitality," 321–341.
292. Malherbe, *Social Aspects*, 96, n. 11. Also in the Septuagint (see 1 Esd 4:47; Jdt 10:15; 1 Macc. 12:4; 2 Macc. 6:23; Wis 19:2).
293. Bauer, *Greek-English Lexicon*, s.v. "προπέμπω" (original emphasis); see Acts 15:3; Rom 15:24; 1 Cor 16:6, 11; 2 Cor 1:16; Titus 3:13; 3 John 6.
294. Marshall, *Epistles of John*, 85–86.
295. Arterbury, *Entertaining Angels*, 51.
296. Stählin, "ξένος," 5:22; see Riddle, "Early Christian Hospitality."
297. For temples as centers of learning, see Bonner, *Education in Ancient Rome*, 117.

believers were enjoined to show hospitality to one another, the needy fellow believers, traveling strangers, as well as itinerant missionaries and church leaders. Home- or household-based hospitality, hence, played a vital role in the mission and expansion of the early faith communities. The contexts (namely, social, cultural, economic, and political) of the first century may be different from our present days. The contexts may also be different in each corner of the world that we live in now. However, the injunction to Christians to practice hospitality remains unchanged. Hence, theological educators need to consider how they can practice Christian hospitality within their faith communities – the theological institutions – and, especially, to their students.

Summary

This chapter has examined the motif of hospitality from a biblical perspective. It first examined the metaphor of God as host through Israel's testimony about God as a gracious host and provider. Having practiced hospitality as a way of life, the Israelites could relate to and testify of God's gracious providential care throughout their history – from Adam and Eve, to the wilderness experience under the leadership of Moses, to the land of milk and honey, and in the age to come. The promised land of milk and honey was Israel's inheritance. Yet, it was still God's land. Living as strangers, aliens, and tenants in God's land, they were obligated to show hospitality to aliens and strangers – a reminder that they were strangers before in the land of Egypt and a reflection of the hospitality they had received from God.

The second section focused first on Jesus Christ as a host ministering to the people and his disciples, then as a dinner guest in many homes, and lastly as the guest-turned-host, sharing gifts with his hosts. His eating habits earned him the label of "a friend of tax collectors and sinners." By eating with people of questionable purity, he had upset the Pharisees' sense of purity and social propriety, having erased social boundaries and overturned the social hierarchy. Jesus broke down the wall of exclusivism to redefine the kingdom of God – as inclusive, status-leveling, and honor-sharing. And by sending his disciples on mission, carrying with them the bare necessities, Jesus was teaching them to depend on the hospitality of others and experience God as host for themselves. For him, extending a helping hand to the stranger, the poor and the needy was essentially a ministry to him. The weak or the stranger was none other than Christ himself.

The final section examined the role of hospitality in the life of early faith communities. Besides the apostolic command to practice hospitality, which could be an encounter with the divine, the political and social conditions of the first century also made it necessary for household-based hospitality. Private residences or households became places of hospitality to welcome traveling Christian workers and needy fellow believers – friends or strangers. In addition to the provision of food and lodging, one showed hospitality by sending guests on their way, providing them with supplies adequate for them to reach their next destination. By doing so, one becomes a partner with others in the ministry and mission of Jesus – "to seek out and to save the lost" (Luke 19:10).

Though the biblical texts do not portray hospitality as a context or paradigm for teaching and learning, yet the expressions of hospitality as gleaned from these images can definitely inform how theological educators can be hospitable hosts in their respective faith communities, that is, the learning communities of the theological institutions where they minister.[298] The biblically informed and theologically grounded metaphor can teach theological educators how they can mirror the divine and Christian activity of hospitality and "become a visible exemplar" to students, showing them tangibly what it means to receive hospitality and to share that hospitality

---

298. One examiner of this dissertation highlighted that Thomas H. Groome used the two disciples' encounter with Jesus Christ on the road to Emmaus (Luke 24:13–35) as the educational paradigm for his shared praxis approach to religious education (*Christian Religious Education*, 135–136; *Sharing Faith*, 306–307, 511, n. 15). Groome described his approach as "*a group of Christians sharing in dialogue their critical reflection on present action in light of the Christian Story and its Vision toward the end of lived Christian faith*" (*Christian Religious Education*, 184 [original emphasis]). From the Emmaus narrative, he outlined five movements for shared praxis: (1) present action, (2) critical reflection, (3) Story and its Vision, (4) dialectic between Story and stories, and (5) dialectic between Vision and visions. Groome's dialogical approach is certainly worthy of future consideration, especially under the section pertaining to reciprocity, dialogue, and partnership (see below p. 250). However, in my opinion, this one incident, though related to hospitality, does not present hospitality as a paradigm for teaching and learning. Although Groome interpreted this narrative from an educational perspective, he did not perceive it in relation to hospitality (*Sharing Faith*, 306). Instead, he wrote that a hospitable environment is vital for shared praxis (*Christian Religious Education*, 226–227; *Sharing Faith*, 168–170), and that a religious educator must be hospitable ("Spirituality of the Religious Educator," 16–18).

with others.[299] This biblical perspective of hospitality also provides some theologically grounded principles for us to critique the extent to which existing conceptions and contemporary parallel practices of hospitality in higher education reflect biblical themes, and is therefore relevant to theological education and theological educators in their conceptualizing of their task towards the holistic formation of students. This is our focus in the next chapter.

---

299. Davies, "Walking in God's Ways," 103.

5

A Critical Dialogue towards the Application of the Motif of Hospitality in Theological Education

This book seeks to show how the motif of hospitality can be applied in theological education for creating an environment to facilitate the holistic formation of students. In chapters 2 and 3, I have shown how the concept of hospitality, first conceived by Henri J. M. Nouwen and Parker J. Palmer as a viable corrective for the hostile teaching-learning environment, has been used by educators in Christian, theological, and higher education arenas to help them examine their work and rethink their teaching practices. The examination of the biblical practice of hospitality in chapter 4 has provided a description of biblical hospitality and the biblical basis to critique the extent to which existing conceptions and contemporary parallel practices of hospitality in higher education can be utilized by theological educators to conceptualize their educational task in ways that are consistent with their theological beliefs. In the light of the work done so far in chronicling the history and development of the concept of hospitality, and in setting out a biblical basis for judging this literary phenomenon and contemporary educational practices, this chapter seeks to assess four constitutive elements of hospitality (drawn from the foregoing discussions) and explore how they can be translated into practice by theological educators to transform the teaching-learning environment in theological education for holistic transformation of students.

Hospitality as a Cluster Concept

The lexical definition of the Greek word *philoxenia* is hospitality. Etymologically, it would mean "love of strangers" (see above p. 191). However, such a simple definition fails to adequately explicate the usage of hospitality. As seen in the previous chapters, modern authors have each given their own understanding of what hospitality means or how it can be expressed. Hence, I would like to contribute to this ongoing conversation on hospitality by using John Hospers' concept of a "*quorum* feature of definitions"[1] and Max Black's "range concept" or "cluster concept."[2] In his discussion on definition, Hospers acknowledged that vagueness makes it difficult to give a precise definition of a word. Sometimes, a word could have "*multiple criteria* for its application":[3]

> A term may be associated with characteristics A, B, C, D, and E. But if a thing has A, B, and C, the term may apply without D or E. Or, it can have B, C, D, and E but not A and still apply. As long as it has some of the features, the term is applicable. But there may be no one feature that *all* members of the class have in common; the term may be applicable no matter which feature is absent as long as all or most of the others are there. And the others needn't have the same *weight*: having D may count more heavily than having E.[4]

Similarly, Black's "range concept" or "cluster concept" is concerned with a cluster of constitutive elements, "none of them being separated necessary or sufficient, but each of them relevant in the sense of potentially counting toward the proper application of the concept."[5] Thus, in this chapter, rather than defining hospitality in a single statement, I would present biblical hospitality as "love for the other," and discuss hospitality in terms of a cluster concept of four key constitutive elements: (1) inclusion, (2) presence, (3)

---

1. Hospers, *Introduction*, 3rd ed., 122 (original emphasis).
2. Black, "How Do Pictures Represent?" 128. For a more detailed explanation of this concept, see Max Black's earlier essay, "Definition, Presuppositions, and Assertion."
3. Although John Hospers did not use the term *quorum feature of definitions* in the fourth edition of his book, *An Introduction to Philosophical Analysis*, his discourse on vagueness in definition, correlates with what he had written in the third edition.
4. Hospers, *Introduction*, 4th ed., 22 (original emphasis).
5. Black, "How Do Pictures Represent?" 128.

Critical Dialogue towards the Application of the Motif of Hospitality   205

care, and (4) reciprocity. The choice of these four constitutive elements is not random: it is based on the ideas that have emerged from the discussion in the preceding chapters. This approach is also not intended to be fully inclusive of all the various developments of the concept of hospitality that have been discussed thus far in this book, especially in chapters 2 and 3, but it encapsulates the essential essence of the concept in the choice of these four constitutive elements, as the ensuing discussion shows.

Constitutive Element 1: Inclusion

Diversity is a reality. Inclusion is a choice. Diversity of all sorts is indeed a reality in this globalized world. However, individuals have to make their own choice as to whom they would like to include in their circle of concern. In the practice of hospitality in theological education, the constitutive element of inclusion is about creating a more welcoming environment that seeks to include rather than exclude. Here, it is discussed under the following sub-themes: (1) hosts rather than hostages, (2) boundaries as horizons, and (3) intentional marginality. In the examination of each theme, I have included some thoughts on how inclusion could be used as a principle of practice in the classrooms of theological institutions to create an inclusive environment that facilitates the holistic formation of students.

Hosts Rather than Hostages

In several of the works reviewed in this book, the authors turned to Jacques Derrida's notion of hospitality, particularly the unquestioning or unconditional welcome of the visitor, when discussing inclusion – of persons,[6] or ideas,[7] or both.[8] Derrida, in his discussion with Richard Kearney, defined unconditional hospitality as "openness to whomever, to any newcomer."[9] Unconditional hospitality would "say *yes to who or what turns up*" at one's door/shore – "a foreigner, an immigrant, an invited guest, or an uninvited guest, whether or

---

6. Ibrahim, "Question of the Question."
7. Phipps and Barnett, "Academic Hospitality"; Kuokkanen, "What Is Hospitality"
8. Quinn, "No Room."
9. Kearney, "Desire of God," 133.

not the new arrival is the citizen of another country, a human, animal, or divine creature, a living or dead thing, male or female."[10]

However, Derrida's call for unconditional hospitality, "in *receiving without invitation*, beyond or before the invitation"[11] which he thought might be quite consistent to the hospitality of the infinite, of God, is quite unlike Jesus' call for hospitality to receive the poor, sick, prisoners, and the outcasts.[12] For Derrida, radical hospitality must be "where the welcoming . . . is second, no longer subject to the visit, to the visitation, and where one becomes, prior to being the *hôte*, the hostage of the other."[13] Hence, hospitality becomes a paradox because one needs to be the master of the house in order to extend hospitality and welcome whoever shows up at the door and allow them to make themselves at home. Yet in Derrida's logic, the master (namely, the inviting host) becomes the hostage, and the guest (namely, the invited hostage) becomes the master; that is, "the guest (*hôte*) becomes the host (*hôte*) of the host (*hôte*)."[14] As a result, "an infinite cycle takes place wherein the positions of both host and hostage are simultaneously assumed,"[15] making "everyone into everyone else's hostage."[16]

Derrida's reversal of the roles of host and guest is comparable to the biblical use of *xenos* which can be translated as "stranger" or "host." A brief etymological study of two key Greek hospitality-related words reveals that the noun *xenos* occurs fourteen times in the New Testament and is often translated as "stranger" or "foreigner" (Matt 25:35, 38, 43, 44; 27:7; Acts 17:18, 21; Eph 2:12, 19; Heb 11:13; 3 John 1:5).[17] However, it is translated once as "host" in Romans 16:23. The same polysemous meanings are found in the verb *xenizō*. Used in the active sense, it means "to entertain as a host" (Acts 10:23; 28:7;

---

10. Derrida and Dufourmantelle, *Of Hospitality*, 77 (original emphasis).
11. Derrida, "Hostipitality," 360 (original emphasis).
12. Ibid., 365.
13. Ibid. In Jacques Derrida's usage, the word *hôte* can mean either "guest" or "host" (Derrida and Dufourmantelle, *Of Hospitality*, 125; see above p. 114, n. 172). In this context, it probably means "host."
14. Derrida and Dufourmantelle, *Of Hospitality*, 123, 125.
15. Leung and Stone, "Otherness and Hospitality," 196.
16. Derrida and Dufourmantelle, *Of Hospitality*, 125.
17. All word studies are done with *BibleWorks 9* (2013).

Heb 13:2), in the passive, "to be entertained as a guest" (Acts 10:6, 18; 21:16).[18] The shared etymology of host and stranger/guest, and hosting and guesting implies that the roles of host and guest are interchangeable. This fluidity of the roles of host and guest has also been brought up by many authors, and often, in the context of reciprocity (see below p. 244, "Constitutive Element 4: Reciprocity").[19]

Derrida also described the guest, the invited hostage, as someone appearing from the horizon as a liberator, holding the keys of freedom for the host.[20] As Molly Quinn put it, "He [Derrida] underscores the heart of hospitality as simultaneously poison and remedy ..., risk and possibility – required, perhaps even redemptive, and potentially reckless."[21] No doubt, hospitality can be potentially risky (discussed below p. 209, "Boundaries as Horizons") – "we do not know what we will discover about the other person or ourselves and how that will impact our lives."[22] We can choose to be held hostage to potential dangers. Or, we can look forward to pleasant delights[23] – surprises, gifts, promises, truth, even new life.[24]

Nonetheless, with Derrida's use of the terms *host* and *hostage*, "hospitality, which typically carries a genial connotation, quickly morphs into hostility when deconstructed, namely, into xenophobia."[25] The negative connotation associated with the term *hostage* can make one wary of strangers. The idea of one being a hostage of the other is clearly not found in Jesus' welcome of the other. Jesus, the guest-host, in enacting inclusion and God's all-embracing grace through his inclusive table fellowship, would say "yes" to whoever came to share his table but he never regarded himself as being a hostage to his guests (see above p. 179, "Jesus' intentional acts"). He remained, always, a

---

18. The verb can also mean "to surprise." When used with this sense, it carries a negative connotation (e.g. Acts 17:20; 1 Pet 4:4, 12). The element of surprise comes from the presence of a strange person or thing (Koenig, *New Testament Hospitality*, 8).
19. E.g. Nouwen, *Reaching Out*, 67; Palmer, *Company of Strangers*, 78; Kuokkanen, "What Is Hospitality," 76–77; Larson, "Creating a Space," 2; Shaw, "Welcome Guest," 21; Burwell and Huyser, "Practicing Hospitality," 10; Hagstrom, "Role of Charism," 4–5.
20. Derrida and Dufourmantelle, *Of Hospitality*, 121, 123.
21. Quinn, "No Room," 106.
22. Newman, "Hotel or Home," 92.
23. Quinn, "No Room," 111.
24. Nouwen, *Reaching Out*, 66–67; Palmer, *Company of Strangers*, 64–65; Bennett, *Academic Life*, 54; Shaw, "Welcome Guest," 21; Hagstrom, "Role of Charism," 6.
25. Fox and Reece, "Impossible Decision," 262.

gracious host who lovingly served his guests, invited or uninvited. In fact, just days before his betrayal by his disciple Judas Iscariot, Jesus acted as the host/servant and washed the feet of all his disciples, even Judas Iscariot (John 13:4–5).[26] Despite knowing that he soon would become a hostage of Judas, Jesus still performed this welcoming act of hospitality towards him. In spite of knowing the suffering he had to endure to welcome all, he still set his face to the cross. As phrased by Marjorie J. Thompson, "Jesus' arms stretched on the beam – extended to release our sin, to receive all in love, to invite us to new life – are the very image of God's unaccountably gracious hospitality to us."[27]

Hospitality should not begin with the fear of being held hostage by or coming under the servitude of the other. Instead, hospitality should begin with theological educators standing ready with a basin of water and a towel at the door, waiting to wash the feet of any student that crosses the threshold into their classrooms. This welcoming stance of a servant-host – mental or physical – should be the overture of hospitality that theological educators can extend to their students. But a word of caution is needed here. Overly eager teacher-hosts can make student-guests feel like hostages. Theological educators need to strike a delicate balance in this regard, carefully considering the social and cultural milieu of their students.

In seeking to create a hospitable learning environment, theological educators must also heed Elizabeth Newman's reminder that "hospitality is a practice ultimately in service to God and to God's truth."[28] Our theological conviction – that "the other is a worthy child of God, no matter how much we might fail to see this" – should give us the courage to do the risky business and welcome "the other in all of his or her particularity, even to the point of being willing to *suffer* at the hands of the other."[29] The atmosphere of inclusiveness begins when looking at "the misshapen and the well-proportioned . . . empty faces, and noble faces in indiscriminate confusion, . . . the glance of the educator accepts and receives them all."[30]

---

26. See Arterbury, *Entertaining Angels*, 91, 184.
27. Thompson, *Soul Feast*, 131.
28. Newman, "Hospitality and Christian," 87.
29. Newman, "Faith-Knowledge Dichotomy," 145–146 (original emphasis).
30. Buber, *Between Man and Man*, 112. For Martin Buber, inclusion does not end here. It is a developing I-Thou relationship whereby "the teacher must really *mean* him [the student] as the definite person he is in his potentiality and his actuality; . . . he must be aware of him as a whole being and affirm him in this wholeness" (*I and Thou*, 131–132 [original emphasis]).

Boundaries as Horizons

Just as Newman as well as others have admitted, hospitality is risky business: Hospitality may entail suffering at the hands of the other.[31] As Derrida put it, "For unconditional hospitality to take place you have to accept the risk of the other coming and destroying the place, initiating a revolution, stealing everything, or killing everyone" because you do not know if the "who" or "what" that turns up at the door is a good person or the devil.[32] This is the disconcerting picture of hospitality. And Derrida is right to say that "if you exclude the possibility that the newcomer is coming to destroy your house – if you want to control this and exclude in advance this possibility – there is no hospitality."[33] Thus, the challenge before theological educators is "to calculate the risks, yes, but without closing the door on the incalculable, that is, on the future and the foreigner."[34]

Through his deconstruction, Derrida has given "a clear-eyed corrective to a tendency to over-spiritualize the struggle that characterizes hospitality" – an assessment of John Blevins with which I agree.[35] Hospitality is certainly not about "soft sweet kindness, tea parties, bland conversations and a general atmosphere of coziness."[36] Having said that, it would then seem that unconditional hospitality, as extolled by Derrida and advocated by some of the authors, represents an unattainable ideal, an impossible possibility that Jesus, and maybe a few others like the late Mother Teresa, could achieve.[37] I

---

31. Newman, "Faith-Knowledge Dichotomy," 145; Pohl, "Mysterious and Mundane," 5; Haswell, Haswell, and Blalock, "College Composition Courses," 708; Quinn, "No Room," 110; Call, "Rough Trail," 66.
32. Derrida, "Hospitality, Justice," 70, 71.
33. Ibid., 70.
34. Derrida, "Principle of Hospitality," 6.
35. Blevins, "Hospitality Is a Queer Thing," 113.
36. Nouwen, *Reaching Out*, 66.
37. From the Scriptures, we know that Jesus did not draw any boundaries when extending welcome to all, even though he was aware of the potential risks involved. The one who betrayed him was one of his chosen disciples. The same can be said of the late Mother Teresa. A missionary to India, Mother Teresa worked among the sick, dying, lepers, and abandoned children. Through the order she founded, the Missionaries of Charity, she established a leper colony outside the city of Calcutta and built many leper clinics in Calcutta. "The Missionaries of Charity were not to wear gloves to touch the maggot-ridden bodies of the dying, any more than they were to hold the lepers at arm's length because they were tending the body of Christ" (Spink, *Mother Teresa*, 69). While others would avoid lepers like the plague, lepers were the only ones who were allowed to kiss Mother Teresa (Greene, *Mother Teresa*, 120).

believe that most people, to minimize risks so as to protect themselves, are more inclined to draw the limits and boundaries to the "who" and "what" can be welcomed. When analyzed closely, it is fear – the fear of strangers, abuses, violence – that leads people to draw up social codes and political laws, stipulating who can arrive and how they should behave.[38]

Drawing limits and boundaries in the practice of hospitality is a perennial problem. As discussed in chapter 4 (see above p. 197), the first-century Christian communities had to set guidelines regarding the practice of hospitality to protect the identity and integrity of their communities (2 John 9–11; 3 John 5–10; *Did.* 11–12) as safeguards against exploitation (e.g. 2 Tim 3:6; Jude 12). That depicts more the reality of the world we live in. As finite beings, we are constrained by many limitations, such as time, resources, and space.[39] Furthermore, our gracious hospitality could be exploited by the other. Herein lies the dilemma: "Boundaries and hospitality . . . are in a necessary but irresolvable tension with each other."[40]

Ultimately, theological educators have to acknowledge the need for boundaries in their practice of hospitality.[41] However, boundary lines need to be drawn with extreme care because "boundaries both foster and inhibit freedom; they both protect and violate life."[42] On the one hand, boundaries can serve to make a place "physically and psychologically safe."[43] They can also give "a point of orientation and a frame of reference" that allows for critical engagement with others (see below p. 225, "Articulate Presence to the Other").[44] "*Without a boundary, we have nothing to which we can invite or*

---

38. Derrida and Bennington, "Politics and Friendship."
39. This is a real concern of host countries when they deal with immigrants, refugees, and asylum seekers but this area is beyond the scope of this work. Suffice here to say that Derrida was aware of the realities of immigration issues but he still advocated unconditional hospitality ("Hospitality, Justice," 70–71; Kearney, "Desire of God," 133). Christine D. Pohl too believed that "although hospitality is inadequate as a total response to the needs of strangers, immigrants, refugees and asylum seekers, it is a crucial component of any response." ("Responding to Strangers," 83).
40. Westerhoff, *Good Fences*, xii.
41. See Pohl, *Making Room*, ch. 7; Westerhoff, *Good Fences*; Thompson, "Boundaries," Wrobleski, *Limits of Hospitality*.
42. Connolly, *Ethos of Pluralization*, 163.
43. Pohl, *Making Room*, 140.
44. Nouwen, *Reaching Out*, 98.

welcome anyone else."[45] Yet, on the other hand, boundaries can be hostile and intrusive. As pointed out by Derrida, even supposedly welcoming questions such as "Who are you? Where do you come from? What do you want?" can become "unnecessary, if not outright violent."[46] Boundaries, thereby, become "a fortress of exclusion and self-protection."[47]

Thus, Palmer's paradoxical tension in the teaching-learning space becomes a useful tool for our consideration of boundaries: "The space should be bounded and open."[48] Or, as Jessica Wrobleski put it, there must be "a balance between a generous openness and the safety of boundaries."[49] For instance, in the classroom of theological institutions, boundaries formed by a question or text related to the subject would prevent the space from becoming a "chaotic void" and "a place no learning is likely to occur."[50] Yet, the space must also be open – open to surprises, new discoveries, new paths of learning.[51] Seen from this perspective, and as expressed by Martin Heidegger, "a boundary is not that at which something stops but, as the Greeks recognized, the boundary is that from which something *begins its essential unfolding. That is why the concept is that of horismos*, that is, the horizon, the boundary."[52] New possibilities and opportunities await us at the edge of the horizon as we are challenged to transcend familiar boundaries, to struggle with vulnerability as we welcome the other into our own world, "allowing his or her strangeness and unfamiliarity to affect and engage us."[53] And if truth is our guest, then "the risk we feel is not really the risk of error; it is the challenge of transformation that comes as we allow ourselves to be mastered by truth."[54] This is pertinent to theological education where truth

---

45. Westerhoff, *Good Fences*, 7 (original emphasis).
46. Derrida and Dufourmantelle, *Of Hospitality*, 131; see Ibrahim, "Question of the Question," 150. For Derrida, these questions are especially hostile when they are asked at the immigration checkpoints.
47. Bouma-Prediger and Walsh, "Education for Homeless or Homemaking," 67.
48. Palmer, *Courage to Teach*, 76.
49. Wrobleski, *Limits of Hospitality*, xii.
50. Palmer, *Courage to Teach*, 77; see *To Know as We Are Known*, 72.
51. Palmer, *Courage to Teach*, 77.
52. Heidegger, *Basic Writings*, 356 (original emphasis).
53. Bennett, "Hospitality and Collegial," 93; see *Collegial Professionalism*, 36.
54. Palmer, *To Know as We Are Known*, 117.

– the Word of God – is the foundation for holistic formation of students: to form and transform the way they think, do, live, and feel (see above p. 4).

When theological educators envision boundaries as horizons, "the wideness of God's mercy and generosity of God's welcome must frame [their] thinking about limits and boundaries."[55] The Trinitarian perichoretic hospitality proposed by the theologian Amos Yong serves to illustrate this point. "God as Giver [Father], Given [Son], and Giving [Holy Spirit] … initiates, sustains, and solicits, rather than requiring (by law or otherwise) our own giving."[56] As such, theological educators should "allow the gifts poured out to overflow through their lives into those of others because of the boundless hospitality of an excessively gracious God."[57] Having said that, it is also important to note that Christian hospitality "is not hospitality without boundaries or limits but rather hospitality that enacts such limits while *minimizing* violence or harm to those who may be excluded," rather than minimizing the violence and harm that the one doing the excluding would experience.[58] This is not to obliterate the issue of risks faced by the host in a naïve manner but, rather, to serve as a reminder of the vulnerability of the stranger or guest. Moreover, the risks and dangers of receiving and welcoming strangers can be reduced considerably through wise practices, such as offering hospitality within the context of a larger educational community, having the initial meeting at public places, community rituals, or small group meetings.[59] In the context of theological education, events such as the admissions interview, the orientation session, chapel services and the celebration of the Holy Communion, and communal meals can become threshold places and the means to help reduce the risk factor for the both students and teachers.[60]

In the theological education setting, some boundaries are already prescribed by the institution, such as the entry requirements for admission, course description, members of mentoring groups, even the size and physical layout of the classroom. Though theological educators may be somewhat

---

55. Pohl, *Making Room*, 129.
56. Yong, "Guests, Hosts," 79.
57. Ibid.
58. Wrobleski, *Limits of Hospitality*, 22 (original emphasis).
59. See Pohl, "Hospitality from the Edge," 134; *Making Room*, 93–98.
60. See Jacobs, "Audacity of Hospitality," 573–574, for student and faculty orientations.

reluctant to accept last-minute changes to their class enrollment, I would say that it is easier to transgress these given boundaries than those "invisible" boundaries created by gender stereotypes, racial and cultural prejudices, personal grievance and resentment, and doctrinal differences. On their first day of class, how wide are their arms stretched out to welcome the student standing before them? The rough-looking unkempt student who looks like a potential troublemaker? The student from an underdeveloped country who applied for financial aid? The student who has been labeled by other faculty members as an underachiever and one who often lodges complaints against faculty? The student who comes from a church whose theological beliefs are vastly divergent from them? The extent to which theological educators can see the horizon unfolding would largely depend on the extent they allow "the wideness of God's mercy and generosity of God's welcome" to erase these boundary lines, to enable them to explore new frontiers and experience new joys in the presence of the other.[61] Ultimately, our personal experience of "the wideness of God's mercy and generosity of God's welcome" should humble us and guide us as we navigate the delicate balance between inclusion and exclusion in our practice of hospitality. We must always remember that "the stranger at our door can be both gift and challenge, human and divine."[62]

Intentional Marginality

Another aspect of inclusion in the practice of hospitality is the idea of intentional marginality. For the purpose of our discussion, "the marginality of hosts is more properly characterized as distance from, rather than detachment from, prevailing social institutions, hierarchies, and values."[63] Unless we ourselves have experienced living life at the margins, we are not able to effectively minimize the pain and hurt of those who have been excluded.[64] The supreme example of a host who practiced intentional marginality is our Lord Jesus Christ: Jesus, the guest-host, emptied himself and became "like his brothers and sisters in every respect, so that he might be a merciful and

---

61. Pohl, *Making Room*, 129.
62. Pineda, "Hospitality," 29.
63. Pohl, "Hospitality from the Edge," 123.
64. Johnson, "Reshaping," 347; Pohl, "Hospitality from the Edge," 129–130; *Making Room*, 123–124.

faithful high priest in the service of God, to make a sacrifice of atonement for the sins of the people. Because he himself was tested by what he suffered, he is able to help those who are being tested" (Heb 2:17–18). Having tasted suffering himself, Jesus is able to empathize with our weaknesses, pain, and suffering (Heb 4:15).

It has to be an intentional experience of marginality because many people have moved away "from a marginal identity to a respectable and settled status" and are now "situated so centrally" that they may not be able to fully understand and to reach out to the vulnerable and marginalized.[65] In fact, not having experienced marginality or vulnerability, they "often find it easier to be hosts than guests" and may even "insist on being hosts even in the domain of another."[66] Rendering help from such a privileged location is dangerous.

> Under the guise of acting generously, they avoid the questions of maldistribution of power and resources and reinforce existing patterns of status and wealth. They make others, especially poor people, passive recipients in their own families, churches, or communities. Such hospitality is a form of control that disempowers the guest. It can keep people homeless and powerless by pretending to provide connections or by connecting them to larger communities in superficial ways. . . . This kind of hospitality keeps people needy strangers while fostering an illusion of relationship and connection.[67]

Many scholars have shown concern over the hegemony of white Western males in the areas of pedagogy, scholarship, and theology.[68] Frans Wijsen, writing on intercultural theology, highlighted the tendency that "often European theologians eagerly take up contextual theologies from Africa, Asia and Latin America but they do not change their Western outlook and view of theology. They treat Third World theologies as if they are exotic fruit to supplement their traditional European dishes."[69] This sort of attitude

---

65. Pohl, "Hospitality from the Edge," 132; *Making Room*, 123.
66. Pohl, "Hospitality, a Practice," 41; "Hospitality from the Edge," 135.
67. Pohl, "Hospitality from the Edge," 135.
68. E.g. Freire, *Pedagogy of the Oppressed*; Gutiérrez, *Theology of Liberation*; Fiorenza, *Rhetoric and Ethic*; Norton, "Interview"; Tiénou, "Christian Theology"; Tan, "Feminist Biblical Studies"; Shaw, "New Treasures."
69. Wijsen, "Intercultural Theology," 173, citing Franz Weber.

also prevails in the political arena. Yvonne Scruggs-Leftwich wrote about the discord captured by reporters attending the "World Conference against Racism, Racial Discrimination, Xenophobia and Related Intolerance" held in Durban (South Africa). In her opinion, the heated confrontations were "fueled by Western nations' determination to have their own way and to play only by their rules."[70] In Tite Tiénou's proposal for change in Christian scholarship, he encouraged Northern/Western theologians and scholars to move to the margins, to learn Southern languages, even languages of the minorities, so that they can engage in conversations away from their center of assumed superiority and power.[71]

Likewise, the practice of inclusion in Christian hospitality must entail the experience of marginality so that theological educators, the hosts, will gain a sense of their own marginality and vulnerability that will then allow them to "bond sympathetically with vulnerable guests."[72] For example, theological educators can experience intentional marginality by joining a community that is culturally different from theirs, living in a foreign land for a period of time, visiting a new campus, moving around the campus for a day using crutches or a wheelchair, enrolling in a course to learn a new language or skill, or teaching a subject outside their discipline.[73]

Even if it is not feasible for theological educators to put themselves in situations where they could personally experience marginality, they should at least ask, and listen closely to, those who have had experienced life at the margin about their experiences.[74] As a case in point, theological educators who performed exceptionally well in their studies and won numerous academic awards when they were students should periodically interact with students who are struggling in their classes. Without such feedback, such theological educators will never fully understand the frustrations of the students nor be able to make the necessary changes to help these students.

Definitely, the process of experiencing marginality in unfamiliar settings and of learning the unfamiliar could challenge and stretch their limits. Yet, it

---

70. Scruggs-Leftwich, "Racism, Terror."
71. Tiénou, "Christian Theology," 50.
72. Pohl, "Hospitality from the Edge," 133.
73. See Palmer, *To Know as We Are Known*, 114–115; Pohl, "Hospitality from the Edge," 136; *Making Room*, 123–124; Larson, "Welcoming and Restoring," 50.
74. Pohl, "Grace Enters."

could lead to the creation of a more inclusive learning environment, resulting in the holistic formation of students, as theological educators "become more conscious of and to model for their students their own strategies for learning, to show how they strive to situate themselves in a conversation that is new and strange to them."[75] Moreover, practicing intentional marginality is not just a hospitable act of inclusion. One's "individual experiences of marginality or vulnerability rein[force] the impact of the larger historical and theological identity of the people of God as aliens."[76] The Israelites, as tenants living in God's land, were commanded to love the stranger for they were strangers before in the land of Egypt (Deut 10:19) (see above p. 162, "Israel's Moral Obligation in Relation to God as Host"). The first-century Christian communities, having experienced ostracism and persecution, opened their homes to itinerant preachers and Christians fleeing from persecutions, took care of the widows and orphans, and visited those in prison (see above p. 185, "The Early Faith Communities as Hosts"). So, the starting point of intentional marginality is when theological educators have a sense of their alien status as God's people whose citizenship is in heaven (Phil 3:20). Yong even posited that "the Christian condition of being aliens and strangers in this world means both we are perpetually guests, first of God and then of others, and that we should adopt postures appropriate to receiving hospitality – from God through others – even when we find ourselves as hosts."[77] Theological educators must constantly remind themselves of their marginal position so that, as hosts in the classrooms, they do not become so settled that they "own" the classroom space, making it difficult for them to welcome vulnerable guests – the students.

In summary, when theological educators practice inclusion in their classrooms, they become servant-hosts and extend their personal experience of God's generous hospitality to their students. By intentionally experiencing life at the margins, the heightened awareness of vulnerability will enable them to understand what it means to be hospitable hosts to their students, especially those living at the margins – intellectually, and even physically.

---

75. Gallagher, "Welcoming the Stranger," 140.
76. Pohl, "Hospitality from the Edge," 133.
77. Yong, "Guests, Hosts," 79; see Pohl, "Hospitality," 5.

Constitutive Element 2: Presence

The second constitutive element of hospitality is presence. Presence is simply "being there." To be a hospitable host is to be "present" to the guest, to be there with the guest physically, intellectually, and psychologically/spiritually. To be present is to let our *self*, our holistic *self* show up (emphasis mine). This section explores two themes of presence that have emerged from the preceding discussions: (1) embodied presence of self, and (2) articulate presence to the other.[78] Both themes present presence as a posture that theological educators as hosts need to assume in the practice of Christian hospitality – to be present to the other with all that they are and all that they believe.[79] In the exploration of each theme, I have included some thoughts on how presence could be used as a principle of practice in the classrooms of theological institutions to create an authentic environment that facilitates the holistic formation of students. In an authentic environment, we are "true to who we are and what we believe."[80]

Embodied Presence of Self

An aspect of presence, which was discussed and variously described by some authors, is what I term *embodied presence*.[81] The embodied presence of self requires a presence that is "fully conscious and aware in the present moment"; thus, enabling one to connect with the self within us as well as

---

78. My discussion of presence in hospitality may bear slight similarity to the theory of presence in teaching as proposed by Carol R. Rodgers and Miriam B. Raider-Roth ("Presence in Teaching"); specifically, presence as being present to oneself (see this page, "Embodied Presence of Self"). Their concept of presence as relational and pedagogical is more related to my third constitutive element of hospitality – caring.

79. I present presence as a posture here because the actual engagement of presence in terms of dialogue and attending is discussed under the constitutive elements of reciprocity and caring respectively.

80. Larson, "Welcoming and Restoring," 51.

81. I coined this term after reading Rachael Kessler's article, "The 'Teaching Presence.'" In it, she explored how teachers could "embody a 'presence' that carries the class to a place where minds and hearts are moved and genuine connections occur" (ibid., 7). She called that presence the "teaching presence" (ibid.). Though similar in some aspects, her concept of the teaching presence is not identical to the embodied presence of self that I discuss here.

with the other before us.⁸² With an embodied presence of the self, we are present to the other both *physically* and *psychologically/spiritually* (emphasis mine). Since "what precedes the move toward hospitality to others is … the achievement of a hospitality toward and knowledge of oneself," we begin our discussion with the embodied presence as connection to self, followed by the embodied presence as connection to others.⁸³

Embodied Presence as Connection to Self

"We teach who we are."⁸⁴ In fact, "*consciously, we teach what we know; unconsciously, we teach who we are.*"⁸⁵ "The 'who we are' facet of our teaching personality contributes significantly to the positive or negative tone of a classroom and, certainly, to students' receptivity to teaching."⁸⁶ Therefore, it is imperative for theological educators to be authentic, "to be true to who [they] are," in the presence of their students.⁸⁷ The truth of the matter, however, is that "there is a great gulf between the way my ego wants to identify me, with its protective masks and self-serving fictions, and my true self."⁸⁸

John B. Bennett also believed that hospitable teachers do not separate their personal and professional lives.⁸⁹ "Presence to the other points up the importance of self-knowledge … [which] involves how to make sense of one's life – how to connect the complex and often disparate facts of professional and personal experience."⁹⁰ However, to attain self-knowledge is not an easy task. We need discernment, courage, and perseverance because the process of uncovering our deep inner self involves a gamut of issues, as Bennett so described in much detail:

---

82. Senge et al., *Presence*, 13. This was the basic understanding of presence for Peter Senge and his colleagues (ibid., 13–14). But their understanding of presence eventually evolved to "deep listening," "letting go," and ultimately, "letting come." I am using their basic understanding in my discussion here.
83. Rud, "Learning in Comfort," 123.
84. Palmer, *Courage to Teach*, xi, 2.
85. Hamachek, "Effective Teachers," 209 (original emphasis).
86. Ibid., 209–210.
87. Larson, "Welcoming and Restoring," 51; see Brookfield, *Skillful Teacher*, 67–73.
88. Palmer, *Let Your Life Speak*, 5.
89. Bennett, "Academy and Hospitality," 26–27; "Hospitality and Collegial," 94.
90. Bennett, *Academic Life*, 78.

It includes naming, celebrating, and using one's talents and gifts; accepting oneself and relinquishing habits of self-denigration or self-hate, as well as those of perpetual self-congratulation; attending to one's testimony, confronting illusions, and examining motivations. It involves living out of our academic knowledge, as well as bringing our true selves to our profession – not separating person and work. It means combating our culturally invasive consumerism as well as identifying and attending to those questions most worthy of pursuit. It requires practicing discernment about the truth of our lives and our individual and corporate situations.[91]

In short, to know our inner self is to know "our shadows and limits, our wounds and fears, ... our strengths and potentials,"[92] including our self-doubts and feelings of impostership (namely, feeling that one is less competent and intelligent than others think).[93] Knowing who we are within helps us to become more whole, "*but wholeness does not mean perfection.*"[94] "Hosts who recognize the woundedness in themselves and their ongoing need for grace and mercy, and yet continue to open their lives to others, find God their sufficiency."[95] Nouwen was such a host. He was a restless soul who struggled with his passions and weaknesses but penned his inner conflicts with the hope that his writings would help him to confront the cries of his inner self and help him to practice what he had taught (see above p. 24).[96]

Another host who struggled with his inner self was Jesus when he performed the greatest hospitable act for us – dying for the sins of the whole world so that everyone could be invited to partake at the Great Banquet (see above p. 167). At Gethsemane, knowing the suffering that was awaiting him, Jesus grappled with his human frailty and vulnerable self (Matt 26:36–46; Mark 14:32–42). The inner struggle must have had been intense for "his sweat became like great drops of blood falling down on the ground" (Luke

---

91. Ibid.
92. Palmer, *Courage to Teach*, 13.
93. Kets de Vries, *Reflections*, 98; Brookfield, *Skillful Teacher*, 81–82; for more, see Clance and Imes, "Imposter Phenomenon."
94. Palmer, *Courage to Teach*, 14 (emphasis mine).
95. Pohl, "Hospitality," 41.
96. Nouwen, *Reaching Out*, under "Foreword."

22:44). Ultimately, he found God his sufficiency and was able to open his life to humanity.

Here, it is crucial to note that embodied presence as connection to self focuses on self-knowledge and self-awareness, and does not necessitate *full* self-disclosure to others (emphasis mine), even though teacher self-disclosure has a positive effect on students' affective learning, attendance, participation, motivation, teacher clarity, and out-of-class communication.[97] According to Lawrence R. Wheeless and Jams Grotz, "a self-disclosure is any message about the self that a person communicates to another" and involves five dimensions: (1) conscious intent, (2) amount, (3) valence (i.e. positive/negative), (4) honesty, and (5) intimacy.[98] Jacob L. Cayanus and his colleague, Matthew M. Martin focused instead on three dimensions: (1) amount, (2) valence, and (3) relevance.[99] To these, Bob Eckhart added the dimensions of discretion, character, intent, and venue.[100]

Cayanus opined, and I agree, that "although the teacher-student relationship is an interpersonal relationship, a degree of professionalism needs to be maintained."[101] Knowing that self-disclosure is multi-dimensional in nature, we must exercise wisdom and discretion in our self-disclosure to students, especially regarding controversial issues.[102] For instance, Nouwen did not mention his struggle with homosexuality in his writings or speeches, even though he openly admitted his constant need for affection and intimacy (see above p. 24), possibly because of its controversial nature.[103] As Dierdre LaNoue correctly observed, "Nouwen was an open book in many ways, but on this particular subject, he sought to be wise in what he revealed and what he

---

97. Cayanus, "Effective Instructional Practice"; Cayanus and Martin, "Instructor Self-Disclosure Scale"; "Teacher Self-Disclosure"; Cayanus, Martin, and Goodboy, "Teacher Self-Disclosure." For positive and negative effects of self-disclosure of feelings of impostership, see Brookfield, *Skillful Teacher*, 79, 82.

98. Wheeless and Grotz, "Conceptualization and Measurement," 338, 342; see Cayanus, Martin, and Goodboy, "Teacher Self-Disclosure," 106.

99. Cayanus, "Effective Instructional Practice"; Cayanus and Martin, "Teacher Self-Disclosure."

100. Eckhart, "To Share or Not to Share," 46.

101. Cayanus, "Effective Instructional Practice," 8; see Frymier and Houser, "Teacher-Student Relationship."

102. See Eckhart, "To Share or Not to Share," 44–46.

103. LaNoue, *Spiritual Legacy*, 84–85.

kept private."[104] Likewise, Jesus, too, did not openly share his inner struggles with his disciples although he did ask them to pray, in view of the troubled days ahead (Luke 22:39–46). Indeed, self-disclosure presents the teacher as a "flesh-and-blood human being with a life and identity outside the classroom" and this is essential in a hospitable classroom, but the teacher should exercise discretion and not make the classroom a public confession box.[105]

Various authors have suggested ways to reach the center of our lives. We can practice: (1) concentration, that is, meditation and contemplation;[106] (2) listening and taking notes of our lives – our words, "our actions and reactions, our intuitions and instincts, our feelings and bodily states of being";[107] and (3) listening to what others have to say about us, even their criticisms about us.[108] All these practices will help us to "open a space for truth within ourselves."[109] It is when we are more aware of who we are and are able to accept ourselves, that is, "being personally inviting with oneself," that we will be open, honest, and inviting to the other.[110]

Theological educators must deliberately set aside time to discover the center of our lives. Spending time to talk and listen to colleagues and students, both present and former, will help them see a facet of themselves which may be hidden to them. Sometimes, looking at what students have written in the course evaluations, if their comments were carefully thought out, sincere and truthful, could also be helpful. Cultivating a habit of journaling and being a reflective teacher are also ways by which theological educators can know their hidden inner self. Going on personal retreats, meeting God in prayer, reflecting on all that they have listened to and have written in their

---

104. Ibid., 85.
105. Brookfield, "Authenticity and Power," 10; *Skillful Teacher*, 71–72. It must be noted that Stephen D. Brookfield discussed self-disclosure under "Personhood" ("Authenticity and Power," 10–11; *Skillful Teacher*, 71–73). For Brookfield, full-disclosure refers to "the teacher's regularly making public the criteria, expectations, agendas, and assumptions that guide her practice" ("Authenticity and Power," 8; *Skillful Teacher*, 69–70).
106. Nouwen, *Wounded Healer*, 90.
107. Palmer, *Let Your Life Speak*, 2.
108. Bennett, *Academic Life*, 79. Listening is an important discipline for self-knowledge. We need to listen to be at home with oneself and "to pay attention to the strangeness in our own lives" (Rud, "Learning in Comfort," 122, citing Cavell, *Senses of Walden*, 55). The act of listening is discussed in greater detail in the pursuing discussion on caring and reciprocity.
109. Palmer, *To Know as We Are Known*, 105.
110. Rud, "Learning in Comfort," 126; Bennett, *Academic Life*, 78.

journals in his presence, will give them the spiritual strength to overcome their weaknesses and grace to receive their strengths. And as Nouwen wrote, "when we have found the anchor places for our lives in our own center, we can be free to let others enter into the space created for them and allow them to dance their own dance, sing their own song and speak their own language without fear."[111]

Embodied Presence as Connection to the Other

I have argued in chapter 3 that emotion and cognition are interconnected in the learning process (see above p. 99). Teaching and learning are emotional practices, so much so that just the perceptual availability, as well as perceptual care, of the teacher will increase both the students' affective and cognitive learning. The concept of an embodied presence in hospitality, as connection to the other, is closely related to that of immediacy, the perceptual availability of the host to the guest.

As seen in chapter 3 (see above p. 102) from the work done by researchers, the verbal and nonverbal immediacy behaviors of teachers help to reduce both the physical and psychological distance between them and their students. In order for theological educators to connect with their students in a hospitable manner, they need an embodied presence that will make their students feel welcome. A way to achieve this is to practice the simple nonverbal immediacy behaviors cues that were proposed by Albert Mehrabian: (1) touching, (2) distance, (3) forward lean, (4) eye contact, and (5) body orientation.[112] An incident I witnessed illustrates the role such immediacy behavior cues can play in our embodied presence. A student in a theological institution came into the faculty room to seek clarification from a teacher regarding the term paper requirements. The teacher, who was in the midst of searching for some lost papers, said this, without even looking at the student: "Just tell me what you need. I am listening . . . even though I am busy looking for something right now. I am good at multi-tasking." In my opinion, that teacher had a disembodied presence and showed inhospitality to the student, who looked rather dejected after hearing that reply. Nouwen's words serve as a good reminder for all busy theological educators: "When we are always 'over there'

---

111. Nouwen, *Wounded Healer*, 91–92; see *Reaching Out*, 72.
112. Mehrabian, "Some Referents and Measures," 203.

between people, ideas, and worries of this world, how can we possibly create the room and space where someone else can enter freely without feeling himself an unlawful intruder?"[113] As Nel Noddings put it, "What I must do is to be totally and unselectively present to the student – to each student – as he addresses me. The time interval may be brief but the encounter is total."[114] It is only when we are entirely and genuinely present with our students that we are able to have their full presence.[115]

We can see Jesus, the guest-host, entertaining interruptions with his embodied presence through a close reading of the gospel stories. While he was on his way to Jairus' house, he was interrupted by a woman who had been suffering from bleeding for twelve years (Matt 9:20–22; Mark 5:25–34; Luke 8:43–48). The Markan and Lukan accounts recorded that there was a big crowd following him and the people were pressing in on him (Mark 5:24; Luke 8:42). Yet, Jesus sensed that his power left him when the woman touched the fringe of his cloak. He stopped in his tracks and took time to minister to the sick woman. In the Matthean account, the woman did not touch Jesus (Matt 9:20–22). Rather, it seemed like Jesus could read the sick woman's mind. "For she was just saying to herself: 'If I only touch His garment, I will get well.' But Jesus turning and seeing her said, 'Daughter, take courage; your faith has made you well'" (Matt 9:20–22 NASB).[116] Leon Morris put it this way, "So Jesus *turned and saw her*; he gave her his full attention."[117] In another episode, while walking in the city of Jericho, at the exact spot where Zacchaeus was, perched in a sycamore tree, *Jesus looked up* and requested to be a guest at Zacchaeus' house (Luke 19:2–5) (emphasis mine). Jesus' embodied presence was always there: he took the little children, whom the disciples thought were too insignificant for his attention, into his arms (see Mark 10:13–16), he touched the untouchable leper (Matt 8:3), the eyes of the blind (Matt 9:29;

---

113. Nouwen, *Wounded Healer*, 90.
114. Noddings, *Caring*, 180. However, it must be noted that in the sentence preceding this quotation, Nel Noddings wrote: "I do not need to establish a deep, lasting, time-consuming personal relationship with every student." On this point, I disagree (see discussion on "Being a Friend to the Other" in below p. 234).
115. Farber, "Teaching and Presence," 215.
116. The translation from NASB is preferred here because it retains the Greek participles "turning" and "seeing" in verse 22, separating it from the main verb "said." Compare this with the translation from the NRSV, "Jesus turned, and seeing her he said . . ."
117. Morris, *Matthew*, 230 (original emphasis and expresses my intent too).

20:34), and he even put his fingers into the ears of a deaf man and touched the man's tongue with his saliva (Mark 7:33).

Students interrupting teachers while the latter are busy with something is a daily occurrence in schools. Nouwen recounted a conversation he had with an experienced professor in the University of Notre Dame. "And while we strolled over the beautiful campus, he said with a certain melancholy in his voice, 'You know, . . . my whole life I have been complaining that my work was constantly interrupted, until I discovered that my interruptions were my work.'"[118] If theological educators see interruptions as an essential part of their teaching ministry and service to God, they would be more careful to practice an embodied presence before the other. How they respond to such "interruptions" will also indicate how hospitable they are. Does their embodied presence show a slight hint of irritation? Do they speak to the student while their eyes are still glued to the computer screen? Or do they stand up to meet the student or even invite him/her to sit down so that their eyes can meet while they talk? In the classroom, they must also be conscious where they physically position themselves. Are they standing behind the desk/podium or where the students are seated when they teach? While students are engaged in a task or discussion, do theological educators sit by themselves in the teacher's chair or do they walk among the students to see if they need help, or even sit down and join a group in their discussion? The closer the gap, the closer their connection to their students will be. And, although it is not the ultimate solution, removing the teacher's desk, and re-arranging the furniture and the seating arrangement of the classroom may help to reduce both the physical and psychological distances between teachers and students.[119]

However, negotiating immediacy is a delicate matter because the appropriateness of one's behavior is largely determined by culture, including age, gender, and religion.[120] Most Asian cultures are generally high in context but low in immediacy (i.e. low in contact orientation). According to communication researchers, people from high-context cultures communicate through nonverbal codes where meanings are internalized and

---

118. Nouwen, *Reaching Out*, 52.
119. Haskins, "Ethos and Pedagogical Communication"; see Shaw, "Welcome Guest," 20.
120. E.g. Riedel, "Communication"; Wilson et al., "Touching Your Students"; Wolfe and Waters, "Exploring Higher Education."

communication is "vague, indirect, and implicit,"[121] and people in low-contact cultures prefer low sensory involvement (e.g. standing apart and touch less).[122] Research done on Asian societies, such as China, Korea, Japan, and Taiwan, has shown that they are high-context[123] and low-contact cultures.[124] Thus, Peter A. Andersen was able to conclude that "compared to the rest of the world, Asia is an extreme noncontact culture."[125] Asians tend to avoid physical contact, even eye contact. They may feel uncomfortable if someone stands too close to them or looks at them in the eye while talking,[126] especially if they are of the opposite gender. So, it is imperative for theological educators to bear these unwritten cultural rules in mind in their practice of embodied presence to the other. Theological educators are only hospitable when their immediacy cues are not perceived as intrusive or offensive.

Articulate Presence to the Other

If embodied presence is *being there physically and psychologically*, then articulate presence is *being there intellectually* (emphasis mine). We are to be true not only to who we are but also to what we believe.[127] Working among people of other religious traditions in Christian colleges/universities, Newman and Aurelie A. Hagstrom were concerned about the loss of Christian identity in such higher learning institutions. Newman deplored the faith-knowledge dichotomy in higher education which is essentially gnostic in nature.[128] This dualism is exacerbated by the modern and deconstructive postmodern approaches to learning which are "caught in the bind between an objectivist presentation of facts and a relativistic, aesthetic appreciation

---

121. Samovar, Porter, and McDaniel, *Communication between Cultures*, 216; see Hall, *Beyond Culture*, 91.
122. Andersen, "Different Dimensions," 247; see Hall, *Hidden Dimension*.
123. Hall, *Beyond Culture*.
124. E.g. McDaniel and Andersen, "International Patterns"; Zhang et al., "Teacher Immediacy Scales."
125. Andersen, "Different Dimensions," 248.
126. Georgakopoulos and Guerrero, "Student Perceptions of Teachers," 5.
127. Larson, "Welcoming and Restoring," 51.
128. Newman, "Who's Home Cooking," 9; "Faith-Knowledge Dichotomy," 148; "Hospitality and Christian," 77–81; "Hotel or Home," 96–97.

of difference."[129] Newman believed that "a hospitality shaped by relativism would have no profound reason or moral obligation to welcome another beyond personal preference."[130] At the same time, "an objectivistic hospitality – by denying our own particularity – is [also] unable to welcome the other as truly other."[131] In both instances, we privatize our religious convictions and, instead of embracing and celebrating diversity, we are merely tolerating another person's point of view. Such tolerance is what Newman labeled as "hotel hospitality"[132] and what Hagstrom, quoting Stanley Fish, described as "boutique multiculturalism."[133] Tolerance works on the principle of mutual non-interference.[134] As an expression of mutual respect, it does not challenge the opinions of others. Instead, it "reduces us to silence and inactivity, because to add to and seek to change what others think is by definition intolerant."[135] Furthermore, "tolerance is simply another expression of privilege."[136] The corrective for this is articulate presence, a term borrowed from Nouwen (see above p. 17).

Based on the discussion of boundaries in the constitutive element of inclusion, I acknowledge that the space that we welcome the other into does have boundaries. Nouwen even said that a "space can only be a welcoming space when there are clear boundaries."[137] However, such boundaries – boundaries of our articulate presence – are different from boundaries drawn to exclude the other. They are flexible "limits between which we define our position."[138] They are "boundaries that mark our identity."[139] We do not just welcome and receive the other into our space; we also have "to confront them by an unambiguous presence, not hiding ourselves behind neutrality but

---

129. Newman, "Faith-Knowledge Dichotomy," 141; see "Who's Home Cooking," 11; "Hospitality and Christian," 77–81.
130. Newman, "Who's Home Cooking," 11.
131. Ibid.
132. Newman, "Hotel or Home," 101.
133. Hagstrom, "Christian Hospitality," 121, quoting Fish, "Boutique Multiculturalism," 378.
134. Young, *Inclusion and Democracy*, 230.
135. Bretherton, *Hospitality as Holiness*, 147.
136. Eck, *Encountering God*, 192.
137. Nouwen, *Reaching Out*, 98.
138. Ibid.
139. Volf, "Trends in American Religion."

showing our ideas, opinion and life style clearly and distinctly."[140] Receptivity without confrontation, without our articulate presence, is akin to welcoming a guest into an empty house, which soon becomes a ghost house.[141] By confronting the other with our beliefs and values, we "offer the boundaries that challenge strangers to become aware of their own position and to explore it critically."[142] Otherwise, the "indiscriminate openness . . . may be just as bad as manipulative objectivism or murky subjectivism."[143] "Welcome without critique is like staying in an empty house where the fridge is full but there's no one to eat with."[144]

Though worded differently, several of the authors also put forth the idea of confrontation in terms of one's articulate presence before the other. For instance, Newman rejected "epistemological and pedagogical strategy [that] endorses an aesthetic, or *non-committal*, appreciation of 'otherness.'"[145] In her opinion,

> Christian hospitality, however, is not shaped by such dualistic convictions (objectivism/relativism). Rather, it flows from the conviction that we are creatures and "guests" of God, inhabitants of God's household and thus recipients of God's steadfast love. Given this fact, our "presence" is best understood in terms of faithfulness. We are called to be faithfully present to God in and through our interaction with others.[146]

In fact, "hospitality as faithful presence might well involve challenge or resistance, even conflict, with certain ideas, particularly those that would undercut the very practice itself."[147] It is through our hospitable full presence, together with "our own particularity," that we are able to engage others.[148] And, "because the finite is capable of bearing the infinite, human

---

140. Nouwen, *Reaching Out*, 99; see Losito, "Education as Hospitality," 67; Pohl, "Hospitality, a Practice," 42–43; "Hospitality," 10.
141. Nouwen, *Reaching Out*, 99.
142. Ibid.
143. Rud, "Learning in Comfort," 125.
144. Hershberger, "Response."
145. Newman, "Faith-Knowledge Dichotomy," 141 (original emphasis).
146. Newman, "Who's Home Cooking," 11.
147. Ibid., 13.
148. Ibid., 11.

places always contain the possibility of being epistemologically revelatory."[149] Similarly, Susanne Johnson believed that "the strategy of unqualified *relativism*, or a *simple pluralism*" is inadequate for dialogue among diverse religions, hermeneutical options, or cultures.[150] Instead, she proposed critical pluralism because "it celebrates diversity and plurality while it also pursues and heightens a sense of particularity."[151] As for Hagstrom, she believed that "it is only the clear identity of the host that makes the guest feel secure and welcome."[152] Leaving a space empty with "free-floating unconditionality impinges on the integrity of both host and guest."[153]

The concepts of receptivity and confrontation can be seen in the hospitality practiced by Jesus, the guest-host. He both received and confronted. Acting as a guest, he requested a drink from a Samaritan woman (John 4:7). By talking to her – a Jewish man to a Samaritan woman – he opened his arms and welcomed her as his guest (John 4:9). However, his articulate presence confronted her beliefs and lifestyle (John 4:10–26) and she, in turn, was so challenged that she left behind her water jar and went back to the city to share the good news to her fellow Samaritans (John 4:28–29). This pattern of receptivity and confrontation is repeated throughout the gospel narratives, such as Jesus' encounters with Zacchaeus, the rich chief tax collector (Luke 19:1–10), with the woman who had been caught in adultery (John 8:1–11), and with Simon the Pharisee as well as the "sinful" woman who anointed his feet when he had dinner in Simon's house (Luke 7:36–50). Jesus showed courage in his practice of hospitality "because, whether in his role as guest or host, he does not waver from speaking and living the truth in love."[154]

To have an articulate presence in the classrooms of theological institutions, as Newman would suggest, calls for patience, courage, and charity with humility.[155] Besides these virtues, Susanne Johnson proposed critical pluralism which is "a strategy, or a posture of practice and theory, that situates itself in critical dialogue among or between different hermeneutical,

---

149. Ibid., 15.
150. Johnson, "Reshaping," 340 (original emphasis).
151. Ibid.
152. Hagstrom, "Christian Hospitality," 125.
153. Ibid.
154. Newman, "Hospitality and Christian," 86.
155. Ibid., 86–87.

cultural, religious, or theological options."[156] Theological educators should not impose their personal views and values on their students. Neither should they keep absolutely silent, revealing nothing about what they believe while hiding behind the screen of neutrality. When the occasion presents itself, they should let their students hear their views, values, and beliefs. This is akin to Brian V. Hill's "committed impartiality" whereby teachers "foster critical analysis and discussion of the grounds for various beliefs and values, and . . . exhibit their own beliefs as additional data for analysis, provided that their procedures for teaching and assessing remain impartial."[157] "As God is present to us, we too are called to be fully present in our engagement with others, refusing to privatize or abandon those parts of our identity that might sound odd in the world of so-called rational discourse."[158] Having said that, theological educators should also take care not to present *my* perspective as *the* authoritative perspective (emphasis mine). This is especially so for students from cultures where teachers are perceived as the "fount of knowledge."[159] Dilin Liu described these cultures as having "a long tradition of unconditional obedience to authority,"[160] for example, those cultures in East Asia that have Confucian ethics and values.[161] However, with globalization, this mindset is changing somewhat.[162]

Theological educators also need to consider another aspect of articulate presence which was highlighted by Nouwen, but neglected by others, when he stressed that "confrontation is much more than 'speaking up.'"[163] For him, even the objects in his home have an articulate presence because

> when we have lived a while the walls of our lives have become marked by many events – world events, family events, personal events – as well as by our responses to them. These marks speak their own language and often lead to a dialogue, sometimes

---

156. Johnson, "Reshaping," 340.
157. Hill, "Teacher Commitment," 334.
158. Newman, "Who's Home Cooking," 11.
159. Holliday, *Appropriate Methodology*, 59.
160. Liu, "Ethnocentrism in TESOL," 5.
161. Wang, "Teaching Asian Students."
162. Littlewood, "Asian Students"; Xiao, "Bridging the Gap."
163. Nouwen, *Reaching Out*, 100.

limited to the heart, but occasionally expressed in words and gestures.[164]

I agree with Nouwen that objects around us can speak up for us. But, more than that, the way we live our lives can also speak up for us. Here, I would like to use Miroslav Volf's understanding of Christian beliefs and practices forming and shaping each other and relate it to the practice of articulate presence.[165] If our Christian beliefs shape our practices, that is, our way of life, then how we live our lives can also be considered an aspect of our articulate presence.[166] By living out their Christian beliefs, theological educators are also confronting their students with their articulate presence. Hence, they must be mindful of how they are modeling and "imaging God" through their lives.[167] Volf illustrated his point with this example, "Rightly to espouse the belief that God is 'the God of peace' (Rom 15:33), for instance, *is*, among other things, to commit oneself to the pursuit of peace."[168] If we believe that God is a "father of orphans and protector of widows" (Ps 68:5; see James 1:27), how have we incarnated God's care for the orphans and widows in our own faith communities? How have we exhibited the fruit of the Spirit, the virtues of "love, joy, peace, patience, kindness, generosity, faithfulness, gentleness, and self-control" in our daily living (Gal 5:22–23)? If "the spiritual formation and development of seminary students begins with, and is dependent upon, the spiritual formation and development of the faculty," then one's articulate presence – how one lives his or her life as a God-fearer – is a matter of importance to theological educators.[169]

In summary, hospitable theological educators practicing presence must acknowledge and confront their inner selves as well as be genuinely present and available to their students. Besides an embodied presence, they must have an articulate presence, speaking up for and living out their convictions in humility, with patience, courage, and love.

---

164. Ibid.
165. Volf, "Theology for a Way of Life," 250–254.
166. See Kessler, "Teaching Presence," 7.
167. Volf, "Theology for a Way of Life," 253.
168. Ibid. (original emphasis).
169. Edwards, "Spiritual Formation," 8; see Herring and Deininger, "Challenges and Blessings," 137.

Constitutive Element 3: Care

For most educators, the word *care* is often associated with Noddings' ethics of care in moral education. However, my understanding of the third constitutive element of hospitality, care, unlike Noddings', is grounded in the providential care of God towards his creation (see discussion on "God as Host" in ch. 4, above p. 152).[170] Unlike presence which has been presented as a posture, caring is the actual engagement of presence in terms of attending to the other (see above p. 217, n. 79).

In Noddings' works on care, her focus is on the ethic of care in moral education, addressing the need to teach students to care about people, learning, and even the created order of plants and animals. When incorporated into a curriculum, it should include the components of modeling, dialogue, practice, and confirmation.[171] Several educators have deliberated on how this ethic of care could inform the curriculum in K–12 schools[172] and colleges.[173] However, this book does not approach the constitutive element of care from this perspective. Instead, it reflects further on what Anthony G. Rud Jr. has highlighted in his essay, which explored the feasibility of practicing hospitality in schools. Stating that Noddings' notion of care was seen as a parallel to hospitality in educational practice with some explanation, Rud instead highlighted the need for teachers, rather than the students, to be hospitable. His reason, like mine, is that "in education, at least, the onus of responsibility is upon the teacher."[174] Hence, this discussion focuses on the expressions of care that theological educators show to their students rather than a curriculum based on the ethic of care. Furthermore, it involves both caring for students as individuals (a personal priority) and caring for student learning (a professional priority).[175]

---

170. Noddings *Caring*, 28–29. Noddings included both the one-caring and the one-cared-for. The one-cared-for is not discussed because it is beyond the scope of this work. However, I would like to point out that in Christian hospitality, the caring relation should take place even if the one-cared-for does not respond or reciprocate (cf. ibid., 150).
171. Noddings, *Caring*, ch. 8; *Challenge to Care*, 22–27.
172. Rogers and Webb, "Ethic of Caring"; Pang, Rivera, and Mora, "Ethic of Caring."
173. Goralnik et al., "Environmental Pedagogy"; Shotsberger, "Christian Ethic of Care."
174. Rud, "Learning in Comfort," 127.
175. See Frego, "Authenticity," 43. I concur with Katherine A. Frego on this issue and have adopted the distinction that she has made concerning teacher caring.

Realizing the important role emotions play in students' learning has led many researchers to conduct empirical studies so as to inform educational policy and practice in the past few decades. Jason J. Teven, sometimes in collaboration with other researchers, conducted several studies to investigate how perceived teacher caring affected students' perceptions of their teachers. Using James C. McCroskey's understanding of perceived care as "good will," or "intent toward receiver,"[176] Teven's initial research with McCroskey positioned teacher caring as "empathy, understanding, and responsiveness."[177] In a subsequent study, Teven associated the behaviors perceived by students as caring with teacher's nonverbal immediacy, responsiveness, assertiveness, and the absence of verbal aggressiveness.[178] Verbally aggressiveness can take the form of "character attacks, competence attacks, background attacks, physical appearance attacks, malediction, teasing, ridicule, threats, swearing, [and] nonverbal emblems."[179] In a research done with Trudy L. Hanson, Teven included the element of verbal caring messages, and the results showed that college teachers who were less nonverbally immediate but voiced their care verbally were perceived to be more credible by students. In their introduction, they also listed the works of others who used other indicators to measure teaching caring; such as being able to teach in a clear manner, using humor and sharing personal narratives, and building positive interpersonal relationships with students.[180] And in a more recent research Teven categorized caring behaviors as:

> behaviors demonstrating teachers' concern for student performance and/or grades; behaviors demonstrating teachers' concern for their own classroom performance; solicitation of and responses to student questions and feedback; behaviors associated with attempts to build interpersonal relationships with students; and the use of nonverbal immediacy behaviors.[181]

---

176. McCroskey and Teven, "Goodwill," 90.
177. Teven and McCroskey, "Relationship," 2; see also McCroskey and Teven, "Goodwill," 92.
178. Teven, "Relationships."
179. Myers, "Perceived Instructor Credibility," 358.
180. Teven and Hanson, "Impact of Teacher Immediacy," 42.
181. Teven, "Teacher Caring," 446, n. 1.

Critical Dialogue towards the Application of the Motif of Hospitality 233

As seen from these empirical researches, there are many different ways to measure whether or not a teacher cares for the students. I would like to join in this ongoing discourse by presenting my perspective of teacher caring that is based on the metaphor of God as host discussed in chapter 4.

In Noddings' ethic of care, attention and motivational displacement are both necessary to caring. The one-caring not only gives "nonselective attention or total presence to the other"[182] but also directs his or her energy "toward the welfare, protection, or enhancement of the cared-for."[183] As Noddings put it, "to care . . . requires some action in behalf of the cared-for."[184] It is interesting to note that results of a research done by Teven and Joan Gorham indicated that "students' perceptions of teacher caring largely emphasized 'nitty-gritty' rather than 'warm and fuzzy' elements of class interaction: if you care about me, you will do your job and help me do mine."[185] It is task-related. This is also how I perceive attentive caring to be: It is more than feeling; it is love in action. And this is what care is for God.

Our discourse on God as host in chapter 4 reveals God showing his care by being both the provider and protector of his people, Israel, and even more so the marginalized orphans, widows, and strangers living among them. In turn, Israel's moral obligation to God was, by following his example, to protect and care for the marginalized among them while remembering that they too once were the marginalized, "strangers in the land of Egypt" (Deut 10:19). "The practice of [care in] hospitality is, therefore, both a reflection and an extension of God's own hospitality – God's sharing of the love of the triune life with those who are dust,"[186] providing the theological basis for teacher caring within the context of theological education. Such hospitality involved the provision of food and clothing (see Deut 10:17–18), and defense of the defenseless orphans and widows (Isa 1:17). Translated into the theological classroom context, it could mean taking care of the needs of the students – physical, psychological, and intellectual needs. However, we must first know what their needs are before we can take of them. Hence, the two key practices that will help theological educators to care for their students in ways that

---

182. Noddings, "Ethic of Caring," 219–220.
183. Noddings, *Caring*, 23.
184. Ibid., 12.
185. Teven and Gorham, "Qualitative Analysis," 295.
186. Hütter, "Hospitality and Truth," 219.

would meet their needs are: (1) being a friend to the other, and (2) listening to the other. In my discussion of these key practices of care, where applicable, I have included some thoughts on how caring could be used as a principle of practice in the classrooms of theological institutions to create a caring environment that facilitates the holistic formation of students.

Being a Friend to the Other

The importance of teachers building a positive relationship with the students in relation to the constitutive element of care cannot be underestimated. It is used as an indicator of teacher caring,[187] and its effect on the students towards learning, teachers, and schools has been a subject of interest to researchers.[188] David Giles made this statement: "Once a student has enrolled in a particular course, the teacher and student are 'always' in relationship; ontologically, they cannot exist in any other way."[189] There is a Chinese saying that goes, "Once a teacher, always a father" (一日为师,终身为父 *yīrì wéishī, zhōngshēn wéifù*; meaning, "being a teacher for one day entitles one a lifelong respect from the student that befits his father").[190] The kinship between teacher and student begins when the student walks into the classroom to attend the first class and lasts a lifetime. Though the source of this popular saying is unknown, the use of the father-son relationship analogy reflects Confucian values[191] and implies an acceptance of power distance, "the extent to which the less powerful person in society accepts inequality in power and considers it as normal."[192]

---

187. E.g. Teven and Gorham, "Qualitative Analysis"; Teven and Hanson, "Impact of Teacher Immediacy"; Teven, "Teacher Caring."
188. E.g. Churukian, "Perceived Learning"; Frymier and Houser, "Teacher-Student Relationship"; Brekelmans, Wubbels, and Den Brok, "Teacher Experience"; Den Brok, Brekelmans, and Wubbels, "Interpersonal Teacher Behavior"; Zhan and Le, "Interpersonal Relationship"; Wubbels and Brekelmans, "Two Decades of Research"; Docan-Morgan and Manusov, "Relational Turning Point Events"; Zhang, "Study on the Satisfaction"; Spilt, Koomen, and Thijs, "Teacher Wellbeing."
189. Giles, "Relationships Always Matter," 89.
190. Wu, "Dynamics," 98.
191. Flowerdew and Miller, "On the Notion of Culture," 357; see Hofstede and Bond, "Confucius Connection," 8; Ng, "From Confucian Master Teacher," 315.
192. Hofstede, "Cultural Relativity," 390.

Critical Dialogue towards the Application of the Motif of Hospitality 235

In Confucian teaching, "one's teacher is on a par with one's father in terms of the loyalty and deference that is one expected to show."[193] Hence, the acknowledgment of power distance is common in "cultures of the East Asian countries . . . rooted in the teachings of Confucius."[194] In such Confucian heritage cultures, when "the less powerful person in a society accepts inequality in power and considers it as normal," the degree of power distance is higher.[195] Students from such cultures prefer a more formal teacher-student relationship as a sign of their respect for teachers.[196] This concept is unlike the Western understanding of teaching that advocates an informal relationship and mutual respect between students and teachers.[197] A teacher wishing to establish a more personal relationship with students from Confucian heritage cultures may encounter some degree of rejection by those who are cognizant of this power distance.

The situation is compounded when we include the cultural dimension of masculinity/femininity.[198] Students coming from masculine cultures with highly differentiated gender roles could find it difficult to accept the leadership of women. A case in point comes from my personal experience. At a theological institution where I taught, a male Korean student was struggling in the Greek 1 class that I was teaching. I offered to coach him after class but he never took up the offer. At the end of the semester, he was called to the academic dean's office because of his failing grade. After much probing, he told the dean that he did not take up my offer of help because I was a female teacher. In such an instance, it was difficult to establish a close relationship with the student. Though this is a legitimate concern, the high acceptance of power distance and masculinity by students can be changed over time with wise discernment, loving patience, and sincere efforts of teachers. The crux

---

193. Flowerdew and Miller, "On the Notion of Culture," 357.
194. Hofstede and Bond, "Confucius Connection," 6, 11; see Hofstede, "Cultural Relativity," 391.The term *neo-Confucian* was coined by Herman Kahn (ibid., 6). A study conducted by IBM in the 1970s showed that "neo-Confucian countries generally score fairly high on Power Distance" (ibid., 11).
195. Hofstede, "Cultural Relativity," 390.
196. Burba, Petrosko, and Boyle, "Appropriate and Inappropriate Instructional Behaviours," 279.
197. Dunn and Wallace, "Australian Academics Teaching," 300.
198. Hofstede, "Cultural Relativity," 390.

of the discussion is the importance of the teacher-student relationship in the students' learning and life.

Patricia Cranton proposed that teacher-student relationships can be based on respectful distance, collegiality, or closeness:

> When respectful distance is the basis of knowing students, the relationship occurs primarily through the subject area and focuses on the learning. In collegial relationships, the educator views the learner as a future or a current colleague, works collaboratively, and engages in mutual sharing of experience and expertise. In a close relationship, teachers and students come to know each other as people both inside and outside the classroom.[199]

Although Cranton encouraged educators to choose the style of relationship "that is comfortable for them and congruent with their values, beliefs, and philosophy of teaching," I am of the opinion that a hospitable caring teacher should strive particularly to build relationships that can foster a closer relationship with the students both inside and outside the classroom, and that relationship building is essentially a function of time spent together and the sharing of lives, both inside and outside of the classroom.[200]

Jesus, the guest-host, was such an exemplary teacher even though he did not have a formal classroom. "He modeled interpersonal connectedness by living and working closely with his disciples and other followers."[201] He even called his disciples "friends" (John 15:15). However, some participants in Lori Price Aultman, Meca R. Williams-Johnson, and Paul A. Schutz's phenomenological research on boundaries in teacher-student relationships indicated that they drew a line between "being 'friends' and 'being friendly.'"[202] One participant said, "I think you can be friendly with your students, but you don't need to be one of their friends."[203] Noddings even felt that there is no need for the teacher "to establish a deep, lasting, time-consuming personal relationship with every student."[204] In my opinion, in the context of theological

---

199. Cranton, "Fostering Authentic Relationships," 9–10.
200. Ibid., 10.
201. Morr, "Friendship in Spiritual Formation," 46.
202. Aultman, Williams-Johnson, and Schutz, "Boundary Dilemmas," 642.
203. Ibid.
204. Noddings, *Caring*, 180.

education, within a learning community that seeks the holistic formation of students, teachers should develop a close relationship with students, even treating them as friends. Yet, at the same time, they must remember that there is also the danger of them losing control or crossing/violating boundaries in such friendships.[205] Besides taking into consideration cultural factors, and institutional rules and regulations, theological educators must be careful not to cross over boundaries of communication, emotional, personal, financial, temporal, financial, curricular, and expertise.[206]

A common objection to such close teacher-student relationships or friendships is the potential display of bias that could interfere with the teacher's impartial judgment towards their "favorite" students and their work.[207] This is indeed possible because teachers are human beings with emotions and may be more drawn to some students than others for some reason or other. However, as Amy Shuffelton commented, "good teaching always involves overcoming inclinations and preferences, and a good teacher develops this capacity."[208] As with the other boundary issues which teachers have to negotiate, sometimes on a daily basis, consulting with other teachers may help them to gain the wisdom and knowledge needed to make wise decisions in their interactions with students.[209]

Being a friend to students is important in teacher caring because it allows us to know them and their needs better; thus, enabling us to care for them in more relevant ways. To know students better as friends, theological educators can begin by knowing and addressing each student by his or her name.[210] This is one of the many verbal immediacy behaviors, indicated by Gorham, that can take place inside or outside the classroom.[211] Taking the cue from Gorham's list, theological educators can also make an effort to initiate conversations with individual students, not just to get feedback about their teaching or to find out how the students are coping with their studies,

---

205. See Aultman, Williams-Johnson, and Schutz, "Boundary Dilemmas," 645.
206. Ibid., 640–644; see also Frego, "Authenticity and Relationships," 46.
207. Hill and Zinsmeister, "Becoming an Ethical Teacher," 131.
208. Shuffelton, "Ethics," 85.
209. Aultman, Williams-Johnson, and Schultz, "Boundary Dilemmas," 645.
210. Jacob Stratman has proposed that "a pedagogy of hospitality begins . . . by knowing their [students'] names" ("What's In a Name," 35).
211. Gorham, "Relationship," 44.

but also to know more about them – their families, their work and ministry, their spiritual and personal lives. Even if they are casually chit-chatting along the theological institution's corridors, they can still pause and pray for the students and their personal concerns. Words of praise, affirmation, and encouragement can sometimes make their day. However, for those students who are in need, the offer to help may be even more useful than mere words. Hence, some of these practical caring acts would demand a sacrifice of time. But as Christine D. Pohl put it, in our slowing down to be present to the other, "it means that we view individuals as human beings rather than as embodied needs or interruptions."[212]

Jane Vella is right when she wrote that to develop friendships, "time is paramount."[213] Giving and spending time with students is essential for cultivating friendships with students. Following Vella's example, it is good practice for teachers to allocate time before or after class to meet students for reflection or consultation.[214] Vella organized sit-down meals, potluck dinners, and picnics for her students so that there was more time to get to know one another better and an opportunity to develop networks of friends. Here, Vella practiced one of the most fundamental acts of hospitality – eating together. To get to know a person takes time. The casual informal act of eating together somehow offers "people ways to be themselves and to reduce self-consciousness."[215] It is a time and an opportunity for us to open our hearts and share our lives with the other, and to bond as a learning community.[216] Writing on the cultural differences in the way we eat, Margaret Visser noted that "eating round a table is an ethnocentric way for us to express a bonding mechanism which is common to very human society: that of mealtime sharing."[217] It is like what Larry Rasmussen wrote about, that "the perennial Christian strategy, someone has said, is to gather the folks, break the bread, and tell the stories."[218] Furthermore, when theological educators practice

---

212. Pohl, "Hospitality," 40.
213. Vella, *Learning to Listen*, 89.
214. Ibid.
215. Ginsberg and Wlodkowski, *Diversity and Motivation*, 108.
216. See Banks, *Reenvisioning Theological Education*, 204.
217. Visser, *Rituals of Dinner*, 83; see Quinn, "No Room," 113, n. 14.
218. Rasmussen, "Shaping Communities," 117; see Shea, *Stories of God*, 8. Both John Shea and Larry Rasmussen did not cite the source of this statement.

Critical Dialogue towards the Application of the Motif of Hospitality 239

Jesus' "radically inclusive, status-leveling, and honor-sharing fellowship at table" (see above p. 172, "The Intent of Jesus' Table Fellowship"), they too will be proclaiming the openness of God's welcoming grace to all their students. "There are no more classes: 'all sit at the same table.'"[219] However, the practice of teachers sitting only with teachers at specially designated tables in the college canteen certainly does not reflect this idea of everyone being equal at the table.

Also, as Julie A. P. Walton and Matthew Walters pointed out:

> At the table, we can't hide. For a few precious minutes we sit face-to-face as equals, thankful together for God's provision. We not only satisfy our physical hunger; we learn of the dreams, hopes and concerns of our image-bearing neighbors. This is what a meal at the table affords: the very moment we notice and understand how precious our tablemates are to Jesus, we are free to leave behind our self-indulgent, even tyrannical fears and suspicions.[220]

It is more than eating physical food; it is "the offering of our minds, entertaining together conceptual 'food' for thought."[221] Understandably, where there is no college canteen it may be difficult for a whole class to eat together on a regular basis, considering our conflicting personal schedules and the logistics if it involves the entire class. Some teachers instead practice bringing snacks or food to class and serving them during break times.[222] It is interesting to note that in a research done in Manitoba (Canada) in two community-based adult literacy programs, several learners indicated that "the provision of refreshments in the classroom was proof that they were being treated as adults in an adult learning environment."[223] The act of eating together could perhaps "create a loose mortar of care" for teachers and students to bond together, making room for everyone to get better acquainted with one another.[224] Carolyn Call shared that her simple act of bringing food to class was voluntarily taken over by the students after the second week of

---

219. Newman, "Hotel or Home," 101, quoting Gerhard Lohfink.
220. Walton and Walters, "Eat This Class," 101.
221. Quinn, "No Room," 107.
222. See Call, "Rough Trail," 68–69, 72–73; Rhoads, "Hospitality in the Classroom," 261.
223. Terry, "Importance of Interpersonal Relations," 40.
224. Call, "Rough Trail," 68–69.

the semester. At the end of the semester, in the course evaluations, students indicated that "the sharing of food [was] the central element of a shared sense of community."²²⁵ Another possible practice is to invite a couple of students at a time on a rotating basis, or sometimes impromptu, for lunch or dinner, or to a café for a cup of tea or coffee. Here, I would like to clarify that when an Asian invites another person for a meal, it means that he or she will act as the host and foot the bill, unless specified otherwise from the outset. For example, "let's have tea together" would be considered an invitation whereby the one who initiated it would act as the host. Therefore, it is important that the teacher initiates the invitation. Since all these hospitable acts, sometimes beyond the classroom and class contact time, require a commitment of time and effort, are theological educators willing make the sacrifices needed to become a friend to their students?

Listening to the Other

In the discussion on presence as connection to self (see above p. 218), I argued that we need to listen to ourselves and others in order to discover the center of our life. Here, my focus is on listening to the other, to his or her story as an expression of our hospitable care. In our classrooms, we do a lot of listening. However, as William D. Lindsey lamented:

> Our theological education places a premium on our ability to make critical distinctions, but gives scarcely an emphasis to helping us develop the skills to listen. Seeking to dismantle arguments of opponents and make critical distinctions envisages a state of perpetual battle, in which we must be poised to listen to our opponent's argument primarily to spot the flaw in it, the Achilles heel. Such listening is hardly listening at all, since we listen only for our chance to enter the fray and outwit our opponent.²²⁶

Mary Rose O'Reilley shared similar sentiments when she noted that "in academic culture, most listening is critical listening. We tend to pay attention only long enough to develop a counterargument; we critique the student's

---

225. Ibid., 73.
226. Lindsey, "Crossing the Postmodern Divide," 61.

or the colleague's ideas; we mentally grade and pigeonhole each other."[227] Listening for content is not listening to the other. Instead of listening so that we can reach out to help the other, this sort of listening is just so we can pounce on and tear the other apart.

Several authors have highlighted the need for the discipline of listening in hospitable classrooms.[228] To care is to listen. Caring, also referred to as attending, "begins with an attitude of openness that enables us to set aside our preoccupations in order to turn our attention to others. This is followed by a response."[229] "Attending, therefore, includes the ability to listen accurately and to respond with accurate understanding."[230] This would be akin to O'Reilley's "deep listening" – the "deep, openhearted, unjudging reception of the other."[231] "Attention: deep listening. People are dying in spirit for lack of it."[232] We all need a "soul friend" who will listen to us.[233]

In Palmer's opinion, students have chosen to be silent because "implicitly and explicitly, young people are told that they have no experience worth having, no voice worth speaking, no future of any note, no significant role to play."[234] This often is also true of female students in theological education. Finding themselves in an alienating educational environment, they "respond in the self-condemning acts of impatience and despair."[235] Hence, there is a need to "hear people to speech":

> Behind their fearful silence, our students want to find their voices, speak their voices, have their voices heard. A good teacher is one who can listen to those voices even before they are spoken – so that someday they can speak with truth and obedience. ... [T]o listen to a voice before it is spoken ... means making space for the other, being aware of the other, paying attention

---

227. O'Reilley, *Radical Presence*, 19.
228. Nouwen, *Reaching Out*, 95–97; Palmer, *Courage to Teach*, 45–47; Conde-Frazier, "From Hospitality to Shalom," 178–188; Hagstrom, "Christian Hospitality," 128.
229. Conde-Frazier, "From Hospitality to Shalom," 184.
230. Ibid.
231. O'Reilley, *Radical Presence*, 17.
232. Ibid., 19.
233. Ibid., 16.
234. Palmer, *Courage to Teach*, 46.
235. McAvoy, "Hospitality," 22.

to the other, honoring the other. It means not rushing to fill our students' silences with fearful speech of our own and not trying to coerce them into saying the things that we want to hear. It means entering empathetically into the students' world so that he or she perceives you as someone who has the promise of being able to hear another person's truth.[236]

For O'Reilley, it is to *"listen someone into existence."*[237] "We all have a story. We **are** a story."[238] "But our stories are caught in our throats. We need someone to listen to our stuttering, stammering plea to be heard. We need deep listening. We need good, welcoming silence … When this attentive silence opens to me, I gather the courage to speak, to be heard, to hear myself."[239] Therefore, when we hear people to speech or "listen someone to existence," we are making room for "a stronger self to emerge or a new talent to flourish. Good teachers listen this way, as do terrific grandfathers and similar heroes of the spirit."[240] Hagstrom also highlighted that "to welcome the other means to let the other tell his or her story. So listening becomes a basic attitude of hospitality."[241] Caring by deep listening thus allows theological educators to know their students better even as they help the students find the center of their lives, and express the dreams and aspirations that God has planted in their individual hearts. In this way, theological educators open up the possibility of "relationships of equality."[242]

Theological educators are more poised to listen attentively to their students when they are fully present to them. Whether it is Elizabeth Conde-Frazier's attending or O'Reilley's deep listening, to listen is simply to give undivided attention to students as we "listen for content, feeling, and context," even for

---

236. Palmer, *Courage to Teach*, 47, quoting Nelle Morton.
237. O'Reilley, *Radical Presence*, 21 (original emphasis).
238. Guenther, *Holy Listening*, 31 (original emphasis).
239. O'Reilley, *Radical Presence*, 26; see Conde-Frazier, "From Hospitality to Shalom," 171–172.
240. O'Reilley, *Radical Presence*, 21.
241. Hagstrom, "Christian Hospitality," 128, quoting Richard, *Living the Hospitality of God*, 12.
242. Jacobs, "Audacity of Hospitality," 576.

the unspoken words.[243] We may also have to listen patiently with our eyes and our heart because it takes time for the self to reveal itself. This is especially true for Asians. Kim Joo Yup and Nam Sang Hoon noted that "Asians have 'two faces': one reflecting the 'authentic self' (e.g. feelings, intentions, and attitudes) and the other reflecting the 'public self' (e.g. social status)."[244] Asians tend to hide the authentic self behind the public self, that is, the face (面子 miànzi), "the positive, respectable public self-image that a person, a family or a community claims for themselves in social interaction."[245] As a result, they may be hesitant to disclose their personal issues and problems so as to preserve their self-image. This is attested by Mary Sylvia Fernandez's study on Asian attitude towards counseling. Counselors in the United States have noted that Southeast Asians are less inclined to share their personal problems because they do not want to be looked down upon by others.[246] However, the sense of trust and safety in a close teacher-student relationship will provide the hospitable space for theological educators to truly listen to their students. "There is so much in life that is potentially dehumanizing. Listening is the most hospitable thing to do, and if we do no other thing than to train ourselves to listen to others, we will have taken great steps in hospitality."[247] "Careful, nonjudgmental listening is the way the heart offers hospitality" that cares.[248] After all, in our practice of care in hospitality, it invites "soul work for broken bodies" and "body work for bruised and battered souls."[249]

---

243. Conde-Frazier, "From Hospitality to Shalom," 185. Neither Elizabeth Conde-Frazier nor Mary Rose O'Reilley cited Carl Rogers in their works but their descriptions of attending and deep listening respectively bear close similarities to Rogers' active or attentive listening in person-centered therapy (e.g. giving total and undivided person to the other; listening with one's ears, eyes, mind, heart, and imagination; listening to the words and the unspoken messages behind the words) (for a more detailed description, see McWhinney and Freeman, *Textbook of Family Medicine*, 129).

244. Kim and Sang, "Concept and Dynamics," 526.

245. Wu, "Dynamics," 91. The concept of "face" is complex and beyond the scope of the work. Suffice to note that the public self-image (面子 miànzi) is inextricably tied with one's reputation and is to be differentiated from respect that is derived from the integrity of one's moral character (脸 liǎn) (ibid.; see Hu, "Chinese Concepts," 61; Ho, "On the Concept of Face," 867–870).

246. Fernandez, "Issues in Counselling," 163.

247. Homan and Pratt, *Radical Hospitality*, 216–217; see Justes, *Hearing beyond the Words*, ch. 1.

248. Thurston, "*Soli Deo Placere Desiderans*," 15.

249. Westfield, *Dear Sisters*, 70.

In summary, the hospitable practice of care is not confined to the four walls of the classroom but extends far beyond the classroom as theological educators cultivate friendships with and take time to listen to their students.

Constitutive Element 4: Reciprocity

The fourth constitutive element of hospitality is reciprocity, a concept that can be derived from its etymology. Embedded in the concept of reciprocity is the idea of fluidity of roles in the host-guest relationship and the possibility of mutual sharing of gifts and partnership between host and guest.[250] Hence, I explore reciprocity along two sub-themes: (1) reciprocity, role sharing, and gift sharing; and (2) reciprocity, dialogue, and partnership.[251] In the exploration of each theme, I have included my personal thoughts on how presence could be used as a principle of practice in the classrooms of theological institutions to create a reciprocal environment that fosters partnership between teachers and student, thus contributing to the holistic formation of students.

Reciprocity, Role Sharing, and Gift Sharing

As I have shown previously (see above p. 206, discussion on *xenos* and verb *xenizō*), there is no sharp etymological distinction between the stranger/guest and the host. This "signals the essential mutuality that is at the heart of hospitality": hosts become guests, and guests, hosts.[252] Herein lies the idea of reciprocity.

In relation to reciprocity, authors have made reference to various Bible stories to show that "in the context of hospitality guest and host can reveal their most precious gifts and bring new life to each other."[253] Abraham's three

---

250. My concept of reciprocity is not related in any way to the idea of one reciprocating in kind after receiving a gift from another. It is vastly different from reciprocity in a patron-client relationship or friendship between social equals of the first century (see deSilva, "Patronage and Reciprocity").

251. In tandem with what authors have written about reciprocity in hospitality, my thoughts regarding the sub-themes of reciprocity are also guided by Thomas W. Ogletree's understanding of hospitality as a way to guide our moral life (*Hospitality to the Stranger*, 1–9). Authors such as Susanne Johnson ("Reshaping"), Rud ("Learning in Comfort"), and Stratman ("Toward a Pedagogy") also cited Ogletree's work.

252. Pineda, "Hospitality," 33.

253. E.g. Nouwen, *Reaching Out*, 67; Losito, "Education as Hospitality," 65; Shaw, "Welcome Guest," 21.

guests brought to him the promise of a son (Gen 18:1–15). Elijah, the guest of the widow of Zarephath, raised her son from the dead (1 Kgs 17:9–24). Jesus, whom the two disciples invited to stay with them in the village of Emmaus, revealed to them that he was the risen Lord and Savior (Luke 24:13–35) (see above pp. 14, 32). With reference to this incident in Luke, an episode which Andrew Arterbury identified as having the standard features of a hospitality encounter,[254] Pohl alluded to the idea of role reversal, or what I perceive as role sharing, with these words: "Jesus comes to them as a stranger (they do not recognize him), but they welcome him as a guest, and in breaking bread together, Jesus becomes their host."[255] Hence, reciprocity involves the mutual sharing of roles and gifts between the guest and host.

In sharing our gifts, we establish "a reciprocal relationship – reciprocal as in gift circulation, not in obligated, restricted exchange – characterized by hospitality."[256] This idea runs contrary to Derrida's notion of the impossibility of the gift because once a gift is recognized as a gift, "this simple recognition suffices to annul the gift."[257] I can agree with the idea that "the gift exceeds the realms of both economy and exchange."[258] However, the reciprocal relationship as described by Rauna Kuokkanen stems from her Sami philosophy and "takes the form of circular reciprocity and sharing, sometimes also called 'ceremonial reciprocity,'" within a community that encompasses both human and the natural worlds. This is not my perception of reciprocity in Christian hospitality.[259] Neither do I perceive reciprocity in terms of exchange whereby receiving a gift can be a burden "for it implies owing something of at least equal value to the giver."[260] As Pohl pointed out, "within the Christian tradition, there was a normative emphasis in the practice of hospitality that involved offering welcome to 'the least,' to those who could not do the host any material or social good."[261] We show hospitality without expecting to be reciprocated in kind. My focus, rather, is on reciprocal giving between

---

254. Arterbury, *Entertaining Angels*, 146–147.
255. Pohl, *Making Room*, 31.
256. Kuokkanen, "Toward a New Relation," 286.
257. Derrida, *Given Time*, 13.
258. Kuokkanen, "Logic of the Gift," 258.
259. Kuokkanen, "Gift as a Worldview," 89; see "Gift Logic," 71–72.
260. Kuokkanen, "Gift as a Worldview," 88.
261. Pohl, "Hospitality from the Edge," 128.

persons, based on the theological understanding we are all created in the image of God, endowed with gifts that are to be shared with others.

It was only recently that I had an "aha moment" of what sharing and receiving a gift is all about. At a forum for Christian educators that I attended, an experienced college professor allayed the anxiety of a young female seminary teacher who was tasked to lead the next morning's devotion with these words: "Don't stress yourself over it. *Whatever you prepare is already a gift to us*" (paraphrased and emphasis mine). Frankly, I had never seen class participation and presentation, Greek translation exercises, term papers, even examinations, in this light before. I had never received them as gifts from the students – carefully prepared, at the expense of many sacrifices, and sometimes with sweat and tears. They were, to me, merely course requirements – expected, to be duly submitted on time, and if at all possible, done to near perfection. So, this is what reciprocity is about – receiving students' efforts as gifts. In appreciation of the gift, theological educators, as Chris Rust would suggest, could begin their feedback with a positive comment to encourage the student.[262] Graham Cheesman also suggested that feedback should begin on a positive note, with the teacher thanking the student for his or her work.[263] In his lecture on assessment at the Centre for Theological Education (November 3, 2009 in Belfast, UK), he revealed that his personal practice is to then give three positive comments before he gives his negative comments and, whenever possible, he would try to end his feedback on a positive note. David Jaques and Gilly Salmon even posed this question for the teachers' consideration: "Can it [feedback] be regarded by the receiver as a 'gift'?"[264] Perceived in that light, class lectures, responses to queries, feedback, evaluations are gifts to the students. Theological educators should be careful then to present them as such.

If theological educators practice reciprocity in the tradition of Christian hospitality, they would then be able to mutually share, and receive these, and many other seemingly trivial things (e.g. time, presence, prayer), as gifts with thankfulness and gratefulness in their hearts. It does not mean that they compromise on academic scholarship and standards, which was a concern

---

262. Rust, "Impact of Assessment," 152, citing an unpublished workshop handout of David Jaques.
263. Cheesman, "Assessment."
264. Jaques and Salmon, *Learning in Groups*, 218.

raised by some authors.²⁶⁵ Instead, as empirical research has shown, a positive hospitable environment is a more conducive learning environment that would increase student motivation and achievement. To practice a hospitable role and gift sharing, theological educators need to cultivate a fresh perspective of looking at the mundane things in their academic work. Even a warm "Thank you for sharing your gift with us (meaning, the class as a whole)" becomes significant because it not only affirms that they have received the gift but the giver as well, thus, allowing for positive student learning outcomes.²⁶⁶

Everyone has stories to tell, gifts to share. "Sharing personal narratives draws people toward hospitable kinship and is, in fact, gift exchange."²⁶⁷ Such stories and gifts have the potential to "open up our narrow, provincial worlds," even transforming the power dynamics in a host-guest relationship.²⁶⁸ As the theologian Thomas W. Ogletree so aptly described:

> When the stranger stands before me in his vulnerability, there is at least an inequality of power in our relationship. . . . However, when the stranger begins to tell her stories, a new kind of asymmetry appears. With regard to the world of meaning which is uncovering, she enjoys a level of authority that wholly surpasses my own. I am the novice, she the expert. I can only sit at her feet to learn. That the stranger and I enjoy an equal dignity emerges concretely only as our interactions unfold over time.²⁶⁹

This is echoed by Rud: "When you listen to a student, the student becomes the teacher. This reversal of roles is important for teachers to realize, to allow their own learning, and to put oneself in the role of the student."²⁷⁰ Role reversal or role sharing requires humility, what Nouwen referred to as the spiritual virtue of poverty of mind and of heart,²⁷¹ because we must be willing "to place ourselves under the authority or truth of another."²⁷² "The teacher

---

265. E.g. Schrag, "Beautiful Minds"; Johns, "Love and Hospitality."
266. Wimberly, "Hospitable Kinship," 6.
267. Ibid., 9; see Nouwen *Reaching Out*, 107.
268. Ogletree, *Hospitality to the Stranger*, 2.
269. Ibid., 3–4.
270. Rud, "Learning in Comfort," 121.
271. Nouwen, *Reaching Out*, 102–107.
272. Newman, "Hospitality and Christian," 86.

who lacks humility will be unable to create a space for any voice except his or her own."²⁷³ Since teachers have inherent power over their students in the classroom, it is the responsibility of the teacher to make room for students to be hosts, to create learning activities and opportunities for increased student participation/involvement/voice.

Speaking on behalf of students, Nouwen wrote:

> We will never believe that we have anything to give unless there is someone who is able to receive. Indeed, we discover our gifts in the eyes of the receiver. Teachers who can detach themselves from their need to impress and control, and who can allow themselves to become receptive for the news that their students carry with them, will find that it is in receptivity that gifts become visible.²⁷⁴

Rud was even more descriptive when he wrote, "If one casts off the mantle of pedagogical invincibility, a teacher probably learns more from students than students learn from the teacher."²⁷⁵ However, it may be difficult for teachers to cast off their mantle of pedagogical invincibility because they have been put on the pedestal by the prevailing social and cultural structures and perceived, either by themselves or others, as a "fount of knowledge, which is delivered without any concession to students."²⁷⁶ I believe that both teachers and students need to change their perspectives here. A traditional teacher-centered teaching (as practiced by teachers) or learning (as practiced by students) situation does not have a place for role and gift sharing.

In practicing reciprocity, theological educators working with culturally diverse students need to carefully study the communication patterns of different cultures. For instance, some teachers include class participation as a component in the course grading. However, what constitutes class participation? Does it mean that students will be penalized if they do not speak out in class? Much research has been done on passive and reticent students, especially those from "Confucian heritage culture . . . such as

---

273. Palmer, *To Know as We Are Known*, 109. Although this statement was made in relation to the need to pay attention to the other person or idea, and silence rather than reciprocity, the idea is also applicable here (see ibid., 108).
274. Nouwen, *Reaching Out*, 103–104.
275. Rud, "Learning in Comfort," 124.
276. Holliday, *Appropriate Methodology*, 59.

China, Vietnam, Singapore, Korea and Japan."²⁷⁷ There is a conception, or misconception, that "overseas Asian students typically take a low profile, rarely asking questions or volunteering answers, let alone make public observations or criticisms of course content."²⁷⁸ It is true that silence is normal in high-context Asian cultures. Silence can be a sign that the person "is thinking, is showing deference, or is simply taking the time to respond while observing the reactions" of the other person.²⁷⁹ The perceived student reticence and passivity could also be due to: (1) respect for the teacher, (2) fear of being seen as being unknowledgable and losing face, and (3) fear of disrupting group harmony.²⁸⁰ Although teachers need to be aware that silence is linked to culture, they must also realize that there are other factors involved as well.

Some researchers have argued that "if passiveness of Asian students is indeed observed in both Asian and English-speaking countries, it is more because of situation-specific factors of teaching methodologies, learning requirements, learning habits and language proficiency rather than cultural factors," including individual personalities.²⁸¹ In an interview conducted by Thi Tuyet Tran, in responding to the popular thinking that Asian students are passive, a respondent retorted: "Are all Asian students the same? I am Singaporean, and I don't think I am the same like Vietnamese, Thai, or Japanese students.²⁸² And even in the same class in Singapore, we may have some very active students and some very passive ones." Even David A. Watkins, who wrote about the Chinese learner, stated that he and his colleague John Biggs "do not, of course, claim *all* Chinese students are the same but [they] do believe from the research evidence that many Chinese students, because of their cultural heritage, approach education in a different way to most Western students."²⁸³ Hence, for whatever reasons, some students may be reluctant to speak up in class. Thus, theological educators need wisdom, patience, and a large repertoire of strategies to draw the students out of their

---

277. Nguyen, Terlouw, and Pilot, "Cooperative Learning," 403.
278. Biggs, "Western Misperceptions," 47; see Volet and Renshaw, "Chinese Students," 215.
279. Tuleja, *International Communication*, 38–39.
280. For more, see Zhou, Knoke, and Sakamoto, "Rethinking Silence," 288–289.
281. Tran, "Learning Approach," 58; see Volet and Renshaw, "Chinese Students"; Liu and Littlewood, "Students Appear Reluctant"; Cheng, "Asian Students"; Wong, "Learning Styles"; cf. Chan, "Chinese Learner"; Watkins, "Learning and Teaching."
282. Tran, "Learning Approach," 62.
283. Watkins, "Learning and Teaching," 171 (original emphasis).

reticence, showing them that they can share their gifts and become a teacher for even just a moment.

In their research involving primary and middle school classrooms in China, Lixian Jin and Martin Cortazzi observed that students preferred "talking of the known rather than talking to know."[284] Hence, in relation to asking questions, such students would "ask questions after learning because they feel that asking should be on the basis of knowledge, as confirmation . . . [rather than as] a way of knowing."[285] Research done on Singapore university students yielded similar results.[286] "Discovery learning (from the unknown to the known) often appear to elicit minimal response from Asian students because they need to be sure of the 'known' first" in order to appear as knowledgable before the class.[287] Questions need to be prepared ahead of time and the students "'have got to be sure' that things are right when communicating with their lecturers."[288] Hence, these students rarely participate actively in class by speaking up and voicing their opinions. However, it is not uncommon for them to seek teachers out after their class to discuss.[289] Since this is the case, theological educators should look for other platforms that can create space for student participation, such as reflection papers, journals, online discussions and blogs, and email correspondences. Therefore, rather than restricting reciprocity to participation in class from students, reciprocity in role and gift sharing should be perceived more widely as engagement both inside and outside the classroom, making it more urgent for theological educators to develop positive relationships with their students, thereby allowing the latter to seek them out for further discussion.

Reciprocity, Dialogue, and Partnership

Reciprocity is not just about sharing roles and gifts. Indeed, "the equality of host and stranger . . . shows itself in reciprocal acts of hospitality that reflect

---

284. Jin and Cortazzi, "Dimensions of Dialogue," 743.
285. Ibid., 753.
286. The majority of these Singaporean students were Chinese but there were other races as well (Dunn and Wallace, "Australian Academics Teaching," 293). As a whole, the class population reflected the population demographic of Singapore.
287. Dunn and Wallace, "Australian Academics," 300.
288. Ibid., 297, 299.
289. See Jin and Cortazzi, "Dimensions of Dialogue," 752–753.

reversals in the relational order."[290] However, "my readiness to welcome the other into my world must be balanced by my readiness to enter the world of the other."[291] "Hospitality to the stranger points toward an ongoing dialectic of host and stranger. It expresses a fundamental recognition of the world's plurality. The point is . . . that I can have my world in a moral way only as I learn to relate it positively to the contrasting worlds of others."[292] This is especially true in the world we live in which is made up of a diverse array of peoples and cultures. That is why, as seen in chapter 3, several educators have highlighted the need for dialogue,[293] conversation,[294] or questioning[295] as possible strategies for welcoming diversity of thought and ideas, beliefs and cultures.

For Hagstrom, in the context of a Christian host community and non-Christian guests, "the spiritual activity of conversation or dialogue is not about argument, contention, or controversy" but is characterized by "gratuitousness, welcome, receptivity, and a recognition of interdependency with others."[296] Quoting Lucien Richard, Hagstrom highlighted that in dialogue "I must let the other tell me who he or she is. Hospitality decenters our perspective; my story counts but so does the story of the other . . . To welcome the other means the willingness to enter the world of the other, to let the other tell his or her story."[297] With the attitude of *kenosis* (i.e. emptying; see Phil 2:7) exemplified by Jesus Christ our Lord, we can engage in genuine dialogue because it "creates an inner receptive charity that can become the space for mutual exchange of gifts."[298] Kuokkanen exhibited a similar stance when she argued that indigenous people, in helping others to learn about their indigenous epistemes, should "guide others in listening, in listening to learn, in becoming a guest instead of automatically assuming

---

290. Ogletree, *Hospitality to the Stranger*, 4.
291. Ibid.
292. Ibid.
293. E.g. Rud, "Learning in Comfort"; Hagstrom, "Christian Hospitality."
294. E.g. Bennett, "Academy and Hospitality"; *Academic Life*; Phipps and Barnett, "Academic Hospitality."
295. E.g. Quinn, "No Room."
296. Hagstrom, "Christian Hospitality," 128.
297. Ibid., quoting Richard, *Living the Hospitality of God*, 12.
298. Hagstrom, "Christian Hospitality," 129.

the role of the host or a host-guest."²⁹⁹ "The question of who is the host and who is the guest in the academy cannot be definitely answered – both the official representatives of the institution and indigenous people occupy the roles of the host and guest simultaneously and concurrently (however differently and disparately)."³⁰⁰ Using Michael Oakeshott's terminology of conversation in relation to liberal education, Bennett expresses essentially what dialogue to Hagstrom and Kuokkanen is.³⁰¹ A conversation requires an other. "There must be a multitude of important others – bearing substantial gifts of different perspective and experience."³⁰² Besides, conversation helps us to be present to ourselves because "we need others to whom we must listen carefully to learn more about ourselves – what we really think and who we are" (see above p. 218, "Embodied Presence as Connection to Self").³⁰³ For Bennett, hospitable conversation involves: (1) "the offering to share and to receive," and (2) "the provision of feedback on the position exchanged."³⁰⁴ In such hospitable conversations, we respect and treat others as equals. Such "mutual interaction and reciprocity . . . promises the possible transformation and fulfillment of both host and guest."³⁰⁵ Reflecting further on Bennett's proposal of conversation, Alison Phipps and Ronald Barnett added:

> Conversation – in the form of seminar, symposium, conference, the chat in the corridor or the deeper encounters of extremis as life presses and scours out its shape through academic life – enacts hospitality. It gives, speaking, and receives, listening. In the more formal modalities, it ponders, debates, contests, critiques, celebrates and most of all it communicates.³⁰⁶

So it is also for questioning. "Questioning requires the art of hospitality wherein we are not only open to the radical other it may introduce – listening to, learning from, the stranger who comes even as we question or critique

---

299. Kuokkanen, "Toward a New Relation," 282–283.
300. Kuokkanen, "What Is Hospitality," 76–77.
301. Oakeshott, *Voice of Liberal Learning*, 109–110.
302. Bennett, *Academic Life*, 103.
303. Ibid.
304. Bennett, "Academy and Hospitality," 24.
305. Ibid., 25.
306. Phipps and Barnett, "Academic Hospitality," 253.

Critical Dialogue towards the Application of the Motif of Hospitality 253

her; but also caring for this other, extending and offering our 'there' to him as well."[307] At the heart of all these three modes of hospitable exchanges – dialogue, conversation, questioning – is the concept of reciprocity, of sharing roles and gifts. Paulo Freire described this dialectical relationship between teacher and students as follows:

> Through dialogue, the teacher-of-the-students and the students-of-the-teacher cease to exist and a new term emerges: teacher-student with students-teachers. The teacher is no longer merely the-one-who-teaches, but one who is himself taught in dialogue with the students, who in turn while being taught also teach. They become jointly responsible for a process in which all grow.[308]

Bennett suggested that conversation or dialogue should go beyond "performative utterances" to include acts, that is, gestures and deeds.[309] Though Bennett was somewhat abstract in his explanation, his idea that we see conversation beyond utterances is worth our reflection. "The voice reveals human presence and bears story and temporality. Deeds carry a similar weight in enabling and conveying attention to the other."[310] I even believe that theological educators should express reciprocity, their interest in the stories of their students, not just through their deeds but through all available avenues. In this respect, the forms of dialogue put forth by the Pontifical Council for Interreligious Dialogue to facilitate interreligious dialogues among Catholics and those of other faiths help to reinforce my argument:

- The *dialogue of life*, where people strive to live in an open and neighborly spirit, sharing their joys and sorrows, their human problems and preoccupations
- The *dialogue of action*, in which Christians and others collaborate for the integral development and liberation of the people
- The *dialogue of theological exchange*, where specialists seek to deepen their understanding of their respective religious heritages, and to appreciate each other's spiritual values

---

307. Quinn, "No Room," 108.
308. Freire, *Pedagogy of the Oppressed*, 80.
309. Bennett, *Academic Life*, 106.
310. Ibid.

- The *dialogue of religious experience*, where persons, rooted in their own religious traditions, share their spiritual riches, for instance with regard to prayer and contemplation, faith and ways of searching for God or the Absolute[311]

I will take these ideas from its context of interreligious dialogue and apply it to the discussion at hand. With slight modifications, I propose reciprocity as a fourfold "dialogue of partnership" between teachers and students that incorporates: (1) dialogue of life (sharing life together), (2) dialogue of action and collaboration (doing things together), (3) dialogue of ideas (exchanging ideas and views), and (4) dialogue of experiences (reflecting on life experiences and spiritual experiences together).

As seen from chapter 4, hospitality played an important role in the mission efforts and growth of the early church (see above p. 195). Besides other reasons, Paul wrote to the believers in Rome because he hoped to add them to "his list of 'sponsors'" of his mission work to Spain.[312] In requesting "to be sent on" by them (Rom 15:24; see discussion on *propempō* in above p. 199), Paul was using a vocabulary related to hospitality. In supplying Paul and his travel companions all that they needed for the journey, they practiced hospitality and participated in his mission. They became his partners in ministry.

For teachers in theological institutions involved in the work of equipping men and women for the service of God, reciprocity in the form of dialogue of partnership is another way of being hospitable teachers. Theological educators should not stop at just telling and sharing of stories and dreams. They should view their work as a partnership with their students, as their way of empowering the students and providing the students with all that they need for their journey, for the service or ministry that God has called them to. It should also not stop the minute the students graduate. Theological educators should continue the dialogue of partnership even when the students are out "there" serving the God who called them to his harvest field. It could just be writing a note of encouragement or counsel, a sharing of resources, a personal visit to their place of ministry, or an invitation to co-teach with them. As Pohl put it, "as much as possible, hospitality relationships should always be

---

311. Arinze and Tomko, "Dialogue and Proclamation," 227–228 (original emphasis).
312. Moo, *Romans*, 17.

moving toward friendship and partnership models; long-term guest status becomes disempowering."[313]

In summary, the practice of reciprocity allows theological educators to share their pedagogical space with students, allowing them to be hosts and to share their gifts with all. The concept of reciprocity is made richer by the concept of dialogue, not just in speech, but of partnership – a dialogue of life, action and collaboration, ideas, and experiences.

Summary

Recognizing the multifaceted dimensions of hospitality, this chapter began with the presentation of the cluster concept to discuss the motif of hospitality in theological education. Based on the work done in the preceding three chapters, it then presented the four constitutive elements of hospitality as: (1) inclusion, (2) presence, (3) care, and (4) reciprocity.

The first constitutive element of hospitality is inclusion. In the face of global diversity, a hospitable learning environment must be inclusive and welcoming. While knowing that hospitality can be risky business, hospitable theological educators can choose not to be held hostage by fear, by their student-guests, but to willingly take on the form of a servant-host, like Jesus, the guest-host, to welcome students into their classrooms. Following the example of Jesus' practice of open commensality inclusive, theological educators can trust in the magnanimity of God's gracious welcome to guide them as they negotiate boundaries, especially invisible boundaries that alienate individuals from each other. Moreover, by intentionally moving away from their privileged positions to experience marginality periodically, they can better understand exclusion. Consequently, they can better practice inclusion. Ultimately, it is their spiritual status as aliens-passing-through in this world that will enable theological educators to be ever mindful of their vulnerable student-guests.

The second constitutive element of hospitality is presence. To be hospitable hosts in their classrooms, theological educators need to be present to their student-guests, with all that they are (namely, embodied presence)

---

313. Pohl, "Mysterious and Mundane," 13.

and all that they believe (namely, articulate presence). Having an embodied presence would mean that theological educators need first to be connected to the center of their inner self and to be personally inviting with themselves, their strengths and their weaknesses. Only then can they be inviting to their students and be fully present to them. This is especially important since emotion and cognition are inextricably linked in the learning process and they affect learning outcomes. Through their nonverbal immediacy behaviors, students can sense whether their teachers are present to them or not. Besides an embodied presence, theological educators must speak up – with words and exemplary lives – in order to establish a hospitable learning environment.

The third constitutive element of care is a reflection of God the host who provides and cares for his created beings, especially the defenseless. To properly care for their students, theological educators need to be a friend to them and to listen to them. A positive teacher-student relationship of care plays a crucial role in mediating student success in college. The process of befriending students may be time-consuming, but it allows theological educators to care for the students in ways that are specifically attuned to their needs. That means theological educators need to listen attentively to the stories, concerns, and dreams of their students, as well as the silence that punctuates their conversations. Such hospitable care, practiced within and beyond classrooms, creates an inviting and trusting space for learning.

Finally, the constitutive element of reciprocity is framed by the understanding of biblical hospitality as was practiced since the days of Abraham – the fluidity and mutuality in hospitality, and the act of sending off of guests (especially as seen in practice of the early faith communities). The idea of reciprocity begins with the possibility of the host becoming the guest and the guest becoming the host, with the host and guest sharing gifts with each other. As hosts, theological educators can sometimes play the role of guests and receive the gifts borne by their students. To learn and to receive from others requires dialogue and questioning. But, more than that, as in the act of sending off of guests where hosts become mission partners with their guests, to learn and to receive from others requires a dialogue of partnership. This dialogue of partnership is fourfold in nature. Theological educators and their students become partners. They share their lives with one another. They do things together. They exchange ideas and views. Together, they reflect on their life and spiritual experiences. In so doing, they practice reciprocity, allowing each other to be the other's host and guest.

The discussion of the four constitutive elements of hospitality includes personal observations and suggestions for application. Where relevant, cultural dimensions such as masculinity/femininity, high/low context, power distance, and silence are also considered. When at least one of these constitutive elements is present, theological educators are then able to create a hospitable teaching-learning environment that can facilitate the holistic formation of their students.

In conclusion, the presence of at least one of these constitutive elements in a teaching-learning situation constitutes a hospitable teaching-learning environment that promotes learning and positive student outcomes. Hence, the motif of hospitality can be applied in theological education to create an effective environment that facilitates the holistic formation of students in theological institutions.

6

Conclusion

This chapter summarizes the key findings of this study by first reviewing its research statement and hypotheses. It then explains the significance and limitations of this research, and offers some recommendations for further study.

Research Statement, Hypotheses, and Findings

This study arose from a desire to see changes to the climate of cold professionalism that prevails in theological institutions. Chance encounters with the concept of hospitality in education in the works of Henri J. M. Nouwen and Parker J. Palmer gave me the impetus to investigate further. Hence, the purpose of this work was to investigate the motif of hospitality as a viable concept for theological education and how it can be used by teachers in theological institutions to create an environment for facilitating the holistic formation of students.

The research has been guided by four hypotheses and the findings of these hypotheses are summarized as follows:

Hypothesis 1:
That the growing body of literature on hospitality in Christian higher education and theological education reveals an emerging literary phenomenon that deserves examination and assessment

The literature review on hospitality in Christian higher education and theological education in chapter 2 shows that conceptualization of hospitality in education began in the 1970s and 1980s with the works of Nouwen and Palmer respectively. Since the 1990s, Nouwen's and Palmer's initial conceptualization of hospitality as the creation of a space that welcomes the other, a person or an idea, has taken on new subtle nuances when educational professionals from Christian colleges/universities and theological institutions began to use the metaphor of hospitality to address emerging issues in higher education. The literature review also reveals gaps in current research. Besides the dominance of Western voices, there is also the lack of a biblically informed metaphor of hospitality that can inform theological educators in their efforts aimed at the holistic formation of students.

Hypothesis 2:
That hospitality appears to be a recurring concept in higher education literature, and that the usage finds parallels in the emotional and relational aspects of learning in contemporary educational practices

The findings of chapter 3 demonstrate that there has been an emerging shift towards the emotional and relational aspects of learning. To address the missing emotional and relational dimensions in the teaching-learning process, many educational professionals in higher education have also used the metaphor of hospitality to re-envision the work of higher education. In their works, the practices of care, dialogue, and inclusion were discussed as possible hospitable educational practices for creating a more relational and supportive learning environment in higher education. The findings of this chapter not only lend support to the need for a more hospitable learning environment for positive student outcomes but also provide some constitutive elements for defining hospitality.

Hypothesis 3:
That an understanding of the biblical concept of hospitality can inform teachers in theological institutions in their goal of education

The examination of key biblical passages where hospitality is encountered reveals God as a host who cares and provides for his created beings, especially for the defenseless – orphans, widows, and strangers. It also reveals Jesus both as a host and a guest who welcomes and eats with everyone, even the marginalized of society. Lastly, it shows that the believers of the early faith communities were hosts who lived out the command to show hospitality in their worship and care for the needy. The discussion of these three images

– God as host, Jesus as guest-host, the early faith communities as hosts – provides the conceptual framework to approach the application of hospitality in chapter 5 as well as some constitutive elements for defining hospitality.

Hypothesis 4:
That the motif of hospitality can be applied in theological education to create an effective environment for facilitating the holistic formation of students

Chapter 5 articulates four constitutive elements of hospitality that are drawn from the foregoing chapters – inclusion, presence, care, and reciprocity. Informed by the conceptual framework of biblical hospitality, it critiques the extent to which existing conceptions and contemporary parallel practices of hospitality in higher education can be applied in theological education. It proposes ways theological educators can practice at least one, if not more, of the constitutive elements to create an effective environment for facilitating the holistic formation of their students.

Significance, Limitations, and Areas for Further Research

This research contributes to the existing discourse on hospitality in education by presenting a biblically informed metaphor of hospitality for our consideration. As acknowledged in chapters 2 and 3, a weakness of this research is the paucity of literature from non-Westerners. This research thus provides another perspective of hospitality in higher education – more specifically, theological education – from the lens of an Asian female theological educator living in Singapore. Although some of my observations and examples may be culture-specific, the general principles for application are broadly applicable in Asian and non-Asian settings.

Several other limitations of this research need also to be acknowledged and recommendations proposed for further research:

- The focus of this research is largely on the role of the teacher as host and student as guest since this book holds the opinion that the onus is on the teacher to initiate changes in the teaching-learning environment. It would be beneficial to expand the conversation on the constitutive element of reciprocity (see above p. 244) and investigate how students can play the role of host in the contexts of both within and outside the classrooms of theological institutions.

- The research concentrates on the relationship between teacher and students in the creation of a hospitable teaching-learning environment. Since the theological institution constitutes a learning community, further research can be done on how the relationships between members of different ranks in this learning community (e.g. leadership with staff, administrative staff with teacher/student) can impact the institution-wide learning environment, and institution-wide strategies proposed to promote a more hospitable environment.
- Issues in relation to other faiths, and sexual orientation and gender identity were not addressed because these were considered as beyond the scope of the present analysis. The gay culture is slowly gaining momentum in Singapore as evidenced by recent events related to gay rights. On 28 June 2014, several Muslim and Christian groups joined the Wear White campaign in protest against an annual LGBT gathering where the attendees were asked to dress in pink.[1] Currently, this is just an emerging issue but, in years to come, it will probably challenge the exclusivist admission policies generally upheld by theological institutions. There is, therefore, a definite need for further research in this area, especially to examine the issue of boundaries in relation to the practice of hospitality in theological education.
- In a workshop where I presented the images of God as host and Jesus as guest-host, a question was raised regarding the omission of the role of the Holy Spirit as host. In this research, as stated in chapter 1 (see above p. 6), I did not portray the Holy Spirit as a host or a guest because I perceive him as the one who empowers and enables us to be hosts and guests. Without his enabling power, our efforts to be Christian hosts and guests may be futile. A future study investigating the role of the Holy Spirit as host could add new insights to the current research.
- Since this study is conceptual in nature, further research using empirical methods could provide more definitive evidence of

---

1. Au-Yong and Nur Asyiqin, "Religious Teacher"; Aw, "Big Turnout"; Nur Asyiqin, "Muslim Student Group"; "Police Issue Public Advisory"; "WP's Faisal Supports Wear White"; Singapore Straits Times, "Church Groups' Followers"; Wong, "Police Reject Road Closure."

how the constitutive elements of inclusion, presence, care, and reciprocity do create a hospitable environment for facilitating the holistic formation of students. Furthermore, since the practice of hospitality is culture-bound, such empirical research could also investigate what constitutes appropriate expressions of inclusion, presence, care, and reciprocity in a given cultural context. This research has clearly shown that the practice of hospitality is prescriptive for theological educators since all Christians are enjoined to practice hospitality. However, how hospitality is to be practiced is largely descriptive and may vary from culture to culture. Hence, such empirical findings may prove useful to theological educators working in diverse multicultural environments and desiring to practice hospitality to their students in ways that are deemed appropriate.

Endword

While preparing this book for submission, I had the opportunity to conduct three workshops on "Education as Hospitality, the Teacher as Host" to three different audiences (Master's students, postgraduate students, and faculty and staff members) in three different theological institutions. It was a revelation to many participants in these workshops that hospitality is *not* (emphasis mine) just one of the many spiritual gifts listed in Romans 12:13 and given only to some members in the body of Christ. It was also a revelation to them that hospitality is a moral responsibility of every believer and a practice that can extend far beyond one's home and the dinner table – into the theological institution and its classrooms.

As evidenced by the responses in these workshops, hospitality in education is still a relatively new concept to many in the theological education arena. I am thus grateful to those educators who have opened the doors of their minds and allowed me to journey with them to explore how hospitality, when practiced in theological classrooms, can create an effective environment for facilitating the holistic formation of students. I hope that this book provides a sound and integrated biblical, theological, and educational rationale to inform theological educators in their quest to transform the teaching/learning process so that they can more effectively equip, form, and transform their students for participation in God's mission of reconciliation.

Bibliography

Achtemeier, Paul J. *1 Peter*. Hermeneia. Minneapolis, MN: Fortress Press, 1996.

Adams, Colin. "Introduction." In *Travel and Geography in the Roman Empire*, edited by Colin Adams and Ray Laurence, 1–6. London: Routledge, 2001.

Airasian, Peter W., and Mary E. Walsh. "Constructivist Cautions." *Phi Delta Kappan* 78, no. 6 (1997): 444–449.

Albright, William Foxwell, and C. S. Mann. *Matthew*. Anchor Bible 26. Garden City, NY: Doubleday, 1971.

Allen, Willoughby C. *A Critical and Exegetical Commentary on the Gospel according to Saint Matthew*. Repr. ed. International Critical Commentary. Edinburgh: T & T Clark, 1985.

Ameny-Dixon, Gloria M. "Why Multicultural Education Is More Important in Higher Education Now than Ever." *International Journal of Scholarly Academic Intellectual Diversity* 6, no. 1 (2004): 1–9. http://www.nationalforum.com/Journals/IJSAID/IJSAID.htm.

Andersen, Peter A. "In Different Dimensions: Nonverbal Communication and Culture." In *Intercultural Communication: A Reader*, edited by Larry A. Samovar and Richard E. Porter, 10th ed., 239–251. Belmont, CA: Wadsworth/Thompson Learning, 2003.

Anderson, David W. "Hospitable Classrooms: Biblical Hospitality and Inclusive Education." *Journal of Education and Christian Belief* 15, no. 1 (2011): 13–27.

Anderson, Lynne E., and John Carta-Falsa. "Factors That Make Faculty and Student Relationships Effective." *College Teaching* 50, no. 4 (2002): 134–138.

Anderson, Robert C., ed. *Graduate Theological Education and the Human Experience of Disability*. Binghamton, NY: Haworth Pastoral Press, 2003.

Andrzejewski, Carey E., and Heather A. Davis. "Human Contact in the Classroom: Exploring How Teachers Talk about and Negotiate Touching Students." *Teaching and Teacher Education* 24, no. 3 (2008): 779–794.

Anidjar, Gil. "A Note on 'Hostipitality.'" In *Acts of Religion*, edited by Gil Anidjar, 356–357. New York: Routledge, 2002.

Ansari, Daniel, Donna Coch, and Bert De Smedt. "Connecting Education and Cognitive Neuroscience: Where Will the Journey Take Us?" *Educational Philosophy and Theory* 43, no. 1 (2011): 37–42.

Anthias, Floya. "Beyond Feminism and Multiculturalism: Locating Difference and the Politics of Difference." *Women's Studies International Forum* 25, no. 3 (2002): 275–286.

Antone, Hope, Wati Longchar, Hyunju Bae, Huang Po Ho, and Dietrich Werner, eds. *Asian Handbook for Theological Education and Ecumenism*. Regnum Studies in Global Christianity. Eugene, OR: Wipf & Stock, 2013.

Arias, Martimer. "Centripetal Mission or Evangelization by Hospitality." *Missiology* 10, no. 1 (1982): 69–81.

Arinze, Francis, and Jozef Tomko. "Dialogue and Proclamation: Reflection and Orientations on Interreligious Dialogue and the Proclamation of the Gospel of Jesus Christ." In *Dialogue and Proclamation: Reflections and Orientations on Interreligious Dialogue and the Proclamation of the Gospel of Jesus Christ*, 210–250. Vatican City: Pontifical Council for Interreligious Dialogue, 1991. http://www.pcinterreligious.org/dialogue-and-proclamation_131.html.

Arterbury, Andrew E. *Entertaining Angels: Early Christian Hospitality in Its Mediterranean Setting*. New Testament Monographs 8. Sheffield: Sheffield Phoenix Press, 2005.

Ascough, Richard S. "Welcoming Design: Hosting a Hospitable Online Course." *Teaching Theology and Religion* 10, no. 3 (2007): 131–136.

Aultman, Lori Price, Meca R. Williams-Johnson, and Paul A. Schutz. "Boundary Dilemmas in Teacher-Student Relationships: Struggling with 'the Line.'" *Teaching and Teacher Education* 25, no. 5 (2009): 636–646.

Au-Yong, Rachel, and Mohamad Salleh Nur Asyiqin. "Religious Teacher Launches 'Wear White' Online Campaign." *Singapore Straits Times*, 20 June 2014. Online.

Aw, Cheng Wei. "Big Turnout at Pink Dot Gathering." *Singapore Straits Times*, 29 June 2014. Online.

Badley, Graham. "Against Fundamentalism, for Democracy: Towards a Pedagogy of Tolerance in Higher Education." *Teaching in Higher Education* 10, no. 4 (2005): 407–419.

Badley, Ken, and Harro Van Brummelen, eds. "Metaphors: Unavoidable, Influential, and Enriching." In *Metaphors We Teach By: How Metaphors Shape What We Do in Classrooms*, edited by Ken Badley and Harro Van Brummelen, 1–15. Eugene, OR: Wipf & Stock, 2012.

———. *Metaphors We Teach By: How Metaphors Shape What We Do in Classrooms*. Eugene, OR: Wipf & Stock, 2012.

Bailey, Kenneth E. *Jesus through Middle Eastern Eyes: Cultural Studies in the Gospels*. Downers Grove, IL: InterVarsity, 2008.

Baker, Gideon. "The 'Double Law' of Hospitality: Rethinking Cosmopolitan Ethics in Humanitarian Intervention." *International Relations* 24, no. 1 (2010): 87–103.

Ball, Nathan. "A Covenant of Friendship." In *Befriending Life: Encounters with Henri Nouwen*, edited by Beth Porter, Susan M. S. Brown, and Philip Coulter, 90–99. New York: Image Books, 2001.

Banks, Robert. *Reenvisioning Theological Education: Exploring a Missional Alternative to Current Models*. Grand Rapids, MI: Eerdmans, 1999.

Barnette, Sean Michael. "Houses of Hospitality: The Material Rhetoric of Dorothy Day and the Catholic Worker." PhD dissertation, University of Tennessee, 2011. http://trace.tennessee.edu/cgi/viewcontent.cgi?article=2272&context=utk_graddiss.

Barr, Robert B., and John Tagg. "From Teaching to Learning – a New Paradigm for Undergraduate Education." *Change* 27, no. 6 (1995): 12–25.

Bartchy, S. Scott. "The Historical Jesus and Honor Reversal at the Table." In *The Social Setting of Jesus and the Gospels*, edited by Wolfgang Stegemann, Bruce J. Malina, and Gerd Theissen, 175–183. Minneapolis, MN: Fortress Press, 2002.

———. "Table Fellowship." In *Dictionary of Jesus and the Gospels*, edited by Joel B. Green, Scot McKnight, and I. Howard Marshall, 796–800. Downers Grove, IL: InterVarsity, 1992.

———. "Table Fellowship: Gospels." In *The IVP Dictionary of the New Testament*, edited by Daniel G. Reid, 1063–1067. Downers Grove, IL: InterVarsity, 2004.

Bauer, Walter. *A Greek-English Lexicon of the New Testament and Other Early Christian Literature*. 3rd ed. Revised and edited by Frederick William Danker. Chicago, IL: University of Chicago Press, 2000.

Baumgartner, Lisa M., and Juanita Johnson-Bailey. "Fostering Awareness of Diversity and Multiculturalism in Adult and Higher Education." *New Directions for Adult and Continuing Education* 120 (Winter 2008): 45–53.

Beck, Clive, and Clare Kosnik. *Innovations in Teacher Education: A Social Constructivist Approach*. SUNY Series, Teacher Preparation and Development. Albany, NY: State University of New York Press, 2006.

Beech, Thomas F. "Reflections." In *Living the Questions: Essays Inspired by the Work and Life of Parker J. Palmer*, edited by Sam M. Intrator, 81. San Francisco, CA: Jossey-Bass, 2005.

Bellinger, William H., and Andrew E. Arterbury. "'Returning' to the Hospitality of the Lord: A Reconsideration of Psalm 23:5–6." *Biblica* 86, no. 3 (2005): 387–395.

Bennett, John B. *Academic Life: Hospitality, Ethics, and Spirituality*. Eugene, OR: Wipf & Stock, 2003/2008.

———. "The Academy, Individualism, and the Common Good." *Liberal Education* 83, no. 4 (1997): 16–23.

———. "The Academy and Hospitality." *Cross Currents* 50, no. 1–2 (2000): 23–35.

———. "Civic and Moral Virtues: Teaching by Practicing Hospitality." *Journal of College and Character* 1, no. 6, article 2 (2000). http://www.tandfonline.com/doi/pdf/10.2202/1940-1639.1291.

———. *Collegial Professionalism: The Academy, Individualism, and the Common Good*. American Council on Education/Oryx Press Series on Higher Education. Phoenix, AZ: American Oryx Press, 1998.

———. "Constructing Academic Community: Power, Relationality, Hospitality, and Conversation." *Interchange* 34, no. 1 (2003): 51–61.

———. "Educational Spiritualities: Parker J. Palmer and Relational Metaphysics." In *A Different Three Rs for Education: Reason, Relationality, Rhythm*, edited by George Allan and Malcolm D. Evans, 169–183. Value Inquiry Book Series 176. Amsterdam: Rodopi B. V, 2006.

———. "Hospitality and Collegial Community: An Essay." *Innovative Higher Education* 25, no. 2 (2000): 85–96.

———. "Liberal Learning as Conversation." *Liberal Education* 87, no. 2 (2001): 32–39. *MasterFILE Premier*, EBSCO*host*.

———. "Teaching with Hospitality." *Toward the Best in the Academy* 12, no. 1 (2000–2001). http://podnetwork.org/content/uploads/V12-N1-Bennett.pdf.

Bentley, Joanne P., Mari Vawn Tinney, and Bing Howe Chia. "Intercultural Internet-Based Learning: Know Your Audience and What It Values." *Educational Technology Research and Development* 53, no. 2 (2005): 117–127.

Béthune, Pierre-François de. "Interreligious Dialogue and Sacred Hospitality." *Religion East and West* 7 (2007): 1–22.

Beumer, Jurjen. *Henri Nouwen: A Restless Seeking for God*. Translated by David E. Schlaver and Nancy Forest-Flier. New York: Crossroad, 1997.

Biggs, John. "Western Misperceptions of the Confucian-Heritage Learning Culture." In *The Chinese Learner: Cultural, Psychological and Contextual Influences*, edited by David A. Watkins and John Biggs, 45–67. Hong Kong: CERC, 1996.

Billson, Janet Mancini, and Richard G. Tiberius. "Effective Social Arrangements for Teaching and Learning." *New Directions for Teaching and Learning* 45 (1991): 87–109.

Binnie, Jon, and Christian Klesse. "'Because It Was a Bit Like Going to an Adventure Park': The Politics of Hospitality in Transnational Lesbian, Gay, Bisexual, Transgender and Queer Activist Networks." *Tourist Studies* 11, no. 2 (2011): 157–174.

Birbeck, David, and Kate Andre. "The Affective Domain: Beyond Simply Knowing." In *Assessment in Different Dimensions: Conference Papers*, 40–47. ATN Assessment Conference 2009. Melbourne: RMIT University, 2009.

Black, Max. "Definition, Presupposition, and Assertion." *Philosophical Review* 61, no. 4 (1952): 532–550.

———. "How Do Pictures Represent?" In *Art, Perception, and Reality*, 95–130. Baltimore, MD: John Hopkins University Press, 1972.

Blevins, John. "Hospitality Is a Queer Thing." *Journal of Pastoral Theology* 19, no. 2 (2009): 104–117.

Blomberg, Craig L. *Contagious Holiness: Jesus' Meals with Sinners*. New Studies in Biblical Theology 19. Downers Grove, IL: InterVarsity, 2005.

———. "Jesus, Sinners, and Table Fellowship." *Bulletin for Biblical Research* 19, no. 1 (2009): 35–62.

———. *Matthew*. New American Commentary 22. Nashville, TN: Broadman, 1992.

Boersma, Hans. "Irenaeus, Derrida and Hospitality: On the Eschatological Overcoming of Violence." *Modern Theology* 19, no. 2 (2003): 163–180.

———. "Liturgical Hospitality: Theological Reflections on Sharing in Grace." *Journal for Christian Theological Research* 8 (2003): 67–77.

Boggs, George R. "The Learning Paradigm." *Community College Journal* 66, no. 3 (1995–1996): 24–27.

Boice, James Montgomery. *Psalms: Vol. 1; Psalms 1–41*. Grand Rapids, MI: Baker, 1994.

Bolchazy, Ladislaus J. *Hospitality in Antiquity: Livy's Concept of Its Humanizing Force*. Rev. ed. Chicago, IL: Ares, 1977/1995.

Boler, Megan. "Disciplined Emotions: Philosophies of Educated Feelings." *Educational Theory* 47, no. 2 (1997): 203–227.

———. *Feeling Power: Emotions and Education*. New York: Routledge, 1999.

Bonner, Stanley F. *Education in Ancient Rome: From the Elder Cato to the Younger Pliny*. Routledge Library Editions, Education 91. New York: Routledge, 1977/2012.

Borg, Marcus J. *Conflict, Holiness and Politics in the Teachings of Jesus*. 2nd ed. Harrisburg, PA: Trinity Press, 1998.

———. *Jesus, a New Vision: Spirit, Culture, and the Life of Discipleship*. San Francisco, CA: Harper & Row, 1987.

Bouma-Prediger, Steve, and Brian Walsh. "Education for Homeless or Homemaking? The Christian College in a Postmodern Culture." *Journal of Education and Christian Belief* 8, no. 1 (2004): 53–70.

Breitenbach, Louise M. "Pompeian Wall-Scribblings." *School Review* 14, no. 7 (1906): 529–534.

Brekelmans, Mieke, Theo Wubbels, and Perry Den Brok. "Teacher Experience and the Teacher-Student Relationship in the Classroom Environment." In *Studies in Educational Learning Environments: An International Perspective*, edited by Goh Swee Chiew and Myint Swe Khine, 73–99. Singapore: World Scientific, 2002.

Brekelmans, Mieke, Theo Wubbels, and Jan van Tartwijk. "Teacher-Student Relationships across the Teaching Career." *International Journal of Educational Research* 43, no. 1–2 (2005): 55–71.

Bretherton, Luke. *Hospitality as Holiness: Christian Witness amid Moral Diversity.* Aldershot, UK: Ashgate, 2006/2010.

———. "Tolerance, Education and Hospitality: A Theological Proposal." *Studies in Christian Ethics* 17, no. 1 (2004): 80–103.

Briggs, Charles Augustus, and Emilie Grace Briggs. *A Critical and Exegetical Commentary on the Book of Psalms: Vol. 1.* Repr. ed. International Critical Commentary. Edinburgh: T & T Clark, 1976.

Brookfield, Stephen D. "Authenticity and Power." *New Directions for Adult and Continuing Education* 111 (Fall 2006): 5–16.

———. *The Skillful Teacher: On Technique, Trust, and Responsiveness in the Classroom.* 2nd ed. San Francisco, CA: Jossey-Bass, 2006.

Brown, Raymond E. *The Epistles of John.* Anchor Bible 30. Garden City, NY: Doubleday, 1982.

———. *The Gospel according to John 13–21.* Anchor Bible 29A. Garden City, NY: Doubleday, 1970.

Brown, Tom H. "Beyond Constructivism: Navigationism in the Knowledge Era." *On the Horizon* 14, no. 3 (2006): 1.

Broyles, Craig C. *The Conflict of Faith and Experience in the Psalms: A Form-Critical and Theological Study.* Journal for the Study of the Old Testament Supplement Series 52. Sheffield: Sheffield Press, 1989.

Bruce, F. F. *The Epistle to the Hebrews.* New International Commentary on the New Testament. Grand Rapids, MI: Eerdmans, 1964.

Brueggemann, Walter. *The Message of the Psalms: A Theological Commentary.* Augsburg Old Testament Series. Minneapolis, MN: Augsburg, 1984.

———. *Theology of the Old Testament: Testimony, Dispute, Advocacy.* Minneapolis, MN: Fortress, 1997.

Buber, Martin. *Between Man and Man.* Translated by Ronald Gregor-Smith. London: Routledge & Kegan Paul, 1947/2004.

———. *I and Thou.* Translated by Ronald Gregor-Smith. New York: Scribner's Sons, 1958.

Buchanan, George Wesley. *To the Hebrews.* 2nd ed. Anchor Bible 36. Garden City, NY: Doubleday, 1972.

Bulkeley, Kelly. *The Wondering Brain: Thinking about Religion with and beyond Cognitive Neuroscience.* New York: Routledge, 2005.

Bultmann, Rudolf. *The Johannine Epistles: A Commentary on the Johannine Epistles.* Translated by R. Philip O'Hara, Lane C. McGaughy, and Robert W. Funk. Hermeneia. Philadelphia, PA: Fortress, 1973.

Burba, Fengjiao Ji, Joseph Petrosko, and Mike A. Boyle. "Appropriate and Inappropriate Instructional Behaviours for International Training." *Human Resource Development Quarterly* 12, no. 3 (2001): 267–283.

Burbules, Nicholas C. "The Limits of Dialogue as a Critical Pedagogy." In *Revolutionary Pedagogies: Cultural Politics, Instituting Education, and the Discourse of Theory*, edited by Peter Trifonas, 251–274. New York: Routledge, 2000.

Burbules, Nicholas C., and Suzanne Rice. "Dialogue across Differences: Continuing the Conversation." *Harvard Educational Review* 61, no. 4 (1991): 393–416.

Burwell, Rebecca, and Mackenzi Huyser. "Practicing Hospitality in the Classroom." *Journal of Education and Christian Belief* 17, no. 1 (2013): 9–24.

Caine, Geoffrey, and Renate Nummela Caine. "Meaningful Learning and Executive Functions of the Brain." *New Directions for Adult and Continuing Education* 110 (Summer 2006): 53–61.

Caird, G. B. *The Language and Imagery of the Bible*. Philadelphia, PA: Westminster Press, 1980.

Cairns, Earle E. *Christianity through the Centuries: A History of the Christian Church*. 3rd ed. Grand Rapids, MI: Zondervan, 1996.

Call, Carolyne. "The Rough Trail to Authentic Pedagogy: Incorporating Hospitality, Fellowship, and Testimony in the Classroom." In *Teaching and Christian Practices: Reshaping Faith and Learning*, edited by David I. Smith and James K. A. Smith, 61–79. Grand Rapids, MI: Eerdmans, 2011.

Campbell, Barth L. "Honor, Hospitality and Haughtiness: The Contention for Leadership in 3 John." *Evangelical Quarterly* 77, no. 4 (2005): 321–341.

Carcopino, Jérôme. *Daily Life in Ancient Rome: The People and the City at the Height of the Empire*. Edited by Henry T. Rowell. Translated by E. O. Lorimer. Repr. ed. Middlesex: Penguin, 1974.

Carley, Kathleen. "Knowledge Acquisition as a Social Phenomenon." *Instructional Science* 14, no. 3–4 (1986): 381–438.

Carr, David. "Personal and Interpersonal Relationships and Education and Teaching: A Virtue Ethical Perspective." *British Journal of Educational Studies* 53, no. 3 (2005): 255–271.

Casson, Lionel. *Travel in the Ancient World*. Baltimore, MD: John Hopkins University Press, 1994.

Cavell, Stanley. *The Senses of Walden: An Expanded Edition*. Chicago, IL: University of Chicago Press, 1974/1992.

Cayanus, Jacob L. "Effective Instructional Practice: Using Teacher Self-Disclosure as an Instructional Tool." *Communication Teacher* 18, no. 1 (2004): 6–9.

Cayanus, Jacob L., and Matthew M. Martin. "An Instructor Self-Disclosure Scale." *Communication Research Reports* 21, no. 3 (2004): 252–263.

———. "Teacher Self-Disclosure: Amount, Relevance, and Negativity." *Communication Quarterly* 56, no. 3 (2008): 325–341.

Cayanus, Jacob L., Matthew M. Martin, and Alan K. Goodboy. "The Relation between Teacher Self-Disclosure and Student Motives to Communicate." *Communication Research Reports* 26, no. 2 (2009): 105–113.

Chan, Sally. "The Chinese Learner: A Question of Style." *Education + Training* 41, no. 6 (1999): 294–305.

Chang, Mitchell J., Nida Denson, Victor Sáenz, and Kimberly Misa. "The Educational Benefits of Sustaining Cross-Racial Interaction among Undergraduates." *Journal of Higher Education* 77, no. 3 (2006): 430–455.

Cheesman, Graham J. "Assessment." Lecture Handout, Centre for Theological Education, Belfast Bible College, Belfast. 3 November 2009.

———. "A Conversation with Henri Nouwen about Theological Education." Lecture Handout, Centre for Theological Education, Belfast Bible College, Belfast. 20 November 2009.

Cheng, Xiaotang. "Asian Students' Reticence Revisited." *System* 28, no. 3 (2000): 435–446.

Chia, Mun Onn. "Major Differences between Eastern and Western Philosophies as the Basis for Adult Education: The Singapore Experience." *EAEA (European Association for the Education of Adults)* n.d. Online.

Childs, Brevard S. *Isaiah: A Commentary*. Old Testament Library. Louisville, KY: Westminster John Knox Press, 2001.

Chilton, Bruce. *Jesus' Baptism and Jesus' Healing*. Harrisburg, PA: Trinity Press, 1998.

Chory, Rebecca M., and James C. McCroskey. "The Relationship between Teacher Management Communication Style and Affective Learning." *Communication Quarterly* 47, no. 1 (1999): 1–11.

Christensen, Duane L. *Deuteronomy 1–11*. Word Biblical Commentary 6A. Dallas, TX: Word, 1991.

———. *Deuteronomy 21:10–34:12*. Word Biblical Commentary 6B. Waco, TX: Word, 2002.

Christophel, Diane M. "The Relationships between Teacher Immediacy Behaviors, Student Motivation, and Learning." *Communication Education* 39, no. 4 (1990): 323–340.

Churukian, George A. "Perceived Learning in the Classroom and Teacher-Student Interpersonal Relationships." Paper presented at Teacher Education 80–90 International Seminar, Groningen, the Netherlands, April 1982. (ERIC Reproduction Service No. 218273).

Cicero. *Against Verres*. Translated by C. D. Yonge. In Perseus Digital Library, 1903. http://www.perseus.tufts.edu/hopper/text?doc=Cic.+Ver.+2.4.48&fromdoc=Perseus%3Atext%3A1999.02.0018.

———. *Divination*. Translated by William Armistead Falconer. In Perseus Digital Library, 1923. http://www.perseus.tufts.edu/hopper/text?doc=Perseus%3Atext%3A2007.01.0043%3Abook%3D1%3Asection%3D57.

———. *For King Deiotarius*. Translated by C. D. Yonge. In Perseus Digital Library, 1891. http://www.perseus.tufts.edu/hopper/text?doc=Cic.+Deiot.+6.18&fromdoc=Perseus%3Atext%3A1999.02.0020.

———. *The Letters of Cicero*. Translated by Evelyn S. Shuckburgh. In Perseus Digital Library, 1899. http://www.gutenberg.org/files/21200/21200-h/21200-h.htm.

Clance, Pauline Rose, and Suzanne Ament Imes. "The Imposter Phenomenon in High Achieving Women: Dynamics and Therapeutic Intervention." *Psychotherapy: Theory, Research and Practice* 15, no. 3 (1978): 241–247.

Clare, Roberta. "Review of *A Hidden Wholeness: The Journey toward an Undivided Life*, by Parker J. Palmer." *Journal of Adult Theological Education* 2, no. 1 (2005): 86–87.

Coady, Frank. "Hospitality in the Liturgy." *Liturgical Ministry* 11 (2002): 182–186.

Conde-Frazier, Elizabeth. "From Hospitality to Shalom." In *A Many Colored Kingdom: Multicultural Dynamics for Spiritual Formation*, edited by Elizabeth Conde-Frazier, S. Steven Kang, and Gary A. Parrett, 167–210. Grand Rapids, MI: Baker, 2004.

———. "A Spirituality for a Multicultural Ministry." *Perspectivas/Occasional Papers* 7 (Fall 2003): 57–82.

Connolly, William E. *The Ethos of Pluralization*. Borderlines 1. Minneapolis, MN: University of Minnesota Press, 1995.

Constable, Olivia Remie. *Housing the Stranger in the Mediterranean World: Lodging, Trade, and Travel in Late Antiquity and the Middle Ages*. Cambridge: Cambridge University Press, 2003.

Cooper, Marlene E. "I Was a Stranger and You Welcomed Me: Exploring Godly Hospitality and Its Implications for Christian Education." *Lutheran Theological Journal* 30, no. 3 (1996): 120–130.

Cozolino, Louis, and Susan Sprokay. "Neuroscience and Adult Learning." *New Directions for Adult and Continuing Education* 110 (Summer 2006): 11–19.

Craigie, Peter C. *Psalms 1–50*. Word Biblical Commentary 19. Waco, TX: Word, 1983.

Cranfield, C. E. B. *A Critical and Exegetical Commentary on the Epistle to the Romans: Vol. 2*. Repr. ed. International Critical Commentary. Edinburgh: T & T Clark, 1979.

Cranton, Patricia. "Fostering Authentic Relationships in the Transformative Classroom." *New Directions for Adult and Continuing Education* 109 (Spring 2006): 5–13.

Cross, Frank Moore, Jr. *The Ancient Library of Qumran and Modern Biblical Studies.* Rev. ed. Grand Rapids, MI: Baker, 1980.

Cutri, Ramona Maile, Dolores Delgado Bernal, Anne Powell, and Claudia Ramirez Widerman. "'An Honorable Sisterhood': Developing a Critical Ethic of Care in Higher Education." *Transformations* 9, no. 2 (1998): 100–117.

Dahood, Mitchell. *Psalms 1:1–50.* Anchor Bible 16. Garden City, NY: Doubleday, 1966.

Dalgleish, Tim. "The Emotional Brain." *Nature Reviews Neuroscience* 5 (2004): 582–589.

Damasio, Antonio R. "A Second Chance for Emotion." In *Cognitive Neuroscience of Emotion*, edited by Richard D. Lane and Lynn Nadel. Series in Affective Science, 12–23. New York: Oxford University Press, 2000.

Davids, Peter H. *The First Epistle of Peter.* New International Commentary on the New Testament. Grand Rapids, MI: Eerdmans, 1990.

Davies, Eryl W. "Walking in God's Ways: The Concept of *Imitatio Dei* in the Old Testament." In *In Search of True Wisdom: Essays in Old Testament Interpretation in Honour of Ronald E. Clements*, edited by Edward Ball, 99–115. Journal for the Study of the Old Testament Supplement Series 300. Sheffield: Sheffield Academic Press, 1999.

Davies, W. D., and Dale C. Allison. *A Critical and Exegetical Commentary on the Gospel according to Saint Matthew: Vol. 2; Matthew 8–18.* Repr. ed. International Critical Commentary. London: T & T Clark, 2004.

DeFelice, John. "Inns and Taverns." In *The World of Pompeii*, edited by John Joseph Dobbins and Pedar William Foss, 474–486. London: Routledge, 2007.

Den Brok, Perry, Mieke Brekelmans, and Theo Wubbels. "Interpersonal Teacher Behavior and Student Outcomes." *School Effectiveness and School Improvement* 15, no. 3–4 (2004): 407–442.

Denaux, Adelbert. "The Theme of Divine Visits and Human (Inhospitality) in Luke-Acts: Its Old Testament and Graeco-Roman Antecedents." In *The Unity of Luke-Acts*, edited by Jozef Verheyden, 255–279. Bibliotheca Ephemeridum Theologicarum Lovaniensium 142. Leuven, Belgium: Leuven University Press, 1999.

Denzin, Norman K. *On Understanding Emotion.* San Francisco, CA: Jossey-Bass, 1984.

Derrida, Jacques. *The Gift of Death.* Translated by David Wills. Chicago, IL: University of Chicago Press, 1995.

———. *Given Time: 1. Counterfeit Money.* Translated by Peggy Kamuf. Chicago, IL: Chicago University Press, 1992.

———. "Hospitality, Justice and Responsibility: A Dialogue with Jacques Derrida." In *Questioning Ethics: Contemporary Debates in Philosophy*, edited by Richard Kearney and Mark Dooley, 65–83. London: Routledge, 1999.

———. "Hostipitality." Translated by Barry Stocker and Forbes Morlock. *Angelaki: Journal of the Theoretical Humanities* 5, no. 3 (2000): 3–18.

———. "Hostipitality." In *Acts of Religion*, edited and translated by Gil Anidjar, 358–420. New York: Routledge, 2002.

———. *On Cosmopolitanism and Forgiveness*. Translated by Mark Dooley and Michael Hughes. London: Routledge, 2001.

———. *The Politics of Friendship*. Translated by George Collins. London: Verso, 1997.

———. "The Principle of Hospitality." *Parallax* 11, no. 1 (2005): 6–9.

Derrida, Jacques, and Geoffrey Bennington. "Politics and Friendship: A Discussion with Jacques Derrida." In Centre for Modern French Thought, University of Sussex, 1997. http://hydra.humanities.uci.edu/derrida/pol+fr.html.

Derrida, Jacques, and Anne Dufourmantelle. *Of Hospitality: Anne Dufourmantelle Invites Jacques Derrida to Respond*. Translated by Rachel Bowlby. Cultural Memory in the Present. Stanford, CA: Stanford University Press, 2000.

deSilva, David A. *Despising Shame: Honor Discourse and Community Maintenance in the Epistle to the Hebrews*. Rev. ed. SBL 21. Atlanta, GA: SBL, 2008.

———. *An Introduction to the New Testament: Contexts, Methods and Ministry Formation*. Downers Grove, IL: InterVarsity, 2004.

———. "Patronage and Reciprocity: The Context of Grace in the New Testament." *Ashland Theological Journal* 31 (1999): 32–84.

———. *Perseverance in Gratitude: A Socio-Rhetorical Commentary on the Epistle "to the Hebrews."* Grand Rapids, MI: Eerdmans, 2000.

Dewey, John. *Democracy and Education*. Electronic Classics Series. University Park, PA: Penn State University, 2001. Online.

Dikeç, Mustafa. "*Pera Peras Poros*: Longings for Spaces of Hospitality." *Theory, Culture and Society* 19, no. 1–2 (2002): 227–247.

Dirkx, John M. "The Meaning and Role of Emotions in Adult Learning." *New Directions for Adult and Continuing Education* 120 (Winter 2008): 7–18.

Docan-Morgan, Tony, and Valerie Manusov. "Relational Turning Point Events and Their Outcomes in College Teacher-Student Relationships from Students' Perspectives." *Communication Education* 58, no. 2 (2009): 155–158.

Donahue, John R. "The 'Parable' of the Sheep and the Goats: A Challenge to Christian Ethics." *Theological Studies* 47 (1986): 3–31.

———. "Tax Collectors and Sinners: An Attempt at Identification." *Catholic Biblical Quarterly* 33, no. 1 (1971): 39–61.

Douglas, Mary. "Deciphering a Meal." *Daedalus* 101, no. 1 (1972): 61–81.

———. *Natural Symbols: Explorations in Cosmology*. 2nd ed. London: Routledge, 1970/1996.

———. *Purity and Danger: An Analysis of Concepts of Pollution and Taboo*. London: Routledge, 1966.

Driver, S. R. *A Critical and Exegetical Commentary on the Book of Deuteronomy*. 3rd ed. International Critical Commentary. Edinburgh: T & T Clark, 1986.

Dunn, James D. G. *Jesus Remembered*. Christianity in the Making: Vol. 1. Grand Rapids, MI: Eerdmans, 2003.

———. "Jesus, Table-Fellowship, and Qumran." In *The Christ and the Spirit: Collected Essays of James D. G. Dunn; Vol. 1, Christology*, 96–111. Grand Rapids, MI: Eerdmans, 1998.

———. *Romans 9-16*. Word Biblical Commentary 38B. Dallas, TX: Word, 1988.

Dunn, Lee, and Michelle Wallace. "Australian Academics Teaching in Singapore: Striving for Cultural Empathy." *Innovations in Education and Teaching International* 41, no. 3 (2004): 291–304.

Durback, Robert, ed. *Seeds of Hope: A Henri Nouwen Reader*. 2nd ed. New York: Image Books, 1997.

Dykstra, Craig R., and Dorothy C. Bass. "Times of Yearning, Practices of Faith." In *Practicing Our Faith: A Way of Life for a Searching People*, edited by Dorothy C. Bass, 2nd ed., 1–12. San Francisco, CA: John Wiley & Sons, 2010.

———. "A Way of Thinking about a Way of Life." In *Practicing Our Faith: A Way of Life for a Searching People*, edited by Dorothy C. Bass, 2nd ed., 203–217. San Francisco, CA: John Wiley & Sons, 2010.

Eck, Diana L. *Encountering God: A Spiritual Journey from Bozeman to Banaras*. 2nd ed. Boston, MA: Beacon Press, 2003.

Eckhart, Bob. "To Share or Not to Share: Cancer and What Teachers Should Tell Students about It." *Talking about Teaching* 5 (2011): 43–50. https://works.bepress.com/bobeckhart/1/.

Economides, Anastasios. "Culture-Aware Collaborative Learning." *Multicultural Education and Technology Journal* 2, no. 4 (2008): 243–267.

Edgar, Don W. "Learning Theories and Historical Events Affecting Instructional Design in Education: Recitation Literacy toward Extraction Literacy Practices." *Sage Open* 2, no. 4 (2012): 1–9.

Edwards, Renee, and Terre Allen. "Perspectives on Teacher Evaluation." In *Power in the Classroom: Communication, Control, and Concern*, edited by Virginia P. Richmond and James C. McCroskey, 177–193. Hillsdale, NJ: Lawrence Erlbaum Associates, 1992.

Edwards, Tilden, Jr. "Spiritual Formation in Theological Schools: Ferment and Challenge." *Theological Education* 17, no. 1 (1980): 1–52.

Efklides, A., and Simone Volet. "Emotional Experiences during Learning: Multiple, Situated and Dynamic." *Learning and Instruction* 15 (2005): 377–380.

Elbow, Peter. "The Believing Game." In *Nurturing the Peacemakers in Our Students: A Guide to Writing and Speaking Out about Issues of War and of Peace*, edited by Chris Weber, 16-25. Portsmouth, NH: Heinemann, 2006.

———. *Writing without Teachers*. London: Oxford University Press, 1973.

Ellingworth, Paul. *The Epistle to the Hebrews*. New International Greek Testament Commentary. Grand Rapids, MI: Eerdmans, 1993.

Elliott, John H. *1 Peter*. Anchor Bible 37B. Garden City, NY: Doubleday, 2000.

Ellsworth, Elizabeth. "Why Doesn't This Feel Empowering? Working through the Resistant Myths of Critical Pedagogy." *Harvard Educational Review* 59, no. 3 (1989): 297–324.

Epictetus. *Epictetus: Vol. 1; Discourses (Books 1 and 2)*. Translated by W. A. Oldfather. Repr. ed. Loeb Classical Library. Cambridge, MA: Harvard University Press, 1956.

———. *Epictetus: Vol. 2; The Discourses as Reported by Arrian: The Manual, and Fragments*. Translated by W. A. Oldfather. Repr. ed. Loeb Classical Library. Cambridge, MA: Harvard University Press, 1952.

Farber, Jerry. "Teaching and Presence." *Pedagogy* 8, no. 2 (2008): 215–225.

Farr, Bernard C. "Introduction: On Being Theologically Educated: Ten Key Characteristics." In *Christianity and Education: Shaping Christian Thinking in Context*, edited by David Emmanuel Singh and Bernard C. Farr, 9–30. Regnum Studies in Global Christianity. Oxford: Regnum International, 2011.

Fee, Gordon D. *The First Epistle to the Corinthians*. New International Commentary on the New Testament. Grand Rapids, MI: Eerdmans, 1987.

Fernandez, Mary Sylvia. "Issues in Counselling Southeast Asian Students." *Journal of Multicultural Counselling and Development* 16, no. 4 (1988): 157–166.

Ferrari, Michel. "What Can Neuroscience Bring to Education?" *Educational Philosophy and Theory* 43, no. 1 (2011): 31–36.

Filson, Floyd V. "The Significance of the Early House Churches." *Journal of Biblical Literature* 58, no. 2 (1939): 105–112.

Fiorenza, Elizabeth Schüssler. *Rhetoric and Ethic: The Politics of Biblical Studies*. Minneapolis, MN: Fortress Press, 1999.

Firebaugh, W. C. *The Inns of Greece and Rome*. Repr. ed. New York: Benjamin Blom, 1928/1972.

Fish, Stanley. "Boutique Multiculturalism, or Why Liberals Are Incapable of Thinking about Hate Speech." *Critical Inquiry* 23, no. 2 (1997): 378–395.

Fishback, Sarah Jane. "Learning and the Brain." *Adult Learning* 10, no. 2 (1998–1999): 18–22.

Fitzmyer, Joseph A. *The Gospel according to Luke 1–9*. 2nd ed. Anchor Bible 28. Garden City, NY: Doubleday, 1981.

———. *Romans*. Anchor Bible 33. Garden City, NY: Doubleday, 1993.

Flesher, Paul Virgil McCracken. "Palestinian Synagogues before 70 C.E.: A Review of Evidence." In *Ancient Synagogues: Historical Analysis and Archaeological Discovery*, edited by Dan Urman and Paul Virgil McCracken Flesher, 1:27–39. Studia Post-Biblica 47. Leiden, the Netherlands: Brill, 1998.

Flowerdew, John, and Lindsay Miller. "On the Notion of Culture in L2 Lectures." *TESOL Quarterly* 29, no. 2 (1995): 345–373.

Forbes, Clarence A. "Expanded Uses of the Greek Gymnasium." *Classical Philology* 40, no. 1 (1945): 32–42.

Ford, Michael. *Wounded Prophet: A Portrait of Henri J. M. Nouwen*. London: Darton, Longman & Todd, 1999.

Foster, Charles R. "Diversity in Theological Education." *Theological Education* 38, no. 2 (2002): 15–37.

Foucault, Michel. *The Archaeology of Knowledge and the Discourse on Language*. Translated by A. M. Sheridan Smith. New York: Pantheon Books, 1972.

Fox, Melodie J., and Austin Reece. "The Impossible Decision: Social Tagging and Derrida's Deconstructed Hospitality." *Knowledge Organization* 40, no. 4 (2013): 260–265.

France, R. T. *The Gospel of Matthew*. New International Commentary on the New Testament. Grand Rapids, MI: Eerdmans, 2007.

Frego, Katherine A. "Authenticity and Relationships with Students." *New Directions for Adult and Continuing Education* 111 (Fall 2006): 41–50.

Freire, Paulo. *Pedagogy of Freedom: Ethics, Democracy, and Civic Courage*. Translated by Patrick Clarke. Lanham: Rowman & Littlefield, 1998.

———. *Pedagogy of the Oppressed*. Translated by Myra Bergman Ramos. 30th anniversary ed. New York: Continuum, 1970/2000.

Freyne, Seán. *Galilee from Alexander the Great to Hadrian, 323 BCE to 153 CE: A Study of Second Temple Jerusalem*. University of Notre Dame Center for the Study of Judaism and Christianity in Antiquity No. 5. Wilmington, DE: Michael Glazier, 1980.

———. "Herodian Economics in Galilee: Searching for a Suitable Model." In *Modelling Early Christianity: Socio-Scientific Studies of the New Testament in Its Context*, edited by Philip F. Esler, 22–44. London: Routledge, 1995.

Frier, Bruce Woodward. "The Rental Market in Early Imperial Rome." *Journal of Roman Studies* 67 (1977): 27–37.

Frymier, Ann Bainbridge, and Marian L. Houser. "The Teacher-Student Relationship as an Interpersonal Relationship." *Communication Education* 49, no. 3 (2000): 207–219.

Gaff, Jerry G. *Toward Faculty Renewal*. San Francisco, CA: Jossey-Bass, 1975.

Gafni, Isaiah M. "The Historical Background." In *The Jewish People in the First Century: Historical Geography, Political History, Social, Cultural and Religious Life and Institutions; Vol. 1*, edited by M. Safrai, 1–34. Compendia Rerum Iudaicarum Ad Novum Testamentum. Philadelphia, PA: Fortress, 1974.

Gallagher, Eugene V. "Welcoming the Stranger." *Teaching Theology and Religion* 10, no. 3 (2007): 137–142.

Gascho, Victoria. "Parker Palmer and Christian Nurture." *Christian Education Journal* 2NS, no. 1 (1998): 91–113.

Geelan, David R. "Epistemological Anarchy and the Many Forms of Constructivism." *Science and Education* 6, no. 1–2 (1997): 15–28.

Gehring, Roger W. *House Church and Mission: The Importance of Household Structures in Early Christianity*. Peabody, MA: Hendrickson, 2004.

Geldenhuys, Norval. *The Gospel of Luke*. New International Commentary on the New Testament. Grand Rapids, MI: Eerdmans, 1951.

Georgakopoulos, Alexia, and Laura K. Guerrero. "Student Perceptions of Teachers' Nonverbal and Verbal Communication: A Comparison of Best and Worst Professors across Six Cultures." *International Education Studies* 3, no. 2 (2010): 3–16.

Gergen, Kenneth J. "The Social Constructionist Movement in Modern Psychology." *American Psychologist* 40, no. 3 (1985): 266–275.

Gilbert, Jane. "Catching the Knowledge Wave: Redefining Knowledge for the Post-Industrial Age." *Education Canada* 47, no. 3 (2010): 4–8. Online.

Gilbert, Jen. "'Let Us Say Yes to Who or What Turns Up': Education as Hospitality." *Journal of the Canadian Association for Curriculum Studies* 4 , no. 1 (2006): 25–34.

Gilbert, Marlea M. "Hospitality in Sacred Space." *Liturgy* 25, no. 1 (2009): 21–29.

Giles, David. "Relationships Always Matter: Findings from a Phenomenological Research Inquiry." *Australian Journal of Education* 36, no. 6, Article 6 (2011): 80–91.

Gilligan, Carol. *In a Different Voice: Psychological Theory and Women's Development*. Cambridge, MA: Harvard University Press, 1982/1993.

———. "In a Different Voice: Women's Conception of Self and Morality." *Harvard Educational Review* 47, no. 4 (1977): 481–517.

Ginsberg, Margery B., and Raymond J. Wlodkowski. *Diversity and Motivation: Culturally Responsive Teaching in College*. 2nd ed. San Francisco, CA: Jossey-Bass, 1995/2009.

Gittins, Anthony J. "Beyond Hospitality? The Missionary Status and Role Revisited." *Currents in Theology and Mission* 21, no. 3 (1994): 164–182.

Glaser, Chris. "Henri's Greatest Gift." In *Befriending Life: Encounters with Henri Nouwen*, edited by Beth Porter, Susan M. S. Brown, and Philip Coulter, 125–133. New York: Image Books, 2001.

Glasersfeld, Ernst von. *Radical Constructivism: A Way of Knowing and Learning*. London: Falmer, 1995.

Goh Chor Boon, and Saravanan Gopinathan. "The Development of Education in Singapore since 1965." In *Toward a Better Future: Education and Training for Economic Development in Singapore since 1965*, edited by Lee Sing Kong, Goh Chor Boon, Birger Fredriksen, and Tan Jee Peng, 12–38. Singapore: NIE, 2008.

Good, Ron. "The Many Forms of Constructivism." *Research in Science Teaching* 30, no. 9 (1993): 1015.

Gopinathan, Saravanan. "Fourth Way in Action? The Evolution in Singapore's Education System." *Educational Research for Policy and Practice* 11, no. 1 (2012): 65–70.

Goralnik, Lissy, Kelly F. Millenbah, Michael P. Nelson, and Laurie Thorp. "An Environmental Pedagogy of Care: Emotion, Relationships, and Experience in Higher Education Ethics Learning." *Journal of Experiential Education* 35, no. 3 (2012): 412–428.

Gordon, Cyrus H. "Fratriarchy in the Old Testament." *Journal of Biblical Literature* 54, no. 4 (1935): 223–231.

Gorham, Joan. "The Relationship between Verbal Teacher Immediacy Behaviors and Student Learning." *Communication Education* 37, no. 1 (1988): 40–53.

Gorham, Joan, and Diane M. Christophel. "Students' Perceptions of Teacher Behaviors as Motivating and Demotivating Factors in College Classes." *Communication Quarterly* 40, no. 3 (1992): 239–252.

Gorham, Joan, and Walter R. Zakahi. "A Comparison of Teacher and Student Perceptions of Immediacy and Learning: Monitoring Process and Product." *Communication Education* 39, no. 4 (1990): 354–368.

Goswami, Usha. "Principles of Learning, Implications for Teaching: A Cognitive Neuroscience Perspective." *Journal of Philosophy of Education* 42, no. 3–4 (2008): 381–399.

Grabow, Brandy Lyn. "Expanding the Metaphor: A Pragmatic Application of Hospitality Theory to the Field of Writing Studies." PhD dissertation, University of North Carolina at Greensboro, 2013. https://libres.uncg.edu/ir/uncg/listing.aspx?id=10019.

Graff, Gerald, and Cathy Birkenstein. *They Say/I Say: The Moves That Matter in Academic Writing*. New York: W. W. Norton & Co, 2007.

Graham, Stephen R., ed. "Issue Focus: Christian Hospitality and Pastoral Practices in a Multifaith Society." *Theological Education* 47, no. 1 (2012).

———, ed. "Issue Focus: Christian Hospitality and Pastoral Practices in a Multifaith Society: Reports and Reflections." *Theological Education* 47, no. 2 (2013).

Grant, Barbara. "Improvising Together: The Play of Dialogue in Humanities Supervision." *Arts and Humanities in Higher Education* 9, no. 3 (2010): 271–288.

Gray, George Buchanan. *A Critical and Exegetical Commentary on the Book of Isaiah 1–27*. Repr. ed. International Critical Commentary. Edinburgh: T & T Clark, 1912/1980.

Gray, Jeremy R., Todd S. Braver, and Marcus E. Raichle. "Integration of Emotion and Cognition in the Lateral Prefrontal Cortex." *Proceedings of the National Academy of Sciences of the United States of America* 99, no. 6 (2002): 4115–4120.

Gredler, Margaret E. *Learning and Instruction: Theory into Practice*. 6th ed. Upper Saddle River, NJ: Pearson, 2008.

Greene, Meg. *Mother Teresa: A Biography*. Greenwood Biographies. Westport, CT: Greenwood Press, 2004.

Greenstein, Edward L. "Mixing Memory and Design: Reading Psalm 78." *Prooftexts* 10, no. 2 (1990): 197–218.

Greenstone, Juilius H. "Hospitality." In *The Jewish Encyclopedia*, edited by Isidore Singer, repr. ed., 6:480–481. New York: KTAV Publishing House, 1964.

Greer, Rowan A. *Broken Lights and Mended Lives: Theology and Common Life in the Early Church*. University Park, PA: Pennsylvania State University, 1986.

Gregory, Marshall. "Curriculum, Pedagogy, and Teacherly Ethos." *Pedagogy* 1, no. 1 (2001): 69–89.

Griffin, Gail B. *Calling: Essays on Teaching in the Mother Tongue*. Pasadena, CA: Trilogy Publications, 1992.

Groome, Thomas H. *Christian Religious Education: Sharing Our Story and Vision*. San Francisco, CA: Jossey-Bass, 1980.

———. *Sharing Faith: A Comprehensive Approach to Religious Education and Pastoral Ministry; The Way of Shared Praxis*. Eugene, OR: Wipf & Stock, 1991.

———. "The Spirituality of the Religious Educator." *Religious Education* 83 no. 1 (1988): 9–20.

Grossmark, Tziona. "The Inn as a Place of Violence and Danger in Rabbinic Literature." In *Violence in Late Antiquity: Perceptions and Practices*, edited by Harold Allen Drake, 57–68. Aldershot, UK: Ashgate, 2006.

Guelich, Robert A. *Mark 1–8:26*. Word Biblical Commentary 34A. Dallas, TX: Word, 1989.

Guenther, Margaret. *Holy Listening: The Art of Spiritual Direction*. London: Darton, Longman & Todd, 1992.

Gundry-Volf, Judith M., and Miroslav Volf. *A Spacious Heart: Essays on Identity and Belonging*. Christian Mission and Modern Culture. Harrisburg, PA: Trinity Press, 1997.

Gupta, Tania Das. "The Challenges of a 'Multicultural' Classroom: Some Reflections." *Atlantis* 35, no. 2 (2011): 118–127. http://journals.msvu.ca/index.php/atlantis/article/view/924.

Gurin, Patricia, Eric L. Dey, Sylvia Hurtado, and Gerald Gurin. "Diversity and Higher Education: Theory and Impact on Educational Outcomes." *Harvard Educational Review* 72, no. 3 (2002): 330–366.

Guskin, Alan E. "Reducing Student Costs and Enhancing Student Learning: Part 2, Restructuring the Role of Faculty." *Change* 26, no. 5 (1994): 16–25.

Gutiérrez, Gustavo. *A Theology of Liberation: History, Politics, and Salvation*. Translated by Caridad Inda and John Eagleson. Rev. ed. with a new introduction. Maryknoll, NY: Orbis Books, 1973/1988.

Hagner, Donald A. *Matthew 1–13*. Anchor Bible 33A. Dallas, TX: Word, 1993.

———. *Matthew 14–28*. Word Biblical Commentary 33B. Dallas, TX: Word, 1995.

Hagstrom, Aurelie A. "Christian Hospitality in the Intellectual Community." In *Christianity and the Soul of the University: Faith as a Foundation for Intellectual Community*, edited by Douglas V. Henry and Michael D. Beaty, 119–131. Grand Rapids, MI: Baker, 2006.

———. "The Role of Charism and Hospitality in the Academy." *Integritas* 1, no. 1 (2013): 1–14. http://ejournals.bc.edu/ojs/index.php/integritas/issue/view/562.

Hall, Edward T. *Beyond Culture*. New York: Anchor Books, 1976.

———. *The Hidden Dimension*. Garden City, NY: Doubleday, 1982.

Halverson, Delia. *The Gift of Hospitality: In Church, in the Home, in All of Life*. St. Louis, MO: Chalice Press, 1999.

Hamachek, Don. "Effective Teachers: What They Do, How They Do It, and the Importance of Self-Knowledge." In *The Role of Self in Teacher Development*, edited by Richard P. Lipka and Thomas M. Brinthaupt, 189–224. SUNY Series, Studying the Self. Albany, NY: State University of New York Press, 1999.

Han, Sang-Ehil, Paul Louis Metzger, and Terry C. Muck. "Christian Hospitality and Pastoral Practices from an Evangelical Perspective." *Theological Education* 47, no. 1 (2012): 11–31.

Hansen, Chad. *A Daoist Theory of Chinese Thought: A Philosophical Interpretation*. Oxford: Oxford University Press, 1992.

Hardiman, Mariale M. "Connecting Brain Research with Dimensions of Learning." In *Taking Sides: Clashing Views in Educational Psychology*, edited by Leonard Abbeduto and Frank Symons, 5th ed., 265–271. Boston, MA: McGraw-Hill, 2008.

Hardina, Donna, Jane Middleton, Salvador Montana, and Roger A. Simpson. *An Empowering Approach to Managing Social Service Organizations*. New York: Springer, 2007.

Hargreaves, Andy. "Emotional Geographies of Teaching." *Teachers College Record* 103, no. 6 (2001): 1056–1080.

———. "The Emotional Practice of Teaching." *Teaching and Teacher Education* 14, no. 8 (1998): 835–854.

———. "Mixed Emotions: Teacher's Perceptions of Their Interactions with Students." *Teaching and Teacher Education* 16, no. 8 (2000): 811–826.

Harkness, Allan G. "De-schooling the Theological Seminary: An Appropriate Paradigm for Effective Pastoral Formation." In *Tending the Seedbeds: Educational Perspectives on Theological Education in Asia*, edited by Allan G. Harkness, 103–128. Quezon City, Philippines: ATA, 2010.

———. "Introduction." In *Tending the Seedbeds: Educational Perspectives on Theological Education in Asia*, edited by Allan G. Harkness, 7–22. Quezon City, Philippines: ATA, 2010.

Harrington, Daniel J. *The Gospel of Matthew*. Sacra Pagina 1. Collegeville, MN: Liturgical Press, 1991.

Hartley, John E. *Leviticus*. Word Biblical Commentary 4. Dallas, TX: Word, 1992.

Haskins, William. "Ethos and Pedagogical Communication: Suggestions for Enhancing Credibility in the Classroom." *Current Issues in Education* 3, no. 4 (2000). http://cie.asu.edu/ojs/index.php/cieatasu/article/view/1616.

Hassan, Aminuddin, Nur Syuhada Jamaludin, Tajularipin Sulaiman, and Roselan Baki. "Western and Eastern Educational Philosophies." In *40th Conference of the Philosophy of Education Society of Australasia*, 1–9. Murdoch University, Perth, Australia, 2010. http://psasir.upm.edu.my/17675/.

Haswell, Janis, Richard Haswell, and Glenn Blalock. "Hospitality in College Composition Courses." *College Composition and Communication* 60, no. 4 (2009): 707–727.

Hawk, Thomas F., and Paul R. Lyons. "Please Don't Give Up on Me: When Faculty Fail to Care." *Journal of Management Education* 32, no. 3 (2008): 316–338.

Heard, Matthew. "Hospitality and Generosity." *JAC* 30, no. 1–2 (2010): 315–335.

Heidegger, Martin. *Basic Writings*. Edited by David Farell Krell. Revised and expanded ed. New York: HarperCollins, 1992.

———. *Being and Time*. Translated by John Macquarrie and Edward Robinson. New York: Harper & Row, 1927/1962.

Heil, John Paul. *The Meal Scenes in Luke-Acts: An Audience-Oriented Approach*. Society of Biblical Literature Monograph Series 52. Atlanta, GA: SBL, 1999.

Helms, Jeffrey L., and Daniel T. Rogers. *Majoring in Psychology: Achieving Your Educational and Career Goals*. West Sussex: Wiley-Blackwell, 2011.

Henrey, Robert. "Hospitality in Pastoral Care." *Religion East and West* 7 (2007): 29–38.

Herring, Richard, and Fritz Deininger. "The Challenges and Blessings of Spiritual Formation in Theological Education." In *Educating for Tomorrow: Theological Leadership for the Asian Context*, edited by Manfred Waldemar Kohl and A. N. Lal Senanyake, 125–138. Bangalore: SAIACS Press, 2002.

Hershberger, Michele. "Response to 'Beautiful Minds, Crucified Minds, and Hospitable Hearts.'" *Mennonite Life (Online)* 58, no. 1 (March 2003). https://ml.bethelks.edu/issue/vol-58-no-1/article/response-to-beautiful-minds-crucified-minds-and-ho/.

Hill, Brian V. "Teacher Commitment and the Ethics of Teaching for Commitment." *Religious Education* 76, no. 3 (1981): 322–336.

Hill, G. William, IV, and Dorothy D. Zinsmeister. "Becoming an Ethical Teacher." In *Effective College and University Teaching: Strategies and Tactics for the New Professoriate*, edited by William Buskist and Victor A. Benassi, 125–133. Los Angeles, CA: SAGE Publications, 2012.

Hinton, Christina, Koji Miyamoto, and Bruno Della-Chiesa. "Brain Research, Learning and Emotions: Implications for Education Research, Policy and Practice." *European Journal of Education* 43, no. 1 (2008): 87–103.

Ho, David Yau-fai. "On the Concept of Face." *American Journal of Sociology* 81, no. 4 (1976): 867–884.

Hock, Ronald F. "Cynics." In *Anchor Bible Dictionary*, edited by David Noel Freedman, 1:1221–1226. Garden City, NY: Doubleday, 1992.

———. *The Social Context of Paul's Ministry: Tentmaking and Apostleship*. Philadelphia, PA: Fortress, 1980.

Hoffman, Karen L., and Joan E. Scott. "Review of *The Courage to Teach: Exploring the Inner Landscape of the Teacher's Life*, by Parker J. Palmer." *Michigan Journal of Community Service Learning* 6, no. 1 (1999): 138–141.

Hofstede, Geert. "Cultural Relativity of the Quality of Life Concept." *Academy of Management Review* 9, no. 3 (1984): 389–398.

Hofstede, Geert, and Michael Harris Bond. "The Confucius Connection: From Cultural Roots to Economic Growth." *Organizational Dynamics* 16, no. 4 (1988): 5–21.

Holliday, Adrian. *Appropriate Methodology and Social Context*. Cambridge Language Teaching Library. Cambridge: Cambridge University Press, 1994.

Homan, Daniel, and Lonni Collins Pratt. *Radical Hospitality: Benedict's Way of Love*. Brewster, MA: Paraclete Press, 2002.

Homer. *Odyssey*. Translated by A. T. Murray. In Perseus Digital Library, 1919. http://www.perseus.tufts.edu/hopper/text?doc=Hom.+Od.+17.484&fromdoc=Perseus%3Atext%3A1999.01.0136.

hooks, bell. *Teaching to Transgress: Education as the Practice of Freedom*. New York: Routledge, 1994.
Horner, Thomas Marland. "Changing Concepts of the 'Stranger' in the Old Testament." *Anglican Theological Review* 42, no. 1 (1960): 49–53.
Hospers, John. *An Introduction to Philosophical Analysis*. 3rd ed. London: Routledge, 1990.
———. *An Introduction to Philosophical Analysis*. 4th ed. London: Routledge, 1997.
Hu, Hsien Chin. "The Chinese Concepts of 'Face.'" *American Anthropologist*, New Series 46, no. 1 (1944): 45–64.
Hultgren, Arland. "The Johannine Footwashing (13:1–11) as a Symbol of Eschatological Hospitality." *New Testament Studies* 28, no. 4 (1982): 539–546.
Hussain, Irshad. "Use of Constructivist Approach in Higher Education." *Creative Education* 3, no. 2 (2012): 179–184.
Hütter, Reinhard. "Hospitality and Truth: The Disclosure and Practices in Worship and Doctrine." In *Practicing Theology: Beliefs and Practices in Christian Life*, edited by Miroslav Volf and Dorothy C. Bass, 206–227. Grand Rapids, MI: Eerdmans, 2002.
Ibrahim, Awad. "The Question of the Question Is the Foreigner: Towards an Economy of Hospitality." *Journal of Curriculum Theorizing* 21, no. 4 (2005): 149–162.
Iliško, Dzintra. "Educational Encounters and Interreligious Education: A Latvian Case Study for Expanding the Borders of Hospitality." In *International Handbook of Inter-Religious Education*, edited by Kath Engebretson, Marina de Souza, Gloria Durka, and Liam Gearon, 191–203. International Handbooks of Religion and Education 4. Dordrecht, the Netherlands: Springer, 2010.
Imel, Susan. *Effect of Emotions on Learning in Adult, Career, and Career-Technical Education*. Eric Clearinghouse on Adult, Career, and Vocational Education: Trends and Issues Alert 43. Columbus, OH: Ohio State University, 2003.
Immordino-Yang, Mary Helen. "Implications of Affective and Social Neuroscience for Educational Theory." *Educational Philosophy and Theory* 43, no. 1 (2011): 98–103.
Immordino-Yang, Mary Helen, and Antonio R. Damasio. "We Feel, therefore We Learn: The Relevance of Affective and Social Neuroscience to Education." *Mind, Brain, and Education* 1, no. 1 (2007): 3–10.
Intrator, Sam M. "A Journey of Questions: The Life and Work of Parker J. Palmer." In *Living the Questions: Essays Inspired by the Work and Life of Parker J. Palmer*, edited by Sam M. Intrator, xvii–lix. San Francisco, CA: Jossey-Bass, 2005.
Isenbarger, Lynn, and Michalinos Zembylas. "The Emotional Labour of Caring in Teaching." *Teaching and Teacher Education* 22, no: 1 (2006): 120–134.
Jacobs, Dale. "The Audacity of Hospitality." *JAC* 28, no. 3–4 (2008): 563–581.

———. "What's Hope Got to Do with It? Towards a Theory of Hope and Pedagogy." *JAC* 25, no. 4 (2005): 783–802.
Janzen, Waldemar. *Old Testament Ethics: A Paradigmatic Approach*. Louisville, KY: Westminster John Knox Press, 1994.
Jaques, David, and Gilly Salmon. *Learning in Groups: A Handbook for Face-to-Face and Online Environments*. 4th ed. London: Routledge, 2007.
Jarvis, Peter, John Holford, and Colin Griffin. *The Theory and Practice of Learning*. 2nd ed. London: Kogan Page, 2003.
Jashemski, Wilhelmina F. "A Pompeian *Copa*." *Classical Journal* 59, no. 8 (1964): 337–349.
Jeremias, Joachim. *Jerusalem in the Time of Jesus: An Investigation into Economic and Social Conditions during the New Testament Period*. Philadelphia, PA: Fortress, 1975.
———. *New Testament Theology*. Translated by John Bowden. London: SCM Press, 1971.
———. *The Parables of Jesus*. 3rd rev. ed. London: SCM Press, 1972.
Jin, Lixian, and Martin Cortazzi. "Dimensions of Dialogue: Large Classes in China." *International Journal of Educational Research* 29, no. 8 (1998): 739–761.
Jobes, Karen H. *1 Peter*. Baker Exegetical Commentary on the New Testament. Grand Rapids, MI: Baker, 2005.
Johns, Loren L. "Love and Hospitality in Mennonite Higher Education: Negotiating Culture in a Competitive World." *Mennonite Life (Online)* 58, no. 1 (March 2003). https://ml.bethelks.edu/issue/vol-58-no-1/article/love-and-hospitality-in-mennonite-higher-education/.
Johnson, Helen. "Cross-Cultural Differences: Implications for Management Education and Training." *Journal of European Industrial Training* 15, no. 6 (1991): 13–16.
Johnson, Luke Timothy. *The Writings of the New Testament: An Interpretation*. 3rd ed. Minneapolis, MN: Fortress, 2010.
Johnson, Sandra. "The Neuroscience of the Mentor-Learner Relationship." *New Directions for Adult and Continuing Education* 110 (Summer 2006): 63–69.
Johnson, Susanne. "Reshaping Religious and Theological Education in the 90s: Toward a Critical Pluralism." *Religious Education* 88, no. 3 (1993): 335–349.
Johnstone, David M. "Review of *Academic Life: Hospitality, Ethics, and Spirituality*, by John B. Bennett." *Journal of Education and Christian Belief* 13, no. 2 (2009): 178–179.
Jonas, Robert A., ed. *Beauty of the Beloved: A Henri J. M. Nouwen Anthology*. London: Darton, Longman, & Todd, 1999.
Jones, Alison. "The Limits of Cross-Cultural Dialogue: Pedagogy, Desire, and Absolution in the Classroom." *Educational Theory* 49, no. 3 (1999): 299–318.

de Jong, Ton, Tamara van Gog, Kathleen Jenks, Sarah Manlove, Janet van Hell, Jelle Jolles, Jeroen van Merriënboer, Theo van Leeuwen, and Annemarie Boschloo. *Explorations in Learning and the Brain: On the Potential of Cognitive Neuroscience for Educational Science*. New York: Springer, 2009.

Just, Arthur A., Jr. *The Ongoing Feast: Table Fellowship and Eschatology at Emmaus*. Collegeville, MN: Liturgical Press, 1993.

Justes, Emma J. *Hearing beyond the Words: How to Become a Listening Pastor*. Nashville, TN: Abingdon Press, 2006.

Kaiser, Otto. *Isaiah 13–39: A Commentary*. Translated by R. A. Wilson. Old Testament Library. Philadelphia, PA: Westminster Press, 1974.

Kameniar, Barbara. "Dilemmas in Providing Hospitality to Others in the Classroom: Stories about One Christian Religious Education Teacher." *Transnational Curriculum Inquiry* 4, no. 3 (2007): 1–11. http://ojs.library.ubc.ca/index.php/tci/article/view/31.

Kang, Namsoon. "From Colonial to Postcolonial Theological Education: Envisioning *Postcolonial* Theological Education; Dilemmas and Possibilities." In *Handbook of Theological Education in World Christianity: Theological Perspectives, Ecumenical Trends, Regional Surveys*, edited by Dietrich Werner, David Esterline, Namsoon Kang, and Joshva Raja, 30–41. Regnum Studies in Global Christianity. Eugene, OR: Wipf & Stock, 2010.

Karris, Robert J. *Luke: Artist and Theologian; Luke's Passion Account as Literature*. Edited by Lawrence Boadt. Theological Inquiries: Studies in Contemporary Biblical and Theological Problems. New York: Paulist Press, 1985.

Käsemann, Ernst. *Commentary on Romans*. Edited and translated by Geoffrey W. Bromiley. Grand Rapids, MI: Eerdmans, 1980.

Kaufmann, Jodi Jan. "The Practice of Dialogue in Critical Pedagogy." *Adult Education Quarterly* 60, no. 5 (2010): 456–476.

Kearney, Richard. "Desire of God and Discussion." In *God, the Gift, and Postmodernism*, edited by John D. Caputo and Michael J. Scanlon, 112–163. Indiana Series in the Philosophy of Religion. Bloomington, IN: Indiana University Press, 1999.

Keener, Craig S. *A Commentary on the Gospel of Matthew*. Grand Rapids, MI: Eerdmans, 1999.

Keifert, Patrick R. *Welcoming the Stranger: A Public Theology of Worship and Evangelism*. Minneapolis, MN: Fortress, 1992.

Keller, Philip. *A Shepherd Looks at Psalm 23*. Grand Rapids, MI: Zondervan, 1970.

Kellermann, D. "גּוּר gûr." In *Theological Dictionary of the Old Testament*, edited by G. Johannes Botterweck and Helmer Ringgren, translated by John T. Willis, 2:439–449. Grand Rapids, MI: Eerdmans, 1974–2006.

Kelly, J. N. D. *A Commentary on the Epistle of Peter and of Jude*. Repr. ed. Harper's New Testament Commentaries. Peabody, MA: Hendrickson, 1988.

Keogh, Siobhan. "My Adopted Father." In *Befriending Life: Encounters with Henri Nouwen*, edited by Beth Porter, Susan M. S. Brown, and Philip Coulter, 155–162. New York: Image Books, 2001.

Kessler, Rachael. "The 'Teaching Presence.'" *Virginia Journal of Education* (November 2000): 7–10.

Kets de Vries, Manfred F. R. *Reflections on Character and Leadership*. San Francisco, CA: Jossey-Bass, 2009.

Kim, Joo Yup, and Sang Hoon Nam. "The Concept and Dynamics of Face: Implications for Organizational Behavior in Asia." *Organization Science* 9, no. 4 (1998): 522–534.

Kirylo, James D. *Paulo Freire: The Man from Recife*. Counterpoints: Studies in the Postmodern Theory of Education 385. New York: Peter Lang, 2011.

Klawans, Jonathan. *Impurity and Sin in Ancient Judaism*. Oxford: Oxford University Press, 2000.

Knauth, R. J. D. "Alien, Foreign Resident." In *Dictionary of the Old Testament: Pentateuch*, edited by T. Desmond Alexander and David W. Baker, 26–33. Downers Grove, IL: InterVarsity, 2003.

Kneipp, Lee B., Kathryn E. Kelly, Joseph D. Biscoe, and Brandon Richard. "The Impact of Instructor's Personality Characteristics on Quality of Instruction." *College Student Journal* 44, no. 4 (2010): 901–905.

Knight, George W., III. *The Pastoral Epistles*. New International Greek Testament Commentary. Grand Rapids, MI: Eerdmans, 1992.

Koenig, John. *New Testament Hospitality: Partnership with Strangers as Promise and Mission*. Repr. ed. Eugene, OR: Wipf & Stock, 1985/2001.

Koester, Craig R. *To the Hebrews*. Anchor Bible 36. Garden City, NY: Doubleday, 2001.

Kolb, Anne. "The Conception and Practice of Roman Rule: The Example of Transport Infrastructure." *Geographia Antiqua* 20–21 (2011–2012): 53–70.

Konkel, A. H. "תּוֹשָׁב." In *New International Dictionary of Old Testament and Exegesis*, edited by Willem A. VanGemeren, 4:284–285. Grand Rapids, MI: Zondervan, 1997.

Konrath, Sara H., Edward H. O'Brien, and Courtney Hsing. "Changes in Dispositional Empathy in American College Students over Time: A Meta-analysis." *Personality and Social Psychology Review* 15, no. 2 (2011): 180–198.

Koyama, Kosuke. "'Extend Hospitality to Strangers': A Missiology of *Theologia Crucis*." *Currents in Theology and Mission* 20, no. 3 (1993): 165–176.

Kraus, Hans-Joachim. *Psalms 1–59: A Continental Commentary*. Translated by Hilton C. Oswald. Minneapolis, MN: Fortress, 1993.

Kuh, George D., Katie Branch Douglas, John P. Lund, and Jackie Ramin-Gyurnek. *Student Learning Outside the Classroom: Transcending Artificial Boundaries.* ASHE-ERIC Higher Education Report 8. Washington, DC: George Washington University, Graduate School of Education & Human Development, 1994.

Kumi-Yeboah, Alex, and Waynne B. James. "The Relevance of Multicultural Education for Adult Learners in Higher Education." *International Forum of Teaching and Studies* 7, no. 1 (2011): 10–15.

Kuokkanen, Rauna. "The Gift as a Worldview in Indigenous Thought." In *The Gift, Il Dono: A Feminist Analysis*, edited by Genevieve Vaughan, 81–95. Rome: Meltemi Press, 2004.

———. "The Gift Logic of Indigenous Philosophies in the Academy." In *Women and the Gift Economy: A Radically Different Worldview Is Possible*, edited by Genevieve Vaughan, 71–83. Toronto: Inanna, 2007.

———. "The Logic of the Gift: Reclaiming Indigenous Peoples' Philosophies." In *Re-ethnicizing the Mind? Cultural Revival in Contemporary Thought*, edited by Thorsten Botz-Bornstein, 251–271. Amsterdam: Rodopi B. V., 2006.

———. "Toward a New Relation of Hospitality in the Academy." *American Indian Quarterly* 27, no. 1–2 (2003): 267–295.

———. "What Is Hospitality in the Academy? Epistemic Ignorance and the (Im)possible Gift." *Review of Education, Pedagogy, and Cultural Studies* 30, no. 1 (2008): 60–82.

Lake, Kirsopp, trans. *The Apostolic Fathers: Vol. 1; 1 Clement, 2 Clement, Ignatius, Polycarp, Didache, Barnabas.* Repr. ed. Loeb Classical Library. Cambridge, MA: Harvard University Press, 1965.

Lamont, Michèle. *How Professors Think: Inside the Curious World of Academic Judgment.* Cambridge, MA: Harvard University Press, 2009.

Lamport, Mark A. "Student-Faculty Informal Interaction and the Effect on College Student Outcomes: A Review of the Literature." *Adolescence* 28, no. 112 (1993): 971–990.

Lane, William L. *Commentary on the Gospel of Mark.* New International Commentary on the New Testament. Grand Rapids, MI: Eerdmans, 1974.

———. *Hebrews 9–13.* Word Biblical Commentary 47B. Dallas, TX: Word, 1991.

LaNoue, Dierdre. *The Spiritual Legacy of Henri Nouwen.* New York: Continuum, 2000.

Larson, Marion H. "Classroom Dialogue as Embrace." *Academic Exchange Quarterly* 12, no. 3 (2008): 6–10. http://rapidintellect.com/AEQweb/cho4096j8.htm.

———. "Creating a Space for Practicing a Community of Truth." *On Teaching and Learning* 21, no. 2 (2008): 1–4.

———. "Welcoming and Restoring, Dwelling and Sending: Creating a Space for Hospitality in Faculty Development." *Journal of Faculty Development* 23, no. 1 (2009): 48–53.

Lashley, Conrad, Paul Lynch, and Alison Morrison. "Hospitality: An Introduction." In *Hospitality: A Social Lens*, edited by Conrad Lashley, Paul Lynch, and Alison Morrison, 1–15. Amsterdam: Elsevier, 2007.

Lea, Susan J., David Stephenson, and Juliette Troy. "Higher Education Students' Attitudes to Student Centred Learning: Beyond 'Educational Bulimia.'" *Studies in Higher Education* 28, no. 3 (2003): 321–334.

LeDoux, Joseph. "Cognitive-Emotional Interactions: Listen to the Brain." In *Cognitive Neuroscience of Emotion*, edited by Richard D. Lane and Lynn Nadel, 129–155. Series in Affective Science. New York: Oxford University Press, 2000.

Lee, Mo-Yee, and Gilbert J. Greene. "A Social Constructivist Framework for Integrating Cross-cultural Issues in Teaching." *Journal of Social Work Education* 35, no. 1 (1999): 21–37.

———. "A Teaching Framework for Transformative Multicultural Social Work Education." *Journal of Ethnic and Cultural Diversity in Social Work* 12, no. 3 (2003): 1–28.

Lenschow, Rolf Johan. "From Teaching to Learning: A Paradigm Shift in Engineering Education and Lifelong Learning." *European Journal of Engineering Education* 23, no. 2 (1998): 155–161.

Leung, Angela Ka-yee, and Chi-yue Chiu. "Multicultural Experience, Idea Receptiveness, and Creativity." *Journal of Cross-Cultural Psychology* 41, no. 5–6 (2010): 723–741.

Leung, Gilbert, and Matthew Stone. "Otherness and Hospitality: A Disputation on the Relation of Ethics to Law and Politics." *Law and Critique* 20, no. 2 (2009): 193–206.

Levine, Lee I. *The Ancient Synagogue: The First Thousand Years*. 2nd ed. New Haven: Yale University Press, 2005.

Lieu, Judith M. *1, 2, & 3 John: A Commentary*. New Testament Library. Louisville, KY: Westminster John Knox Press, 2008.

Lin, Min. *Certainty as a Social Metaphor: The Social and Historical Production of Certainty in China and the West*. Contributions in Philosophy. Westport, CT: Greenwood Press, 2001.

Lindsey, William D. "Crossing the Postmodern Divide: Some Implications for Academic Theology." *Theology and Sexuality* 4, no. 7 (1997): 53–69.

Lingenfelter, Judith E., and Sherwood G. Lingenfelter. *Teaching Cross-culturally: An Incarnational Model for Learning and Teaching*. Grand Rapids, MI: Baker Academic, 2003.

Linnenbrink, Elizabeth A. "Emotion Research in Education: Theoretical and Methodological Perspectives on the Integration of Affect, Motivation, and Cognition." *Educational Psychology Review* 18, no. 4 (2006): 307–314.

Lipiński, E. "נָחַל." In *Theological Dictionary of the Old Testament*, edited by G. Johannes Botterweck, Helmer Ringgren, and Heinz-Josef Fabry, translated by David E. Green, 9:319–335. Grand Rapids, MI: Eerdmans, 1974–2006.

Liston, Daniel P. "Contemplating Teaching's Conflicts and Paradoxes." *Educational Theory* 60, no. 1 (2010): 29–38.

———. "Intellectual and Institutional Gaps in Teacher Education." In *The Educational Conversation: Closing the Gap*, edited by James W. Garrison and Anthony G. Rud Jr., 129–142. SUNY Series, The Philosophy of Education. Albany, NY: State University of New York Press, 1995.

Littlewood, William. "Do Asian Students Really Want to Listen and Obey?" *ELT Journal* 54, no. 1 (2000): 31–36.

Liu, Dilin. "Ethnocentrism in TESOL: Teacher Education and the Neglected Needs of International TESOL Students." *ELT Journal* 52, no. 1 (1998): 3–10.

Liu, Ngar-Fun, and William Littlewood. "Why Do Many Students Appear Reluctant to Participate in Class Learning Discourse?" *System* 25, no. 3 (1997): 371–384.

Loden, Marilyn, and Judy Rosener. *Workforce America! Managing Employee Diversity as a Vital Resource*. New York: McGraw-Hill, 1990.

Loewenberg, Frank M. *From Charity to Social Justice: The Emergence of Communal Institutions for the Support of the Poor in Ancient Judaism*. New Brunswick: Transaction Publishers, 2001.

Losito, William F. "Education as Hospitality: The Reclamation of Cultural Metaphor and Narrative." In *In Other Voices: Expanding the Educational Conversation*, edited by Warren Strandberg, 62–69. Richmond: SAPES, 1992.

Lottes, John D. "Toward a Christian Theology of Hospitality to Other Religions on Campus." *Currents in Theology and Mission* 32, no. 1 (2005): 26–38.

Lyman, Linda L. *How Do They Know You Care: The Principal's Challenge*. New York: Teachers College Press, 2000.

Lynch, Paul, Jennie Germann Molz, Alison McIntosh, Peter Lugosi, and Conrad Lashley. "Theorizing Hospitality." *Hospitality and Society* 1, no. 1 (2011): 3–24. http://dx.doi.org/10.1386/hosp.1.1.3_2.

Makkhado, Samson B. K., and Dean Spalding. "Community and Hospitality in Multicultural Classrooms." *Journal of Education and Christian Belief* 5, no. 2 (2001): 135–144.

Malherbe, Abraham J. *Social Aspects of Early Christianity*. 2nd ed. Philadelphia, PA: Fortress Press, 1983.

Malina, Bruce J. *The New Testament World: Insights from Cultural Anthropology*. Rev. ed. Louisville, KY: Westminster John Knox Press, 1993.

———. "The Received View and What It Cannot Do: III John and Hospitality." *Semeia* 35 (1986): 171–194.

Malina, Bruce J., and Jerome H. Neyrey. "Jesus the Witch: Witchcraft Accusations in Matthew 12." In *Social-Scientific Approaches to New Testament Interpretation*, edited by David G. Horrell, 29–67. Edinburgh: T & T Clark, 1999.

Manen, Max van. *The Tact of Teaching: The Meaning of Pedagogical Thoughtfulness*. Albany, NY: State University of New York Press, 1991.

Mann, C. S. *Mark*. Anchor Bible 27. Garden City, NY: Doubleday, 1986.

Mann, Sarah J. "A Personal Inquiry into an Experience of Adult Learning On-Line." *Instructional Science* 31, no. 1–2 (2003): 111–125.

Marcel, Gabriel. Homo Viator: *Introduction to a Metaphysic of Hope*. Translated by Emma Craufurd. Chicago, IL: Henry Regnery Co, 1951.

Marmon, Ellen L. "Teaching as Hospitality." *Asbury Theological Journal* 63, no. 2 (2008): 33–39.

Marshall, I. Howard. *1 Peter*. IVP New Testament Commentary Series. Downers Grove, IL: InterVarsity, 1991.

———. *The Epistles of John*. New International Commentary on the New Testament. Grand Rapids, MI: Eerdmans, 1978.

———. *The Gospel of Luke*. New International Greek Testament Commentary. Grand Rapids, MI: Paternoster, 1978b.

Marshall, I. Howard, and Philip H. Towner. *A Critical and Exegetical Commentary on the Pastoral Epistles*. Repr. ed. International Critical Commentary. London: T & T Clark, 1999.

Marshall, Molly T. "One Student at a Time: The Hospitality of Multicultural Theological Education." *Review and Expositor* 109 (Winter 2012): 51–59.

Martínez, Florentino García, and Eibert J. C. Tigchelaar, eds. *The Dead Sea Scrolls Study Edition*. 2nd ed. Leiden, the Netherlands: Brill, 1999.

Martínez, María A., Narcís Sauleda, and L. Huber Güenter. "Metaphors as Blueprints of Thinking about Teaching and Learning." *Teaching and Teacher Education* 17 (2001): 965–977.

Martinsons, Maris G., and Aelita Brivins Martinsons. "Conquering Cultural Constraints to Cultivate Chinese Management Creativity and Innovation." *Journal of Management Development* 15, no. 9 (1996): 18–35.

Matthews, Michael R. "Constructivism and Science Education." *Journal of Science and Technology Education Research* 2, no. 1 (1993): 359–370.

———. "Introductory Comments on Philosophy and Constructivism in Science Education." *Science and Education* 6, no. 1–2 (1997): 5–14.

Matthews, Victor H. *Old Testament Turning Points: The Narratives That Shaped a Nation*. Grand Rapids, MI: Baker, 2005.

Mayo, Joseph A. "Dialogue as Constructivist Pedagogy: Probing the Minds of Psychology's Greatest Contributors." *Journal of Constructivist Psychology* 15, no. 4 (2002): 291–304.

McAvoy, Jane. "Hospitality: A Feminist Theology of Education." *Teaching Theology and Religion* 1, no. 1 (1998): 20–26.

McCroskey, James C., Joan M. Fayer, Virginia P. Richmond, Aino Sallinen, and Robert A. Barraclough. "A Multi-Cultural Examination of the Relationship between Nonverbal Immediacy and Affective Learning." *Communication Quarterly* 44, no. 3 (1996): 297–307.

McCroskey, James C., and Virginia P. Richmond. "Increasing Teacher Influence through Immediacy." In *Power in the Classroom: Communication, Control, and Concern*, edited by Virginia P. Richmond and James C. McCroskey, 101–119. Hillsdale, NJ: Lawrence Erlbaum Associates, 1992.

McCroskey, James C., and Jason J. Teven. "Goodwill: A Reexamination of the Construct and Its Measurement." *Communication Monographs* 66, no. 1 (1999): 90–103.

McDaniel, Ed, and Peter A. Andersen. "International Patterns of Interpersonal Tactile Communication: A Field Study." *Journal of Nonverbal Behavior* 22, no. 1 (1998): 59–73.

McDaniel, Karen L. "Review of *The Courage to Teach: Exploring the Inner Landscape of the Teacher's Life*, by Parker J. Palmer." *The Clearing House* 82, no. 3 (2009): 153–154.

McDonnell, Thomas P., ed. *A Thomas Merton Reader*. Doubleday Image ed. New York: Image Books, 1996.

McEwen, Bruce S., and Robert M. Sapolsky. "Stress and Cognitive Function." *Current Opinion in Neurobiology* 5, no. 2 (1995): 205–216.

McGowan, Andrew. "The Meals of Jesus and the Meals of the Church: Eucharistic Origins and Admission to Communion." In *Studia Liturgica Diversa: Essays in Honor of Paul F. Bradshaw*, edited by Maxwell E. Johnson and L. Edward Phillips, 101–115. Portland, OR: Pastoral Press, 2003.

McIntyre, Sheila. "Studied Ignorance and Privileged Innocence: Keeping Equity Academic." *Canadian Journal of Women and the Law* 12, no. 1 (2000): 147–196.

McKinlay, Judith E. "To Eat or Not to Eat: Where Is Wisdom in This Choice." *Semeia* 86 (1999): 73–84.

McLeod, Douglas B. "Research on Affect in Mathematics Education: A Reconceptualization." In *Handbook of Research on Mathematics Teaching and Learning*, edited by D. A. Grows, 575–596. New York: Macmillan, 1992.

McManus, Dean A. "The Two Paradigms of Education and the Peer Review of Teaching." *Journal of Geoscience Education* 49, no. 5 (2001): 423–434.

McWhinney, Ian R., and Thomas Freeman. *Textbook of Family Medicine*. 3rd ed. Oxford: Oxford University Press, 2009.

Meagher, Robert E. "Strangers at the Gates: Ancient Rites of Hospitality." *Parabola* 2, no. 4 (1977): 10–15.

Mehrabian, Albert. "Inference of Attitudes from the Posture, Orientation, and Distance of a Communicator." *Journal of Consulting and Clinical Psychology* 32, no. 3 (1968): 296–308.

———. *Silent Messages*. Belmont, CA: Wadsworth, 1971.

———. "Some Referents and Measures of Nonverbal Behavior." *Behavioral Research Methods and Instruments* 1, no. 6 (1969): 203–207.

Merrill, A. L. "Psalm 23 and the Jerusalem Tradition." *Vetus Testamentum* 15, Fasc. 3 (1965): 354–360.

Merton, Thomas. *The Sign of Jonas*. San Diego, CA: Harvest Book, 1979/1981.

Meyer, Debra K., and Julianne Turner. "Discovering Emotion in Classroom Motivation Research." *Educational Psychologist* 37, 2 (2002): 107–114.

Mezirow, Jack. "Transformative Learning Theory." In *Transformative Learning in Practice: Insights from Community, Workplace, and Higher Education*, edited by Jack Mezirow and Edward W. Taylor, 18–32. San Francisco, CA: John Wiley & Sons, 2009.

Michaels, J. Ramsey. *1 Peter*. Word Biblical Commentary 49. Waco, TX: Word, 1988.

Michel, Otto. "τελώνης." In *Theological Dictionary of the New Testament*, edited by Gerhard Kittel and Gerhard Friedrich, translated by Geoffrey W. Bromiley, 8:88–105. Grand Rapids, MI: Eerdmans, 1964–1976.

Miller, Jennifer, Alex Kostogriz, and Margaret Gearon, eds. *Professional Ethics in Multicultural Classrooms: English Hospitality and the Other*. Perspectives on Language and Education. Bristol, UK: Multilingual Matters, 2009.

Miller, Patrick D. "Israel as Host to Strangers." In *Israelite Religion and Biblical Theology: Collected Essays*, edited by David J. A. Clines and Philip R. Davies, 548–571. Journal for the Study of the Old Testament Supplement Series 267. Sheffield: Sheffield Academic Press, 2000.

Miller-McLemore, Bonnie J. "Contemplation in the Midst of Chaos: Contesting the Maceration of the Theological Teacher." In *The Scope of Our Art: The Vocation of the Theological Teacher*, edited by Gregory L. Jones and Stephanie Paulsell, 48–74. Grand Rapids, MI: Eerdmans, 2002.

Mitchell, Margaret M. "'Diotrephes Does Not Receive Us': The Lexicographical and Social Context of 3 John 9–10." *Journal of Biblical Literature* 117, no. 2 (1998): 299–320.

———. "New Testament Envoys in the Context of Greco-Roman Diplomatic and Epistolary Conventions: The Example of Timothy and Titus." *Journal of Biblical Literature* 111, no. 4 (1992): 641–662.

Mitchell, Theodore. "Review of *Collegial Professionalism: The Academy, Individualism, and the Common Good*, by John B. Bennett." *Library Quarterly* 69, no. 3 (1999): 409–411.

Mogabgab, John S. "The Spiritual Pedagogy of Henri Nouwen." *Reflection* 78, no. 2 (1981): 4–6.

Moo, Douglas J. *The Epistle to the Romans*. New International Commentary on the New Testament. Grand Rapids, MI: Eerdmans, 1996.

Moore, George Foot. *Judaism in the First Centuries of the Christian Era: The Age of Tannaim; Vols. 2 and 3*. Peabody, MA: Hendrickson, 1997.

Morgenstern, Julian. "Psalm 23." *Journal of Biblical Literature* 65, no. 1 (1946): 13–24.

Morr, Christy. "The Role of Friendship in Spiritual Formation." *Christian Education Journal* 4NS, no. 2 (2000): 45–62.

Morris, Leon. *The Gospel according to Matthew*. Grand Rapids, MI: Eerdmans, 1992.

Mosteller, Sue. "Introduction." In *Home Tonight: Further Reflections on the Parable of the Prodigal Son*, by Henri J. M. Nouwen, edited by Sue Mosteller, vii–xi. Garden City, NY: Doubleday, 2009.

Muller, Chandra, Susan Roberta Katz, and L. Janelle Dance. "Investing in Teaching and Learning: Dynamics of the Teacher-Student Relationship from Each Actor's Perspective." *Urban Education* 34, no. 3 (1999): 292–337.

Mulvaney, Robert J. "Hospitality and Its Discontents: A Response to Losito." In *In Other Voices: Expanding the Educational Conversation*, edited by Warren Strandberg, 70–72. Richmond, VA: SAPES, 1992.

Myers, Bryant L. *Walking with the Poor: Principles and Practices of Transformational Development*. Maryknoll, NY: Orbis Books, 1999.

Myers, Scott A. "Perceived Instructor Credibility and Verbal Aggressiveness in the College Classroom." *Communication Research Reports* 18, no. 4 (2001): 354–364.

Nagel, Thomas. *The View from Nowhere*. New York, NY: Oxford University Press, 1986.

Naus, Peter. "A Man of Creative Contradictions." In *Befriending Life: Encounters with Henri Nouwen*, edited by Beth Porter, Susan M. S. Brown, and Philip Coulter, 78–88. New York, NY: Image Books, 2001.

Neusner, Jacob. *In Quest of the Historical Pharisees*. Edited by Jacob Neusner and Bruce D. Chilton. Waco, TX: Baylor University Press, 2007.

———. *The Mishnah: A New Translation*. New Haven, CT: Yale University Press, 1988.

———. "Mr. Sander's Pharisees and Mine." *Bulletin for Biblical Research* 2 (1992): 143–169.

Newberry, Melissa, and Heather A. Davis. "The Role of Elementary Teachers' Conceptions of Closeness to Students on their Differential Behaviour in the Classroom." *Teaching and Teacher Education* 24, no. 8 (2008): 1965–1985.

Newman, Elizabeth. "Beyond the Faith-Knowledge Dichotomy: Teaching as Vocation." In *Professing in the Postmodern Academy: Faculty and the Future of Church-Related Colleges*, edited by Stephen R. Haynes, 131–148. Waco, TX: Baylor University Press, 2002.

———. "Hospitality and Christian Higher Education." *Christian Scholar's Review* 33, no. 1 (2003): 75–93.

———. "Hotel or Home? Hospitality and Higher Education." In *Conflicting Allegiances: The Church-Based University in a Liberal Democratic Society*, edited by Michael Budde and John Wright, 91–105. Grand Rapids, MI: Brazos Press, 2004.

———. "The Politics of Higher Education: How the *Love* of Hospitality Offers an Alternative." In *The Scholarly Vocation and the Baptist Academy: Essays on the Future of Baptist Higher Education*, edited by Roger Ward and David P. Gushee, 166–196. Macon, GA: Mercer University Press, 2008.

———. *Untamed Hospitality: Welcoming God and Other Strangers.* Edited by David S. Cunningham and William T. Cavanaugh. Christian Practice of Everyday Life Series. Grand Rapids, MI: Brazos Press, 2007.

———. "Who's Home Cooking? Hospitality, Christian Identity and Higher Education." *Perspectives in Religious Studies* 26, no. 1 (1999): 7–16.

Neyrey, Jerome H. "Ceremonies in Luke-Acts: The Case of Meals and Table-Fellowship." In *The Social World of Luke-Acts: Models for Interpretation*, edited by Jerome H. Neyrey, 361–387. Peabody, MA: Hendrickson, 1991.

———. "The Idea of Purity in Mark's Gospel." In *Social-Scientific Criticism of the New Testament and Its Social World*, edited by John H. Elliott, 91–128. *Semeia* 35. Decatur, GA: Scholars Press, 1986.

Ng, Greer Anne Wenh-In. "From Confucian Master Teacher to Freirian Mutual Learner: Challenges in Pedagogical Practice and Religious Education." *Religious Education* 95, no. 3 (2000): 308–319.

Ng, David Foo Seong. "Strategic Management of Educational Development in Singapore (1965–2005)." In *Toward a Better Future: Education and Training for Economic Development in Singapore since 1965*, edited by Lee Sing Kong, Goh Chor Boon, Birger Fredriksen, and Tan Jee Peng, 39–68. Singapore: NIE, 2008.

Ng Pak Tee. "Educational Reform in Singapore: From Quantity to Quality." *Educational Research for Policy and Practice* 7, no. 1 (2008): 5–15.

———. "Students' Perception of Change in Singapore Education System." *Educational Research for Policy and Practice* 3, no. 1 (2004): 77–92.

Nguyen, Phuong-Mai, Cees Terlouw, and Albert Pilot. "Cooperative Learning vs Confucian Heritage Culture's Collectivism: Confrontation to Reveal Some Cultural Conflicts and Mismatch." *Asia Europe Journal* 3, no. 3 (2005): 403–419.

Nichols, Joe D. "Empowerment and Relationships: A Classroom Model to Enhance Motivation." *Learning Environments Research* 9, no. 2 (2006): 149–161.

Noddings, Nel. *Caring: A Feminine Approach to Ethics and Moral Education*. 2nd ed. Berkeley, CA: University of California Press, 1984/2003.

———. *The Challenge to Care in Schools: An Alternative Approach to Education*. 2nd ed. Advances in Contemporary Educational Thought. New York, NY: Teachers College Press, 1992/2005.

———. "Complexity in Caring and Empathy." *Abstracta, Special Issue* 5 (2010): 6–12.

———. "An Ethic of Caring and Its Implications for Instructional Arrangements." *American Journal of Education* 96, no. 2 (1988): 215–230.

———. "The Language of Care Ethics." *Knowledge Quest* 40, no. 4 (2012): 53–56.

———. "Teaching Themes of Caring." *Education Digest* 61, no. 3 (1995): 24–28.

Nolland, John. *The Gospel of Matthew*. New International Greek Testament Commentary. Grand Rapids, MI: Eerdmans, 2005.

———. *Luke 1–9:20*. Word Biblical Commentary 35A. Dallas, TX: Word, 1989.

Norton, Michael Burns. "An Interview with Elisabeth Schüssler Fiorenza: Critical Reflections on Philosophy and Theology." *Journal of Philosophy and Scripture* 1, no. 2 (2004): 27–31.

Nouwen, Henri J. M. *Creative Ministry: Beyond Professionalism in Teaching, Counseling, Organizing and Celebrating*. Garden City, NY: Image Books, 1971/1991.

———. "Education to the Ministry." *Theological Education* 9, no. 1 (1972): 48–57.

———. "Hospitality." *Monastic Studies* 10 (1974): 1–28.

———. *The Inner Voice of Love: A Journey through Anguish to Freedom*. Garden City, NY: Doubleday, 1996.

———. *Intimacy*. New York: HarperSanFrancisco, 1969/1981.

———. *Letters to Marc about Jesus: Living a Spiritual Life in a Material World*. Translated by Hubert Hoskins. Pasay City, Philippines: Saint Paul Publications, 1988.

———. *Reaching Out: The Three Movements of the Spiritual Life*. Garden City, NY: Doubleday, 1975/1986.

———. *Sabbatical Journey: The Diary of His Final Year*. Mumbai, India: St. Pauls, 1998.

———. *The Way of the Heart: Desert Spirituality and Contemporary Ministry*. New York, NY: HarperOne, 1981/1991

———. *The Wounded Healer: Ministry in Contemporary Society.* New York: Image Books, 1972/1990.
Nur Asyiqin, Mohamad Salleh. "Muslim Student Group Backs 'Wear White.'" *Singapore Straits Times*, 25 June 2014. Online.
———. "Police Issue Public Advisory to 'Keep Peace' at Pink Dot Event." *Singapore Straits Times*, 27 June 2014. Online.
———. "WP's Faisal Supports Wear White." *Singapore Straits Times*, 3 July 2014. Online.
Oakeshott, Michael. *The Voice of Liberal Learning.* Indianapolis, IN: Liberty Fund, 1989/2001.
Oatley, Keith, Dacher Keltner, and Jennifer M. Jenkins. *Understanding Emotions.* 2nd ed. Malden, MA: Blackwell, 2006.
O'Banion, Terry. *A Learning College for the 21st Century.* Phoenix, AZ: Oryx Press, 1997.
Oden, Amy, ed. *And You Welcomed Me: A Sourcebook on Hospitality in Early Christianity.* Nashville, TN: Abingdon Press, 2001.
Ogletree, Thomas W. *Hospitality to the Stranger: Dimensions of Moral Understanding.* Louisville, KY: Westminster John Knox Press, 1985/2003.
O'Laughlin, Michael. *God's Beloved: A Spiritual Biography of Henri Nouwen.* Maryknoll, NY: Orbis Books, 2004.
———. *Henri Nouwen: His Life and Vision.* Maryknoll, NY: Orbis Books, 2005.
———. "Henri the Teacher." In *Remembering Henri: The Life and Legacy of Henri Nouwen*, edited by Gerald Sean Twomey and Claude Pomerleau, 1–10. Maryknoll, NY: Orbis Books, 2006.
Olsson, Andreas. "Emotion and Motivation in Learning: Current Research, Future Directions, and Practical Implications. Abstract." *Lund University Cognitive Studies* 112 (2003): 1–35. http://www.lucs.lu.se/LUCS/112/LUCS.112.pdf.
O'Reilley, Mary Rose. *Radical Presence: Teaching as Contemplative Practice.* Portsmouth, NH: Boynton/Cook Publishers, 1998.
Orner, Mimi. "Interrupting the Calls for Student Voice in 'Liberatory' Education: A Feminist Poststructivist Perspective." In *Feminisms and Critical Pedagogies*, edited by Carmen Luke and Jennifer Gore, 74–89. New York: Routledge, 1992.
Oswalt, John N. *The Book of Isaiah: Chapters 1–39.* New International Commentary on the Old Testament. Grand Rapids, MI: Eerdmans, 1986.
Ovid. *Metamorphoses: Vol. 1; Books 1–8.* Translated by Frank Justus Miller. Repr. ed. Loeb Classical Library. Cambridge, MA: Harvard University Press, 1971.
Pacheco, José Augusto. *Whole, Bright, Deep with Understanding: Life Story and Politics of Curriculum Studies; In-Between William Pinar and Ivor Goodson.* Rotterdam, the Netherlands: Sense Publishers, 2009.

Palmer, Parker J. "Action and Insight: An Interview with Parker Palmer." *Christian Century* 112, no. 10 (1995): 326–329.

———. *The Active Life: Wisdom for Work, Creativity, and Caring*. San Francisco: HarperSanFrancisco, 1991.

———. "The Broken-Open Heart: Living with Faith and Hope in the Tragic Gap." *Weavings* 24, no. 2 (2009): 1–12. http://www.couragerenewal.org/PDFs/PJP-WeavingsArticle-Broken-OpenHeart.pdf.

———. "Community, Conflict, and Ways of Knowing: Ways to Deepen Our Educational Agenda." *Change* 19, no. 5 (1987): 20–25. http://www.couragerenewal.org/parker/writings/community-conflict/.

———. *The Company of Strangers: Christians and the Renewal of America's Public Life*. New York: Crossroad, 1981.

———. *The Courage to Teach: Exploring the Inner Landscape of a Teacher's Life*. 10th anniversary ed. San Francisco, CA: John Wiley & Sons, 1998/2007.

———. *Healing the Heart of Democracy: The Courage to Create a Politics Worthy of the Human Spirit*. San Francisco, CA: Jossey-Bass, 2011.

———. *A Hidden Wholeness: The Journey toward an Undivided Life*. San Francisco, CA: Jossey-Bass, 2004.

———. *Let Your Life Speak: Listening for the Voice of Vocation*. San Francisco, CA: Jossey-Bass, 2000.

———. *The Promise of Paradox: A Celebration of Contradictions in the Christian Life*. 3rd ed. San Francisco, CA: Jossey-Bass, 1980/2008.

———. *To Know as We Are Known: Education as a Spiritual Journey*. New York: HarperSanFrancisco, 1983/1993.

———. "Toward a Philosophy of Integrative Education." In *The Heart of Higher Education: A Call to Renewal; Transforming the Academy through Collegial Conversations*, by Parker J. Palmer, Arthur Zajonc, and Megan Scribner, 19–33. San Francisco, CA: Jossey-Bass, 2010.

———. "Toward a Spirituality of Higher Education." In *Faithful Learning and the Christian Scholarly Vocation*, edited by Douglas V. Henry and Bob R. Agee, 75–84. Grand Rapids, MI: Eerdmans, 2003.

———. "Truth Is Personal: A Deeply Christian Education." *Christian Century* 98, no. 33 (1981): 1051–1055.

———. "The Violence of Our Knowledge: Toward a Spirituality of Higher Education." Paper presented at the Michael Keenan Memorial Lecture: The Seventh Lecture, Berea College, Berea, KY, 1993. http://www.kairos2.com/palmer_1999.htm.

Palmer, Parker J., and Arthur Zajonc. "Introduction." In *The Heart of Higher Education: A Call to Renewal; Transforming the Academy through Collegial*

Conversations, by Parker J. Palmer, Arthur Zajonc, and Megan Scribner, 1–17. San Francisco, CA: Jossey-Bass, 2010.

Pang, Valerie Ooka, John Rivera, and Jill Kerper Mora. "The Ethic of Caring: Clarifying the Foundation of Multicultural Education." *Educational Forum* 64, no. 1 (1999): 25–32.

Park, Joon-Sik. "Hospitality as Context for Evangelism." *Missiology* 30, no. 3 (2002): 385–395.

Pascarella, Ernest T. "Student-Faculty Informal Contact and College Outcomes." *Review of Educational Research* 50, no. 4 (1980): 545–595.

Patten, Kathryn E. "The Somatic Appraisal Model of Affect: Paradigm for Educational Neuroscience and Neuropedagogy." *Educational Philosophy and Theory* 43, no. 1 (2011): 87–97.

Pekrun, Reinhard, Thomas Goetz, Wolfram Titz, and Raymond P. Perry. "Positive Emotions in Education." In *Beyond Coping: Meeting Goals, Visions, and Challenges*, edited by Erica Frydenberg, 149–173. Oxford: Oxford University Press, 2002.

Perrin, Norman. *Rediscovering the Teaching of Jesus*. New York: Harper & Row, 1976.

Perry, Bruce D. "Fear and Learning: Trauma-Related Factors in the Adult Education Process." *New Directions for Adult and Continuing Education* 110 (Summer 2006): 21–27.

Pessoa, Luiz. "On the Relationship between Emotion and Cognition." *Nature Reviews Neuroscience* 9, no. 2 (2008): 148–158. http://lce.umd.edu/publications_files/Pessoa_NRN_2008.pdf.

Phelan, Anne M. "Review of *The Educational Conversation: Closing the Gap*." *Studies in Philosophy and Education* 17, no. 1 (1998): 63–70.

Phillion, JoAnn. "Response to Molly Quinn: Why Is the Notion of Hospitality So Radically Other? Hospitality in Research, Teaching, and Life." In *Curriculum Studies Handbook: The Next Moment*, edited by Erik Malewski, 118–121. New York: Routledge, 2010.

Phillips, D. C. "The Good, the Bad, and the Ugly: The Many Faces of Constructivism." *Educational Researcher* 24, no. 7 (1995): 5–12.

———. "An Opinionated Account of the Constructivist Landscape." In *Constructivism in Education: Opinions and Second Opinions on Controversial Issues*, edited by D. C. Phillips, 1–16. Chicago, IL: National Society for the Study of Education, 2000.

Philo. *Philo: Supplement 1; Questions and Answers on Genesis*. Translated by Ralph Marcus. Repr. ed. Loeb Classical Library. Cambridge, MA: Harvard University Press, 1953.

Philostratus, F. C. *The Life of Apollonius of Tyana*. Translated by F. C. Conybeare. Repr. ed. 2 vols. Loeb Classical Library. London: Heinemann, 1921.

Phipps, Alison, and Ronald Barnett. "Academic Hospitality." *Arts and Humanities in Higher Education* 6, no. 3 (2007): 237–254.

Phiri, Isabel Apawo, and Dietrich Werner, eds. *Handbook of Theological Education in Africa*. Regnum Studies in Global Christianity. Oxford, UK: Regnum Books, 2013.

Pinar, William F. *What Is Curriculum Theory?* Studies in Curriculum Theory. New York: Erlbaum, 2004.

Pineda, Ana Maríe. "Hospitality." In *Practicing Our Faith: A Way of Life for a Searching People*, edited by Dorothy C. Bass, 38–56. San Francisco, CA: Jossey-Bass, 1997.

Pitt-Rivers, Julian. "The Stranger, the Guest, and the Hostile Host: Introduction to the Study of the Laws of Hospitality." In *Contributions to Mediterranean Sociology: Mediterranean Rural Communities and Social Change*, edited by J. G. Peristiany, 13–30. Paris: Mouton, 1968.

Pliny. *Pliny: Natural History*. Translated by H. Rackham. Repr. ed. Loeb Classical Library. Cambridge, MA: Harvard University Press, 1967.

Pohl, Christine D. "Grace Enters with the Stranger." Interview by Faith and Leadership. 22 November 2010. https://www.faithandleadership.com/multimedia/christine-d-pohl-grace-enters-the-stranger.

———. "Hospitality, a Practice and a Way of Life." *Vision* 3, no. 1 (2002): 34–43.

———. "Hospitality from the Edge: The Significance of Marginality in the Practice of Welcome." *Annual of the Society of Ethics* 15 (1995): 122–136.

———. "Hospitality: Mysterious and Mundane." *Reformed Review* 57, no. 2 (2003): 1–14. http://www.electronicsandbooks.com/eab1/manual/Magazine/R/Reformed%20Review,%20Theological%20Journal%20of%20Western%20Theological%20Seminary%20Holland%20MI%20US/win0304vol57no2.pdf.

———. *Making Room: Recovering Hospitality as a Christian Tradition*. Grand Rapids, MI: Eerdmans, 1999.

———. "Responding to Strangers: Insights from the Christian Tradition." *Studies in Christian Ethics* 19, no. 1 (2006): 81–101.

Pope, Mary Elizabeth. "The Teacher as Hostess: Celebrating the Ordinary in Creative Nonfiction Workshops." *Pedagogy* 5, no. 1 (2005): 105–107.

Powell, Katherine C., and Cody J. Kalina. "Cognitive and Social Constructivism: Developing Tools for an Effective Classroom." *Education* 130, no. 2 (2009): 241–250.

Pribyl, Charles B., Masahiro Sakamoto, and James A. Keaten. "The Relationship between Nonverbal Immediacy, Student Motivation, and Perceived Cognitive

Learning among Japanese College Students." *Japanese Psychological Research* 46, no. 2 (2004): 73–85.

Priest, J. "A Note on the Messianic Banquet." In *The Messiah: Developments in Earliest Judaism and Christianity*, edited by James H. Charlesworth, J. Brownson, M. T. Davis, S. J. Kraftchick, and A. F. Segal, 222–238. Princeton Symposium on Judaism and Christian Origins 1. Minneapolis, MN: Augsburg Fortress, 1992.

Pritchard, Alan, and John Woollard. *Psychology for the Classroom: Constructivism and Social Learning*. London: Routledge, 2010.

Purkey, William W., and John Novak. *Inviting School Success: A Self-Concept Approach to Teaching and Learning*. 2nd ed. Belmont, CA: Wadsworth, 1984.

Quinn, Jerome D. *The Letter to Titus*. Anchor Bible 35. Garden City, NY: Doubleday, 1990.

Quinn, Jerome D., and William C. Wacker. *The First and Second Letters to Timothy: A New Translation with Notes and Commentary*. Grand Rapids, MI: Eerdmans, 2000.

Quinn, Molly. "'No Room in the Inn?' The Question of Hospitality in the Post(Partum)-Labors of Curriculum Studies." In *Curriculum Studies Handbook: The Next Moment*, edited by Erik Malewski, 101–117. New York: Routledge, 2010.

Rad, Gerhard von. *Old Testament Theology: Vol. 1; The Theology of Israel's Historical Traditions*. Translated by D. M. G. Stalker. New York: Harper & Row, 1962.

Raffel, Stanley. "On Generosity." *History of the Human Sciences* 14, no. 4 (2001): 111–128.

Raiser, Konrad. "Fifty Years of Ecumenical Formation: Where Are We? Where Are We Going?" *Ecumenical Review* 48, no. 4 (1996): 440–451.

Ramaley, Judith, and Andrea Leskes. *Greater Expectations: A New Vision for Learning as a Nation Goes to College*. Washington, DC: American Association of Colleges & Universities, 2002.

Ramsay, William M. "Roads and Travel (in NT)." In *A Dictionary of the Bible*, edited by James Hastings and John Selbie. Repr. from the 1898 ed., 5:375–402. Peabody, MA: Hendrickson, 1988.

Ramsden, Paul. *Learning to Teach in Higher Education*. London: Routledge, 1992.

Rankin, Susan R. "Campus Climates for Sexual Minorities." *New Directions for Student Services* 111 (Fall 2005): 17–23.

Rapske, Brian M. "Acts, Travel and Shipwreck." In *Vol. 2: The Book of Acts in Its Graeco-Roman Setting*, edited by David W. J. Gill and Conrad Gempf, 1–47. The Book of Acts in Its First Century Setting. Grand Rapids, MI: Eerdmans, 1994.

Rasmussen, Larry. "Shaping Communities." In *Practicing Our Faith: A Way of Life for a Searching People*, edited by Dorothy C. Bass, 117–130. San Francisco, CA: John Wiley & Sons, 1997.

Ratcliffe, Krista. *Rhetorical Listening: Identification, Gender, Whiteness.* Studies in Rhetorics and Feminisms Series. Carbondale, IL: Southern Illinois University Press, 2005.

Rengstorf, Karl Heinrich. "ἁμαρτωλός." In *Theological Dictionary of the New Testament*, edited by Gerhard Friedrich, translated and edited by Geoffrey W. Bromiley, 1:317–335. Grand Rapids, MI: Eerdmans, 1964–1976.

Renn, Kristen. "LGBT and Queer Research in Higher Education: The State and Status of the Field." *Educational Researcher* 39, no. 2 (2010): 132–141.

Rensberger, D. *The Epistles of John.* Westminster Bible Companion. Louisville, KY: Westminster John Knox Press, 2001.

Reynolds, Thomas E. "Improvising Together: Christian Solidarity and Hospitality as Jazz Performance." *Journal of Ecumenical Studies* 43, no. 1 (2008): 45–66.

———. "Toward a Wider Hospitality: Rethinking Love of Neighbour in Religions of the Book." *Irish Theological Quarterly* 75, no. 2 (2010): 175–187.

Rhoads, David M. "Hospitality in the Classroom." *Currents in Theology and Mission* 40, no. 4 (2013): 255–261.

Richard, Lucien. *Living the Hospitality of God.* New York: Paulist Press, 2000.

Richards, Janet C. "The Challenges of Nurturing Graduate Education Majors' Ethic of Relational Care Vital to Culturally Responsive Teaching." *Journal of Multiculturalism in Education* 7, no. 3 (2012): 1–27. Online.

Richardson, Troy, and Sofia Villenas. "'Other' Encounters: Dances with Whiteness in Multicultural Education." *Educational Theory* 50, no. 2 (2000): 255–277.

Richardson, Virginia. "Constructivist Pedagogy." *Teachers College Record* 105, no. 9 (2003): 1623–1640.

Richmond, Virginia P., Joan Gorham, and James C. McCroskey. "The Relationship between Selected Immediacy Behaviors and Cognitive Learning." In *Communication Yearbook 10*, edited by M. McLauglin, 574–590. Beverly Hills, CA: SAGE, 1987.

Ricoeur, Paul. *Freedom and Nature: The Voluntary and the Involuntary.* Translated by Erazim V. Kohák. Evanston, IL: Northwestern University Press, 1966.

———. *The Hermeneutics of Action.* Edited by Richard Kearney. Philosophy and Social Criticism. London: SAGE Publications, 1996.

———. *On Translation.* Translated by Eileen Brennan. London: Routledge, 2006.

Riddle, Donald Wayne. "Early Christian Hospitality: A Factor in the Gospel Transmission." *Journal of Biblical Literature* 57, no. 2 (1938): 141–154.

Riedel, Sharon L. "Communication." In *Multinational Military Operations and Intercultural Factors*, edited by Angela R. Febbraro, Brian McKee, and Sharon L. Riedel, 6.1–6.20. Neuilly-sur-Seine Cedex, France: RTO/NATO, 2008.

Riesner, Rainer. "Synagogues in Jerusalem." In *Vol. 4: The Book of Acts in Its Palestinian Setting*, edited by Richard Bauckham, 179–211. The Book of Acts in Its First Century Setting. Grand Rapids, MI: Eerdmans, 1995.

Ringgren, Helmer. "נכר nkr." In *Theological Dictionary of the Old Testament*, edited by G. Johannes Botterweck, Helmer Ringgren, and Heinz-Josef Fabry, translated by David E. Green, 9:423–432. Grand Rapids, MI: Eerdman, 1974–2006.

Rodgers, Carol R., and Miriam B. Raider-Roth. "Presence in Teaching." *Teachers and Teaching: Theory and Practice* 12, no. 3 (2006): 265–287.

Rogers, Dwight, and Jaci Webb. "The Ethic of Caring in Teacher Education." *Journal of Teacher Education* 42, no. 3 (1991): 173–181.

Rosenfeld, Ben-Zion. "Innkeeping in Jewish Society in Roman Palestine." *Journal of the Economic and Social History of the Orient* 41, no. 2 (1998): 133–158.

Rosiek, Jerry, and Ronald A. Beghetto. "Emotional Scaffolding: The Emotional and Imaginative Dimensions of Teaching and Learning." In *Advances in Teacher Emotion Research: The Impact on Teachers' Lives*, edited by Paul A. Schutz and Michalinos Zembylas, 73–91. New York: Springer, 2009.

Ross, Colin A. "Brain Self-Repair in Psychotherapy: Implications for Education." *New Directions for Adult and Continuing Education* 110 (Summer 2006): 29–33.

Rossing, Barbara. "Why Luke's Gospel? Daily Bread and 'Recognition' of Christ in Food-Sharing." *Currents in Theology and Mission* 37, no. 3 (2010): 225–229.

Rud, Anthony G., Jr. "Learning in Comfort: Developing an Ethos of Hospitality in Education." In *The Educational Conversation: Closing the Gap*, edited by James W. Garrison and Anthony G. Rud Jr., 119–128. SUNY Series, The Philosophy of Education. Albany, NY: State University of New York Press, 1995.

———. "More Than Words: Response to Phelan." *Studies in Philosophy and Education* 17, no. 1 (1998): 71–72.

Russell, Letty M. *Just Hospitality: God's Welcome in a World of Difference*. Edited by Shannon Clarkson and Kate M. Ott. Louisville, KY: Westminster John Knox Press, 2009.

Rust, Chris. "The Impact of Assessment on Student Learning: How Can the Research Literature Practically Help to Inform the Development of Departmental Assessment Strategies and Learner-Centred Assessment Practices?" *Active Learning in Higher Education* 3, no. 2 (2002): 145–158.

Sachs, Dalia, and Naomi Schreuer. "Inclusion of Students with Disabilities in Higher Education: Performance and Participation in Student's Experiences."

Disability Studies Quarterly 31, no. 2 (2011). http://dsq-sds.org/ article/view/1593/1561.

Safrai, Zeev. "The Communal Functions of the Synagogue in the Land of Israel in the Rabbinic Period." In *Ancient Synagogues: Historical Analysis and Archaeological Discovery*, edited by Dan Urman and Paul Virgil McCracken Flesher, 2:181–204. Studia Post-Biblica 47. Leiden, the Netherlands: Brill, 1998.

Saldarini, Anthony J. *Pharisees, Scribes and Sadducees in Palestinian Society: A Sociological Approach*. Grand Rapids, MI: Eerdmans, 1988.

Samovar, Larry A., Richard E. Porter, and Edwin R. McDaniel. *Communication between Cultures*. 7th ed. Boston, MA: Wadsworth, Cengage Learning, 2010.

Sanders, E. P. *Jesus and Judaism*. Philadelphia, PA: Fortress Press, 1985.

———. "Jesus and the Sinners." *Journal for the Study of the New Testament* 19 (October, 1983): 5–36.

Sarason, Seymour B. *The Predictable Future of Educational Reform: Can We Change Course before It's Too Late?* San Francisco, CA: Jossey-Bass, 1990.

Schiewer, Tana M. "Teacher-Student Relationships: A Model of Hospitality." *Pedagogy* 13, no. 3 (2013): 544–548.

Schiffman, Lawrence H. "Communal Meals at Qumran." *Revue de Qumran* 10, no. 1 (1979): 45–56.

———. "The Eschatological Community of the Serekh Ha-'Edah." *Proceedings of the American Academy for Jewish Research* 51 (1984): 105–129.

Schmidt, Stephen A. "Review of *The Courage to Teach: Exploring the Inner Landscape of the Teacher's Life*, by Parker J. Palmer." *Religious Education* 93, no. 4 (1998): 496–499.

Schoorman, Dilys, and Ira Bogotch. "Conceptualisations of Multicultural Education among Teachers: Implications for Practice in Universities and Schools." *Teaching and Teacher Education* 26, no. 4 (2010): 1041–1048.

Schrag, Dale R. "Beautiful Minds, Crucified Minds, and Hospitable Hearts." *Mennonite Life (Online)* 58, no. 1 (March, 2003). https://ml.bethelks.edu/issue/vol-58-no-1/article/beautiful-minds-crucified-minds-and-hospitable-hea/.

Schreiner, Thomas R. *Romans*. Baker Exegetical Commentary on the New Testament. Grand Rapids, MI: Baker Books, 1998.

Schutz, Paul A., Ji Y. Hong, Dionne I. Cross, and Jennifer N. Osbon. "Reflections on Investigating Emotion in Educational Activity Settings." *Educational Psychology Review* 18, no. 4 (2006): 343–360.

Schutz, Paul A., and Sonja L. Lanehart. "Introduction: Emotions and Education." *Educational Psychologist* 37, no. 2 (2002): 67–68.

Schutz, Paul A., and Reinhard Pekrun, eds. *Educational Psychology: Emotion in Educating*. Burlington, MA: Academic Press, 2007.

Schutz, Paul A., and Michalinos Zembylas, eds. *Advances in Teacher Emotion Research: The Impact on Teachers' Lives*. London: Springer, 2009.

Scruggs-Leftwich, Yvonne. "Racism, Terror: A Connection?" *Chicago Tribune*, 26 September 2001. http://articles.chicagotribune.com/2001-09-26/features/0109260355_1_poor-nations-racism-declaration.

Senge, Peter, C. Otto Scharmer, Joseph Jaworski, and Betty Sue Flowers. *Presence: Exploring Profound Change in People, Organizations, and Society*. London: Nicholas Brealey Publishing, 2005.

Seymour, Jack L., Margaret Ann Crain, and Joseph V. Crockett. *Educating Christians: The Intersection of Meaning, Learning, and Vocation*. Nashville, TN: Abingdon, 1993.

Sfard, Anna. "On Two Metaphors for Learning and the Dangers of Choosing Just One." *Educational Researcher* 27, no. 2 (1998): 4–13.

Shaw, Perry W. H. "Education as Hospitality: A Christian Approach to Teaching and Learning." *Theological Review* 23, no. 2 (2002): 95–124.

———. "'New Treasures with the Old': Addressing Culture and Gender Imperialism in High Level Theological Education." In *Tending the Seedbeds: Educational Perspectives on Theological Education in Asia*, edited by Allan G. Harkness, 47–74. Quezon City, Philippines: ATA, 2010.

———. "Review of *To Know as We Are Known: A Spirituality of Education*, and *The Courage to Teach: Exploring the Inner Landscape of the Teacher's Life*, by Parker J. Palmer." Theological Educator 4, no. 2 (2011): 42–44. Online.

———. "A Welcome Guest." *Christian Education Journal*, Ser. 3, 8 (Spring 2011): 8–26.

———. "A Welcome Guest: Theological Education as an Act of Hospitality." Paper presented at the Institute for Excellence in Christian Leadership Development, Arab Baptist Theological Seminary, Beirut, Lebanon. 30 October 2009.

Shea, John. *Stories of God*. Chicago, IL: Thomas More Press, 1978.

Sheckley, Barry G., and Sandy Bell. "Experience, Consciousness, and Learning: Implications for Instruction." *New Directions for Adult and Continuing Education* 110 (Summer 2006): 43–52.

Shotsberger, Paul. "How a Christian Ethic of Care Can Inform the Organization and Structure of Schools of Education." *ICCTE Journal* 7, no. 2 (2012): https://icctejournal.org/issues/v7i2/v7i2-shotsberger/.

Showalter, Shirley H. "Reflections." In *Living the Questions: Essays Inspired by the Work and Life of Parker J. Palmer*, edited by Sam M. Intrator, 165. San Francisco, CA: Jossey-Bass, 2005.

Shryock, Andrew. "Breaking Hospitality Apart: Bad Hosts, Bad Guests, and the Problem of Sovereignty." *Journal of the Royal Anthropological Institute* 18, S1 (June, 2012): S20–S33.

———. "Hospitality Lessons: Learning the Shared Language of Derrida and the Balga Bedouin." *Paragraph* 32, no. 1 (2009): 32–50.

———. "The New Jordanian Hospitality: House, Host, and Guest in the Culture of Public Display." *Comparative Studies in Society and History* 46, no. 1 (2004): 35–62.

Shuffelton, Amy. "On the Ethics of Teacher-Student Friendships." *Philosophy of Education* (2011): 81–89.

Shun, Kwong-Loi. *Mencius and Early Chinese Thought*. Stanford, CA: Stanford University Press, 1997.

Singapore Straits Times. "Church Groups' Followers Wear White to Make Stand." *Singapore Straits Times* 2 July 2014. http://news.asiaone.com/news/singapore/church-groups-followers-wear-white-make-stand.

Skinner, John. *A Critical and Exegetical Commentary on Genesis*. 2nd ed. International Critical Commentary. Edinburgh: T & T Clark, 1980.

Slattery, Patrick. *Curriculum Development in the Postmodern Era*. 2nd ed. New York: Routledge, 2006.

Smalley, Stephen S. *1, 2, 3 John*. Rev. ed. Word Biblical Commentary 51. Nashville, TN: Thomas Nelson, 2007.

Smit, Peter-Ben. *Fellowship and Food in the Kingdom: Eschatological Meals and Scenes of Utopian Abundance in the New Testament*. Wissenschaftliche Untersuchungen Zum Neuen Testament 2 Reihe 234. Tübingen, Germany: Mohr Siebeck, 2008.

Smith, David I., and Barbara Carvill. *The Gift of the Stranger: Faith, Hospitality, and Foreign Language Learning*. Grand Rapids, MI: Eerdmans, 2000.

Smith, Dennis E. "Dinner with Jesus and Paul: The Social Role of Meals in the Greco-Roman World." *Biblical Archaeology Review* 20, no. 4 (2004): 30–39.

———. *From Symposium to Eucharist: The Banquet in the Early Christian World*. Minneapolis, MN: Fortress Press, 2003.

———. "Messianic Banquet." In *Anchor Bible Dictionary*, edited by David Noel Freedman, 4:788–791. Garden City, NY: Doubleday, 1992.

———. "The Messianic Banquet Reconsidered." In *The Future of Early Christianity: Essays in Honor of Helmut Koester*, edited by Birger Albert Pearson, 64–74. Minneapolis, MN: Fortress Press, 1991.

Soh, Christina. *The Use of Information Technology for the Management of Education in Singapore*. Commonwealth Case Studies in Education. London: Commonwealth Secretariat, 2001.

Souter, Alexander. "Roads and Travel." In *Dictionary of the Apostolic Church*, edited by James Hastings, 4:393–399. Grand Rapids, MI: Baker Book House, 1906–1918.

Spencer, John R. "Sojourn." In *Anchor Bible Dictionary*, edited by David Noel Freedman, 6:103–104. Garden City, NY: Doubleday, 1992.

Spilt, Jantine L., Helma M. Y. Koomen, and Jochem T. Thijs. "Teacher Wellbeing: The Importance of Teacher-Student Relationships." *Educational Psychology Review* 23, no. 4 (2011): 457–477.

Spink, Kathryn. *Mother Teresa: An Authorized Biography*. Rev. and updated ed. New York: HarperCollins, 2011.

Spivak, Gayatri Chakravorty. *In Other Worlds: Essays in Cultural Politics*. New York: Methuen, 1987.

———. *The Post-Colonial Critic: Interviews, Strategies, Dialogues*. Edited by Sarah Harasym. London: Routledge, 1990.

Stählin, Gustav. "ξένος." In *Theological Dictionary of the New Testament*, edited by Gerhard Kittel and Gerhard Friedrich, translated by Geoffrey W. Bromiley, 5:1–36. Grand Rapids, MI: Eerdmans, 1964–1976.

———. "φιλέω." In *Theological Dictionary of the New Testament*, edited by Gerhard Kittel and Gerhard Friedrich, translated by Geoffrey W. Bromiley, 9:113–171. Grand Rapids, MI: Eerdmans, 1964–1976.

Stallman, Robert C. "Divine Hospitality and Wisdom's Banquet in Proverbs 9:1–6." In *The Way of Wisdom: Essays in Honor of Bruce K. Waltke*, edited by J. I. Packer and Sven K. Soderlund, 117–133. Grand Rapids, MI: Zondervan, 2000.

———. "Divine Hospitality in the Pentateuch: A Metaphorical Perspective on God as Host." PhD dissertation, Westminster Theological Seminary, 1999. http://eagle.northwestu.edu/faculty/bob-stallman/dissertation/.

Stambaugh, John, and David L. Balch. *The New Testament in Its Social Environment*. Library of Early Christianity. Philadelphia, PA: Westminster Press, 1986.

Steele, Richard B. "Accessibility or Hospitality: Reflections and Experiences of a Father and Theologian." *Journal of Religion in Disability and Rehabilitation* 1, no. 1 (1994): 11–26.

Steffen, Daniel S. "The Messianic Banquet and the Eschatology of Matthew's Gospel." *Global Journal of Classical Theology* 5, no. 2 (2006). http://www.galaxie.com/article/gjct05-2-03.

Stock, St. George. "Hospitality (Greek and Roman)." In *Encyclopaedia of Religion and Ethics*, edited by James Hastings, repr. ed., 6:808–812. Edinburgh: T & T Clark, 1994.

Storbeck, Justin, and Gerald L. Clore. "On the Interdependence of Cognition and Emotion." *Cognition and Emotion* 21, no. 6 (2007): 1212–1237. http://www.ncbi.nlm.nih.gov/pmc/articles/PMC2366118/pdf/ nihms40350.pdf.

Storm, M. R. 1993. "Diotrephes: A Study of Rivalry in Apostolic Church." *Restoration Quarterly* 35 (4): 193–202.

Stratman, Jacob [Jake]. "Toward a Pedagogy of Hospitality: Empathy, Literature, and Community Engagement." *Journal of Education and Christian Belief* 17, no. 1 (2013): 25–59.

———. "What's in a Name: The Place of Recognition in a Hospitable Classroom." *International Journal of Christianity and Education* 19, no. 1 (2015): 27–37.

Strecker, George. *The Johannine Letters*. Edited by Harold Attridge. Translated by Linda M. Maloney. Hermeneia. Minneapolis, MN: Fortress Press, 1996.

Sullivan, Bernie. "A Practice of Inclusion as the Transcendence of Models of Assimilation and Integration." In *The Transformative Potentials of Our Self-Studies for a New Epistemology of Scholarship in Our University*. Educational Studies Association of Ireland Conference. University College Cork, Ireland, 2005. http://www.jeanmcniff.com/items.asp?id=74&term=Bernie+sullivan.

Supple, Briony, and Joseph Abgenyega. "Developing the Understanding and Practice of Inclusion in Higher Education for International Students with Disabilities/Additional Needs: A Whole Schooling Approach." *International Journal of Whole Schooling* 7, no. 2 (2011): 93–108. http://www.wholeschooling.net/Journal_of_Whole_Schooling/articles/7-2c%20Supple%20Agbenyega.pdf.

Sylwester, Robert. "How Emotions Affect Learning." *Educational Leadership* 52, no. 2 (1994): 60–65.

Tan, Amelia. "'Teach Less, Learn More' Now at NTU: Fewer Classes, More Overseas Exchange Trips for New Intake." *Singapore Straits Times*, 16 March 2011.

Tan, Charlene. "Creating Thinking Schools through 'Knowledge Inquiry': The Curriculum Challenges for Singapore." *The Curriculum Journal* 17, no. 1 (2006): 89–105.

Tan, Ivan. "Loving Strangers: Practising Hospitality as a Community." *Church and Society in Asia Today* 1, no. 3 (2008): 79–86.

Tan, Nancy Nam-Hoon. "Feminist Biblical Studies: Resident Alien Seeking Citizen." *Journal of Feminist Studies in Religion* 25, no. 2 (2009): 133–137.

Tan, Sharon M. "Theological Diversity in a Liberal Seminary: United Theological Seminary of the Twin Cities." *Theological Education* 47, no. 1 (2012): 111–118.

Tappy, Ron E. "Psalm 23: Symbolism and Structure." *Catholic Biblical Quarterly* 57, no. 2 (1995): 255–280.

Taylor, Kathleen. "Brain Function and Adult Learning: Implications for Practice." *New Directions for Adult and Continuing Education* 110 (Summer 2006): 71–85.

Terenzini, Patrick T., Alberto F. Cabrera, Carol L. Colbeck, Stefani A. Bjorklund, and John M. Parente. "Racial and Ethnic Diversity in the Classroom: Does It Promote Student Learning?" *Journal of Higher Education* 72, no. 5 (2001): 509–531.

Terenzini, Patrick T., and Ernest T. Pascarella. "Living Myths: Undergraduate Education in America." *Change* 26, no. 1 (1994): 28–32.

Terry, Marion. "The Importance of Interpersonal Relations in Adult Literacy Programs." *Educational Research Quarterly* 30, no. 2 (2006): 30–43.

Teven, Jason J. "The Relationships among Teacher Characteristics and Perceived Caring." *Communication Education* 50, no. 2 (2001): 159–169.

———. "Teacher Caring and Classroom Behavior: Relationships with Student Affect and Perceptions of Teacher Competence and Trustworthiness." *Communication Quarterly* 55, no. 4 (2007): 433–450.

Teven, Jason J., and Joan Gorham. "A Qualitative Analysis of Low-Inference Student Perceptions of Teacher Caring and Non-Caring Behaviors within the College Classroom." *Communication Research Reports* 15, no. 3 (1998): 288–298.

Teven, Jason J., and Trudy L. Hanson. "The Impact of Teacher Immediacy and Perceived Caring on Teacher Competence and Trustworthiness." *Communication Quarterly* 52, no. 1 (2004): 39–53.

Teven, Jason J., and James C. McCroskey. "The Relationship of Perceived Teacher Caring with Student Learning and Teacher Evaluation." *Communication Education* 46, no. 1 (1997): 1–9.

Thiselton, Anthony C. *The First Epistle to the Corinthians*. New International Greek Testament Commentary. Grand Rapids, MI: Eerdmans, 2000.

Thompson, Nancy, and Julie P. Wheeler. "Learning Environment: Creating and Implementing a Safe, Supportive Learning Environment." National Teacher Standards 2, *Journal of Family Consumer Sciences Education* 26 (2008): 33–43. http://www.natefacs.org/Pages/v26Standards2/v26Standards2Std7Thompson.pdf.

Thompson, Steven W. "The Boundaries of Christian Hospitality in a Postmodern Setting." In *Exploring the Frontiers of Faith:* Festschrift *in Honour of Dr. Jan Paulsen*, edited by Borge Schantz and Reinder Bruinsma, 325–342. Lueneburg, Germany: Advent-Verlag, 2009.

Thompson, Marjorie J. *Soul Feast: An Invitation to the Christian Spiritual Life*. Reprint ed. Louisville, KY: Westminster John Knox Press, 2005.

Thoreau, Henry David. *Walden: A Fully Annotated Edition*. Edited by Jeffrey S. Cramer. New Haven, CT: Yale University Press, 1854/2004.

Thurston, Nonnie. "*Soli Deo Placere Desiderans*." In *A Monastic Vision for the 21st Century: Where Do We Go from Here?*, edited by Patrick Hart, 1–22. Monastic Wisdom Series 8. Kalamazoo, MI: Cistercian Publications, 2006.

Thwaites, Tony. "'Vigilant Hospitality': The Online Imperative and Teaching Cultural Studies." *International Journal of Cultural Studies* 5, no. 4 (2002): 479–493.

Thweat, Katherine S., and James C. McCroskey. "Teacher Nonimmediacy and Misbehavior: Unintentional Negative Communication." *Communication Research Reports* 13, no. 2 (1996): 198–204.

Tiénou, Tite. "Christian Theology in an Era of World Christianity." In *Globalizing Theology: Belief and Practice in an Era of World Christianity*, edited by Craig Ott and Harold A. Netland, 37–51. Nottingham, UK: Apollos, 2007.

Toh Kok Aun. "Teacher-Centred Teaching Is Alive and Well." *Teaching and Learning* 15, no. 1 (1994): 12–17.

Toh Kok Aun, Ho Boon Tiong, Charles M. K. Chew, and Joseph P. Riley II. "Teaching, Teacher Knowledge and Construction." *Educational Research for Policy and Practice* 2, no. 3 (2003): 195–204.

Tomlin, Graham. "Evangelism as Catechesis, Hospitality and Anticipation: A Study of the Alpha Course." In "International Perspectives on Christian Education," Special Supplement, *Christian Education Journal*, Ser. 3, 10 (Fall 2013): S91–S102.

Towner, Philip H. *The Letters to Timothy and Titus*. New International Commentary on the New Testament. Grand Rapids, MI: Eerdmans, 2006.

Townsend, John T. "Education (Greco-Roman)." In *Anchor Bible Dictionary*, edited by David Noel Freedman, 2:312–317. Garden City, NY: Doubleday, 1992.

Tran, Thi Tuyet. "Is the Learning Approach of Students from the Confucian Heritage Culture Problematic?" *Educational Research for Policy and Practice* 12, no. 1 (2013): 57–65.

Tremmel, Robert. "Hospitality in the Classroom: The Teaching Stance of the Writers in the Schools." *Journal of Teaching Writing* 3, no. 2 (1984): 191–199.

Trinity Christian College. "Speller Encourages Faculty to Embrace Diversity." 4 October 2005. http://tcc.trnty.edu/new/archive/100604/.

Tuleja, Elizabeth A. *International Communication for Business*. 2nd ed. Managerial Communication Series 4. Mason, OH: South-Western Cengage Learning, 2009.

Twelftree, G. H. "Scribes." In *Dictionary of Jesus and the Gospels*, edited by Joel B. Green, Scot McKnight, and I. Howard Marshall, 732–735. Downers Grove, IL: InterVarsity, 1992.

Twigg, Carol A. "The Need for a National Learning Infrastructure." *Educom Review* 29, no. 4 (1994): 17–24. http://net.educause.edu/ir/library/html/nli0001.html.

Ültanir, Emel. "An Epistemological Glance at Constructivist Approach: Constructivist Learning in Dewey, Piaget, and Montessori." *International Journal of Instruction* 5, no. 2 (2012): 195–212. http://eric.ed.gov/?id=ED533786.

Van Brummelen, Harro. *Walking with God in the Classroom: Christian Approaches to Teaching and Learning*. 3rd ed. Colorado Springs, CO: Purposeful Design Publications, 2009.

Vanier, Jean. "A Gentle Instrument of a Loving God." In *Befriending Life: Encounters with Henri Nouwen*, edited by Beth Porter, Susan M. S. Brown, and Philip Coulter, 259–268. New York: Image Books, 2001.

Vaux, Roland de. *Ancient Israel: Its Life and Institutions*. Translated by John McHugh. Grand Rapids, MI: Eerdmans, 1997.

Velez, Jonathan J., and Jamie Cano. "The Relationship between Teacher Immediacy and Student Motivation." *Journal of Agricultural Education* 49, no. 3 (2008): 76–86.

Vella, Jane. *Learning to Listen, Learning to Teach: The Power of Dialogue in Educating Adults*. Rev. ed. San Francisco, CA: Jossey-Bass, 2002.

Visser, Margaret. *The Rituals of Dinner: The Origins, Evolution, Eccentricities, and Meaning of Table Manners*. London: Penguin Books, 1991.

Vogels, Walter A. "Hospitality in Biblical Perspective." *Liturgical Ministry* 11 (2002): 161–173.

Volet, Simone. "Learning across Cultures: Appropriateness of Knowledge Transfer." *International Journal of Educational Research* 31, no. 7 (1999): 625–643.

Volet, Simone, and Peter Renshaw. "Chinese Students at an Australian University: Adaptability and Continuity." In *The Chinese Learner: Cultural, Psychological and Contextual Influences*, edited by David A. Watkins and John Biggs, 205–220. Hong Kong: CERC, 1996.

Volf, Miroslav. *Exclusion and Embrace: A Theological Exploration of Identity, Otherness, and Reconciliation*. Nashville, TN: Abingdon Press, 1996.

———. "Introduction." In *A Spacious Heart: Essays on Identity and Belonging*, 1–11. Christian Mission and Modern Culture. Harrisburg, PA: Trinity Press International, 1997.

———. "Theology for a Way of Life." In *Practicing Theology: Beliefs and Practices in Christian Life*, edited by Miroslav Volf and Dorothy C. Bass, 245–263. Grand Rapids, MI: Eerdmans, 2002.

———. "Trends in American Religion and the Challenge of Exclusion and Embrace in Christian Practice." Interview, transcript dated 21 February 2002, Resources for American Christianity. http://www.resourcingchristianity.org/sites/default/files/transcripts/interview/MiroslavVolf_American_Religion_Interview.pdf.

———. "'The Trinity Is Our Social Programme': The Doctrine of Trinity and the Shape of Social Engagement." *Modern Theology* 14, no. 3 (1998): 403–423.

———. "A Vision of Embrace: Theological Perspectives on Cultural Identity and Conflict." *Ecumenical Review* 47, no. 2 (1995): 195–205.

Vondey, Wolfgang. "Pentecostal Ecclesiology and Eucharistic Hospitality: Toward a Systematic and Ecumenical Account of the Church." *Pneuma* 32, no. 1 (2010): 41–55.

Wallace, Daniel B. *Greek Grammar beyond the Basics*. Grand Rapids, MI: Zondervan, 1996.

Walton, Julie A. P., and Matthew Walters. "Eat This Class: Breaking Bread in the Undergraduate Classroom." In *Teaching and Christian Practices: Reshaping Faith and Learning*, edited by David I. Smith and James A. A. Smith, 80–101. Grand Rapids, MI: Eerdmans, 2011.

Walton, Martin. "The Welcoming Guest: Practices of Mutual Hospitality in Chaplaincy." In *Encounter in Pastoral Care and Spiritual Healing: Towards an Integrative and Intercultural Approach*, edited by Daniel Louw, Takaaki David Ito, and Ulrike Elsdorfer, 220–234. Münster, Germany: LIT Verlag, 2012.

Wang, Haidong. "Teaching Asian Students Online: What Matters and Why?" *PAACE Journal of Lifelong Learning* 15 (2006): 69–84. http://www.uwyo.edu/education/_files/documents/diversity-articles/wang_2006.pdf.

Wang, Yunping. "Confucian Ethics and Emotions." *Frontiers of Philosophy in China* 3, no. 3 (2008): 352–365.

Watkins, David. "Learning and Teaching: A Cross-Cultural Perspective." *School Leadership and Management* 20, no. 2 (2000): 161–173.

Watts, John D. W. *Isaiah 1–33*. Word Biblical Commentary 24. Waco, TX: Word, 1985.

Webb, Kerry S. "Review of *College Professionalism: The Academy, Individualism, and the Common Good*, by John B. Bennett." *Canadian Journal of Higher Education* 30, no. 1 (2000): 189–214.

Weil, Simone. *Waiting for God*. Capricon Books ed. N.p.: Capricon Books, 1959.

Weiss, Palumbo Ruth. "Emotion and Learning." *Training and Development* 54, no. 11 (2000): 44–48.

Wenham, Gordon J. *Genesis 16–50*. Word Biblical Commentary 2. Dallas, TX: Word, 1994.

Werner, Dietrich. "Challenges and Opportunities in Theological Education in the 21st Century: Pointers for a New International Debate on Theological Education." 2009. http://wocati.org/wp-content/uploads/2012/12/Challenges-and-Opportunities-in-Theological-Education-in-the-21st-Century-Prospects-for-a-New-International-Debate-on-Theological-Education.pdf.

———. "Perspectives on the Future of Theological Education in Asia." In *Asian Handbook for Theological Education and Ecumenism*, edited by Hope Antone, Wati Longchar, Hyunju Bae, Huang Po Ho, and Dietrich Werner, 657–666. Regnum Studies in Global Christianity. Eugene, OR: Wipf & Stock, 2013.

Werner, Dietrich, David Esterline, Namsoon Kang, and Joshva Raja, eds. *Handbook of Theological Education in World Christianity: Theological Perspectives, Ecumenical Trends, Regional Surveys*. Regnum Studies in Global Christianity. Eugene, OR: Wipf & Stock, 2010.

Westerhoff, Caroline A. *Good Fences: The Boundaries of Hospitality*. Harrisburg, PA: Morehouse, 1999.

Westfield, N. Lynne. *Dear Sisters: A Womanist Practice of Hospitality*. Cleveland, OH: Pilgrim Press, 2001.

Wheeless, Lawrence R., and Jams Grotz. "Conceptualization and Measurement of Reported Self-disclosure." *Human Communication Research* 2, no. 4 (1976): 338–346.

Whitsed, Craig, and Simone Volet. "Fostering Intercultural Dimensions of Internationalisation in Higher Education: Metaphors and Challenges in the Japanese Context." *Journal of Studies in International Education* 15, no. 2 (2011): 146–170.

Wijsen, Frans. "Intercultural Theology instead of Missiology: New Wine in Old Wineskins?" *SEDOS Bulletin* 38, no. 7–8 (2004): 171–180.

Williams, Heather. "bell hooks speaks up." *The Sandspur* 112, no. 17 (2006): 1–2.

Wilson, Gerald H. *Psalms: Vol. 1*. New NIV Application Commentary. Grand Rapids, MI: Zondervan, 2002.

Wilson, Janie H., Jonathan R. Stadler, Beth M. Schwartz, and Dennis M. Goff. "Touching Your Students: The Impact of a Handshake on the First Day of Class." *Journal of the Scholarship of Teaching and Learning* 9, no. 1 (2009): 108–117.

Wimberly, Anne E. Streaty. "Hospitable Kinship in Theological Education: Cross-Cultural Perspective on Teaching and Learning as Gift Exchange." *Teaching Theology and Religion* 7, no. 1 (2004): 3–12.

Windschitl, Mark. "Framing Constructivism in Practice as the Negotiation of Dilemmas: An Analysis of the Conceptual, Pedagogical, Cultural, and Political Challenges Facing Teachers." *Review of Educational Research* 72, no. 2 (2002): 131–175.

Witherington, Ben, III. *The Acts of the Apostles: A Socio-Rhetorical Commentary*. Grand Rapids, MI: Eerdmans, 1998.

———. *The Gospel of Mark: A Socio-Rhetorical Commentary*. Grand Rapids, MI: Eerdmans, 2001.

———. *Letters and Homilies for Hellenized Christians: Vol. 2; A Socio-Rhetorical Commentary on Hebrews, 1–2 Peter*. Downers Grove, IL: InterVarsity, 2007.

Witherington, Ben, III, and Darlene Hyatt. *Paul's Letter to the Romans: A Socio-Rhetorical Commentary*. Grand Rapids, MI: Eerdmans, 2004.

Witmer, Timothy Z. "Seminary: A Place to Prepare Pastors?" *Westminster Theological Journal* 69, no. 2 (2007): 229–246.

Wolfe, Kari M., and Susan E. Waters. "Exploring Higher Education Classroom Immediacy: Effects of Biological Sex and Teaching Experience." *International Journal of Arts and Commerce* 2, no. 8 (2013): 95–114.

Wolfe, Patricia. "The Role of Meaning and Emotion in Learning." *New Directions for Adult and Continuing Education* 110 (Summer 2006): 35–41.

Wong, Joseph Kee-Kuok. "Are the Learning Styles of Asian International Students Culturally or Contextually Based?" *International Education Journal* 4, no. 4 (2004): 154–166.

Wong, Tessa. "Police Reject Road Closure for Pink Dot." *Singapore Straits Times*, 22 June 2014. Online.

Wright, Christopher J. H. *Old Testament Ethics for the People of God*. Leicester: InterVarsity, 2004.

Wrobleski, Jessica. *The Limits of Hospitality*. Collegeville, MN: Liturgical Press, 2012.

Wu, Xiaoxin. "The Dynamics of Chinese Face Mechanisms and Classroom Behaviour: A Case Study." *Evaluation and Research in Education* 22, no. 2–4 (2009): 87–105.

Wubbels, Theo, and Mieke Brekelmans. "Two Decades of Research on Teacher-Student Relationships in Class." *International Journal of Educational Research* 43, no. 1 (2005): 6–24.

Xiao, Lixin. "Bridging the Gap between Teaching Styles and Learning Styles: A Cross-Cultural Perspective." *TESL-EJ* 10, no. 3 (2006): 1–15. http://www.tesl-ej.org/wordpress/issues/volume10/ej39/ej39a2/.

Yao, Santos. "The Table Fellowship of Jesus with the Marginalized: A Radical Inclusiveness." *Journal of Asian Mission* 3, no. 1 (2001): 25–41.

Yearley, Lee II. *Mencius and Aquinas: Theories of Virtue and Conceptions of Courage*. Albany, NY: State University of New York Press, 1990.

Yeatts, John R. "Why Are We Doing This? The Relation of Theological Methodology to Christian Education Practice." *Christian Education Journal* 15, no. 3 (1995): 37–53.

Yong, Amos. "Guests, Hosts, and the Holy Ghost: Pneumatological Theology and Christian Practices in a World of Many Faiths." In *The Lord and Giver of Life: Perspectives on Constructive Pneumatology*, edited by David H. Jensen, 71–86. Louisville, KY: Westminster John Knox Press, 2008.

———. *Hospitality and the Other: Pentecost, Christian Practices, and the Neighbor*. Edited by William R. Burrows. Faith Meets Faith Series. Maryknoll, NY: Orbis Books, 2008.

Young, Iris Marion. *Inclusion and Democracy*. Oxford Political Theory. Oxford, UK: Oxford University Press, 2002.

Yount, William R. *Created to Learn*. Nashville, TN: Broadman & Holman, 1996.

Yu, Ning. "The Chinese Heart as the Central Faculty of Cognition." In *Culture, Body and Language: Conceptualizations of Internal Body Organs across Cultures and Languages*, edited by Farzad Sharifian, René Dirven, Ning Yu, and Niemeier, 131–168. Applications of Cognitive Linguistics 7. Berlin, Germany: Mouton de Gruyter, 2008.

Yuen, Chi-Chung, and Seok Noi Lee. "Applicability of the Learning Style Inventory in an Asian Context and Its Predictive Value." *Educational and Psychological Measurement* 54, no. 2 (1994): 541–549.

Zhan, Suxian, and Thao Le. "Interpersonal Relationship between Teachers and Students: An Intercultural Study on Chinese and Australian Universities." Paper presented at Doing the Public Good: Positioning Educational Research Melbourne, Australia. December 2004. http://www.aare.edu.au/data/publications/2004/zha04171.pdf.

Zhang, Lei. "Study on the Satisfaction of the Relationship between Teachers and Students under the Impact of Double Factors in Universities: A Case Study of Empirical Survey among the Students of Seven Universities in China." *International Journal of Psychological Studies* 2, no. 1 (2010): 116–121.

Zhang, Qin, John G. Oetzel, Xiaofang Gao, Richard G. Wilcox, and Jiro Takai. "Teacher Immediacy Scales: Testing for Validity across Cultures." *Communication Education* 56, no. 2 (2007): 228–248.

Zhang, Wenhai, and Jiamei Lu. "The Practice of Affective Teaching: A View from Brain Science." *International Journal of Psychological Studies* 1, no. 1 (2009): 1–7.

Zhou, Yanqiu Rachel, Della Knoke, and Izumi Sakamoto. "Rethinking Silence in the Classroom: Chinese Students' Experiences of Sharing Indigenous Knowledge." *International Journal of Inclusive Education* 9, no. 3 (2005): 287–311.

Zull, James E. "Key Aspects of How the Brain Learns." *New Directions for Adult and Continuing Education* 110 (Summer 2006): 3–9.

Global Hub for Evangelical Theological Education

ICETE is a global community, sponsored by nine regional networks of theological schools, to enable international interaction and collaboration among all those engaged in strengthening and developing evangelical theological education and Christian leadership development worldwide.

The purpose of ICETE is:
1. To promote the enhancement of evangelical theological education worldwide.
2. To serve as a forum for interaction, partnership and collaboration among those involved in evangelical theological education and leadership development, for mutual assistance, stimulation and enrichment.
3. To provide networking and support services for regional associations of evangelical theological schools worldwide.
4. To facilitate among these bodies the advancement of their services to evangelical theological education within their regions.

Sponsoring associations include:
Africa: Association for Christian Theological Education in Africa (ACTEA)

Asia: Asia Theological Association (ATA)

Caribbean: Caribbean Evangelical Theological Association (CETA)

Europe: European Evangelical Accrediting Association (EEAA)

Euro-Asia: Euro-Asian Accrediting Association (E-AAA)

Latin America: Association for Evangelical Theological Education in Latin America (AETAL)

Middle East and North Africa: Middle East Association for Theological Education (MEATE)

North America: Association for Biblical Higher Education (ABHE)

South Pacific: South Pacific Association of Evangelical Colleges (SPAEC)

www.icete-edu.org

Langham Literature and its imprints are a ministry of Langham Partnership.

Langham Partnership is a global fellowship working in pursuit of the vision God entrusted to its founder John Stott –

> *to facilitate the growth of the church in maturity and Christ-likeness through raising the standards of biblical preaching and teaching.*

Our vision is to see churches in the majority world equipped for mission and growing to maturity in Christ through the ministry of pastors and leaders who believe, teach and live by the Word of God.

Our mission is to strengthen the ministry of the Word of God through:
- nurturing national movements for biblical preaching
- fostering the creation and distribution of evangelical literature
- enhancing evangelical theological education

especially in countries where churches are under-resourced.

Our ministry

Langham Preaching partners with national leaders to nurture indigenous biblical preaching movements for pastors and lay preachers all around the world. With the support of a team of trainers from many countries, a multi-level programme of seminars provides practical training, and is followed by a programme for training local facilitators. Local preachers' groups and national and regional networks ensure continuity and ongoing development, seeking to build vigorous movements committed to Bible exposition.

Langham Literature provides majority world preachers, scholars and seminary libraries with evangelical books and electronic resources through publishing and distribution, grants and discounts. The programme also fosters the creation of indigenous evangelical books in many languages, through writer's grants, strengthening local evangelical publishing houses, and investment in major regional literature projects, such as one volume Bible commentaries like *The Africa Bible Commentary* and *The South Asia Bible Commentary*.

Langham Scholars provides financial support for evangelical doctoral students from the majority world so that, when they return home, they may train pastors and other Christian leaders with sound, biblical and theological teaching. This programme equips those who equip others. Langham Scholars also works in partnership with majority world seminaries in strengthening evangelical theological education. A growing number of Langham Scholars study in high quality doctoral programmes in the majority world itself. As well as teaching the next generation of pastors, graduated Langham Scholars exercise significant influence through their writing and leadership.

To learn more about Langham Partnership and the work we do visit **langham.org**

www.ingramcontent.com/pod-product-compliance
Lightning Source LLC
Chambersburg PA
CBHW061932220426
43662CB00012B/1881